Bridging

UNIVERSITY PRESS OF FLORIDA

Florida A&M University, Tallahassee
Florida Atlantic University, Boca Raton
Florida Gulf Coast University, Ft. Myers
Florida International University, Miami
Florida State University, Tallahassee
New College of Florida, Sarasota
University of Central Florida, Orlando
University of Florida, Gainesville
University of North Florida, Jacksonville
University of South Florida, Tampa
University of West Florida, Pensacola

Bridging Race Divides

Black Nationalism, Feminism, and Integration
in the United States, 1896–1935

Kate Dossett

University Press of Florida
Gainesville · Tallahassee · Tampa · Boca Raton · Pensacola
Orlando · Miami · Jacksonville · Ft. Myers · Sarasota

Copyright 2008 by Kate Dossett
Printed in the United States of America
All rights reserved

First cloth printing, 2008
First paperback printing, 2009

Library of Congress Cataloging-in-Publication Data:
Dossett, Kate.
Bridging race divides: Black nationalism, feminism, and integration in the United States, 1896–1935 / Kate Dossett.
p. cm.
Includes bibliographical references and index.
ISBN 978-0-8130-3140-8 (alk. paper)
ISBN 978-0-8130-3495-9 (pbk.)
1. African American women political activists—History—19th century. 2. African American women political activists—History—20th century. 3. African American women political activists—Biography. 4. African American women—Intellectual life. 5. African American women—Social networks. 6. Black nationalism—United States—History. 7. Feminism—United States—History. 8. African American leadership—History. 9. African Americans—Segregation—History. 10. United States—Race relations. I. Title.
E185.6.D69 2007
305.48'8960730090349—dc22
2007016624

The University Press of Florida is the scholarly publishing agency for the State University System of Florida, comprising Florida A&M University, Florida Atlantic University, Florida Gulf Coast University, Florida International University, Florida State University, New College of Florida, University of Central Florida, University of Florida, University of North Florida, University of South Florida, and University of West Florida.

University Press of Florida
15 Northwest 15th Street
Gainesville, FL 32611-2079
http://www.upf.com

For Mum and Dad

Contents

List of Figures ix

Preface xi

List of Abbreviations xv

Introduction 1

1. Laying the Groundwork: Washington, Burroughs, Bethune, and the Clubwomen's Movement 15

2. Black Nationalism and Interracialism in the Young Women's Christian Association 66

3. Luxuriant Growth: The Walkers and Black Economic Nationalism 107

4. Amy Jacques Garvey, Jessie Fauset, and Pan-African Feminist Thought 150

Epilogue 200

Notes 209

Bibliography 241

Index 257

Figures

1. Mary McLeod Bethune and her pupils at Daytona 53
2. Mary McLeod Bethune walking into the White House 63
3. Mary McLeod Bethune portrait 64
4. Madam Walker driving her automobile 115
5. Madam Walker Manufacturing Company advertisement 115
6. Madam Walker and Booker T. Washington 117
7. Walker agents at Villa Lewaro 138
8. A'Lelia Walker's 136th Street Beauty Parlor 139
9. Music room at the 108 West 136th Street Walker home 139
10. A'Lelia Walker receiving a treatment at Lelia College, New York City 140
11. A'Lelia Walker portrait 143

Preface

This book developed out of my fascination with the literary, political, and social networks that black women created across the United States in the late nineteenth and early twentieth centuries. I was struck, initially, by what seemed to be their inconsistent approach to racial uplift. As I delved more into their lives and learned how to listen to their many voices, I discovered they were smart, flexible, and strategic in their thinking. They had to be. At a time when segregation was relentless in its imposition of daily humiliations on African Americans from all walks of life, black women forged connections through their professional and voluntary work, their involvement in race, religious, and women's organizations, and their entrepreneurial endeavors. They sustained these networks with an indefatigable energy that enabled them to endure traveling in uncomfortable and often degrading conditions. They visited each other in their homes, and schools, and met each other at conventions, churches, and community celebrations. Their interactions with each other as revealed by their frequent correspondence suggests they were women whose lives cannot be understand fully through separate studies of them as clubwomen, as Harlem Renaissance writers, as Garveyites, or as successful businesswomen. This project grew out of a desire to understand women's networks across organizational boundaries, but also across the historiographical and chronological boundaries that have seen black women of the Gilded Age, or "Women's Era" as being distinct from black women in the New Negro movement of the 1920 and 1930s. These categorizations and periodizations were not recognized by the women who created these networks in the forty years which bridged the nineteenth and twentieth centuries. Rather they saw themselves as race women, whose ambitions and strategies changed over time but who always depended on their interactions with other race women. This book is a study of how they created and drew strength from these networks. Continually exposed to other members of these networks who may have held different views from them, black women were encouraged to be strategic in their thinking: to challenge white supremacy while also working for and within the race.

Just as black women's networks were diverse in form and content, so were the sources for this study. Many of the sources are private papers and collections of correspondence, including those of Mary Church Terrell, Margaret Murray Washington, Nannie Helen Burroughs, Mary McLeod Bethune, W. E. B. Du Bois, and Booker T. Washington. Jessie Fauset's copious correspondence is scattered around various collections, including the Countee Cullen Papers at the Library of Congress and the Langston Hughes papers held in the Beinecke Library at Yale. The Madam Walker Collection at the Indiana Historical Society contains a wealth of information on the Madam Walker Manufacturing Company, although a good quantity of personal correspondence remains in the possession of Walker's great-great-granddaughter and biographer. Studies of the West 137th Street Colored Branch of the YWCA are hampered by a scarcity of existing records. When the branch was shut down in the early 1960s and amalgamated with the Lexington Avenue YWCA, many records were lost. However, there are still microfilms of the 15th Street and later Metropolitan Board Executive Committee Minutes, thousands of photographs, and some reports by women leaders of the Colored Branch for this period. These are scattered (literally) in boxes over the current New York City Lexington Avenue headquarters in several rooms, corridors, and cupboards and are in serious danger of being lost altogether. I would like to thank Evie Shapiro at the New York City YWCA for helping me shift through piles of abandoned boxes.

Other useful sources include contemporaneous historical accounts, particularly Jane Olcott's *The Work of Colored Women*, written in 1919, and Cecelia Cabaniss Saunders's *A Half Century of the Young Women's Christian Association* (draft typescript, 1955), which had been stolen from the Lexington Avenue YWCA archives; my thanks to Judith Weisenfeld for allowing me to xerox her copy. I have since deposited a copy at the Lexington Avenue Y. Besides personal correspondence, many of the networks between race women were unearthed through reports and sometimes photographs in black newspapers and journals. Particularly helpful in this regard were the *New York Age*, *The Crisis*, the *Negro World*, as well as the publications of black women's organizations, including the NACW's *National Notes* and the YWCA's *Association Monthly*.

There are many archivists who helped me with this project, and I thank them all. I would particularly like to thank Kenneth Chandler at the Bethune Council House. I thank all the organizations who provided financial assistance, which enabled me to embark on regular trips to the United States. These include the Arts and Humanities Research Council, the Gilder Lehrman Foundation, the Sara Norton Fund at Cambridge University, and Columbia University for providing me with a Visiting Fellowship and for facilitating my research in New York City. I am grateful to the History Department at Leeds for funding research trips and for putting their faith in me even before this project was finished. I thank my colleague Katrina Honeyman, for her insightful comments on a section of the manuscript, and for being an inspiring role model. I would particularly like to thank my third-year Harlem Renaissance Special Subject students at Leeds, whose enthusiasm and excitement for the subject inspired me afresh in the last stages of this project. I would also like to thank the members of the Black History Workshop held at Houston University in 2003 for their insightful comments at an early stage of this work.

I appreciate the talents of Michael O'Brien and Tony Badger, who read early drafts of the manuscript, as well as those of the University Press of Florida readers. I thank Derek Krisoff, Eli Bortz, and Jacqueline Kinghorn Brown at UPF for their support and guidance through the final stages of this project. There are a vast number of people who helped me and hosted me in the United States. Particular thanks to Anneli McDowell for sharing her home and family with me. I would also like to thank the late Frank Sieverts for hosting me so graciously in Washington, D.C. My deepest thanks to Chris Sidell for driving me to archives from New York to Atlanta to Indianapolis and far beyond. My sincere thanks go to Zoë Hilton for hosting me on my early trips to New York, and to Jessica Pogson for her always open house in London. I thank Julie for her love and always generous support. Above all my thanks go to Mum and Dad, for their love, constant support, and unfailing patience, and for providing me with four brothers, without whom my feminist consciousness would not have been what it is. Last, but never least, I thank two brave people who read numerous drafts of this manuscript and who never shrank from offering advice: James, my friend and editor, and Robert, my love.

Abbreviations

ASWPL	Association of Southern Women for the Prevention of Lynching
BOD	Minutes of the Board of Directors of the YWCA of New York City
BTW-LOC	Booker T. Washington Papers, Library of Congress
BTW Papers	*The Booker T. Washington Papers,* Louis Harlan, ed.
CCP	Countee Cullen Papers, Library of Congress
CCW	Council on Colored Work Minutes
Du Bois Papers	*The Papers of W. E. B. Du Bois.* Microfilm, University of Massachusetts
ECM	Executive Committee Minutes of the 15th Street Association, YWCA of the City of New York
Gumby Papers	L. S. Gumby Papers, Rare Books and Manuscripts, Columbia University
ICWDR	International Council of Women of the Darker Races
ILPDR	International League of People of the Darker Races
LHP	Langston Hughes Papers, James Weldon Johnson Collection in the Yale Collection of American Literature, Beinecke Rare Book and Manuscript Library, Yale University
LOC	Library of Congress
MCT-LOC	Mary Church Terrell Papers, Library of Congress
MCT-MSRC	Mary Church Terrell Papers, Moorland-Spingarn Research Center, Howard University
MMB-LOC	Mary McLeod Bethune Papers, Bethune Foundation Collection, Library of Congress
MSRC	Moorland-Spingarn Research Center
MWC-IHS	Madam Walker Collection, Indiana Historical Society
NAACP-LOC	National Association for the Advancement of Colored People Papers, Library of Congress
NAACP Papers	*Papers of the NAACP.* University Publications of America, 1982–1997
NACW	National Association of Colored Women
NACWC Papers	National Association of Colored Women's Clubs Papers
NAWE	National Association of Wage Earners

NBA	National Board Archives, YWCA of the USA
NBC	National Baptist Convention
NCNW	National Council of Negro Women
NCNW Papers	National Council of Negro Women's Papers, Series II, Mary McLeod Bethune Council House, Washington, D.C.
NHB-LOC	Nannie Helen Burroughs Papers, Library of Congress
NLRCW	National League of Republican Colored Women
NNBL	National Negro Business League
NYCAA	New York City YWCA Archives
NYPL	New York Public Library
RNNBL	Records of the National Negro Business League, Manuscript Division, Library of Congress
SC	Schomburg Center for Research in Black Culture
TICF	Tuskegee Institute Clippings File, British Newspaper Library
UNIA	Universal Negro Improvement Association
WC	Women's Convention of the National Baptist Convention
YMCA	Young Men's Christian Association
YWCA	Young Women's Christian Association

Introduction

When Zora Neale Hurston suggested in a newspaper interview in 1943 that the segregation of southern blacks from whites was not necessarily undesirable, she provoked an outcry. Her critics charged her with endorsing Jim Crow and providing ammunition to white supremacists. Her friends wondered at her hypocrisy, since she had herself benefited from the blessings of integration through her education at Barnard College. How, wondered Joel A. Rogers, the Afrocentric historian, could Hurston legitimately grab the benefits of integration while advocating black separatism?[1] But Hurston was far from unique; black women had a long history of weaving a course that relied on integrationist and separatist strategies. In early-twentieth-century America, black women sought the benefits of both black separatism and integrationism: at a grassroots level, they became members of both Marcus Garvey's black nationalist Universal Negro Improvement Association (UNIA) and the interracial National Association for the Advancement of Colored People (NAACP); on an individual level, businesswomen like Madam C. J. Walker lent their philanthropy to both separatist and integrationist organizations; at a leadership level, black clubwomen set up pan-African organizations while also joining with white women in interracial movements, such as the Young Women's Christian Association (YWCA).

Bridging Race Divides examines the careers of a group of black women activists, clubwomen, writer-intellectuals, and businesswomen who had multiple affiliations with both black nationalist and interracial organizations, made important contributions to black feminist thought, and, through their use of multiple strategies, shaped debates over the solution to the race problem. Included in this study are three prominent clubwomen, Margaret Murray Washington, Nannie Helen Burroughs, and Mary McLeod Bethune; black women leaders in the YWCA, including Eva Bowles and Cecelia Cabaniss Saunders; Madam C. J. Walker and her daughter A'Lelia Walker, who founded the Walker Manufacturing Company's hair treatment and beauty schools; Amy Jacques Garvey, UNIA leader and *Negro World* journalist; and Jessie Fauset, novelist and literary editor of *The Crisis* during the Harlem Renaissance. Through an examination of the political thought and activism of these women in the years between the founding of the National Association of Colored Women (NACW) in 1896 and the National Council of Negro Women (NCNW) in 1935, this book puts forward three main arguments: first, that these women challenged the dichotomy between black nationalism and integrationism and with it the presumed triumph of an interracial America; second, that black women were at the forefront of black nationalism and worked to shape it within a feminist framework; third, that they made a significant contribution toward the development of a black feminist tradition. As such this study engages with three current historiographical debates: studies that understand black political thought as having overlapping rather than oppositional strands; feminist scholarship that has redefined the meaning of the political and the nature of essentialist feminism; and interdisciplinary studies concerning the role of feminism within nationalist organizations.

Black women in early-twentieth-century America consciously chose to support a range of race and women's organizations, and drew on a variety of strategies to address the "multiple jeopardy" of gender, race, and class. Their flexible approach was manifested in their political groupings, economic initiatives, cultural protests, and organizational strategies, which challenged the integrationist versus black nationalist dichotomy constructed by their contemporaries and built up by later narratives of American history. The religious, literary, social reform, women's rights, antilynching, pan-African, interracial, party political, and myriad other clubs to which these women belonged had wide crossover in their membership, and their activities were faithfully reported and given publicity by women journalists like Fauset in *The Crisis* and Alice Dunbar-Nelson in the *Pittsburgh Courier*.[2] Time and again, Washington, Burroughs, Bethune, the Walkers, Fauset, and many others offered their homes, schools, and wider contacts to help other black women launch new organizations and initiatives. For example, Margaret Murray Washington founded the pan-African International Council of Women of the Darker Races (ICWDR) at Nannie Helen Burroughs's National Training School in Washington, D.C.; Mary McLeod Bethune founded the NCNW at the Colored Branch of the YWCA in Harlem, which was also used as a meeting place for many other local and national black women's initiatives, including the Women's Auxiliary of the NAACP. A'Lelia Walker also hosted the Women's Auxiliary at her 136th Street Studio, while her mother's homes in Indianapolis and at Irvington-on-Hudson had welcomed many prominent clubwomen.[3] In her will Madam Walker left funds to the schools of many of the clubwomen she had come to see as friends, including Bethune, while it was Bethune herself who delivered the eulogy at A'Lelia Walker's funeral in 1931.[4]

In spite of their many close ties, both personal and intellectual, the women who form the substance of this study have often been written about separately, either as integrationists or nationalists. Viewed as part of the narrative of the Harlem Renaissance or the Garvey movement or the black clubwomen's movement, the connections these women forged were for a long time obscured by historiographical boundaries. This meant that scholars of the Harlem Renaissance neglected the organizational records and writings of clubwomen or Garveyites, scholars of Garveyism paid little attention to the novels of black women writers, and historians of clubwomen assumed they had little in common with rank-and-file Garveyites. Just as these women relied on a range of formal and informal networks to enable them to bridge race divisions, historians need to look beyond historiographical boundaries in order to more fully understand their ideological and political worlds. Recent studies in early-twentieth-century black women's history by scholars such as Victoria Wolcott and Michele Mitchell have begun to explore the connections between women from different social and political backgrounds, and it is to this field that *Bridging Race Divides* contributes.[5] This book examines together the private papers and correspondence of black women activists, writers, club members, and race leaders in conjunction with the records of the many organizations to which they belonged, as well as public speeches, newspaper reports, and writings, including journalistic pieces and novels. What becomes clear through listening to the voices of these women is that while they saw integrationism as neither inevitable nor always desirable, they did see it is as compatible with the continuation of oppositional strategies used in the past, including accommodationism, pan-Africanism, and cultural and economic black nationalism. They rarely viewed integrationism as the only solution to the race problem.

Black Nationalism versus Integrationism: A False Dichotomy?

Narratives of American history traditionally pushed African American thought and its political exponents into two camps. Black leaders were viewed as either accommodationists/integrationists on the one hand, or militants/black nationalists on the other. While one group was viewed as conforming to white values, be it through accommodation, assimilation or, later, integration, the other camp resisted white oppression through protest, black nationalism, and pan-Africanism.[6] These dichotomies were usually constructed within the framework of a progressive integrationist narrative which focused on male leadership and the apparent failure of black nationalism and pan-Africanism. While Frederick Douglass continues to be celebrated as the grandfather of civil rights protest, Alexander Crummell and Martin Delany are regarded as ideologically inconsistent thinkers and flawed leaders, whose black nationalist rhetoric disguised their true integrationist feelings; W. E. B. Du Bois outlived Booker T. Washington, and the Tuskegeean's accommodationism lost ground to Du Bois's more militant campaign for civil rights with the integrationist and interracial NAACP. Garvey's arrest and exile removed an important challenge to the integrationist solution to the race problem. While both Malcolm X and Martin Luther King had their lives cut short, King lived on in American memory, as his legacy was transmuted into a celebration of America's interracialism in the form of a national holiday. This celebratory integrationist narrative negated the importance of strategies of black nationalism and pan-Africanism, so prominent in black thought for much of the twentieth century, and instead stressed African Americans' incorporation into mainstream American politics and society through their (albeit segregated) inclusion in the New Deal, the Second World War, and the civil rights movement.[7]

W. E. B. Du Bois was perhaps the first twentieth-century commentator to define the contours of the integrationism-versus-nationalism debate. In his 1903 *Souls of Black Folk*, Du Bois recognized what he called "the contradiction of double aims," a product of the black American's "double consciousness":

> The history of the American Negro is the history of this strife, —this longing to attain self-conscious manhood, to merge his double self into a better and truer self. In this merging he wishes neither of the older selves to be lost. He would not Africanize America, for America has too much to teach the world and Africa. He would not bleach his Negro soul in a flood of white Americanism, for he knows that Negro blood has a message for the world. He simply wishes to make it possible for a man to be both a Negro and American.[8]

Forty years later, in his memoir *Dusk of Dawn*, Du Bois recognized that finding a way to combine integrationist and nationalist sentiments remained one of the greatest challenges facing black leadership.[9] Many of his contemporaries continued to see these two approaches as incompatible. In his 1934 pamphlet *Negro Americans, What Now?* the poet, historian, and NAACP activist James Weldon Johnson suggested that "our entire intellectual history" had been characterized by the debate between integrationists and what he termed isolationists. Integrationism, he believed, would ultimately triumph because separatism could only lead to an unsatisfactory and secondary status for African Americans in the United States.[10] Black intellectuals in the second half of the twentieth century helped to perpetuate this view of incompatibility. While challenging the limited role accorded black nationalism by black intellectuals like Johnson, Harold Cruse in his landmark critique of black intellectuals agreed that "American Negro history is basically a history of the conflict between integrationist and nationalist forces in politics, economics, and culture, no matter what leaders are involved and what slogans are used."[11] Yet even those commentators who understood the importance of black cultural nationalism for the 1960s liberation struggle ironically served to support a liberal integrationist historiography in which nationalism was always the weaker of two competing ideologies. Amiri Baraka, Addison Gayle, and other Black Aesthetic advocates looked back at the failure of past scholarship and cultural endeavor and sought to promote a new black cultural pride. While Baraka and Gayle were arguing against African American integration into what they saw as a corrupt and imperialistic white America, they undermined the very black nationalist legacy upon which they might have built, since their criticism rested on the premise that past black leaders had failed by pursuing integrationist goals in politics and assimilationist values in art.[12] Examining the history of black culture, Afrocentric writers constructed a narrative of failure which could be pinned on a middle-class, integrationist black leadership. The prescriptive judgments of the Black Aesthetic made it easy for later critics to dismiss literary and political forebears as integrationist without any understanding of the historical context. For example, middle-class feminist authors of the Harlem Renaissance were seen as integrationist for writing about middle-class blacks. Clubwomen were likewise viewed as integrationist, because of their rhetoric of racial uplift, and in spite of their long history of separatist and pan-African organizing. The successful black businesswoman Madam Walker was seen as imitating white standards of beauty through her sale of black hair products.[13]

Historians of black nationalist movements have now moved beyond the nationalism-versus-integrationism dichotomy to look at the diverse and complicated array of black nationalisms in the nineteenth century. This study builds on the work of revisionist historians who hold a range of views regarding the success, viability, radicalism, and even existence of black nationalism, but who have been interested in how black nationalism was able to adapt to its circumstances. This is not to suggest as Wilson J. Moses has that black nationalism simply "assumed the shape of its container" and imitated white intellectual movements, but rather to understand as Sterling Stuckey does that: "To enhance effectiveness, to exploit the changing nature of a cruel reality, some elements of the one ideology were combined in the other."[14] While Stuckey argued that black nationalism was radical and grounded in a sense of belonging to a pan-African community which survived slavery, Moses, Tunde

Adeleke, and others have suggested that black nationalism in the nineteenth century was conservative and often assimilationist in its desire to "civilize" Africa.[15] This book does not suggest that the debates concerning the relative benefits of an integrationist or black nationalist solution to the race problem were insignificant, nor deny that they could sometimes be extremely divisive. But we should be wary of replacing the black nationalist–versus–integrationist framework with that of conservative-versus-radical black nationalism, a polarization that can be equally distorting. As an alternative it will be argued in these pages that it is only through analyzing the roles of black women that the extent to which African Americans embraced both integrationist and separatist strategies becomes clear, since black women's leadership roles and overlapping networks made it easier for them to avoid the ideological posturing that often characterized black male leadership roles. By focusing on black women's experiences it becomes evident that black political thought was characterized more by complexity than dichotomy, by multiple rather than singular strategies, and by interdependent rather than mutually exclusive philosophies.

Gender and Nationalism

Black nationalism in the United States has been constantly redefined since the War of Independence, and like many other nationalisms, what characterizes its essential and most successful constituents has been hotly contested. However, the central role played by historians in constructing and sustaining nationalisms has long been acknowledged. As Hobsbawm puts it: "Historians are to nationalism what poppy-growers . . . are to heroin-addicts: we supply the essential raw material for the market."[16] Accepting black nationalism as a constructed, albeit no less significant, worldview, black nationalism can be characterized as a quest for autonomy for black Americans and an understanding that the freedom of all peoples of African descent is interlinked. Indeed, the supranational roots of black nationalism in the international system of African enslavement has meant that black nationalism in the United States has always been closely linked to pan-Africanism, and can be better understood through an imagined community notion of nationalism rather than a Eurocentric nation-state model. Encompassing both an intellectual response to, and a strategic method of dealing with, American racism, black nationalist thought has accommodated both separatist and assimilationist views in the struggle to achieve race solidarity, race pride, and economic and cultural freedom.[17]

Black women in the early twentieth century drew strength from nationalist movements taking place in other parts of the world during what has become known as the "apogee of nationalism." Following World War I and the embedding of self-determination (at least for white peoples) in the League of Nation's mandate, nationalist movements came to be viewed by many as legitimate liberation movements in which women's equality might also be achieved.[18] Black women were inspired not only by contemporaneous movements; they were also able to draw on a long tradition of black nationalist protest in America which linked race and gender oppression. Black feminist nationalists Maria Stewart and Mary Ann Shadd were important contributors and definers of black nationalism in the mid-nineteenth century, arguing for the importance of economic nationalism and sustained political activism. Shadd used her public role as a lecturer and newspaper editor to challenge black men's right to shape black nationalist thought in the antebellum period. An early emigrant to Canada, Shadd was an important voice in the debates concerning emigrationism, playing a leading role in challenging both the American Colonization Society's support for repatriation of free blacks to Africa and Martin Delany's and other black nationalists' advocacy of emigration to Africa or Haiti. Shadd's belief in a black nationalism that was independent of a nation-state reflected her pan-African view of an imagined community of blacks which she promoted through her Canadian newspaper the *Provincial Freeman*, as well as the pragmatic belief that "blacks would be exploited in the sugar cane fields of Latin America and the Caribbean just as they were in the US."[19] A pioneer teacher in western Canada, Shadd strongly opposed segregated schooling, believing that segregation and voluntary separation were very different. Shadd saw no difficulties in arguing for integrated public institutions in Canada while also helping to construct an international network of black activists. Nor did she view her support for black nationalism as being in conflict with her work for women's rights.[20] At the end of the nineteenth century Shadd had become part of a tradition of black women's nationalist activity in North America.

Even so, black feminists in the early twentieth century appear to have been ahead of their time in their willingness to negotiate nationalism and feminism, since both contemporary commentators and later historians have often viewed black nationalist movements, like many other nationalist movements, as inherently patriarchal.[21] Indeed, the very creation of the nation has been viewed as being inextricably connected to the construction of separate spheres: the public life for men and the private for women.[22] Yet visions of a black nation do not have to be patriarchal any more than visions of an integrated society. Indeed integration of black women into white American society in the early twentieth century would hardly have offered them a more liberated or equal status. The notion that black nationalism is inherently incompatible with feminist thought derives from studies of (male) nineteenth-century black nationalists. In *The Black Atlantic*, Paul Gilroy suggests that the nineteenth-century black nationalist Martin Delany was "probably the first black thinker to make the argument that the integrity of the race is primarily the integrity of its male heads of household and secondarily the integrity of the families over which they preside."[23] More problematic than Delany's own views is that by regarding Delany as the founding father of black nationalism, we allow little room for others to represent black nationalist thought.[24] Since historians are so crucial in the construction of nationalisms, we need to take account of the gendered structures that underpin their work before accepting uncritically their notions of who the founding fathers (and it usually is fathers) are. As Hazel Carby argues in her discussion of Du Bois and Cornel West, "We need to expose and learn from the gendered, ideological assumptions which underlie the founding texts and determine that their authors become the *representative* figures of the American intellectual. These authors and their productions are shaped by gendered structures of thought and feeling, which in turn actively shape the major paradigms and modes of thought of all academic discourse."[25] Just as the work of Anthony Smith and Eric Hobsbawm has been canonized in the writing and construction of European nationalisms, so the work of August Meier, Wilson J. Moses, and Tunde Adeleke has been key in constructing male black thinkers as the founders and shapers of black nationalism. These accounts appear to have been little influenced by recent work on gender and nation. Even those recent accounts that acknowledge women's involvement in nationalist movements do not regard a gendered understanding as challenging the main contours of nationalist studies debates.[26] While gender historians such as Michele Mitchell and Ula Taylor have tried to bring the study of gender and nationalism together, it is still the case that black feminist nationalist studies are ghettoized from most mainstream theorizations of nationalism.[27]

There has also been a long tradition of white Western feminists who have viewed nationalism and feminism as incompatible. In *Three Guineas*, Virginia Woolf suggested that "as a woman, I have no country. As a woman I want no country. As a woman my country is the whole world."[28] Woolf saw women as "outsiders and victims of states," and as such she believed that it was difficult for women to support nationalist causes when they were denied equal rights.[29] African American women writing at the same time disagreed, because they saw the two causes as interlinked. How could they be free women when their men were oppressed? Like Woolf, later twentieth-century Western white feminists have also struggled to support women of color engaged in nationalist struggles, while scholars of women and black nationalism, such as Cynthia Enloe, have argued that "nationalism typically has sprung from masculinized memory, masculinized humiliation and masculinized hope."[30]

This study seeks to challenge academic discourse which continues to construct nationalism as a male-centered phenomenon, by examining the historical positioning of black women and their relationships with and within nationalist movements in the early twentieth century. I argue that these women saw themselves as definers of nationalism and feminism, rather than as victims of state or patriarchal nationalism, and that their writings and activities demonstrate their contribution toward "a definition of nationalism that places women at the centre and acknowledges feminist nationalism as a process of interaction developed between women and men, not solely by men."[31] Building on recent studies of feminist nationalists in other periods and other parts of the world, *Bridging Race Divides* explores the creative and sometimes debilitating, but always interlocking, relationship between gender and nation.[32] This study makes a significant contribution to the field of gender and nation studies by analyzing the methods black women employed to negotiate between their gendered and racial identities and by demonstrating how, through their development of pan-African ideas and alliances with other women of color across the Diaspora, they influenced black nationalism.

Developing Black Feminism

Many of the black women who engaged with black nationalism understood it as a central component of the struggle for women's rights. Black feminist thought is an ever-evolving philosophy to which they contributed much in the early decades of the twentieth century. They recognized the importance of self-definition and the interconnected nature of race, gender, and class as sources of oppression. They made connections between their intellectual thought and practical endeavor and celebrated and commemorated the legacy of past struggle. While they recognized that nationalist struggle could help stimulate a feminist consciousness, they realized that institutional transformation was part of the same struggle. All of these were themes which would come to be seen as the defining characteristics of black feminist thought in the latter half of the twentieth century.[33] This book looks beyond essentialist and ahistorical definitions of feminism that developed as part of the second-wave feminist movement and that sought to find one unifying theory. It argues rather for a feminist analysis that explores the mutability of texts and representations, and for a literary and cultural analysis that understands the importance of historical contextualization. In particular it calls for greater understanding of the complex relationship between race and class on the one hand, and the public-private divide on the other, two areas which have often suffered from an ahistorical application of latter-day and essentialist feminist theory.

The attempt to understand the importance of class differentiation in women's history has led, unintentionally, to the creation of a new essentialism. The call to look "beyond the search for sisterhood" was part of the reaction against the essentialism of white feminist history, which had assumed that gender was the most important and equally oppressive criterion in all women's lives.[34] Criticizing women's studies that focused only on elite, northeastern white women, Nancy Hewitt and others called for women's historians to look at the differences characterizing the experiences of women from various classes and ethnicities. The warning not to imagine bonds of sisterhood where there were none led to a welcome and increased awareness of the difference between the experiences of black middle-class and working-class women, and of the danger of allowing articulate middle-class women to speak for all women. It resulted in excellent scholarship by Angela Davis, Tera Hunter, and others who uncovered the voices of working-class women.[35] However, it has also resulted in a reverse essentialism, a class bias which has meant that middle-class women have been deemed less authentic, less worthy of study, and, unlike their poorer sisters, incapable of exhibiting race pride or nationalist sentiment. There is a disturbing tendency to see only working-class voices or rural folk experiences as authentic identifiers of blackness. For example, Houston A. Baker's theory of blues as *the* African American vernacular suggested an essentialist construction of black culture.[36] Feminist critics have questioned this new essentialism. Ann Ducille criticized Baker's work for making the blues, and the way of life the blues represents, the "metonym for authentic blackness." It was not simply that Baker made southern folk experiences the source of all African American culture, rather that "he also makes such sitings an intellectual imperative, arguing that the blues should be privileged in the study of American culture as a way of remapping 'expressive geographies in the US.'"[37] In spite of the attempts by literary critics to revalue the voices of middle-class black women writers like Jessie Fauset and Nella Larsen, the tendency to regard middle-class women as less worthy of study, as inauthentic and instinctively assimilationist, remains. In the same way that the folk or working class have been deemed more "authentic" and therefore worthy of feminist analysis, middle-class black women are often assumed to lack class awareness and accused of imposing their (implicitly white) middle-class values on others. This is a viewpoint put across not only in the feminist scholarship of the 1990s, but also by the masculinist discourse of the Black Aesthetic.[38]

The term *middle class* has undergone intensive scrutiny in recent years. Often the term was used indiscriminately and sometimes pejoratively in discussions of black clubwomen, but now historians have called for a more nuanced understanding of the term when applied to African American communities at the turn of the century, one which requires us to keep in mind the different cultural, economic, and political values that distinguished members of the black and white middle class.[39] To signify this difference historians have variously used "better," "rising," or "aspiring" class."[40] In this study I use the term *black middle class* because recent debates about terminology have served to establish a common understanding of the changing and diverse makeup of the black middle classes: the black middle class was constructed by the black community and differed from a white middle class; members of the black middle class shared a belief in racial uplift and a capacity through education, occupation, or support of family and friends to devote some of their leisure time to advancing the race.[41]

While this emphasis on the cultural beliefs of those who made up the black middle class can help us to recognize class tensions, at the same time we need to understand that respectability was not simply the prerogative of the middle classes, imposed upon the poor. Rather those movements that have been dubbed middle class were sometimes based on "community consensus and cross-class participation."[42] The assumption that black middle-class values, particularly as regards sexual conduct, were not values that working-class black women could develop and adhere to for their own economic and social reasons has been challenged, along with the notion that the sexual life of the blues woman rather than that of the clubwoman was the more typical or identifiable for working-class women. As Victoria Wolcott has demonstrated, an understanding of the interconnectedness of race, class, and gender and how they operated in early-twentieth-century America is central to understanding the politics of respectability as "a foundation of African American women's survival strategies and self-definition irrespective of class."[43] To reflect the diversity of backgrounds and experiences of those who shared these values and whose rise from poverty to race leadership makes a rigid class categorization unhelpful, I also use *race woman*, a term that many of these women used to describe each other and themselves.[44]

Bridging Race Divides argues for greater care in applying the late-twentieth-century race, gender, and class trinity of oppression to the early twentieth century in ways that only emphasize difference, because to do so may deny poor black women agency, and ignore the possibility that the shared threat of racialized and sexual insult was one that might often have helped to bridge divisions among black women. It does not seek to establish sisterhood between all black women, or overlook the importance of class as a source of division, but rather rejects the notion that black culture and politics were shaped only from above.

This book also argues for a definition of feminism in which the relationship between the public and private is handled with greater historical sensitivity. Black feminism in twentieth-century America was not a static concept, but a process of struggle. For the purposes of this study, then, feminist activism is characterized in broad terms by women who strove to promote women's equal rights, who negotiated the private-public sphere divide, and who, while aware that gender is a social construct, also accepted that there were some important environmental and historical differences between the experiences of men and women. Since the 1970s, American women's history has identified strongly with the slogan of the second-wave feminist movement, "the personal is political." Yet recent research in women's studies demonstrates that this concept can be unhelpful when used ahistorically and has called for greater historical contextualization and understanding by feminist scholars of the many restrictions which women face in the private sphere, not only in their relationships with whites but also with black men.[45] In the early decades of the twentieth century, black women pursued feminist goals in their public lives which they were often unable to achieve in their own personal lives, particularly in their marriages. Yet we should be wary of judging them poor feminists on these grounds. Not only were many black women aware of this contradiction, but they also understood that their very ability to project a feminist agenda on race movements sometimes depended on their ability to perform different roles in private.[46] They were aware that the private sphere was far from being an autonomous, free space for men or women and understood that the erection of boundaries between the private and public was essentially a political act.[47] We should not then be put off by the fact that these women seldom self-identified as feminists, since, as Patricia Hill Collins argues, to do so "misses the complexity of how Black feminist practice actually operates."[48] This book argues that it is only by looking at how African American women from a range of political spectrums engaged with feminism, black nationalism, and integrationism that we can really understand how early-twentieth-century black thought "actually operates."

Drawing on a range of private papers, institutional records, fiction, and black newspapers, *Bridging Race Divides* is developed in four chapters. The first two chapters deal with the variety of approaches taken by leading black women activists in the institutional realm of education and women's clubs. Chapter 1 delineates the negotiation of separatist and integrationist strategies on the part of three leading clubwomen, Margaret Murray Washington, Nannie Helen Burroughs, and Mary McLeod Bethune, who created and led the most influential national black women's clubs in the early part of the twentieth century. It pays particular attention to their activities as clubwomen in the 1920s, a decade that has traditionally marked the end of the period known as the Women's Era, but which saw black clubwomen work increasingly with other women of African descent. Steering a course between integrationism and black nationalism, they insisted on being able to choose elements of both strategies, while their pan-Africanist endeavors within the International Council of Women of the Darker Races laid the foundations for the development of black nationalist feminist thought.

Chapter 2 examines African American women who worked within the purportedly interracial (but actually segregated) YWCA, at both the local Colored Branch of the Y in New York City and on the Colored Committees at the national level. Even when African American women worked within an interracial organization, they often pursued policies that promoted race solidarity and black leadership of black women. When it suited their purpose, black women within the YWCA were willing to take from and to exploit, as well as help to define, their own imperatives and agendas in ways that promoted what they conceived of as their own, racially based interests as well as those of the wider black community. Working within segregated organizations like the YWCA was compatible with feminist black nationalism. Indeed the disputes between white and black YWCA workers at both national and local level suggest that black women's experiences of race relations with the YWCA in the early decades of the twentieth century provided impetus for the development of black nationalist feminism in the 1920s. Chapter 2 also examines the impact on the YWCA of pressure from the YMCA to merge in the 1920s. This pressure served to highlight the unique and important role the YWCA played in these years in creating a space where women could work outside and beyond the often more conservative values which governed its male counterpart.

In Chapter 3 the study turns to the activities of the legendary black businesswomen Madam Walker and her daughter A'Lelia. It offers a detailed account of the practical as well as the ideological difficulties encountered by Madam Walker in the establishment of her cosmetics business and examines the ways in which she combined economic incentive with racial uplift to recruit sales agents and hairdressers and to sell her product. It examines the business enterprises, marketing strategies, and political and cultural activities of Walker and her daughter, who managed to swim with both the black nationalist and the integrationist tides. Exploring the methods Madam Walker employed to secure her place within the respectable black elite, the chapter argues that she used her influence in black political circles to promote economic and political opportunities for black women through her network of politicized Walker agents, and examines further how her daughter built on and adapted her mother's legacy for the new consumer age.

The final chapter explores the work of Amy Jacques Garvey and Jessie Fauset, who were writers and activists at the heart of the New Negro movement in Harlem in the 1920s. The chapter shows that through their intellectual and practical endeavors, these women were at the forefront not only of the contemporary debate on the burning, and controversial, issue of black nationalism, but at the forefront of black feminism as well. It seeks to dismantle the fixed boundary between the Harlem Renaissance and the Garvey movement, and examines some of the ways that women played an important role in both movements. Chapter 4 also seeks to domesticate black nationalism in a positive sense and detach it from the gender of its major male spokesmen. Analyzing the role of black women nationalists makes it apparent that nationalism was no extremist, esoteric vision based on utopian fantasies of a return to African or separate black nationhood. Both an intellectual enterprise and sometimes a strategic one, black nationalism was the articulation of a greater shared sympathy among peoples of African descent than between white and black Americans, and one which imagined a community of peoples of African descent whose experiences during and after slavery drew them together in a common destiny.

The study concludes with an epilogue that suggests that what became central to the vision of many black women activists and intellectuals by the late 1930s was a biracialism based on equality rather than integration: that is, a firm belief that African American institutions should have equal access to resources and state provisions; integration could and should wait (potentially for a long time), and certainly until white Americans learned to treat blacks with respect.

1

Laying the Groundwork

Washington, Burroughs, Bethune, and the Clubwomen's Movement

Margaret Murray Washington, Nannie Helen Burroughs, and Mary McLeod Bethune were founders and central actors in the women's club movement of the late nineteenth and early twentieth centuries, who went on to become involved in pan-African and civil rights struggles. This chapter looks at how these three prominent clubwomen operated within the national clubwomen's circuit between the foundation of the National Association of Colored Women (NACW) in 1896 and the creation of the National Council of Negro Women (NCNW) in 1935, focusing particularly on their activities as clubwomen in the 1920s, a decade traditionally perceived as one in which clubwomen were increasingly out of touch with the racial pride that was symbolized by the masculinized New Negro. An analysis of the speeches, correspondence, and organizational activities of black clubwomen reveals that what distinguished them from their male counterparts was their capacity to understand and use both integrationism and black nationalism as weapons in the race struggle rather than as ideological islands that could be held and defended by any one individual. Working sometimes with whites and at other times exclusively with women and men of African descent, black women activists in the early twentieth century laid the foundations for the development of black feminist thought. This chapter seeks to integrate the careers of these three race women into wider interpretations of the clubwomen's movement and to demonstrate that the club movement was versatile, resourceful, and innovative in its capacity to respond to the changing needs of black women in a period of volatile race and gender relations.

The foremost organization of black women from its founding in 1896 until the early 1930s, the NACW was formed by the merger of the National Federation of Afro-American Women and the National League of Colored Women. Designed to unite duplicate national and local clubs into an organization which would be able to take a national approach to the problems facing African American women, the NACW became the central organization for black women's clubs that wanted to partake in social uplift outside of the church.

Starting off with 5,000 members, by 1915 over a thousand clubs were affiliated, with 50,000 total members.[1] The goals and aims of the NACW changed over time, and its membership included a wide variety of women and organizations whose beliefs spanned the political spectrum. For some clubwomen, the very founding of the NACW in 1896 represented a renunciation of the Victorian cult of true womanhood, as a contributor to an early issue of *National Notes*, the official publication of the NACW, explained:

> In the busy whirl of this nineteenth century woman no longer accepts the hearthstone as the circumscribed arena of her activities. Look where we may, we behold her stepping courageously across the threshold ... entering intelligently the various activities of life, working with her hands, her mind and her large sympathetic heart.[2]

As this confident assertion of black woman's capabilities makes clear, in the early years of the twentieth century, clubwomen were challenging the apparent divide between the public and the private sphere, insisting that they would not be confined to problems of the home and other traditional private-sphere activities. Recognizing the separation of the private and public as an essentially political act, clubwoman Christine Smith demanded to know in a 1915 issue of *National Notes* "why should man delegate to himself the power and the right to dictate to woman her sphere, where her development shall begin and where it shall end?" For Smith, it was about time that men woke up to the fact that what constituted the "woman's sphere" would increasingly be defined by women rather than men.[3] But there were others who saw advantage in the construction of a private, woman's sphere, and who continued to define womanhood through motherhood and the responsibilities of the home. In the same issue of *National Notes*, Ellen Key lamented what she saw as a decline in motherhood which she attributed both to the stress of wage labor and a "frivolous desire for pleasure" that made women "dry branches on the tree of life."[4] What comes across clearly from the variety of opinions expressed on the pages of the *National Notes* is that women were defining their own boundaries. Yet there has been a tendency on the part of historians to focus on the arguments of more conservative clubwomen. Too often the NACW is seen as having been hampered by a bourgeois ideology which undermined its capacity to act as an effective vehicle through which to challenge women's assigned role in the private sphere. The assessment that "by feminist standards the NACW was a conservative organization" is one with which many studies have concurred.[5] For example, in Floris Cash's study of black clubwomen and voluntary work in the Progressive Era she argued that not only did black clubwomen embrace patriarchy, but they dealt with this patriarchal society by "placing themselves at the top of a racial hierarchy based on white middle class morality and respectability."[6] This representation of black clubwomen as middle-class elites who were incapable of empathizing with their poorer sisters is supported by some of the earliest literary criticism on black women writers such as Jessie Fauset, who will be discussed later, and who was similarly viewed as unable to represent anything other than a narrow, middle-class viewpoint.[7]

Closely linked to this notion of clubwomen as limited by their middle-class sensibilities is the image of the NACW as a hotbed of bickering women, more concerned with scoring points and punishing enemies than addressing the needs and problems of black women.[8] While the disagreements between Booker T. Washington and W. E. B. Du Bois have been viewed as constituting a clear ideological division, differences of opinion among black women are labeled as petty and personal. Certainly cliques, petty squabbles, and the desire for personal advancement, or what has been termed "mistrissism," were undeniably a part of clubwomen's politics, as surely as of any other group politics. Recent accounts of individual clubwomen have been more understanding of the worlds in which their subjects worked and have placed clubwomen within the context of relationships between men and women, the settlement-house movement, and the wider feminist movement.[9]

Taking this more positive appraisal of clubwomen as a starting point, this chapter builds on the work of Victoria Wolcott, Stephanie Shaw, and others in its exploration of three leading clubwomen and how they developed alliances and networks which allowed them to transcend ideological divisions and establish strong black women's organizations in the first three decades of the twentieth century.[10] The careers of Margaret Murray Washington, Nannie Helen Burroughs, and Mary McLeod Bethune illustrate how clubwomen were capable of coming together time and again, even when they approached problems from very different ideological and social backgrounds, to agree to act together to promote the status of black womanhood. Their careers spanned the years that saw increased migration of black Americans to the North and to cities, World War I, and women's winning of the suffrage. The determination that black women would not be helpless victims of these developments was reflected in the national organizations which Washington, Burroughs, and Bethune built; between 1896 and 1935, they moved increasingly toward formal political organizing for black women, and away from reform activities, such as social welfare and school building, that could legitimately be seen as extensions of their motherhood roles. The growing concentration of black women's organizational headquarters in Washington, D.C., and New York City, the political and cultural capitals of the United States, reflected the increasingly political and national nature of black women's organizing in the early twentieth century. At the same time, by continuing to create new black women's organizations through the 1920s and 1930s, Washington, Burroughs, and Bethune demonstrated the continued importance of separatism, both racial and gendered, for black women in the inter-war era.

Margaret Murray Washington: Clubwoman and Pan-Africanist

Margaret Murray Washington was one of the founders of the national clubwomen's movement. Twice president of the NACW, she edited the NACW's official publication, *National Notes,* and founded the International Council of Women of the Darker Races (ICWDR). She was also the third wife of the "Great Accommodator" and race leader Booker T. Washington, and it is this association which has, mistakenly, come to define her race leadership. Accounts of clubwomen's activities and women's roles at Tuskegee have usually explained Washington in terms of her marital affiliation. At best, she has been dismissed as an elitist uplifter, and at worst, accused of imposing "middle-class" values on poor blacks.[11] Yet this middle-class label, often loaded with an implicit charge of conservatism, obscures the complexity of the beliefs held by women from such diverse backgrounds as the southerner Washington, the northerner Jessie Fauset, and the Jamaican Amy Jacques Garvey. This label also pays insufficient attention to the changing and unstable meaning of middle-class status among African Americans in the early twentieth century. Moreover, Washington has not been allowed to develop from her earlier career as southern educator and wife of Booker T. Washington to a national figure as president of the NACW and founder of the ICWDR in the 1920s. One explanation for this is the continued historiographical prominence of the Du Bois–Booker T. Washington dispute, which has obscured the ideological contributions of black clubwomen to both race and gender debates in the twentieth century.[12]

Washington is better understood if we take her early education and teaching career, rather than her marriage, as the origin of her political activities. Born in Macon, Mississippi, in 1865, Washington was the daughter of a washerwoman. Washington's childhood and adolescence revealed her to be a determined young woman from a far-from-comfortable background. Washington was seven years old when she was sent to live with Quaker teachers following her father's death. By the age of fourteen Washington had become a teacher herself and through part-time teaching was able to put herself through Fisk University, where she was a classmate of W. E. B. Du Bois.[13] She chose her role as race activist when she put herself in the path of Booker T. Washington after his commencement address at Fisk in 1889. The young graduate asked the school founder for a job at Tuskegee. Persuading her future husband to appoint her to the post of lady principal as well as the director of the Domestic Service Department, Washington soon became a key figure in the administration of Tuskegee, a position she consolidated by marrying Tuskegee's founder and president.[14]

Washington's marriage encouraged both her contemporaries and later historians to assume that she shared her husband's views. Yet her partnership also made it easier for her more progressive views to be tolerated by those in the Tuskegee camp, since she was less likely to be targeted as a radical.[15] Furthermore Washington was adept at managing her husband, often making decisions about matters which she presented to her husband as being up for negotiation. For example, in her correspondence with her future husband, Washington halfheartedly suggested she might give up some of her teaching responsibilities upon their marriage:

> If you do not object we will marry here at Martha's. . . . I should lose only a week . . . and I do not think it necessary for me to lose more. . . . Mr. Washington do you think I should go on with the work in the Academic Department? I should so much love to do this and yet I do not wish to be selfish in regard to the cares that come to every wife and that will come to me doubly. I love to work in the class room, and I want to make some money too because I shall need many things for the house.[16]

A woman who can spare only a week for her wedding, Washington suggests that she is unlikely to find contentment as a full-time wife, even with the additional responsibilities that came with being the wife of a race leader and stepmother to his children. After their marriage, Booker T. Washington's frequent absence on speaking tours meant that it was usually Margaret Washington who took decisions about Booker's children and the family finances. This role often extended into taking important decisions about Tuskegee as well, particularly in relation to the recruitment and management of Tuskegee employees.[17]

Washington was aware of the responsibility and prestige attached to becoming the wife of the most prominent black leader in America. Indeed, her own public profile increased when she became Mrs. Booker T. Washington, and she used this position to publicize her own causes. For example, while on their trip to Europe, Margaret Washington insisted on her husband's including an advertisement for the second biennial of the NACW in Chicago in his account of Paris for the *New York Age*.[18] Becoming Booker T. Washington's wife gave her a platform and an audience. Margaret Washington used this platform to speak out against race and gender discrimination, particularly to white Americans, whom she, like many black women, held collectively responsible for their failure to speak out against lynching.[19] She was most critical of "idle" southern women, who, as she complained to a white acquaintance, Ednah Dow Littlehale Cheney, had "little to do except to nurse their prejudices. They do not object to the colored woman who is their servant but they especially object to colored people who are not thus located."[20] Washington, unlike her husband, made few allowances for sectional differences between South and North, dismissing as cowardly northern white women's arguments that they could not challenge lynching as they had their southern white sister's sensitivities over the "race question" to consider. Washington was unsympathetic in her appraisal of white women's organizations such as the National Council of Women and the Women's Christian Temperance Union. She believed that they were more concerned with expanding their organization than with addressing issues of concern to all women and suggested that they deliberately ignored the suffering of black women so as to attract southern white women and boost their coffers through membership subscriptions.[21]

At the same time, Washington had to be careful about how her status as Booker T. Washington's wife affected her role as clubwoman. The same Washington who poured out her heart in protest to a white woman was, at other times, forced to temper her natural instinct to protest publicly when black women were discriminated against. Washington's attachment to her husband could limit her freedom of action, yet it is evident from Washington's role in the women's club movement that she was determined to forge her own career away from her husband and the confines of Tuskegee. While her local club work and social welfare work in and around Tuskegee sometimes provoked conflict with her husband, it was her role as prominent national clubwoman and eventually NACW president that caused the most tension, as Washington tried to implement her own program sometimes regardless of her husband's wishes. As president of the National Federation of Afro-American Women, the precursor to the NACW, Washington had been at the forefront of the move to bring about a national organization of black women. When the National Federation and the National League of Colored Women merged in 1896 to form the NACW, Washington became the chairperson of the Executive Board, a position she held alternately with being vice-president from the NACW's inception, until she was elected president of the NACW in 1912.[22] Washington was an important presence in the NACW from its very foundation. In addition to serving on the Executive Board in the years preceding her presidency, Washington was widely regarded as the voice of the new organization. When suffrage leader Susan B. Anthony asked representatives of national women's organizations to contribute articles for *The History of Woman Suffrage*, Washington, responding on behalf of the NACW, was the only black voice to be included in the volume. In her article, Washington outlined the work of the NACW, but also used the opportunity to criticize segregation laws, lynching, and the other hallmarks of white supremacy in the South.[23] Washington's role on the state and regional club circuit also enhanced her influence within the NACW, as she was the president and founder of both the Alabama Federation of Colored Women and the Southern Federation of Colored Women. Perhaps most important of all, Washington had founded *National Notes*, which she published from Tuskegee and for which she was regularly editor between 1897 and 1922. This position gave her considerable influence over how the meetings and debates held at conventions were presented both to the membership and within the black press.

Washington held a powerful position within the women's club movement, yet her husband was able to restrain her when he felt she compromised his own agenda. For example, in 1904, pressure from her husband led Washington, then vice-president of the NACW, to withdraw her support for a resolution she had introduced at the NACW's Fourth Biennial calling for a boycott of the World's Fair in St. Louis because of discrimination against black women.[24] Besides attempting to rein in her public protest against racial discrimination, Booker and his cohorts also played an important role in the creation and upholding of Margaret Washington as an extension of her husband. In his autobiography, *Up from Slavery*, Booker T. Washington paid tribute to his wife. Carefully defining and circumscribing her role, he described Washington as his helpmate rather than equal partner and national women's leader. Booker claimed that Washington was "completely one with me in the work directly connected with the school, relieving me of many burdens and perplexities."[25] Several years later, in an article written about Washington by her husband's secretary, Emmet J. Scott, this piece of evidence would be recited as confirmation of the couple's ideological closeness.[26] However, a close examination of Margaret's public speeches reveals the degree to which she had a different agenda from that of her husband.

Before she established her own career on the clubwomen's circuit, Washington was often called upon to speak before large audiences because of her status as Booker's wife. In her speeches Margaret Washington blamed slavery for the ignorance, poverty, and intemperance of many rural African Americans. By contrast, her husband spoke of how "it was much better for the colored people to correct and improve their ways within the race than to spend their time abusing another race that is now above it on account of superior education."[27] Margaret Washington's criticism was directed less at the poor and ignorant, and more at the already uplifted women of the race, who neglected their duty to help the downtrodden. Moreover, she used her speeches as an opportunity to redefine black womanhood and encouraged other black women to do the same. Washington rejected white ideals of womanhood as both outdated and demeaning to black women. She defined the black woman as strong, active, and with agency over her own life and insisted that, "It is no longer a compliment to a girl or woman to be of a frail and delicate mold. It is no longer an indication of refinement in woman to possess a weak and fastidious stomach."[28] Washington did not glorify motherhood, nor did she see it as the central task of black women. However, she was concerned with the falling birth rate and rising mortality rate among African Americans. The language Washington used to express her concern with infant mortality positioned her closer to the race-expansion arguments of black nationalists than the cult of true womanhood's emphasis on the duty of women to be mothers and confine their activities to the domestic sphere. Washington was concerned by the high rate of tuberculosis and pneumonia among black Americans because these diseases were "robbing the race of its future race men and women." For Washington, the declining birth rate was worrying because African Americans could not afford to be outnumbered by whites, especially in cities where they were growing in political strength, if they were going to be an equally strong race: "The death rate of our children is something to make us tremble. As long as it is so high we cannot hope for much. Numbers count for a great deal in this country."[29] Sounding more like Marcus Garvey than Booker T. Washington, she called on black women to produce children for the sake of the race. Yet Washington was ambivalent in her attitude toward motherhood, confessing to Booker prior to their marriage that she knew little about bringing up children and suggesting she was not keen to find out more.[30] Perhaps her own child-free status and skepticism as to the joys of raising children made it difficult for her to view motherhood as the defining experience of womanhood, nevertheless she believed that healthy mothers and infants were essential to the survival of the race.

Washington, Suffrage, and the Public Sphere

Washington's speeches and activities within the public sphere promoted the view that black women had much to offer beyond motherhood. She admired "professional and business women whose interests are being pushed so that the woman, who is inclined to be independent of her father and brothers in her struggle for a living, may not be swallowed up."[31] Yet Washington's views on the status of women and the public sphere have often been held up to illustrate the ambivalence of black women toward the suffrage.[32] Historians have pushed Washington into the accommodationist camp alongside her husband, who had long refused to go on record as a supporter of women's suffrage and was only a very late convert.[33] This view of Margaret Washington is usually based on a speech in which she outlined the work that black women had done through the clubwomen's network, and where they should be going in the future. From this speech, Washington has often been quoted out of context as saying: "Personally woman suffrage has never kept me awake at night."[34] Yet in this same speech Washington also put on the record her unequivocal support for women's suffrage: "Colored women, quite as much as colored men, realize that if there is ever to be equal justice and fair play in the protection in the courts everywhere for all races, then there must be an equal chance for all women as well as men to express their preference through their votes."[35] Washington went on to explain that women's suffrage was not the most important goal for which black women should agitate, because the powerful and frequently racist white women's suffrage movement would ensure it would happen anyway. Moreover, Washington's skepticism as to how far the ability to vote would change fundamentally the status of African Americans was a position she shared with Du Bois and other strong supporters of universal suffrage.[36]

Washington was in fact an active supporter of black women's suffrage. She was among the first handful of black American women to vote in Macon County, Alabama, and she encouraged others to join her. It was under Washington's presidency of the NACW that the association voted to endorse the suffrage campaign. In her speeches and journalistic pieces, Washington drew attention to the fact that the NACW had a department of suffrage which held training classes on the Constitution in order to help black women exercise their vote intelligently.[37] Washington also used *National Notes* to support the right of women to vote, as well as to publish the writings of others who favored women's suffrage:

> We have not blown up houses with dynamite, nor have we been engaged in parading the streets in men's attire. . . . but of one thing I am certain, we are reading and studying the great questions which are to make for the good of the country, and when the vote is given to women as it surely will be where it is not already done, we shall be ready to cast our votes intelligently and there shall not be the general accusation that our votes are for sale from all the way from a drink of liquor to two dollars.[38]

Although Washington disassociated herself from the militant suffragettes in England, she urged black women to be prepared to use their vote. Toward this end, Washington also used her work with local women in Tuskegee, through the Tuskegee Women's Club, the Town Night School, and the Russell Plantation, to deliver voter education.[39] At the same time, Washington was implicitly criticizing black men when she declared that women's votes would not be for sale. Washington believed that women had a public role to play in improving their homes, their communities, and therefore the race. However, she was well aware of the restrictions imposed by black men on women's leadership and the necessity of organizing in women-only groups. When Washington was speaking to women-only groups, there was little evidence of accommodationism, either to white racism or black men's authority. On the contrary, for Washington the role of the clubwoman, whether in the local self-help club or the NACW, was "revolutionizing communities and bringing about their moral and civic salvation and so saving the race to itself." Through working together at the national level, representatives of local clubs could achieve wide-reaching reform. The NACW would serve as a "hustling ground to build better homes, to establish good schools, to insist upon a more intelligent ministry, to teach respect for the aged, to bring man and woman, husband and wife, to a realization of their individual responsibility."[40] In other words, the women of the NACW had a role to play in leading the race. Washington's own role as a race leader expanded following her husband's death in 1915. For much of her career, Washington had worked as a social reformer and educator. However, in the late 1910s, she became increasingly interested in political organizing around pan-African issues and understanding the conditions that affected all women of African descent. Having made her mark at the local and national level, Washington's interests, like those of many other black clubwomen, turned increasingly toward international alliances with women of African descent.

Washington and the ICWDR: The Development of Organized Pan-Africanism

Washington's role in bringing leading race women together in one pan-African organization in the early 1920s marked an important moment not only in her intellectual evolution, but also in that of black women's thought and leadership. Headed and in large part inspired by Washington, the International Council of Women of the Darker Races (ICWDR) was a forum designed to facilitate international cooperation through the dissemination of knowledge about the cultures and customs of peoples of African descent.[41] The women who had for so many years made up the backbone of the NACW adapted and contributed to the racial debates of the 1920s through their involvement in the ICWDR. The history of the ICWDR complicates our understanding of the debates about racial identity and black Americans' attitudes to Africa, which have usually been seen as central to the Harlem Renaissance and Garvey movement. Through their pan-African organizing in the 1920s, black women created a platform from which they articulated their own vision and influenced these debates.

The ICWDR was the result of a growing interest in pan-African issues among clubwomen that could be traced back to the beginning of the century. At the national level, the NACW biennial conventions frequently included discussion panels on the needs and status of African women, reflecting a desire for more knowledge of life and conditions of women in Africa and the Caribbean. Discussions ranged from the effects of French and British colonization in Africa and the Caribbean, to the ways in which race and gender oppression served as planks of American colonization in Liberia, Haiti, and the Philippines. Women from around the African Diaspora were often featured as guest speakers at NACW conventions. At the Detroit Convention in 1906, NACW members had the opportunity to learn about the lives of Liberian women from Mrs. De Baptiste-Faulkner, who had come to the convention to request affiliation with the NACW for an organization of women in Liberia.[42] The convention granted permission for affiliation, with a view to developing their international alliances. Delegates to the convention then heard from Ida Gibbs-Hunt, who would later become a member of the Pan-African Congress movement, on the conditions of women in Madagascar. Gibbs-Hunt also spoke on the importance of international alliances among "women of color" and was empowered to set up a Madagascan branch of the NACW.[43] These efforts to create international networks of NACW clubs around the African Diaspora, would, it was hoped, "make a strong self-dependent, self-respecting people."[44]

In the 1910s Washington became increasingly interested in pan-African causes. She had long been a proponent of black history and women's studies, which she promoted through her club work in and around Tuskegee. One of the main achievements of the Tuskegee and Town's Women's Clubs that Washington had set up was to teach black history and encourage local schools to put it on their curriculum.[45] She also influenced the NACW's anticolonial agenda in its critique of European and U.S. imperialism in Africa. It was on her watch as chair of the Executive Board of the NACW that the board voted in 1910 to petition the U.S. Congress to denounce the atrocities committed by the Belgian government in the Congo Free State.[46] The ICWDR's interest in promoting understanding of the achievements of peoples of African descent built on Washington's work within the NACW. At the 1920 biennial held on Washington's home turf, Tuskegee Institute, the NACW passed a resolution to ask black teachers throughout the United States "to teach our boys and girls the lives of the great men and women of our race, who have thus far shaped, and are shaping, our destinies." The convention resolved that local clubs would work to achieve this through putting African American literature as well as works of black history into school libraries.[47]

That the formation of the ICWDR took place at the NACW's 1922 convention was fitting, since it was at this national meeting that pan-African issues took center stage on the convention program. One of the guest speakers at the Richmond convention was Adelaide Casely Hayford, who would later become a member of the ICWDR and delegate to the Fourth Pan-African Congress in New York City. Born into a Creole family in Sierra Leone, Hayford founded the Girls Vocational School in Freetown, served as lady president of the Freetown UNIA, and became a valued member of the international pan-African movement.[48] According to the minutes of the convention, Hayford dressed in "attractive native costume." She apparently "held the audience spell bound, as she pleaded the cause of African womanhood." Emphasizing the importance of motherhood and community life and cooperation in Sierra Leone, Hayford preached an empowering message of black is beautiful, through her description of the beauty of African women. Hayford's appeal evidently worked, since she succeeded in picking up a collection of more than a hundred dollars in less than fifteen minutes.[49]

The NACW's interest in promoting understanding of the cultural heritage and political situation of diasporic Africans was also demonstrated by the presence of James Weldon Johnson and Jessie Fauset at the Richmond convention. James Weldon Johnson, field secretary for the NAACP, spoke on literature and Haiti, while Fauset, novelist and literary editor of *The Crisis*, described the Second Pan-African Congress, which she had attended the previous year. Explaining the purpose of the Congress, Fauset spelled out the serious problems facing peoples of the African Diaspora in an international system geared toward the interests of white people. She explained the difficulty of promoting the interests of peoples of African descent when there was not even an American "colored representative" to the League of Nations. Fauset also spoke of the significance of the Congress meeting at the very centers of African colonization—Paris, Brussels, and London—and described how the Pan-African Congress had excited not just attention and enthusiasm in the pan-African world, but also fear on the part of the white governments of the world.[50]

Two weeks later, in Washington, D.C., the first organizational meeting of the ICWDR was held, with Washington in the chair. With representatives from Africa, Haiti, the West Indies, Ceylon, and the United States, the new council would focus on the "economic, social and political welfare of the women of all darker races."[51] At this initial meeting many of the themes of the early pan-African program of the NACW were continued. The focus of the first year would be the development of an organized plan for the study and dissemination of African American history and literature, and a committee consisting of Addie Dickerson, Nannie Helen Burroughs, and Mary Church Terrell was appointed to draw up a course of study for the year.[52] The meeting agreed upon a list of books that ICWDR women would study in the forthcoming months, including Hubert Anthony Shands's *White and Black*, Stephen Graham's *The Soul of John Brown*, and ICWDR member Elizabeth Ross Haynes's *Unsung Heroes*.[53] The need to introduce courses on African American history and literature in black schools was also discussed, and it was agreed that a start could be made on schools in which members of the ICWDR had links. As educators, many members of the ICWDR had direct access to schools, but they also used their club networks, as well as those of their husbands, to help get black literature into schools. Members of the ICWDR also generated publicity and funds for black schools that developed race pride across the Diaspora.[54]

Following the initial gathering in the summer of 1922, the new organization increasingly became Washington's main focus. By the autumn she had given up for good the editorship of *National Notes* in order to spend more time on the new council. The following August, leading clubwomen from around the country spent three days of discussion at Burroughs's National Training School in Washington, D.C., in the course of which they drew up a constitution and chose officers. Washington was elected president, while Addie Hunton and Mary Church Terrell became vice-presidents. The executive committee, which included Mary McLeod Bethune, was chaired by Burroughs. Other key appointments made in the drawing up of the new council were the heads of the three committees: Addie Dickerson, a successful real estate broker from Philadelphia, leading clubwoman, and well-known pan-Africanist, would head the Committee on International Relations; Atlanta clubwoman Lugenia Burns Hope led the Committee on Social and Economic Conditions; and Mrs. W. T. B. Williams, Tuskegee teacher and clubwoman, would head the Committee on Education. Other associate members included two former NACW presidents, Mary Talbert and Elizabeth Carter, and educator Charlotte Hawkins Brown.[55] Washington believed that self-knowledge was the first step toward greater self-respect and race pride, and as such, one of the aims of the ICWDR was to disseminate information on the culture and customs of peoples of African descent.[56] Toward furthering this goal, the ICWDR formed Committees of Seven in black communities, which studied problems of various regions of the African Diaspora. For example, Washington's own local committee chose to focus on Sierra Leone, Liberia, and Ethiopia, while other committees studied women in Japan. They also published the findings of one of their members on the condition of women and children in Haiti. The ICWDR also kept abreast of incidents of racial discrimination that were attributable to Americans who packed their racism when they traveled abroad. For example, they "express[ed] to the French government our commendation of the democratic stand taken in its recent decision concerning race discrimination."[57] This probably referred to the ejection of Kojo Tovalou Houenon, a Dahomean "prince" and leader of the pan-African movement in France, from a bar in Paris, at the request of white American tourists. Following protests in the National Assembly, the French premier, Poincaré, ordered the bar to be shut down, and banned the screening of *Birth of a Nation*, D. W. Griffith's racist tribute to the Ku Klux Klan.[58]

In 1924, at what would prove to be the last meeting before Washington's death, the ICWDR debated the identity of the organization. Members agreed to extend membership to women who were leaders in fields other than the NACW, including YWCA women Eva Bowles, Helen Curtis, Jane Hunter, and Elizabeth Ross Haynes, as well as the writer Georgia Douglas Johnson and sculptress Augusta Savage.[59] But the question of whether the ICWDR was to become another interracial organization was a more difficult matter to settle. Should the ICWDR, like the NACW, become affiliated with white women's organizations such as the National Council of Women, or should the ICWDR remain devoted to the cause of pan-African sisterhood?[60] ICWDR members held divergent views about whether the organization should pursue links with white women. In a letter sent to the 1924 meeting, Lugenia Burns Hope suggested that council members network with white women's groups. The Atlanta clubwoman, who had a long track record of interracial work in Atlanta, wanted a discussion about whether ICWDR members should seek representation on "all local committees of whites that are particularly interested in colored work."[61] Significantly the conference delegates came to no decision on how they might develop Hope's idea, but gave Washington permission to respond to Hope on their behalf. This Washington did some months later when she expressed some of her own reservations about working with white women, suggesting that "this is not an easy thing to do in some places but it can at least be tried." Washington recognized that many black clubwomen had experienced uncomfortable relationships with white women in the past and so urged ICWDR to think carefully about Hope's suggestion. She recommended that members respond only at a local level and according to each woman's individual experiences of interracial work in their local communities.[62]

Washington's original motivation for forming the ICWDR had more to do with encouraging racial solidarity than interracial cooperation. So while the women of the ICWDR did not turn their backs on individual interracial cooperation, the ICWDR constitution deliberately excluded white women. Pointing to the gulf that existed between white and black women in America because of the fundamental inability of white women to understand the hardships suffered by black women, Washington explained that, "The Anglo-Saxon race [is] barred because of [its] racial antagonism to darker women—not being defamed like women of color, hence [it] would not have the interest and could add nothing to the determined purpose to ameliorate conditions for darker races throughout the world."[63] On the one hand Washington was suggesting that it was futile to try and work with white women because they were incapable of understanding the issues facing black women, but from a pragmatic, leadership point of view, she was happy for individuals to try and seek alliances with white women. That these two planks of the ICWDR could run side by side might appear contradictory. There was clearly no place for white women in an organization that aimed to foster alliances between women who suffered because they were of "the darker races." At the same time ICWDR women could network with white women's organizations if they chose. This was, in effect, what black women had been doing for years: publicizing their cause and attracting funding from whites, while focusing on the pride and achievements of black womanhood.

Because the ICWDR has often been viewed only as a short-lived offshoot of the NACW, accounts that stress the shortcomings of the latter organization tend to view the ICWDR as sharing many of the same limitations, especially in terms of its middle-class membership.[64] The ICWDR served an important bridging function between the NACW and the impetus that led to the formation of the NCNW in 1935. The ICWDR clearly grew out of the NACW in so far as it reflected the National's developing concern for pan-African causes at its biennial meetings. Moreover, the women who came together to form the ICWDR were a combination of women who had been responsible for running the NACW from its inception, through the 1910s, as well as the current leaders, including the then vice-president-at-large, Mary McLeod Bethune, who would become NACW president in 1924. In terms of its personnel, structure, and purpose, the ICWDR was a child of the NACW, particularly its Committee on Peace and Foreign Relations, of which Washington was the national chairman. At the same time, the ICWDR was also an important forebear of the National Council of Negro Women in terms of its international focus, particularly its function as a pressure group and networking organization for African American women.[65]

The women who came together to form the ICWDR and promote a pan-African agenda were taking a radical stance in the early 1920s. The post-war environment in which the ICWDR was founded saw heightened surveillance of black activists by the federal government, a development inspired in part by black Americans' pan-African organizing.[66] Nannie Helen Burroughs and Addie Hunton were among those ICWDR women who were targeted by the Department of Justice in the early 1920s.[67] In the context of post-war race relations, and the rising prominence of J. Edgar Hoover within the intelligence services, the black women who joined the ICWDR and involved themselves in the pan-African movement were categorized as subversive and out of line with more mainstream black leaders. Aligning with the pan-African movement in the 1920s was risky even for prominent civil rights activists such as Du Bois, let alone for less-protected female activists like Hunton and Burroughs.[68]

Historians have generally seen the ICWDR as more or less disappearing in 1925. Certainly the flow of letters among ICWDR members (as members of that organization as opposed to their other affiliations, or in other words, letters on ICWDR letterheads) seems to decrease after 1925. This was, in large part, because of the death of Margaret Washington in 1925. Indeed, Washington's central role within the organization was recognized at the time. An article in the *Tuskegee Messenger* described the inspirational role Washington had played and how her death initially hindered progress. However, the article also noted that the objectives and standards set during Washington's presidency were inspiring the current ICWDR members in a study of conditions in Mexico, and encouraging wider contacts with women across the "darker world."[69] The ICWDR existed until at least 1935. Largely under the guidance of Addie Dickerson, it continued to protest the treatment of Africa and peoples of African descent in the international arena. In 1935 the *Afro-American Ledger* reported on a recent meeting of the ICWDR in which Dickerson, then president of the ICWDR, urged members to register their protest against Italy's invasion of Ethiopia. The ICWDR also sent telegrams to Secretary of State Hull, "urging him to insist that Italy be bound by the Kellogg-Briand Peace Pact." Still active in the ICWDR in 1935 were Burroughs, Bethune, Carter, Hunton, and Terrell, among others.[70] The ICWDR survived the death of its leader, and the pan-African consciousness the ICWDR had developed was channeled into other organizations. The late 1920s were years of great activity on the part of ICWDR members, who, under the auspices of the black women's organization the Circle for Peace and Foreign Relations (CPFR), sponsored the Third and organized the Fourth Pan-African Congresses. Having begun the process of opening up an international dialogue among women of African descent, the energy of the ICWDR was transferred into the Pan-African Congress movement in the late 1920s.

The Pan-African Congress Movement

Women who became active in the ICWDR had been involved in the Pan-African Congress movement from the start. Pan-Africanist Ida Gibbs-Hunt had been a speaker at the first two European-based congresses, and Hunton, vice-president of the ICWDR, had made an address on the role of women in post-war development at the First Pan-African Congress and was also a member of the twelve-person international committee to sign the call for a second Congress.[71] About the time that Hunton was becoming heavily involved in the ICWDR, she was also president of CPFR. Like the ICWDR the CPFR promoted education and dissemination of knowledge about women of the African Diaspora. It was also responsible for promoting and financing the Second and Third Pan-African Congresses.[72]

It was not surprising that women's most high-profile practical contribution to the Pan-African movement took place in the mid to late years of the 1920s, when the ICWDR had laid the groundwork for black women's involvement in pan-African movements. With no stirrings of a Pan-African Congress on the horizon, it was Addie Hunton and the CPFR who decided it was time to organize what would become the Fourth Pan-African Congress. Having gained the reluctant support of Du Bois, the CPFR issued an invitation to the Fourth Pan-African Congress to be held in New York City in August 1927.[73] It was significant that the first ever Pan-African Congress held in the United States would be organized by African American women, and their leading role must be attributed in part to the work of the ICWDR, which encouraged pan-African thought and practice.[74] It was also significant that much of the credit for the success of the Congress would go to men, particularly Du Bois. Yet the correspondence between Du Bois and Hunton reveals that it was Hunton and the CPFR who bore the entire responsibility for organizing the Congress and who should have received the credit for its success.[75] In spite of reports, written mostly by Du Bois and reprinted in the *New York Times,* which would lead readers to conclude that women had been all but absent from the Congress, the women organizers had used their organizing position carefully to ensure that black women gave the majority of the speeches on the first day of the Congress.[76] Introduced by Hunton, Du Bois was, perhaps inevitably, the opening speaker, but the rest of the first day was devoted to speeches by Coralie Franklin Cook, who spoke on conditions in Africa, a panel on African missions including an address by Helen Curtis and Addie Dickerson, and a discussion led by the Reverend Florence Randolph and a Mrs. A. B. Camphor. Meanwhile the reception was hosted by the women of the 137th Street YWCA.[77] While male speakers dominated the rest of the three-day Congress, it was significant that women, who had been sidelined at many of the former Congresses, used their organizational role to promote themselves.

In its manifesto, the Fourth Pan-African Congress echoed many of the concerns and demands of the ICWDR, including the withdrawal of American forces from Haiti and condemnation of the treatment of black South Africans by white South Africans. It also emphasized the importance of forging international alliances with other members of the "colored races" throughout the world in order to bring about meaningful racial justice. Black women's successful organizing was evidenced by the fact that Du Bois, who had been reluctant to encourage Hunton while the preparations for the Congress were in progress, gave a glowing account of it afterwards. In his account Du Bois recognized that the Fourth Congress not only had more delegates than previous Congresses, but "had received the largest amount of carefully catalogued information concerning the peoples of African descent presented to any such session."[78]

The success of the 1927 New York Congress was built upon the development of pan-African thought and organization by members of the NACW and ICWDR. By tracing the connections between the NACW's developing interest in pan-African issues, the formation of the ICWDR, and the CPFR's leadership of the Pan-African Congress movement in the late 1920s, it is evident that the pan-African movement was far from being the "singularly monolithic" movement requiring the "submergence or silencing of gender," as some commentators have argued.[79] The histories of the ICWDR and the organizing committee of the 1927 Congress also reveal the extensive networks which existed between clubwomen and artists who were central to the cultural renaissance that was taking place in New York, Washington, D.C., and other urban centers. Both the ICWDR and the CPFR attracted not only clubwomen but also many feminist writers who were central to the Harlem Renaissance, including Jessie Fauset, Georgia Douglas Johnson, Alice Dunbar-Nelson, Regina Andrews, and Dorothy Peterson.[80] In common with other black women's clubs in the early part of the twentieth century, the ICWDR's membership list included a vast array of women from diverse backgrounds, political perspectives, and organizational affiliations, who embraced a range of approaches along the integrationist-separatist spectrum. Through its personnel and its development of pan-African thought and action, the ICWDR symbolized both the conflict between, and the compatibility of, black nationalism and interracialism within the black clubwomen's movement. At a time when few race organizations explicitly precluded white membership, its deliberate exclusion of white women was unusual. On the other hand, the ICWDR allowed its members to network with white women's organizations on an individual basis. The ICWDR involved black women with pan-Africanism at a time of intense racial consciousness among African Americans and enabled them to take a leadership role within the pan-African movement through their organization of the Third and Fourth Pan-African Congresses. Pan-Africanism in America in the 1920s, as manifested through the Garvey movement, the Pan-African Congresses, and the literary debates about African identity encouraged by the Harlem Renaissance, was the result of years of women's pan-African programs and organizations; it did not spring up suddenly after the war; nor was it the exclusive preserve of male leaders. Washington made a significant contribution to the development of pan-Africanism in the first half of the twentieth century, through her local and national club work and the foundation of the ICWDR. A woman of the South, and wife of the most conservative black leader of the post-Reconstruction era, Washington was at the same time a founding mother of pan-Africanist endeavor among black women in America.

Nannie Helen Burroughs: Educator, Church Leader, and Clubwoman

Often referred to as the female Booker T. Washington, for her leadership of the National Training School (NTS) for girls in Washington, D.C., Nannie Helen Burroughs's reputation has also suffered on account of her being associated with the Tuskegee Wizard. Burroughs frequently shared platforms and correspondence with Booker T. Washington, but she was not afraid to criticize him, an attitude that prompted Melvin Chisum, one of Washington's spies, to label her a "dangerous tramp."[81] On one occasion she wrote to Washington demanding to know why he allowed the vulgar bragging and misleading rags-to-riches stories which male delegates indulged in at his annual National Negro Business League Convention.[82] In fact it is Burroughs's often scathing critiques of white and black men and her powerful voice as secretary of the Woman's Convention (WC) of the National Baptist Convention (NBC), with its tradition of racial separatism, which has led Sharon Harley and others to associate

Burroughs's expressions of race pride with the black nationalism of Marcus Garvey.[83] Evelyn Higginbotham, however, views Burroughs as more of an assimilationist, whose rhetoric of respectability served to reinforce white stereotypes about the black masses and to privatize racial discrimination.[84]

Burroughs also played a central role in black women's organizations outside the church. Besides her religious and educational institutional affiliations, Burroughs was a board member of the National Urban League, the NACW, the ICWDR, and the National League of Republican Colored Women (NLRCW), and was the founder of the National Association of Wage Earners (NAWE). A dark-skinned educator who strived to improve the conditions of black working women and promote cultural pride in blackness long before the onset of the Harlem Renaissance, Burroughs does not fit easily into accounts of clubwomen imposing their own intellectual and sexual standards on others, which perhaps explains why she has not featured prominently in accounts of the NACW and clubwomen in general.[85] Rather, Burroughs has usually been discussed as part of wider studies of the black Baptist movement or of black educators. These studies have examined Burroughs's role in the creation of a separate sphere for black women within the NBC as well as her unique position as a school founder who was not dependent on white philanthropy.[86] This section looks at how the black feminist nationalist perspective that influenced her as a church leader and educator also shaped her work within the clubwomen's movement. Examining how Burroughs brought this perspective to her work as clubwoman over a period spanning more than fifty years, from the woman's era to the modern civil rights movement, helps us move toward a more diverse portrait of black women's organizations in the early decades of the twentieth century.

Nationalism and Feminism within the Black Baptist Church: Burroughs and the Women's Convention

Scholars of the Baptist Church have explored the growth of nationalist sentiment among black Baptists in the aftermath of Reconstruction, and the subsequent creation of a separate black power base in the form of the National Baptist Convention.[87] An important symbol of black separatism throughout the twentieth century, the NBC was formed in 1895 as a result of the growing frustration among African Americans with the discrimination they suffered within the white Baptist Church and associated institutions, particularly Baptist schools.[88] Black women had played an important role within the black Baptist organizations that had proceeded, and pushed for, the creation of the NBC.[89] As Higginbotham has demonstrated, black Baptists' nationalist tendencies were developed in the context of a growing feminist sensibility within the Baptist Church, which at times produced gender tensions. Yet it was this very nationalist discourse with its message of empowerment and separatism which helped to inspire the creation of the Woman's Convention of the NBC.[90] It was difficult for black women to accept the principle of self-determination when they were still being told what to do by black male leaders. As with many other groups of black women who were working within male-controlled institutions in the early twentieth century, Baptist women's feminist consciousness was fostered by the separatist strategies and philosophies they developed alongside black men.

The Woman's Convention was launched in 1900, when a group of Baptist women came together at the annual NBC gathering in Richmond to form a separate organization to represent the interests of women.[91] Burroughs encouraged women to join the WC with her "How the Sisters Are Hindered from Helping" speech, in which she argued for greater gender equality through separate conventions.[92] She would serve the organization first as corresponding secretary, a post she held for forty-eight years until she became president in 1948. The purpose of the WC was to bring black Baptist women from across the United States to work together and develop bonds between women from varied backgrounds within the church. Like the ICWDR and many other African American women's organizations in the early twentieth century, the WC was also international in its outlook and interested in developing links with women of African descent throughout the Diaspora. They paid for African American women to travel to Africa, sent money and food shipments to missionaries already in Africa, and raised funds to pay for the education of African students at black schools in the United States, particularly the NTS.[93] The WC employed other traditions of the clubwomen's movement, including national conferences, which met annually at the same time as the NBC, and at which they shared ideas and developed a common vision of black womanhood. The WC also welcomed speakers of national repute to inspire their membership. Famous race women who addressed WC conventions included the founder of the hair and beauty empire, Madam C. J. Walker, bank president Maggie Lena Walker, and Mary Talbert, former NACW president.[94]

Just as the WC adopted some of the traditions of the NACW, it has also been subject to many of the same criticisms. Although the membership of the WC tended to be of lower social standing than that of the NACW, its officers—Burroughs included—have been viewed as assimilationist in their adoption of "the hegemonic values of white America" and their rejection of the values of the "folk."[95] For Higginbotham, this behavior is encapsulated in what she calls the "politics of respectability," a set of moral codes which served as a guide to blacks' individual public behavior as well as a strategy for improved race relations.[96] Higginbotham views the politics of respectability as a self-defeating strategy, because in attempting to subvert white society's negative constructions of blacks by preaching the importance of clean homes, polite behavior, and sexual abstinence outside marriage, WC officers in fact reinforced racist stereotypes that poor blacks were morally bankrupt and in need of reform. Moreover, by demanding that African Americans reject their "rural folkways of speech, dress, worship and other distinct cultural patterns" in favor of "middle class values and behavioral patterns," Higginbotham argues that black Baptist women only served to heighten class stratification within black communities.[97]

There is a problem, however, with constructing so many dichotomies around contested categories that are by no means independent of each other: folk versus urban, middle class versus working class, accommodation versus resistance. For example, to speak of middle-class values being imposed on working-class women requires us to ignore the different ways in which race, gender, and class intersected for and were understood by white and black middle classes. White middle-class respectability differed from black middle-class respectability, and the latter by no means accepted or shared all the values of the former. For example, it was often the employment of black domestic help that provided the white homemaker with the time to pursue the status that signified middle-class respectability. Yet these same domestic servants were sometimes included in the ranks of the black middle classes. Black Americans from a range of social classes and backgrounds insisted on the sexual propriety of their young black women and emphasized the risk posed to them by years of sexual exploitation at the hands of white men, a fear that was reinforced by white constructions of all black women as sexually promiscuous and easily available. Higginbotham's analysis of respectability accepts that racial uplift through respectability could have been about accommodating white values and resisting gender and racial oppression simultaneously. Nevertheless, for Higginbotham, the politics of respectability carried an implicitly assimilationist message.[98] However, the resistance-versus-accommodation framework does not always help to explain the complex ways in which race, class, and gender intersected in black communities in the early twentieth century. As Wolcott has persuasively argued, the emphasis on black women's sexual respectability was not primarily about assimilating white society's gendered norms; it was in fact resisting racial *and* gendered constructions of black women as sexually immoral.[99]

I argue that we need to understand the racial-uplift activities of black communities within the context of debates about integration and racial solidarity. A leader who frequently employed black nationalist rhetoric, Burroughs focused more on what blacks could do to help themselves than on integration. Indeed, black nationalists have always been vulnerable to the charge that they accommodate white racism. The notion that blacks must have self-respect and agency over their lives to bring about change rather than relying on white power structures to effect change has been regarded as absolving whites of any blame. Yet Burroughs did not deny the responsibility of whites. She protested racial discrimination, argued for institutional change, and was prepared to engage in interracial work with white Baptist women. In concert with white women, she devised strategies for the uplift of the black poor and was ready to accept financial help from those whose skin color meant they had greater access to such resources. But given the deteriorating racial climate of the early twentieth century, a strategy that relied on persuading whites of the humanity of African Americans to thereby secure equal rights seemed increasingly unrealistic. For Burroughs, the race struggle was less about accommodating whites and their expectations of blacks, and more about the importance of self-definition as a means to empowerment. The motto of the National Training School (NTS) encapsulated this belief: "Work. Support thyself. To thine own powers appeal."[100] Burroughs believed that this self-definition could take place in spaces where black women were free from the racial expectations of white men and women and the gendered expectations of black men. In such environments racial uplift could also be based on cross-class cooperation and community consensus.[101] We see evidence of this self-definition and cross-class cooperation in the creation of the NTS, and particularly in the negotiations that took place between parents, teachers, and the WC concerning black women's work and sexuality.

Training Race Women: Burroughs and the National Training School

The NTS was set up by Burroughs under the auspices of the Woman's Convention and chartered independently of the NBC. Opening its doors to its first thirty-one girls in 1909, the school recruited eighty-three students the following year, suggesting that many black parents shared with Burroughs the view that only a girls' school could "give personal attention to the whole life of the girl." Burroughs was passionate in her belief that young black girls benefited from receiving an education in single-sex institutions: "Careful investigation shows that the women who are rendering the most effective service in slum, social settlement, reformatory and mission work were trained in separate schools."[102] Equally adamant in her belief that only the Woman's Convention could offer appropriate supervision of the NTS, Burroughs fought repeatedly, and successfully, the attempts of the male leadership of the NBC to wrest control of and gain credit for the achievements of her school.[103]

The NTS promoted the dignity of women's work both for its own sake and as a means of economic security and political autonomy for black women. Describing her vision for the school to the WC, Burroughs explained that "we . . . are anxious for our girls to learn to think but it is indispensable that they learn how to work." Historians have tended to view Burroughs's educational philosophy through the framework of the Du Bois–Washington dispute over industrial or classical academic education. Higginbotham views Burroughs's school as a natural extension of the Tuskegee industrial school, whereas Johnson focuses on the school's race pride and promotion of black economic nationalism. Wolcott meanwhile views the NTS as a training ground for race activists ready to join in the crusade for civil rights. Burroughs, however, did not believe she had to choose between either Washington's or Du Bois's view of educational uplift, since "an industrial and classical education can be simultaneously attained, and it is our duty to get both."[104] The NTS curriculum reflected this belief, offering what it called trade courses as well as more formal academic subjects. For example, in the first year of the standard four-year high school program, students were required to take classes in the Bible, English, algebra, Negro history, Latin, French, general science, and music, as well as "practical arts," physical education, and homemaking. They could also choose from a variety of trade courses besides domestic science which included business-shorthand, typing, bookkeeping, business practice, dressmaking, designing, printing, automobile mechanics, interior decorating, Christian workers and social service, health service, and practical engineering.[105] Burroughs's ability to attract financial backing from within the black community rather than relying on white philanthropists undoubtedly allowed her more flexibility in shaping the school curriculum than some other school founders. One need only compare the language of Burroughs's school brochure with that of North Carolinian school founder Charlotte Hawkins Brown, who relied heavily on white philanthropy to fund her school, and who was repeatedly frustrated by her patrons' views on the intellectual abilities of African Americans.[106]

In addition to being known for its domestic training courses, Burroughs's school also had a reputation for its philosophy of self-help and racial pride. Its African American History course was a source of particular pride, as Floyd Calvin explained in a 1929 article for the *Pittsburgh Courier*:

> The department of Negro History is of especial pride at the National Training School. . . . Every student must take the course in Negro His-

tory. Recitation every day for two months is held in the subject, then an examination is held, both written and oral. The students then write orations on Negro achivements, and by a process of elimination the two best orators from each class are selected. From these winners an oratorical contest is held annually, at which three awards in gold are made. The contests have created wide interest and a healthy familiarity with Negro history and with current events among Negroes.[107]

Although the NTS offered a variety of subjects and placed high importance on celebrating and commemorating events in black history, the school was criticized for turning out well-trained domestic servants.[108] It is true that NTS literature emphasized domestic science as one of its four major offerings. It was known as "The School of the 3 Bs": "Bible: Clean Lives; Bath: Clean Bodies; Broom: Clean Homes." The school's literature frequently emphasized the importance of domestic science. One such brochure, entitled "Negroes Who Have Helped Themselves," claimed that: "The greatest unmet educational need of the Negro race is for women with trained heads, hands and hearts to develop the social and esthetic taste of its home and church life."[109] But as this reference to black community life suggests, the NTS was not, as Burroughs and her supporters reiterated, primarily about training girls to become domestic servants for whites, but rather inspiring them to serve their communities.[110] Nor did NTS literature emphasize domestic science courses at the expense of other subjects. The same 1930 brochure described its three highest aims as the creation of social workers and Christian leadership, musicians for churches, and businesswomen, secretaries, and professional stenographers. Homemaking courses, although described as the "greatest unmet need," were placed fourth.[111]

The daughter of a domestic, Burroughs refused to follow the same career while its status and working conditions made it one of the most badly paid and low-status jobs available to African American women. Yet she recognized that the majority of black women who worked outside agriculture had few options besides domestic service. The national census showed that in 1910, 22 percent of black females over the age of ten worked in "domestic and personal service," the largest single category outside agriculture, which attracted 55 percent. By 1930, the percentage of black women employed in domestic service had risen to 29 percent, while agricultural employment for black women had fallen to 37 percent.[112] As well as offering girls training in alternative careers, Burroughs believed it was necessary to change the status and conditions of domestic service, and she aimed to do this by presenting her students as highly skilled, professional household managers, rather than as poorly paid menials. Burroughs's emphasis on the skills of black domestic workers was not as unrealistic a strategy as it might appear today. The first half of the twentieth century was, of course, the last moment when housework was regarded as skilled labor.[113]

Closely related to the debate about resistance versus accommodation in black women's work and education is the NTS's emphasis on sexual respectability. Burroughs was always clear that the NTS was a Christian school "good enough for girls who are the best in morals and mind and too good for girls who are below the accepted standard in morals and mental calibre."[114] The emphasis placed on sexual behavior by Burroughs, the WC, and the NTS has contributed toward the view that they tried to impose white middle-class ideas of sexual respectability on an otherwise more sexually liberated black working class. To view hard work and sexual respectability as evidence of accommodation to white middle-class values is problematic, particularly when juxtaposed with the resistance to white middle-class values promoted by the sexually confident blues singers and other representatives of the "folk."[115] As Wolcott has shown, there is evidence in the correspondence between the teachers and parents of NTS pupils that suggests parents wanted their daughters to be taught the importance of sexual abstinence as a means of resisting sexual exploitation. One of the reasons parents preferred their daughters to receive training in skills other than domestic service at the NTS was because of its close association with slavery, and the fear that their daughters would be exposed to sexual exploitation in their white employer's homes as they and their mothers had been. This preference was reflected in the choices of NTS students: 51 percent chose sewing as their major, 29 percent business, with only 15 percent majoring in domestic service.[116] Wolcott and others have challenged the assumption that sexual mores were the preserve of middle-class black women, and have recognized the possibility that "notions of morality, respectability, cleanliness and religiosity were not ideological gifts of the middle class handed down to the poor, but rather part of a pre-existing working class culture."[117] As an unmarried woman in a public leadership role, Burroughs was particularly aware of the difficult sexual stereotypes with which black women had to contend. Most clubwomen and race activists had managed to tuck a marriage into their hectic schedules. Even though many of them, like Burroughs, lived in female households, and away from divorced, dead, or similarly absent husbands, more than one clubwoman found an old marriage convenient in providing her with a less sexually threatening and more-respected status.[118]

Burroughs demonstrated that black women were capable of making their own judgments about what constituted appropriate public behavior for black women which did not conform to hegemonic gender norms. Burroughs's esteemed position among clubwomen and black churchwomen gave her the support she needed to challenge black men publicly. Burroughs had few qualms about taking her quarrels with black Baptist men outside the church and placing them on public view to help her win her cause within the NBC. For example, when the male leadership of the NBC attempted to wrest control of the successful NTS, Burroughs turned to friendly black newspapers to defend her position. With the help of the Oklahoma City *Black Dispatch*, Burroughs defiantly informed those "Men who frowned on effort [who] would now seize big achievement" in no uncertain terms that "Nannie Burroughs is not going to leave the National Baptist Convention, and she is not going to be kicked around like a hound dog." Burroughs was prepared to enlist her male supporters to help maintain her leadership position with the Baptist Church. For example, she persuaded Carter G. Woodson to write an effusive article about her school in the *Afro American*.[119] Yet Burroughs's defiant rhetoric demonstrated that she was guided neither by white nor black men's expectations of what constituted appropriate feminine behavior, but rather by a confidence in her fitness for leadership.

Burroughs exerted her leadership and that of the WC through her close supervision of the NTS. For Burroughs, the NTS was not primarily about accommodation to either white society's demands for obedient servants or to black middle-class Washingtonians, but about providing young women with skills that would enable them to find dignity and race pride through work. Her belief in the dignity of work should be understood in the context of a wider movement on the part of black women to professionalize other traditionally low-status jobs. For example, Burroughs had much in common with Madam C. J. Walker, who professionalized black hair-dressing in the 1910s and '20s. Like Madam Walker, who also used the NBC as well as many other black national organizations to promote the status of black hairdressers, Burroughs tried to market domestic training in ways that would be compatible with race pride, suggesting it was about community building as well as higher wages and skilled employment.[120] As this and later chapters will show, Walker and Burroughs employed similar methods in their efforts to raise the status of their respective professions: both women founded a workers association, both had a training school from which young women graduated with a professional qualification, and both had an official journal. The NTS's publication, *The Worker*, first issued in April 1921, publicized the school's mission, but also addressed pan-African concerns, such as the exploitation of the Congo by Belgium.[121]

Ultimately, however, Burroughs was not successful in marketing domestic service as a means to enhanced status and income for black women in the way that Madam Walker was able to do with the black hair industry. As will be demonstrated in Chapter 3, Madam Walker's success lay in the fact that she offered training in skills that would be used exclusively by and for black women; Burroughs's domestic training furnished young women with the skills needed to serve white homeowners. In spite of this, Burroughs was successful in encouraging students to be race-conscious women who viewed work in both the domestic and the public sphere as appropriate for black women, and an arena in which they could make a difference. This was testified to by the numerous graduates of the NTS who went on to become businesswomen, race activists, and homemakers, options that were never seen as mutually exclusive.[122] The training offered by the NTS encouraged young girls to take on a range of jobs when they graduated and developed the idea that economic independence was something every girl should aspire to, rather than the resort of women whose husbands could not support them. The success of this vision is reflected in the responses to a 1934 survey of former students which revealed that many NTS graduates had avoided domestic service and taken up a variety of jobs within black communities as teachers, stenographers, missionaries, nurses, dressmakers, and "cottage mothers" in black orphanages.[123] Burroughs's promotion of the workplace as an arena in which trained, race-proud black women could find a niche was not shaped primarily by the expectations of white society or the expectations of black men within the NBC, some of whom opposed Burroughs's promotion of women as breadwinners.[124] Rather, in promoting the dignity of women's work, Burroughs was trying to help other women make meaningful choices. The variety of careers taken up by former students shows that the NTS played a considerable part in making choice possible.[125] The growth of institutions—schools, churches, or club organizations—where black women could meet away from white women and men played an important role in providing black women with a sense of agency, choice, and self-definition. In order to fully appreciate this we now need to reconsider the wider context in which Burroughs's school operated, her affiliations with other race and women's movements, and her growing commitment to pursuing nationalist and feminist strategies. Put in this context, Burroughs's preaching on cleanliness, thrift, and sexual abstinence can be seen as more than simply resistance to white representations of black women. It was about racial solidarity and a desire to protect black women and to extend to them the ability to protect themselves. Burroughs's race philosophy was also about building up black communities through developing leadership among young black women. This was a theme emphasized not just in NTS literature, but throughout Burroughs's career as an educator, clubwoman, and race activist.

Burroughs and the NACW

Nannie Burroughs was critical of a certain type of clubwoman, what she called "the kid glove order," who saw work with the poor as being beneath them: "They leave the platform and applause after a flowing paper talk on some burning race question and retire to their parlors where whist and euchre and merry music are indulged in until early morning."[126] Burroughs believed that club life was not simply a way for privileged black women to pass their time but rather was an arena through which women could become involved in actively helping the masses. Her censure of certain aspects of club life came not as an outsider looking in, but as someone who was part of an ongoing dialogue among clubwomen about their purpose, and who as a clubwoman herself was trying to bring her vision of black womanhood and club life to fruition. Burroughs's vocal criticism of certain elements of club life may explain why she has not featured prominently in accounts of clubwomen. Yet Burroughs's was an unignorable voice within the clubwomen's movement: a representative of a million or more black Baptist women, Burroughs carried considerable weight with national organizations, and she used it to press her own priorities on the clubwomen's agenda. For example, in November 1918, Burroughs persuaded Mary Talbert, then president of the NACW, to call a meeting to address the problems affecting industrial women workers.[127] Burroughs's persuasive oratory also made her a powerful force at NACW conventions. One newspaper report of an early NACW convention address by Burroughs described her as "a woman of great oratorical ability" who "carried her audience by storm."[128]

Although Burroughs never served as president of the NACW, her reluctance to accept the top job should not obscure the important role she played in shaping the many organizations to which she belonged. Burroughs served as a guide and mentor for more than one NACW president who was reluctant to take decisions without her support. Mary Talbert and Mary F. Waring were particularly reliant on Burroughs for advice and support during their presidencies, while Bethune regularly consulted her.[129] She also held many leadership positions within the NACW, including head of the Young Women's Work Department and head of the Business Department, as well as serving as a regional president in 1922.[130] As had her predecessors Madam Walker and Maggie Lena Walker, Burroughs used her chairmanship of the Business Department to urge women to create their own economic opportunities. At the 1906 Detroit Convention, Burroughs made a speech in which she advocated black economic nationalism as a means to unite and uplift the race by providing more and better employment opportunities: "The trouble with colored people, is they do not stick together and patronize their own race."[131] Voicing sentiments that Amy Jacques Garvey would echo in her women's page of the *Negro World* twenty years later, Burroughs told the convention of women that there were opportunities being created by black men and women to own homes and businesses, that had been enhanced considerably by the education and training now available in black-run and -owned schools like her own. Burroughs insisted on the power of black people to influence their own fate, in spite of the many obstacles imposed by white America. In common with many black feminists, Burroughs's nationalism was not only compatible with, but an intrinsic part of the feminist outlook she brought to the clubwomen's movement.

Burroughs's approach to club work was also guided by her view of black gender relationships. Like earlier black clubwomen and later female Garveyites, she was critical of black men for their failure to recognize the value of their women and for trying to hold them back. She appealed to black men to "Stop making slaves and servants of our women. We've got to stop singing 'Nobody works but father.' The Negro mother is doing it all. The women are carrying the burden." Burroughs believed that women were responsible for building black communities, churches, and schools through organizations such as the NACW because "men lack manhood and energy." [132] Burroughs used a critique of black manhood to justify women's involvement in the public sphere. As we will see in Chapter 4, this was a well-rehearsed strategy among women who were trying to carve out a space for themselves in the Garvey movement. Burroughs called on black men to glorify black womanhood. But unlike male Garveyites, Burroughs did not want to place black women on a pedestal. Burroughs knew more than most that the majority of black women had to work regardless of their attachment to working men. She called for greater recognition of this fact to be translated into greater respect for women as family wage-earners, valuable employees, and voters. The National League of Republican Colored Women and the National Association of Wage Earners were designed to achieve just that.

The National League of Republican Colored Women: Suffrage and Club Politics

Burroughs did not view the ballot as the one tool capable of transforming the lives of the majority of black women in America. This skepticism was typical of black clubwomen at a time when black women were being excluded from white women's suffrage campaigns. Like many black women, Burroughs had long felt alienated from her white sisters by the racist techniques employed in the struggle to gain the suffrage.[133] For Burroughs, the capacity of white women to bring about meaningful social reform was limited by what they saw as their own rights: "they [white women] want to be able to keep their cooks and house servants in the kitchen for fifteen hours a day."[134] At the same time, Burroughs was in no doubt as to whether black women should have the vote and use it. When a southern white suffragist asked Burroughs "What can the Negro woman do with the ballot?" Burroughs responded "What can she do without it? When the ballot is put into the hands of the American woman the world is going to get a correct estimate of the Negro woman."[135] Yet in her report to the Twentieth Annual Session of the Woman's Convention Auxiliary to the NBC in September 1920 (the year the Nineteenth Amendment, giving women the right to vote, was ratified by the states), Burroughs spoke at length on the limited impact of the ballot on the lives of black working women. Burroughs pointed out that the position of black domestic workers in America had hardly improved in spite of their theoretical right to vote. She gave as an example the minimum-wage laws which had been introduced after the Nineteenth Amendment by the Washington, D.C., government, which failed to include domestic workers. Given that 65 percent of domestic workers were black, the minimum-wage law clearly discriminated against African American women, and showed that a government voted for by predominantly white men *and* women was no less capable of implementing laws that discriminated against black, working women.[136] It was hardly surprising that women's suffrage, which had been won by a racist campaign, was of little use in influencing a government that tolerated and abetted white supremacy. Increasingly, Burroughs came to believe that the only way in which domestic workers could improve their conditions would be by forming unions and working together to promote their own interests in the manner of white labor groups.[137]

Although Burroughs believed that the right to vote would not in itself transform the opportunities available to black women, she was still determined that there should be a woman's voice in black politics. Recalling the strength and determination of her ancestors, Burroughs argued that black women's history of struggle made them fit to use the vote wisely: "she has guided homes through poverty, toil and often shame, from the cradle to the grave. She has pushed back love to support her aged parents and save them from toil. . . . she has kept the home fires burning through a hundred wars." Rather than accepting a boundary between the private and public sphere, Burroughs argued that it was women's very domestic skills that made them valuable participants in the political world. Burroughs's recognition that for all its limitations, black women should try and make the most of the ballot was reflected in her advocacy of suffrage clubs "in every church" to teach women how to use the ballot.[138] It was also reflected in her leadership of the National League of Republican Colored Women (NLRCW). The NLRCW was formed in part in response to criticism that the NACW had compromised its position by taking such an overtly party political stance in the 1924 election. The NACW was meant to be a national force for uniting women from all political and social backgrounds, but at election time it more often became a campaigning tool for the Republican Party. Not only did the *National Notes* frequently editorialize in favor of Republican Party candidates, but in 1924, Hallie Q. Brown, then president of the NACW, also became the national co-coordinator for the Colored Women's Department of the Republican National Committee. Following the successful election of Republican candidate Herbert Hoover in November 1924, Brown used the December issue of *National Notes* to pay tribute to the success and influence of black women in the recent election and to call for a permanent political organization for black women.[139]

Following the 1924 NACW biennial in Chicago, Republican Colored Committee women Mrs. George S. Williams and Mary C. Booze called a meeting of black clubwomen for the purpose of forming a new organization. The aims of the NLRCW were outlined: "to educate and interest women all over the country in the exercise of their citizenship rights and to urge that they use the ballot in an honorable, intelligent manner for the promotion of such candidates and measures as will vouchsafe to the Negro citizens of the country their constitutional rights and privileges."[140] While the desire to maintain the NACW as a nonpartisan forum inspired the creation of the NLRCW, the NLRCW relied on the women's networks that made up the NACW as part of its organizing and campaigning strategy. Estelle Davis, a Republican clubwoman, acknowledged as much in *National Notes*: "our organized club work . . . has not only trained us for service but has created a nation-wide sisterhood through which we know the outstanding women of each state who are able to serve our race in the time of need."[141] Burroughs was appointed president, and other leading NACW members became officers.[142] Although a positive move to bring black women together as a collective voice in black politics, the formation of the NLRCW was also a product of failed interracial cooperation. The new organization reflected the continued racism of white women who refused to come together with black women to form a block that could influence national politics. It also demonstrated how little influence black women were now able to exert on the Republican Party. While Burroughs, as an appointee of the Republican Party's National Speakers' Bureau, was a sought-after speaker, by the end of the 1920s she, like many other clubwomen, had become disillusioned by the party's failure to listen to black women's demands beyond election time. Clubwomen rapidly moved away from the party of black freedom in the 1930s as expectations that Herbert Hoover might be more sympathetic toward race issues soon dissipated.[143] More positively, the NLRCW reflected the growing understanding on the part of black women of the need for a political pressure group that could really influence national politics and that would reach fruition with the creation of Mary McLeod Bethune's National Council of Negro Women in 1935.

It was in the context of the bitterness created by the women's suffrage campaign and of debates about how the suffrage had impacted on black women, that Burroughs brought together leading clubwomen to form the National Association of Wage Earners (NAWE). Organized in 1924, the NAWE was designed to protect the interests of domestic workers.[144] According to its constitution, the purpose of the organization was to "develop and encourage efficient workers," to "assist women in finding the work for which they seem best qualified," to secure a decent wage, to educate black women as to the value of organization, and to influence the passage of legislation to benefit women workers.[145] Once again the personnel of this organization overlapped with that of the NACW, the ICWDR, and the NLRCW. Burroughs was president, with Bethune acting as vice-president and the Richmond banker Maggie Walker as treasurer.[146] Higginbotham suggests that the ideals of the NAWE reflected a "bourgeois reformism," that is, Burroughs was simply seeking a wider place in American capitalism for black women, rather than challenging a system that relied on denying black Americans equal access to the job market. According to Higginbotham, Burroughs was naïve in her belief that if only employers and their employees could sit down and talk to one another face-to-face, they could resolve their differences.[147] Certainly the NAWE was not trying to challenge the capitalist system. Rather, it reflected the principles that governed Burroughs's leadership of the NTS. Burroughs sought to promote race pride by providing black women workers a space of their own where they could share strategies for negotiating with white employers. At the same time, Burroughs recognized that black women's status as voters following the Nineteenth Amendment had little impact on their status as workers, or their ability to effect change through the electoral system. The government continued to exclude domestic workers from the protection of minimum-wage laws.[148] It was imperative therefore that black women continue to organize in separate gender and race groups on issues that affected them as black women.

Burroughs's wide-ranging affiliations meant that she served as an important link between clubwomen and other race organizations.[149] One striking example of this was her role as passionate protestor against the discrimination suffered by black soldiers who were giving up their lives to defend a democracy abroad that they were not privileged to share at home. Burroughs used her report to the Woman's Convention to demand the passage of antilynching legislation and an end to unequal Jim Crow customs. By a majority vote, the WC voted to send Burroughs's report in 1919 to the president as well as to state governors. Under Burroughs's guidance the WC's executive board also agreed that churches throughout the nation should use the Sunday before Thanksgiving to unite in a day of prayer and protest against the "undemocratic and un-Christian spirit of the United States as shown by its discriminating and barbarous treatment of its colored people." The NACW and *The Crisis* played an important role in supporting and advertising the event, and making it a nationwide protest.[150] For all Burroughs's involvement in race-based organizations, she did not completely eschew interracial cooperation, and she was prepared to fight for integration if it would improve the position of African American women. For example, she was a member of several interracial organizations, including the NAACP and National Urban League, and she took part in civil rights protests such as the boycott of Washington's segregated transport system.[151] However, the 1904 report she wrote for the WC on the segregation policies of railroad companies stressed their unfairness in terms of unequal, rather than separate, and called for better toilet facilities for African American women. Burroughs argued that black women wanted the same treatment and quality of facilities available to white women, rather than that they wanted to use the same facilities.[152]

While Burroughs worked with interracial groups, she was more concerned with equal provision for blacks than integration with whites. In numerous speeches delivered to and on behalf of the many clubs with which she was affiliated, her race pride often expressed itself in a black nationalist language which, like the language of many black women active in the club movement in the early years of the twentieth century, became more militant and clearly articulated as the decades passed. For example, in 1933, ten years after Garveyism in the United States had reached its peak, Burroughs delivered a speech that would have received a warm welcome at a UNIA convention. Insisting that "The Negro must serve notice on the world that he is ready to die for justice," Burroughs argued that no compromise was acceptable, no "charity, philanthropy, or . . . manmade institution" could replace the African American's "equal rights."[153] Twenty years later, when she was asked by a group of white women in 1954 what black people in America wanted, Burroughs famously responded: "We don't want your teachers, we have our teachers; we don't want your furniture, nor your clothes, we have plenty of clothes;

we don't want your doctors nor your preachers; we have our doctors and our preachers. . . . What we ask is fair play and to be let alone."[154] Burroughs distinguishes equality, her key demand, from integration, an entirely different issue. For Burroughs, black Americans do not want charity, nor to become more like whites. Rather, they want the removal of those obstacles that make self-sufficiency hard to achieve. At the same time, Burroughs believed that black Americans had an important role to play in developing race pride. They had to stop accepting white oppression. They must "stop apologizing for not being white and rank your race."[155] Burroughs contributed to racial debates of the Harlem Renaissance, insisting that all African Americans, including artists and writers, should be glorifying the beauty of blackness. It was probably for this that Burroughs was praised by the black nationalist Amy Jacques Garvey on the women's page of the *Negro World*. In an article fittingly entitled "A Great Woman of the Race Who Works," Jacques Garvey paid tribute to Burroughs for organizing the NAWE and establishing a worthy school for girls, and encouraged other women to support this "great" race woman.[156] Burroughs spoke the language of the New Negro. She talked of the need for the black American to "wake up spiritually," because only then would he "stop playing white, even on the stage." She spoke of the majesty of his soul, and the need to "glorify the beauty of his own brown skin." Anticipating the Black Arts Movement, Burroughs affirmed her pride in and love for black people everywhere: "I believe it is the Negro's sacred duty to spiritualize American life and popularize his color instead of worshipping the color (or lack of color) of another race. . . . No race is richer in soul quality and color than the Negro. Someday he will realize and glorify them, he will popularize black."[157]

Burroughs's leadership positions within the Baptist church and club organizations placed her at the center of black women's networks in the first half of the twentieth century. She used this influence to push the interests of black working women onto the agenda of the organizations she belonged to, and to create new organizations that would address the concerns of domestic workers. Burroughs's commitment to building race pride and her engagement with New Negro rhetoric made her an important contributor to racial debates during the Harlem Renaissance. It was fitting that Burroughs would host the inaugural meeting of the International Council of Women of the Darker Races at her Training School in Washington, D.C. Burroughs's work with Bethune in the National Association of Wage Earners, and her recognition of the need for politicized black women's organizations, would also lead her to support Bethune's initiative for a separate Council for Black Women in 1935.

Mary McLeod Bethune: Integrationist and Pragmatic Separatist

In an article written for *Who* at the height of her influence as director of Negro affairs within the National Youth Administration, Bethune gave an account of her early life and career. She described her transition from the child of former slaves, to college founder, and eventually to the most powerful black woman in the United States. Exploiting the language of the American dream, Bethune's narrative is replete with the requisite log cabins, an unexpected knock on the door that "changed my life over-night," as well as the usual luck, grit, and determination that characterizes such tales.[158] By engaging in a rags-to-riches discourse, Bethune's account appealed to white liberals, suggesting that black Americans could transcend the obstacles of race, gender, and class. At the same time, Bethune spoke directly to her black audience, justifying on practical grounds the interracial composition of her school's Board of Trustees: "Strongly inter-racial in my ideas, I looked forward to an advisory board of trustees composed of both white and colored people. I did my best missionary work among the prominent winter visitors to Florida."[159] Here Bethune offers two explanations for why her school had an interracial board of trustees. First she suggests she was ideologically committed to interracialism. But she leaves us with the amusing line about missionary work among rich whites, implying that she converted ignorant, uncivilized whites to the Bethune religion. Wealthy, white northerners vacationed in Daytona, Florida, including James Gamble of Procter & Gamble, and she wanted their money for her black girls' school. Bethune suggests her commitment to interracialism was as much strategic as ideological, because she also emphasizes her belief in racial difference. In the same passage, Bethune recalls her African origins, and her pride in her mother's "royal African blood . . . a tribe ruled by matriarchs." For all the interracial sentiments Bethune expressed in this account, she is in the end her mother's daughter; it is her African blood, rather than her American upbringing, that "will not let me rest while there is a single Negro boy or girl without a chance to prove his worth."[160]

Bethune's ability to present herself as an unswerving and committed integrationist, while at other times evoking a black economic and cultural nationalism, is a theme that runs throughout her career. In her educational work, her role as director of Negro affairs for Roosevelt's New Deal programs, and her leadership of clubwomen, Bethune used strategies both of integration and black separatism. Her flexible approach has caused difficulties for historians who have understood Bethune through the framework of the Booker T. Washington–W. E. B. Du Bois debate. For example, Audrey McCluskey views Bethune's reliance on white philanthropy to support her school as evidence of "Bethune's indoctrination into the industrial education movement as championed by Booker T. Washington and the white political-industrial elite who supported him."[161] Certainly Bethune's educational philosophy was influenced by Booker T. Washington. But, as Bethune later explained after visiting Tuskegee, she not only saw much she wanted to emulate, but also what she must do differently:

> I envisioned an institution in which would be taught the essentials of home making, of the skilled trades, but there would also be courses stressing the importance of citizenship and the duty of the citizen using his voting power. These courses must be unduly stressed, as a measure of realizing citizenship in its entirety.[162]

Here we see Bethune's modus operandi, straddling the Du Bois–Washington divide, taking elements of both and adding what she always saw as her crucial ingredient, her leadership: a college head who would be "a modern matriarch, head of the family."[163] To the black community, Bethune presented the girls' school she founded in Daytona, Florida, as a symbol of black women's success at doing things for themselves. For the white philanthropists who funded the school and sat on the board of trustees, Bethune's pupils put on school concerts. The integrated audiences at these performances allowed Bethune to present Daytona as an island of interracial harmony in an otherwise segregated ocean.[164]

Bethune's willingness to combine different approaches, as well as her ability to perform for whites so as to carry out her own agenda while also publicly protesting against discriminatory treatment, has led historians who have concentrated on her educational leadership to describe her position as one of "pragmatic idealism."[165] This label might also be applied to her role as a New Deal administrator. Experiencing at first hand the New Deal's unsatisfactory separate and far-from-equal policy, she nevertheless argued not for integration, but for racial equality, and insisted that African Americans be responsible for directing programs for African Americans. Bethune's policies ensured that some of the benefits of limited federal responsibility for the poorest members of society found their way into the most needy black communities.[166] As was the case for many other black women leaders, including Washington and Burroughs, Bethune's strategy and philosophy depended on the circumstances, the cause, and the audience. At times, Bethune promoted an economic black nationalism. For example, she became a major shareholder in a black-owned business venture at Volusia Beach, near her school in Florida, which was designed not only to exhibit pride in black achievement and allow black Americans to enjoy the beach together, but also to protest discriminatory practices of white beaches.[167] At other times Bethune argued that economic separatism was not a desirable goal: "We must spread out as far and as fast as we can." But she also recognized that "as long as Negroes are hemmed into racial blocs by prejudice and pressure, it will be necessary for them to band together for economic betterment."[168] In common with many other black women, Bethune was adept at performing different racial and gender roles for different audiences. The contrast between how she presented not only the school, but also her own leadership to white and black, male and female audiences struck those of her contemporaries who saw her perform. Lester B. Granger of the National Urban League remarked: "Mrs Bethune had the most marvelous gift of affecting feminine helplessness in order to attain her ends with masculine ruthlessness."[169]

Bethune's role as an educator and her experience in negotiating with white government officials are important, since both helped to shape her contribution to club life. The school at Daytona provided a political power base not simply for Bethune, but also for the many black women who passed through its doors and who would go on to become political activists and educators themselves.[170] Building on those accounts that emphasize Bethune's pragmatic idealism as an educator and New Deal administrator, the rest of this chapter explores Bethune the clubwoman, and suggests that her careful blending of integrationism and black nationalism and her ability to perform differently for white and black audiences characterized her work as a clubwoman throughout the 1920s and 1930s.[171]

Bethune and the NACW

Bethune's first involvement in regional club work came through her association with the Florida Federation of Colored Women. As president of the Florida Federation of Colored Women's Clubs from 1917 to 1924, Bethune built on the experience she had gained and networks she had already established as a school founder and fund-raiser to bring together other state clubs in the region. In 1920, Colored Women's Clubs from Alabama, Georgia, North Carolina, South Carolina, Tennessee, Mississippi, and Virginia formed the South-eastern Federation of Colored Women's Clubs.[172] Through the Southeastern Federation Bethune expanded her sphere of influence and worked with other distinguished clubwomen who had frequently held office at the highest level in the NACW, including Charlotte Hawkins Brown and Lugenia Burns Hope, as well as her "Big Sister" Margaret Murray Washington, with whom Bethune was on intimate terms.[173] Bethune also gained experience of how to use regional club networks to set up new projects. Through local

Figure 1. Mary McLeod Bethune leading her pupils at the Daytona Educational and Industrial Training School for Negro Girls. *School Catalog*, 1910–11. By permission of Florida State Archives.

clubs Bethune raised funds for a home for delinquent girls in Ocala, Florida, in 1921. She also used her contacts in the southern clubwomen's movement to set up local Red Cross chapters and a Circle for Negro War Relief to aid black soldiers and their dependents during World War I.[174]

Younger than Washington, though four years Burroughs's senior, Bethune did not begin to serve her apprenticeship in the national clubwomen's movement until 1912, when she first addressed a NACW convention. According to NACW member and historian of the movement Elizabeth Lindsay Davis, Bethune "made a wonderful impression by telling the story of her early life and her connection with the Girls Training School at Daytona, Florida."[175] Evidently Bethune was already a convincing speaker; on hearing the young Bethune, Madam Walker agreed to head a fund-raising campaign for the struggling school, while NACW president Margaret Washington ordered a collection for the same purpose.[176] Bethune would return Walker's trust, raving in a letter to the successful entrepreneur and beauty culturalist: "For the past four years my girls and myself have been using your Wonderful Hair Grower . . . and would be very glad to place it in our school as a course of study."[177] By 1919 Bethune had become a powerful force within the national organization; in that year she was put in charge of the education department, and from 1922 to 1924 she served as vice-president-at-large under Hallie Q. Brown, a position which traditionally led to the presidency.[178]

Bethune did win the 1924 NACW presidency, but only after a contest which saw her take on and defeat the veteran antilynching campaigner Ida B. Wells. In contrast to the sometimes cantankerous Wells, Bethune was famed for her diplomacy. As president, Bethune would, like Margaret Washington, use *National Notes* as a forum through which to communicate her ideas, ask her readers for their opinions, and endeavor to create a united black womanhood. Bethune believed that the journal played an important role in ensuring NACW officers kept in touch with the membership, particularly at a time when she was in the process of creating a more centralized organization. Appointing a full-time editor, Bethune moved the editorship of the *National Notes* to Daytona, and later to the National Headquarters. Each edition of *Notes* carried a "message from the president," in which Bethune put forward her ambition for a more diverse association. Describing the NACW as a "cosmopolitan body," Bethune claimed that "among its membership may be found women from the humblest walks of life as well as women with the highest degree of culture. By this means the womanhood of the race is being touched in all of its various phases."[179] Certainly Bethune tried to fulfill this vision through instituting a membership drive. Whereas previous and subsequent presidents had relied on a membership of 50,000, Bethune claimed to have a membership in the hundreds of thousands. Bethune's administration also tried to bring the NACW leadership closer to its members by transferring the biennial convention from its traditional East Coast venue to Chicago in 1924 and Oakland in 1926.[180]

Bethune strove to inspire pride among African American women in the achievements of the NACW and a greater sense of unity among members. One of her strategies for realizing this was through the raising of funds for the establishment of permanent headquarters in Washington, D.C. Bethune hoped the new national headquarters would serve as a clearinghouse for "cooperative effort" among African American women, encourage systemization of record keeping, and provide a permanent home for the NACW archives.[181] To celebrate the acquisition of the new headquarters in the nation's capital, a service was held as part of the 1928 biennial meeting, to dedicate the building. Former NACW presidents including Hallie Q. Brown and Elizabeth Carter were allowed a moment of reminiscence before Burroughs dedicated the new headquarters to "the womanhood of the world" and to the "social, moral and spiritual uplift of all women."[182] Bethune also pushed through a revised constitution and published an official guide and directory, written by a collaboration of individual members and departments of the NACW.[183] This new handbook outlined a seven-point platform which reflected well Bethune's careful balancing of black nationalist and interracialist strategies: "Education, Industry, Thrift, Citizenship, Social Service, Racial Solidarity and Interracial Relations."[184] While several of these planks represented traditional strands of uplift, the juxtaposition of the last two was not a coincidence. For many, racial solidarity came first, but was not incompatible with striving to open up more opportunities for black women through improved interracial relations.

Under Bethune's leadership the NACW departments reflected the diverse membership body that Bethune had encouraged. Major departments within the NACW under Bethune included business, publication, young women, health and hygiene, social work, and women in industry. However, Bethune did not abolish all of the more traditional departments, keeping the departments of fine arts, literature, and music. The minor departments, which were more narrowly defined, also reflected a range of interests, including health and education issues that particularly affected poor black communities, such as tuberculosis, hospitals, illiteracy, vocational education, race history, maternity and child welfare, housing, and delinquency.[185] Bethune was keen to use her experience in helping local black communities in Florida through the Florida State Association and South-eastern Federation of Colored Women, to encourage other member organizations of the NACW to raise funds for the building of hospitals and the training and employment of African American medical staff. She publicized the activities of those member organizations that had contributed to the establishment and upkeep of black colleges and health centers, and praised organizations that offered their clubhouses for use as public health clinics.[186] Bethune also used her presidency to encourage discussion of pan-African issues. She invited speakers to NACW meetings to discuss the status and conditions of women in Africa and raised funds to support the work of black women on the African continent. In this way Bethune continued her interest in Africa which dated back to her early thwarted ambitions to become a missionary and which inspired her to become one of the founding members of the ICWDR.[187]

Bethune campaigned against segregation all her life. Yet her presidency of the NACW reveals that her commitment to integration was not at any price, nor was it straightforward. Black women's organizations could help to build race solidarity and develop leadership and enterprise skills. Bethune argued that black Americans "must master the business of taking care of themselves like other races." Bethune also argued for the importance of African Americans using strategies of economic and political nationalism in their leadership, for the sake of "colored people throughout the world." Envisioning a world gathering of "colored women," Bethune wanted the NACW to provide a link to "peoples of color throughout the world." As she explained in her presidential address to the fifteenth biennial of the NACW: "Bred, born and living here under the American Flag we nevertheless bear a relation to others of our blood. Their problems are ours and vice versa." Her involvement in the ICWDR and the pan-African movement helped transform her vision for black people's independence into an international one. Bethune saw the "color question" as "belting the world," particularly through the colonial oppression of African peoples by Western powers.[188] Throughout her presidency of the NACW Bethune insisted on the importance of African American women coming together in organizations to represent one voice for black women. By 1928, however, Bethune believed that there was no single organization that could adequately represent the political interests of black women.

Bethune and the Roots of the NCNW: White Clubwomen and the NACW

Bethune's relationship as president of the NACW with the white National Council of Women reveals much about why she pushed for the creation of a separate black women's council in 1935. The National Council of Women (NCW), founded in 1888, was one of the few white women's federations to offer even token membership to black women's organizations, and in fact the NACW, which joined in 1901, was the only black federated organization of the thirty-eight that made up the NCW in 1925.[189] It was under Bethune's presidency that the NACW had made plans to send representatives to the International Council of Women, through their affiliation with the NCW. Closely tied to the NCW, the International Council of Women was also founded in 1888, and acted as a supranational umbrella organization. In 1925, the NCW served as host at the International Council's conference in Washington, D.C. In spite of Bethune insisting on and being promised interracial seating for the NACW delegation, when the conference got under way, black women were offered only segregated seating. Furious at the way they had been treated, Bethune and her predecessor, Brown, nevertheless won a publicity coup. Using the rhetoric of American patriotism to shame white women in front of the international press, Bethune emphasized the embarrassment that had been caused white and black women alike, to have put American racism on display before the representatives of women from thirty-five countries.[190] The International Council ensured seating was desegregated at future meetings. But the fight to ensure black women's right to be involved in national and international women's movements on an equal basis would continue. However, by 1933, the NCW's relationship with the NACW had deteriorated further. Through crafty maneuvering the NCW rescinded their former recognition of the NACW. By excluding the organization from its official roster, the NCW made it more difficult for black women to get their views heard at NCW meetings.[191]

Black clubwomen's experiences with other white women's organizations also served to heighten their distrust of white women and helped move Bethune and other clubwomen toward circumventing the NCW with a separate black women's council. The founding of the new white Association of Southern Women for the Prevention of Lynching (ASWPL) by Jessie Daniel Ames in 1930 had led some black women to believe that white southern women were finally coming to terms with their own culpability in failing to challenge white supremacy. The ASWPL rejected the view that black men were lynched to protect white women, the justification often used for the lynching of black men in the South. But the ASWPL insisted that education, rather than federal intervention, was the way to bring about change, and refused to endorse the Costigan-Wagner Bill. Black women were keen supporters of the antilynching bill, which would have allowed federal intervention in lynching cases where local justice was unobtainable. Representatives of both sides met in January 1935 to try and resolve their differences, but the ASWPL would not be moved. Many shared the disappointment and disgust of Lugenia Burns Hope who had invested so much faith in interracial work, when she told the meeting: "my heart is so sick and weak over it that I don't know whether I can say anything. I do think that the stand that Southern women took will hold back our interracial work and everything else in the South." Interestingly, Bethune, a strong believer in federal intervention, made no attempt to change the view of ASWPL members, but rather reassured them that "I have only gratitude for what you have done."[192] Giddings argues that the ASWPL's failure to support the bill was in Bethune's interests and that this explains Bethune's equanimity about their decision, compared to the reactions of other clubwomen such as Hope.[193] Once again, at a crucial time, white women had shown that they could not be relied upon to support their black sisters, adding weight to Bethune's argument that a national forum to represent the very different interests of black women's organizations was needed.

In addition to the repeated frustrations with white women's organizations, Bethune's experiences while at the helm of the NACW were also important in the development of a separate and national black women's council. During her presidency Bethune had experienced firsthand the limitations of the association, and it was no coincidence that Bethune was developing her plans for a new council about the same time the NACW was making structural changes to downsize its operation. At its 1930 convention at Hot Springs, the NACW agreed to reduce its number of departments from thirty-eight to just two, "Mother, Home and Child" and "Women in Industry."[194] These two whittled-down departments reflected the need and desire on the part of NACW women to carve out a distinctive niche in a world that was becoming increasingly full of specialized black women's pressure groups, as well as its decreasing capacity to act as a national clearinghouse for all black women's organizations. Many of the functions the NACW had carried out were being subsumed under the newer organizations that NACW women themselves worked for in growing numbers in the 1910s and 1920s. The NAACP and the NUL, as well as the new organizations clubwomen had created, such as the ICWDR and the NLRCW, required the NACW to spell out exactly what its function was.[195] The two new departments suggested that the NACW leadership was no longer entirely sure. Focusing on the welfare of women and children, the Mother, Home, and Child department reflected the voluntarist reforming impulses of the Progressive Era. At the same time, the department of Negro Women in Industry reflected the NACW's desire to address the problems of black working women who were disproportionately affected by the economic crisis of the late 1920s and 1930s. As the Depression continued and Roosevelt's New Deal administration responded to demands that the state assume some responsibility for the poorest members of society, the NACW struggled to define its role, as so many of its traditional functions had been taken over by other organizations, or indeed the state. On the one hand the NACW acknowledged that black women "receive poor wages and have to work under unwholesome conditions and accommodations and many other handicaps" and so pledged to "band themselves to fight drastically for shorter working hours, better wages, wholesome places to work, better accommodations." On the other hand, the NACW hung on to what sounded like an increasingly unrealistic uplift strategy, suggesting that working women should be made to feel that "dividends are not always paid in dollars and cents, but with an inward feeling of contentment and satisfaction when one puts forth his best in every line of work."[196] While this message suggested that black women workers should be more highly valued, at a time when many black women were finding it hard to get any job, and were terribly exploited if they were lucky enough to secure even a day's domestic work, the emphasis on what we would now call job satisfaction seems grossly misplaced. Bethune believed that the struggle between the past legacy of the NACW and the future of black women's organizations could not be overcome within the confines of the NACW structure, particularly not under the cautious leadership of then-president Sallie W. Stewart. By 1930 Bethune was convinced of the need for a separate, more politically focused black women's council. This new organization would encompass all existing black women's organizations, thereby removing the need for the NACW to try and find an equal place within the NCW.

Shortly after the end of her presidency, Bethune was busy hatching plans for a National Council of Negro Women. Writing to leading clubwomen in January 1930, Bethune argued that "Just as the white women's organizations had their National Council of [white] Women, black women should have their own council to represent black women's organizations, and work out ... the many problems which face us as a group."[197] To begin with she met with limited support. Maggie Walker, the Richmond banker and stalwart of club organizations, along with the representatives of twelve national organizations, turned up. But other clubwomen, particularly those from the NACW, were unconvinced that yet another new organization was needed, and they did not respond to Bethune's call in 1930.[198] The silent opposition that Bethune faced in 1930 became vocal when Bethune tried again in 1935. Dr. Mary Waring, the new president of the NACW, had been extremely critical of Bethune's support for NACW withdrawal from the NCW. She was equally skeptical of Bethune's plans for a new Council of Negro Women. Waring even accused Bethune of inaugurating a new council because her preferred candidate, Charlotte Hawkins Brown, had lost the recent NACW presidential election.[199] What was really at stake, however, was whether black women's formal organizing would take an increasingly interracial or black separatist direction. Waring was in favor of staying in the white NCW, but Bethune, like many other black women in the 1920s and 1930s, was increasingly committed to black women working together for each other.

Bethune's support for the NACW's withdrawal from the NCW was clearly related to her plans for her own new black women's council: she would want the NACW to join the National Council of Negro Women, rather than its racist white counterpart.[200] When Waring wrote to the editor of the *New York Age* in December 1935, insisting that black women should "beware of forming organizations which discriminate on the basis of race," and that "Negroes should not segregate themselves," she brought out into a public forum many of the difficulties that African Americans faced in negotiating between integrationism and black nationalism. Waring's argument focused on Bethune's inconsistency. For example, when Bethune held an inaugural dinner for the black women members of what would become the NCNW at the Waldorf-Astoria, they were refused seating. Bethune protested until the women were served. Where, Waring demanded to know, was the "principle" of black separatism then? Did Bethune want integration into American society, or a separate space for black women? When was she going to make up her mind? But Bethune, like many other black clubwomen, believed that both strategies were essential for the survival of black women. Bethune saw no inconsistency between black women organizing together as black women and black women protesting instances of discriminatory treatment on the basis of their race. Defending herself from Waring's criticisms, Bethune insisted the NCNW was essential because the NCW offered "no specific place on their program" for black women's organizations.[201]

In spite of this apparently public falling-out among NACW women, when Bethune convened another meeting that same month at the Harlem branch of the YWCA, the leaders of black club life attended and many of those who were unable to attend sent telegrams, "stating hearty approval of such an organization."[202] Even those who did not support the formation of a new council were present. For example, a founder and first president of the NACW, Mary Church Terrell, expressed frankly her skepticism regarding the feasibility of another organization of black women. Nevertheless, it was she who proposed a resolution to elect Bethune president of the new council. Ever the tactician, Bethune ensured that Terrell was made a vice-president of the National Council of Negro Women. The other women who attended the meeting, many of them New Yorkers, expressed more enthusiasm and included Cecelia Cabaniss Saunders (executive director of the Harlem branch of the YWCA), Eva Bowles (national staff worker for Colored Work in the YWCA), Lillian Alexander (member of the executive board of the NAACP and National Association of College Women representative), Addie Hunton (former YWCA and NAACP worker and on this occasion representative of the National Alpha Kappa Alpha Sorority), Charlotte Hawkins Brown, and Addie Dickerson. On the motion of Hunton, the National Council of Negro Women was unanimously voted into being on December 5, 1935. The overwhelming majority of the founding members of the NCNW were also members of both the ICWDR and the NACW.[203]

The clubwomen who came together to form the NCNW had experience of using both integrationist and separatist methods to bring about equal opportunities for African Americans.[204] The founding of the NCNW, then, was entirely in keeping with the earlier tradition of the club movement that had emphasized the importance of race solidarity and fighting institutional racism. The NCNW was separatist in its structure, in its role as a unifying body for all black women's organizations, and in its refusal to be run or accountable to any national women's group dominated by white women. At the same time, the goals of the NCNW were undeniably integrationist; its program included lobbying to get black women into high-profile government jobs and sending representatives to meetings of political organizations such as the interracial Consumers' League and the League of Women Voters.[205]

The creation of the NCNW in 1935 came at an important juncture, in that it affirmed the continued importance of organizing around race and gender in the inter-war years.[206] The year 1935 was an important one for black leaders within the context of the debate over integrationism versus black nationalism. The NCNW was formed against the backdrop of the bitter and divisive debate between Du Bois and Walter White which was taking place within the NAACP and on the pages of *The Crisis*, and which ultimately led to Du Bois's resignation. At a time when millions of African Americans were hungry and unemployed, Du Bois argued that the end of segregation should no longer be the sole focus of racial organizations such as the NAACP. "Never in the world," he instructed his black readers, "should we fight against association with ourselves."[207] Du Bois worked for an organization that had been fighting for integration since its inception in 1911. This fact, however, did little to stop the battle-weary editor who had endured years of what was often patronizing interracial cooperation. In the January 1934 *Crisis*, Du Bois preached that "there should never be an opposition to segregation pure and simple unless that segregation does involve discrimination."[208] Other NAACP leaders, including Walter White and John P. David, disagreed, arguing that African Americans should not accept funding from New Deal programs that were not integrated. But Du Bois and James Weldon Johnson both argued that African Americans should not refuse federal aid, particularly at a time of economic hardship, simply because it came through separate programs. It was, in the end, the NAACP's perceived need to take a fixed stand on the question of whether interracialism *or* the building of black-owned and financed institutions was the best way forward that finally caused the often-threatened resignation of Du Bois to actually come to pass.[209] Du Bois's increasingly impassioned emphasis on equality rather than integration allowed him to support Bethune in her position as head of Roosevelt's black cabinet, and praise her ability to funnel separate federal funds to black Americans through the National Youth Administration.[210] Rather than viewing Du Bois, Bethune, and the NCNW as pitted against what some historians have viewed as "the rising tide of interracialism," this study demonstrates that clubwomen were part of a growing movement that worked for equality and race pride, rather than integration at any cost. The NCNW was built on both the separatist and interracialist legacies of the early clubwomen's movement, legacies that continued to guide the direction of black women's organizing throughout the 1930s.[211]

"Myriads of Prepared Women": The Achievement of the NCNW

In some ways, the creation of the NCNW demonstrated black women's recognition of the need to go beyond what the localized structure of the NACW could achieve. Yet it was also a reflection of the developments of the clubwomen's movement of the previous forty years, rather than an abrupt change. Not only were some of the founders of the NACW, including its very first president, Terrell, founding members of the new organization, but the NCNW continued to stress racial uplift and the importance of black women working together. Building on the work of the NLRCW and the NACW, the NCNW pushed for legislation that would improve the lives of black women and fought to get black women's concerns represented in the international political process. Continuing the work of the ICWDR, the Peace and Foreign Relations Committee of the NACW, and the CPFR, the NCNW lobbied the U.S. government to join the United Nations in 1945 and to oppose the colonial oppression of native peoples, particularly in Africa. Bethune's international standing as the leader of the NCNW was recognized when she became one of the few women of color to attend the San Francisco conference that launched the United Nations.[212]

Assessments of the NCNW's achievements in its early years are difficult, because it is hard to separate the successes of its charismatic leader from the organization itself. We might for example look at the successful White House conferences that the NCNW convened to address the concerns of African Americans. Bethune proudly recalled the "history-making" episode, which saw sixty-seven African American women "marching to the White House in their own right, standing on their feet expressing what they thought concerning their own people." It was Bethune's relationship with Eleanor Roosevelt and her contacts with high-ranking White House officials that enabled the NCNW to stage high-profile conferences that brought an awareness to African Americans and white society that African American women as well as men were activists and leaders. Previously, according to Bethune, white Americans were unaware of black women's achievements: "They don't know any Black man except Booker T. Washington," she complained: "We want people to understand that there are myriads of prepared women."[213] Certainly Bethune could claim that her new organization had raised the profile of black women leaders in the black and white national press. Measuring the success of the NCNW as a lobbying, awareness-raising organization is problematic, since it is difficult to gauge the impact on black women of seeing other black women as high-profile role models. Yet the NCNW's success in terms of increasing the visibility of powerful black women leaders, gradually, over time,

Figure 2. Mary McLeod Bethune walking into the White House, circa 1950. By permission of Florida State Archives.

both in the eyes of white society and within the black community itself, is not entirely immeasurable. The presidents of the NCNW who succeeded Bethune would continue to play important roles throughout the civil rights struggles of the 1950s and 1960s. While the NCNW struggled to survive in the early 1950s, under the leadership of Dorothy Height from 1958 onwards it did find a place for its work within the civil rights movement. Although the civil rights movement had traditionally been viewed as a movement dominated by male

Figure 3. Mary McLeod Bethune portrait. By permission of Florida State Archives.

leadership, the very existence of the NCNW through the years of civil rights struggle ensured that in national meetings of civil rights leaders, such as the planning convention for the 1963 March on Washington, black women were represented and black women's concerns discussed.[214]

The history of the clubwomen's movement of the first half of the twentieth century helps us understand the relationships between black women and white women in the 1960s and 1970s. The black feminist split from the second-wave feminist movement of the 1970s was part of a long tradition of black women's wary association with, but more frequent separation from, their white sisters, a tradition that had begun with the split over the suffrage in the 1860s and continued through the NACW, ICWDR, NLRCW, and, later, the NCNW. Traditions of black nationalism and feminism in the late nineteenth and early twentieth centuries were shaped by black women's organizations of this period, and carried on through organizational means into the civil rights and black power movements. Operating in the aftermath of Reconstruction when African Americans were segregated from whites, many black women whose lives spanned the turn of the century were interested in building up race pride through women-oriented cultural, political, and economic institutions, as a means to achieving greater freedom within a segregated society. This interest continued with growing force through the 1920s and 1930s, and presented a challenge to the machismo world inhabited by male Garveyites and New Negro men.[215] The careers of Washington, Burroughs, and Bethune within clubwomen's organizations and the ways in which they adapted integrationist and black nationalist strategies over time and within a feminist framework demonstrate the diversity of clubwomen and link them with women writers and activists such as Jessie Fauset and Amy Jacques Garvey who were key figures in the Harlem Renaissance. While the NACW would lose its centrality as the national organization for black women, the programs developed by clubwomen were not lost or abandoned but slowly transferred into other, equally black-women-oriented projects, including the ICWDR, the NLRCW, and the NCNW. We should not view this shift as a completely separate development, or a consequence of the NACW's failure, but rather as a transition that carried over much of the same personnel and continued commitment to working in separate race- and gender-based organizations. Continuity, adaptability, and intergenerational networks, rather than disjuncture, characterized the transition from the Women's Era through the New Negro and beyond.

2

Black Nationalism and Interracialism in the Young Women's Christian Association

> *The Colored women know that our group is much more skeptical about white women than the world knows anything about.*[1]

The black women reformers who, in 1905, came together in New York City to form a Colored Branch of the Young Women's Christian Association (YWCA) were skeptical about working with white women. Yet they chose to work within the interracial YWCA. Building on a tradition of social gospel reform in New York City and on their experiences of club work, black women actively strove to secure the benefits of working within a well-funded, if segregated association. The YWCA's policy of segregating its branches along racial lines had clear, if unintended consequences. Through their experiences in the New York City Colored Branch, a generation of black women increasingly came to see the benefits of organizing separately from white women. Black women grasped opportunities to lead programs and to use funds, which would have been difficult to obtain through solely black networks, to provide services to their communities. Their successful defense of their right to lead black women meant that by the 1920s, the YWCA had become a powerful base for black women to organize together in New York City.[2]

The Colored Branch of the New York City YWCA and the black leaders and committees of the National Board of the YWCA provide an interesting angle from which to look at interracial experiments in the first three decades of the twentieth century. This chapter examines how national black Y leaders and those who worked for one of the best-known Colored Branches in the Y operated within the wider context of relationships with black clubwomen, white women, and the YMCA as well as their involvement in World War I relief programs. Their methods of negotiating these relationships tell a story that does not fit easily into the integrationist narrative that has dominated so much of the literature on race relations in the 1920s. Rather, the disputes between white and black YWCA workers suggest that black women's experiences of race relations within the YWCA in the early decades of the twentieth century provided impetus for the development of black nationalist feminism in the 1920s. This chapter is a case study of African American women who worked for the New York City Colored Branch and black leaders who worked for the National YWCA of the USA, and who were frequently drawn from the same pool. Colored Branches in other northern cities as well as those in the South often had different experiences that owed much to local race relations as well as the National Board's prevarication when it came to defining the relationship of black branches to other regional branches as well as to the National Board itself. Valuable work by Margaret Spratt, Jacqueline Dowd Hall, and Jacqueline Anne Rouse has documented the variety of experiences of black YWCA women in Pittsburgh, Cleveland, and the South.[3] Although the responses of the National Board to conditions in the South and its impact on the branch relationship will be discussed, a consideration of all Colored Branches in the United States is beyond the scope of this study. Rather, this chapter focuses on the conflicts that arose between black and white YWCA workers at two levels of the organization, before, during, and after World War I. It suggests that at the branch level, there were many benefits for black women in establishing and defending a separate branch. The National Board, however, often had different goals, sources of funds, and constituencies, which meant the impact of segregation was often more demoralizing. The war impacted on black Y workers at both levels, boosting the resources of local branches while highlighting the unrelenting racism of white women at the national level. In the aftermath of the war, this combination of powerful separate black branches and growing frustration with the lack of representation at the national level pushed black women increasingly toward black separatism.

"Girls Are Girls, Whatever Their Race or Complexion": The Rhetoric of Interracialism in the YWCA

A central theme of both contemporary and historical accounts of the YWCA has been the story of the gradual, difficult, and yet apparently inevitable process by which the YWCA succumbed to pressure to integrate. This narrative sees white and black YWCA leaders working together through the 1920s and 1930s to sweep away their differences. Guided by its Christian philosophy, goaded by its black members, and pressured by outside black clubwomen, the YWCA overcame the resistance of its white southern membership and signed the Interracial Charter in 1946.[4] According to this interpretation, World War I marked an important turning point for race relations within the YWCA. The movement of thousands of African Americans to urban centers in the

North made race relations a national problem and persuaded the white leadership of the YWCA to take a more serious approach to interracial relations within the association.

Valuable work has been done to uncover the less-than-comfortable story of race relations in the YWCA at the New York City Colored Branch by Judith Weisenfeld, and at the national level by Nancy Robertson. However, these studies tend to depict African American women as working toward, and pressuring reluctant white women to work with them toward, a thoroughly integrated organization.[5] This is by no means the only, or even the most significant, story of race relations within the YWCA. The assumption that African Americans always wanted integration obscures the complexity of race relations within the YWCA in the early decades of the twentieth century. It may well be a product of what appeared to be an integrationist consensus in the late 1910s and 1920s as reflected in the rhetoric of both black and white YWCA leaders. Many black YWCA workers employed the rhetoric of interracialism to pressure a guilty white leadership into granting resources to blacks, and to push the YWCA toward a truly equal as well as separate biracial relationship. For example, Eva Bowles, the most influential black member of the National Board in this period, described the YWCA in 1919 as

> the only organization that is handling the work with all girls alike, and the result of its efforts is bound to be the building up of the confidence of the colored race, not only in the nation itself but in Christianity. With the colored, as with all other women and girls throughout the world, the aim of the YWCA is a constructive foundation of Christian ideals. Girls are girls, whatever their race or complexion.[6]

Included as evidence in Jane Olcott's published report on African Americans in the YWCA, Bowles statement suggests that the YWCA made no discrimination in its handling of black women and girls. As secretary in charge of Colored City Work, and then as head of the Colored Work Committee during World War I, Bowles would frequently use her position to assert publicly the YWCA's commitment to equal opportunities for young women in the association, regardless of race. Yet Bowles herself knew only too well that "girls" were not "girls ... whatever their race or complexion" as far as the YWCA was concerned. By employing an integrationist rhetoric which emphasized the achievements of the YWCA in comparison to other interracial organizations, Bowles was vulnerable to the charge that she was too generous in assessing race relations in the YWCA.[7] She was far from alone: African American women leaders from outside the organization also praised the YWCA publicly for its achievements. In private, however, they revealed a deep distrust of and anger toward the white leadership of the YWCA, and often expressed a preference for working autonomously. For example, Margaret Murray Washington is quoted in Addie Hunton's 1913 account of early association work among African Americans as saying, "I know of no organization doing more for the uplift of our women than the Young Women's Christian Association."[8] Yet on another occasion, when the National YWCA once again ignored the demands of black women for equal representation on the National Board and insisted on maintaining control over regional committees and branches, Washington expressed her long-held frustration with the hypocritical biracialism of the YWCA, remarking to fellow black clubwoman Lugenia Hope Burns, "I am not with these YWCA Women. I am ashamed to say it but I have never been. You would not expect anything different from a business man, a farmer etc. but when the saints come along you expect them to be different."[9]

For most African American YWCA workers integration at any cost was unacceptable. They understood that they could often secure greater advantage through working in biracial or segregated arenas, where they were more insulated from, if not wholly free of, the prejudice and control of white women. Yet the interracial consensus that had become increasingly dominant among white liberal reformers and in some black circles since the formation of the NAACP and the death of Booker T. Washington made it difficult for Bowles and others to present their argument in such a light. However, just because some of their rhetoric appears integrationist we should not be misled into thinking that black YWCA leaders necessarily saw a thoroughly integrated YWCA as the most advantageous for their purposes. Bowles was not unwilling to criticize the YWCA, even if she refrained from denouncing the white leadership in public. Bowles frequently challenged YWCA policies in committee meetings, conferences, and internal publications, and used her contacts in the black clubwomen's network to pressure the white board into securing truly equal, if separate, facilities for African American branches. Given her firm resistance to unequal policies on the inside, it would seem that Bowles's public praise for the YWCA was in order to commit it publicly to equal opportunities and resources, rather than to reward it for good behavior. Although black women within the YWCA battled the unequal provisions that were often the result of segregation, we should not assume that they were therefore committed to integration with white women.[10] Misunderstandings between white and black women as to the meaning, purpose, and desirability of integration came to characterize interracial relations at local and national levels of the YWCA from the founding of the first black branches in the 1890s.

The Contested Status of Black Women in the YWCA

An early official history of the YWCA claimed that "Negro women and girls have always been within the fellowship of the Association."[11] This rather expansive statement contained a truth: African American women had early on been participants in the association, if not equal or even integrated partners and leaders at the national level. The very first (white) YWCAs were formed in Boston and New York City in the 1850s.[12] In the 1870s, these local organizations started to come together to form a national YWCA movement, which culminated in the establishment of the YWCA of the USA in New York City in 1906. Under the leadership of Grace Dodge, the wealthy social reformer, the national YWCA aimed "to establish, develop and unify . . . [the] Associations; to advance the physical, social, intellectual, moral and spiritual interest of young women to participate in the work of the World's YWCA."[13] The first black city associations were formed in the 1890s, although student associations had formed in the 1880s in black colleges including Spelman, Wilberforce, and Tuskegee Institute. Dayton, Ohio, in 1893, saw the first black city association; other cities soon followed, including Philadelphia, Baltimore, Washington, and Brooklyn. The first Colored Branch in New York City was formed in 1905.[14] These black YWCA branches were autonomous until the formation of the National Board in 1906, when they came under the control of the entirely white National Board. Soon after the establishment of the National YWCA, southern associations demanded that there be only one association in each city, and that it should be the white "central" association. The National Board called a conference on race relations in June 1907 which met in Asheville, North Carolina.[15] Composed entirely of southern white women, the conference decided that association work among African American women was not to be promoted in southern cities, because this would mean the attendance of white and black women at conferences, something deemed offensive to southern women. Throughout the country preexisting Colored Branches would become branches of the nearest central—that is, white—branch, while Colored Branches already formed in cities where no white YWCA had yet been founded would come under the direct supervision of the National Board until such time as local white women established their own branch.[16]

The branch relationship established at Asheville was unsatisfactory to black women on two counts. At the national level, it meant that white women alone could determine the pace at which the YWCA expanded its work among African American women. At the local level, it meant that the central association, which held the purse strings, could appoint white women to head the Colored Branch, while the Colored Branch was not allowed its own representation on the central association's board of directors. According to Jane Olcott, a white staff member on the National Board of the Y, this unbalanced branch relationship was at the behest of Eva Bowles.[17] In her 1919 report on "The Work of Colored Women," Olcott described this branch relationship:

> all the YWCA work in any community is directed from a central headquarters, the Central Association being responsible for maintaining the same standards in all divisions of the work. A committee of management of colored women handle the affairs of their own branch Association, but are in constant conference with the white women of the Central Association. This makes it possible for the two races to work together.[18]

However, the history of the Colored Branch of the New York City YWCA up until 1919 reveals that this interpretation of the ideal relationship between the Colored Branch and the central association was not a given, as Olcott claims. Rather, black women of the Colored Branch struggled to be allowed to "handle the affairs of their own branch" in its first two decades.

The struggle by black women to secure leadership of black women for black women was evident in the development of the Colored Branch of the New York City YWCA. Members of the New York City Colored Branch did not fight for integration with the white central association in the early twentieth century. Instead, they formed their own branch before seeking affiliation, rather than integration, with the 15th Street Branch, the largest white branch. The Colored Branch sought affiliation on the same terms as other affiliated branches in New York City, with a view to securing the same access to financial resources and training facilities. Rather than pushing for integration at the local level, the members of the Colored Branch, once affiliated, would struggle to maintain their autonomy and secure their rights to financial support as an equal branch member of what would become the New York City Metropolitan YWCA.

The impetus for the creation of a Colored Branch of the YWCA in New York City came from the African American women's Christian community. The long-established tradition of black women Christian activists working together and with white Christian reformers in New York City has been well documented.[19] As Weisenfeld notes, earlier conflicts between white and black reformers over organizations run for black women, such as the White Rose Mission, the Free Kindergarten, and the Hope Day Nursery, encouraged black women to see the "continuing need for organizations operated entirely within black communities and by African American New Yorkers."[20]

In 1905 a group of African American women came together to form a branch of the YWCA on 53rd Street. When they sent a message to the white 15th Street Branch requesting affiliation, one member responded by reminding her branch that the Brooklyn Colored Branch had successfully affiliated with the white Brooklyn branch. The 15th Street Branch accordingly agreed to affiliate on two conditions: first, that the new Colored Branch realize that it would not, under any circumstances, receive financial aid from the 15th Street Branch, and secondly, that the constitution and bylaws of the new branch be presented for their approval on some future occasion.[21] The Colored Branch rejected these conditions. The delegation they sent to the 15th Street Branch to refuse the terms explained that they already had eighty-five members and that "though they did not intend or propose to become a burden on the Association they would expect to rely on the Association for help if the need for it arose."[22] Although the immediate response of the 15th Street Branch is not recorded in the minutes, after further conference, the white branch agreed to affiliate on the terms proposed by the African American group.[23] While the members of the Colored Branch were clearly pleased to have received official recognition from the 15th Street Branch, they had also demonstrated that they would not accept affiliation on any terms. Other affiliated branches had the safeguard of financial support from the central association and they saw no reason why an exception should be made for them.[24] Nevertheless, the 15th Street Branch exerted its control by appointing a white chairperson of the Colored Branch who would represent the Colored Branch to the Executive Board and in committee meetings, with the right to bring a "colored member of the new branch to meetings at her discretion."[25] Not surprisingly, the woman appointed, a Mrs. Milson, did not last more than seven months before relinquishing the post. Although black women would frequently direct the Colored Branch after 1905, it would be fourteen years before a black woman from the Colored Branch held a position on the Metropolitan Board of the New York City YWCA.[26]

The refusal of the Colored Branch to accept a white woman director eventually led the 15th Street executive committee to hire Eva Bowles as the first African American paid staff worker for the YWCA. Bowles was named general secretary for the New York City Colored Branch in 1907 and was soon elected corresponding secretary for the Committee of Management of the Colored Branch.[27] Addie Waites Hunton, prominent clubwoman and NAACP field-worker, also had her first experience of YWCA work at the Colored Branch in New York City when she was hired by the National Board in 1907 to survey the work among African American members of the YWCA. Hunton's brief included the reorganization of the Colored Branch of the New York City

YWCA, and the search for a permanent African American secretary for the branch following Bowles's departure due to illness.[28] Bowles and Hunton's experience and knowledge of the New York City Colored Branch would prove important for their later roles as Y workers at the national level.

Following the brief involvement of Bowles and Hunton, a succession of general secretaries of the Colored Branch came and went between 1907 and 1911. However, some stability was achieved in 1909 with the election of Emma Ransom as president of the Committee of Management.[29] A woman of vision and determination, Ransom had already edited and published a women's journal and cofounded a Settlement House in Chicago with her husband, Reverdy C. Ransom. Ransom played a crucial role in the development of the Colored Branch of the YWCA through the difficult years of its first decade. As president of the Committee of Management of the Colored Branch, she spent much of the 1910s negotiating with the 15th Street Branch and later the Metropolitan Board for greater financial support while resisting their attempts to take control of the Colored Branch. When the white Harlem and 15th Street Branches merged in 1911 to form the Metropolitan Board of the YWCA of New York City, an attempt was made once again by white YWCA members of the board to take control of the independent Colored Branch.[30] That year, the outgoing Executive Committee of the 15th Street Branch decided that in view of the "conspicuous lack of success" of the Colored Branch, a white secretary should be brought in. A Miss Goodrich, a white social worker, was installed as the secretary of the Colored Branch in an attempt to bring it under the supervision of the new Metropolitan Board.[31] Again, within six months, the white appointed secretary resigned the position, offering as an explanation that "a white secretary is not acceptable to the colored women."[32]

Although they worked within a purportedly interracial organization, black Y workers were keen to retain their independence in segregated branches. Black women did not fight for integration at the branch level, because they understood that integration meant a race-based hierarchy rather than equality. The members of the Colored Branch were an independent body of women who chose to work with what they knew to be a white-dominated association to secure better training and access to resources and funding. These women were experienced enough to recognize that interracial work often involved some level of discrimination. Their struggle was more often to maintain their autonomy over the Colored Branch than to bring about integration. It was increasingly white women who wanted to become more involved in the Colored Branch of the YWCA, albeit in leadership roles. However, their idea of integration with African American women was most often a black membership led by white women. Black women fought against this, believing they would have more control of a segregated black branch than a white-led "integrated" branch. Moreover, in a segregated city such as New York, integration at the branch level of the YWCA would not have made sense to black women. For one thing, their branch would have been dominated by white leadership. What is more, when the Colored Branch moved to Harlem in 1913, African American women would have had to commute downtown for integrated services. This would have undermined what was to become the Harlem-based YWCA's main function as a community center at the heart of a growing black neighborhood.[33] For these reasons, black women in the Colored Branch of the New York YWCA spent much of the 1910s devising strategies to avoid integration.

Throughout the 1910s a fierce battle raged between the Colored Branch of the YWCA and the Metropolitan Board over whether the Colored Branch would be directed by black women or controlled by the white women of the Metropolitan Association. The balance of power certainly seemed to favor the Metropolitan Board; the board had control of central finances, while the Colored Branch lacked representation on the Metropolitan Board. The fact that the Colored Branch was dependent on the Metropolitan Board for some financial support inevitably affected the decisions taken by the Colored Branch. For example, in 1913, when the Colored Branch decided to move from its 53rd Street home to Harlem, the local Harlem community (composed of predominantly white neighborhoods in 1913) objected to the Colored Branch buying a building on 135th Street. Rather than supporting its affiliated branch, the Metropolitan Board asked the Colored Branch to give up the building for the good of the "whole," meaning the hostile white residents of Harlem.[34] Although there is no record of the Colored Branch's response, the fact that the racist sensibilities of non-YWCA members were put before the interests of an affiliated Metropolitan Branch must have caused them considerable frustration. Ultimately the Colored Branch secured two superior buildings not far from the original building they had wished to purchase in Harlem.[35]

The struggle for financial security continued to shape the relationship of the Colored Branch to the Metropolitan Board through the 1910s. Shortly after the Colored Branch moved to Harlem, the New York City YMCA and YWCA launched a joint campaign to raise $4 million, from which the Colored Branch would receive funds to construct its own specially adapted building. Ransom was called to negotiate the amount the Colored Branch would receive from the joint campaign, but when, in discussions with Grace Dodge, she was offered $10,000, she rejected the derisory figure and insisted on a sum no less than $100,000. In his memoir Reverdy Ransom recounted how his wife had handled Grace Dodge. Ransom "squarely faced her [Dodge]" with the "un-Christlike and cowardly attitudes her Board was assuming," and insisted on "nothing less than adequate facilities for the activities of the Colored Women's Branch in that area." Apparently Dodge became so troubled by the disagreement, she suggested the two women pray together: "This they did, Mrs. Ransom doing the praying and Miss Dodge doing the crying, but after prayers and tears, she finally got the pledge from Miss Dodge that they would get the $100,000 sought."[36] The Colored Branch wanted its share of resources from the Metropolitan Association, but not at any price. Ransom was willing to forfeit the insulting sum offered the Branch, rather than accept the Metropolitan Board's inequitable distribution of funds. It was perhaps no coincidence that from this point onwards Ransom appears increasingly frequently in the Metropolitan Board of Directors' minutes, speaking on behalf of the Colored Branch. However, it was not until December 1919 that she was finally given a place on the Board of Directors.[37] Even so, Ransom's promotion in 1919 marked neither the end of discrimination against the Colored Branch nor the beginning of a harmonious era of cooperation. The YWCA's involvement in war relief programs would serve to reinforce the separateness of black and white women within the movement. Although the results of this increased separation would have different operational consequences for black Y workers at the local and national level, in combination it would underscore the futility of interracial activity and the benefits of separatism.

The benefits that black women derived from working separately at the local level were not so evident at the national level. This was in part because segregation at the national level included more obvious slights and humiliations, such as whites' refusal to sit with black women at conferences, and to share hotels and dining areas.[38] Black Y workers at the national level also had to balance two roles. Viewed by Colored Branches as their representatives to the National Board, they were also responsible for implementing and explaining the often discriminatory policies drawn up by the white national leadership, to the Colored Branches. It was after the Asheville Conference, at which white YWCA leaders decided that Colored Branches must affiliate with a white "central" association, that the National Board appointed two black national workers—Addie Hunton and Elizabeth Ross Haynes—to investigate association work among African American women and students. Between 1907 and 1908 Hunton and Haynes had the uncomfortable task of recommending for affiliation those associations that provided services to the constituency that the National YWCA wished to serve—that is, Protestant, hardworking, church-attending young women and girls. Hunton and Haynes were the first of many National Y workers who felt the strain of demanding equal resources for Colored Branches while also trying to defend the YWCA against the criticisms of Colored Branches. Haynes's report for the National YWCA revealed that there were other black YWCA groups that engaged in uplift work for children, the elderly, and the destitute, which fell beyond the remit of the National Y.[39] In her report Haynes confessed she had no answer to their questions as to "why the National Board ha[d] not shown more interest in city work for colored people and [has] refused to encourage one association which sought membership in the National movement."[40] Hunton and Haynes may not have had answers to these questions, but their connections with black clubwomen in the NACW, NAACP, and other organizations did provide them with forums in which they could discuss solutions. The conventions of the various women's and race organizations to which they belonged also provided platforms from which black National Y leaders could articulate the demands of black women and put pressure on the National Board to live up to the social gospel that supposedly guided the YWCA. For example, black Y women delivered reports on the progress being made on race relations within the YWCA at the NACW biennial conventions, and encouraged the NACW to involve itself with the YWCA by endorsing, or sometimes refusing to endorse, Y work among black communities.[41] In 1910 the National Board responded by passing a resolution which gave black Y workers in the South some encouragement: "In certain cities where there is no central association or where the association is weak or where the organization of a branch is not feasible, if the colored population is sufficiently large and able to support its own work, an association called the Colored Young Women's Christian Association shall be organized."[42] Just as importantly, the National Board appointed Eva Bowles (former secretary of the Colored Branch of New York City) as national secretary for Colored City Work, thereby assuring Colored Branches of a full-time paid representative to the National Board. From 1913 onwards Bowles served on the national Sub-Committee for Colored Work, a biracial committee whose purpose was to coordinate the work of Colored Branches, but which in practice did little other than meet.[43] This situation changed when the war broke out; national and local black YWCA workers grasped the opportunity to form a separate national black committee. The Colored Work Committee afforded black women the opportunity to work and plan together on a national scale with unprecedented resources at their disposal. National black committees would play an important role in forging bonds with black women Y workers across the country and in supporting the development of Colored Branches as centers for black women's political organizing during and after the war.

War Relief on the Home Front: Opportunities for Black Women

In 1919 Mary Hopkins, a black YWCA staff worker, described in the YWCA magazine *Association Monthly* the hope and expectation black women had shared at the outbreak of World War I: "They gave joyously, for they believed what they were told by everyone who wanted something from them—that this is the colored women's country as much as the white women's."[44] Opportunities opened up by the war for black women both in the YWCA and in jobs previously closed to black women fed expectations that black women's patriotic contributions to the war effort would yield tangible results in the race struggle. Studies of the impact of the war on the YWCA have reflected this early optimism, suggesting that the war was important in thrusting the YWCA into the national limelight. Race issues within the YWCA became problems for both whites and blacks when the YWCA became involved in war relief work at home.[45] Yet the organizations involved in war relief work rejected efforts at integration both during and after the war. The white leadership of the YWCA actually emphasized racial differences more strongly than ever.[46] Where the war did mark a turning point was in terms of the resources and funds available to Colored Branches through their involvement in war relief work at home.

When the United States had first become involved in the war many black women leaders believed the "colored girl" would be given a chance to show what she was worth. Mary E. Jackson, a Harlem-based Y worker, spoke in the *Association Monthly* of the new opportunities available to black women: "Long has she been denied economic opportunities and restricted to the field of domestic service, but now while the men of her race fight in the trenches, she is taking her rightful place in the 'second line of defense.'" Jackson believed that a war fought in the name of democracy would highlight the discrepancy between the treatment of black and white Americans both on the battlefield and at home: "Everyone realizes that both justice and efficiency demand that white and colored soldiers be treated alike. We are just beginning to awake to the necessity of giving colored girls fair wages and hours, sanitary working conditions, and preliminary training in order that they may make their contribution to the nation."[47] By the war's end, few black leaders were in doubt that the war had provided numerous opportunities for black women to demonstrate their capabilities. Bowles led the praise in a tribute which underscored the importance of black direction of black women: "the War has given the opportunity to the colored woman to prove her ability for leadership. She had her chance and she made good. With all the strength of having suffered she will be able, through the patience born of suffering, to lead the women and girls *whom only she can lead*" (emphasis added).[48]

While neither the National Board of the YWCA nor the federal government viewed the race problem as something that could or should be solved by interracial work during the war, they did accept that black relief work had to be funded and performed by someone. The war drastically expanded the size and scope of YWCA activities and programs for African American women, and nowhere was this more apparent than in the Colored Branch of the New York City YWCA. In 1915 the National YWCA had only 9 paid black workers; in 1919 there were 112. By the end of the war there were 9 paid black staff workers in the New York City Colored Branch alone, 4 of whom were part of the Colored Branch's War Work Council, while another 3 made up the Employment Bureau, which was created in response to the war.[49] This increase was due in part to the significant rise in membership of the YWCA that war-related changes brought about, particularly the migration north of thousands of African Americans encouraged by jobs left vacant by white men and women who were servicing the war effort at home and overseas. On July 1, 1918, the Colored Branch had a membership of 200; one year later, it had expanded to 1,800, including 300 active club members. The national black YWCA membership meanwhile had reached 12,000.[50] As well as the rise in membership, the increased work the YWCA took on in the form of war relief meant that more programs and money were available to the Colored YWCA branch, which in turn impacted on the nature of black women's responsibilities within the YWCA.

The YWCA became involved in war relief work soon after U.S. entry into World War I. The federal government asked the YWCA, along with the National Catholic War Council, the Jewish Welfare Board, the War Camp Community Service, the Salvation Army, and the American Library Association to form the United War Work Council to coordinate war relief. With an appropriation of $4 million the National YWCA formed a War Work Committee to take control of war relief work among women. Bowles formed a separate national Colored Work Committee (CWC) in 1917, drawn from a network of black clubwomen and YWCA workers.[51] Local New Yorkers who joined the staff of the CWC included Addie Hunton, Helen Curtis, Florida Ruffin Ridley, Marie Peek Johnson, and Ethel Kindle. These women, all very well known in their own right, increased the prominence of black women in the YWCA and the YWCA among black women.[52] The creation of the CWC emphasized the separateness of black and white women, even during a time of national emergency. At the same time it furnished Colored Branches with welcome money and resources. The CWC was initially given an appropriation of $200,000 out of the total $4 million appropriation. Its program pledged to African American women "better facilities for recreation, housing protection, and an emphasis on social morality hitherto impossible," as well as offering the "opportunity for a large number of colored women to assume places where fine leadership and strong executive ability are needed."[53] The CWC's budget increased to $400,000 when President Theodore Roosevelt, impressed by Bowles's war relief work among African American women and girls, contributed another $200,00 from his Nobel Peace Prize award.[54] The CWC provided the national black members of the YWCA with a much-needed voice and local branches with much-needed support; the CWC's influence during the war would be of particular importance in helping the Colored Branch in New York City develop into an independent cultural and social center after the war.

The responsibilities of the YWCA during the war were numerous. It established new infrastructure to look after soldiers on leave, but, more naturally, focused on women's involvement in the war. Particularly in the South, but throughout the United States, the question of where to station African American soldiers while not on active duty in France became problematic, as indicated by the sharp rise in lynching both during and after the war.[55] The sight of a black man in American uniform was enough to spark race riots in some localities, and the interaction of black soldiers with the local female populations was a cause of concern for both black and white YWCA workers. The tensions aroused by the presence of black soldiers meant that in many cases they were confined to their camps, which, like all divisions of the army, were strictly segregated. To look after the family and friends who came to visit soldiers, the YWCA set up Hostess Houses. The job of black YWCA war relief workers was made more difficult from the beginning by the insufficient and unequal resources distributed to the black Hostess Houses as well as a belief on the part of white women that African American women could not be trusted to run them on their own. Here, then, was a dilemma for white women, because it was out of the question that they would work with black men themselves. In her report on the war work of black women for the YWCA, Jane Olcott suggested the "biggest difficulty" in setting up the Hostess Houses was "persuading officials that colored women were capable of doing this work and should be placed in camps where colored troops were. The problem was to keep this matter before the proper officials and before the several communities."[56] As Olcott hints here, there was concern on the part of white women that black women, with their supposedly looser morals, could not be trusted near the troops, while white women were naturally seen as a purifying moral influence on white troops. Eva Bowles reacted quickly to the charge that gender relations were only problematic where black Americans were concerned, taking pains to point out in *Association Monthly* that "the dangers are not alone where the colored troops are stationed, but equally so where there are white troops."[57]

In spite of these difficulties, the black YWCA workers controlled and operated a total of sixteen Hostess Houses, which offered cafeterias, libraries, and recreation rooms to African American troops and their visitors. Each was "imbued with a fine spirit of democracy, in which no one was refused service on account of race or rank."[58] Hostess Houses were successful in providing a comfortable, homelike environment for soldiers and a safe and welcoming atmosphere for women visitors. As such they represent an interesting version of the public-private divide. On the one hand, they were a means of policing black soldiers and keeping them away from white public spaces. On the other hand, they provided a public, domestic space where black men and women could meet safe from the threat of white violence, and as such the Hostess House transgressed the gendered public-private divide. Serving black soldiers and the women who wished to visit them, the Hostess Houses nevertheless represented a public space controlled and directed by black women. The Hostess House closest to Harlem was Hostess House Number 3 at Camp Upton, Long Island, where the 367th Infantry was stationed. It opened in November 1917 under the supervision of Lugenia Burns Hope. Founder of Atlanta's Neighborhood Union, Hope had been appointed Special War Secretary by the National Y and was in charge of training black Hostess House workers at Camp Upton.[59] In her description of the Hostess House, Hope stressed the importance of this public space being directed by black women:

> The spacious room was full of soldiers. Every chair and space at all tables were taken and some men were standing.... In one corner apart two of the hostesses were guiding the great hands of the men in copybook exercises. Officers and many men spend the evening in an effort to teach these soldiers, but so many wanted to learn that the hostesses volunteered also. Everyone in the room seemed to be enjoying himself in his own way, yet it was quiet and restful; there was no smoking, no loud talk, yet men, men of all conditions and nationalities were there.[60]

Hope emphasized that these were places where women were in charge. They were responsible for teaching men and ensuring a comfortable presence for women visitors, in spite of the presence of men.

Meanwhile, in Harlem, the Colored Branch of the New York City YWCA was expanding its services rapidly to keep up with the increased demand brought on by the war. Cecelia Cabaniss Saunders recalled how "there came to the Branch new opportunities for cooperation, not merely with neighborhood organizations, as heretofore, but invitations to cooperate in city-wide, state-wide and nation-wide campaigns, making us feel that we, too, were furnishing the sinews of war to this great country."[61] One of the ways in which young girls of the YWCA were encouraged to feel part of the war effort was through the organization of Patriotic Leagues. In New York, Addie Hunton set up a Patriotic League for Colored Girls, whose stated aim was "to give girls through normal, natural activities the habits, insights and ideals which will make them responsible women, capable and ready to help make America more true to its best hopes and traditions." A patriotic sentiment perhaps, but one that suggested there was much work to be done before America lived up to its democratic potential.[62]

Central to the Colored Branch's war work was the establishment of a War Service and Recreation Center. In July 1918, at Emma Ransom's instigation, the Metropolitan Association furnished a building to be used for this purpose. Directed by a black woman, Ruth Fisher, the Recreation Center served as a meeting and resting place for black soldiers and their families. Well positioned on 136th Street, close to the YWCA and the 135th Street library, the Recreation Center housed a canteen on the first floor, and a library furnished by the American Library Association. So popular was the center that even after the canteen was closed down, soldiers continued to come for respite from the city.[63] After the war the Recreation Center offered vocational classes and invited prominent speakers, including Du Bois, to address its members. The Center also became a venue for the staging of cultural events, including amateur dramatics, as well as an exhibition of sculptor May Howard Jackson's work in May 1919.[64]

"A New Era of Industrial Opportunity for the Colored Woman": Black Women and Work

The increased resources furnished by YWCA involvement in war relief also allowed for the expansion of services in other areas. The Colored Branch had concerned itself with women's employment from the beginning. Between 1912 and 1917 approximately five thousand positions were filled through the branch's Employment Bureau. During the war, the Colored Branch upgraded its Employment Bureau and added an employment committee, which registered the details of applicants and employers and worked to secure African American women jobs in factories that had previously employed only white women.[65] The Industrial Committee also helped black women gain access to jobs. It organized an industrial club, whose purpose was to pressure employers into giving black women factory jobs and to represent those women already employed in industry. For example, in 1913, the club persuaded the employers of a bag factory to promote their black female employees, who had previously been confined to the lowest-paid, unskilled tasks, to jobs at motor machines.[66] While the YWCA has been dismissed as a "swim and gym" club, one look at its employment bureaus and services for working women shows that it was far from being the exclusive middle-class club that this epithet suggests.[67]

Black YWCA women at both the local and national levels also played an important role in assessing and trying to address the conditions of black women workers during the war. At the beginning of the twentieth century, the majority of African American women continued to work in the agricultural or domestic-service sectors. However, during the war years black women made small inroads into the industrial sector, a process which the YWCA Colored Branches had encouraged for a number of reasons. The New York City Colored Branch was keen to secure employment for African American women and girls in factories and business houses, not just because these jobs were better paid but also because they helped distance the black working woman from the occupational stereotypes that had restricted them to employment as domestic servants. Working in a factory with white women would also satisfy other goals of the industrial and employment committees of Colored Branches: in theory, it would integrate the factory, as well as giving the colored working woman an opportunity to prove herself, making her more likely to be hired in other jobs. More importantly, however, the factory floor, unlike the isolation and sexual vulnerability of domestic work, encouraged politicization of workers and offered African American women opportunities to club together, form unions, and protect each other in the workplace. As Olcott reported, "The factories were seen as a means, the end being the development of girls into self-respecting women."[68]

At the national level, black women also devoted considerable effort toward promoting black women as valuable workers. Mary E. Jackson was appointed industrial secretary in December 1917. Jackson was well known on the black clubwomen's circuit: she was a member of Bowles's Colored Work Committee and had worked for the Labor Department in Rhode Island. For Jackson, the key task of the employment and industrial committees was to educate the public about the important contributions African American girls were making in these sectors, and to organize girls and women workers into clubs so they would be better able to protect themselves when confronted with unequal treatment in the workplace. The industrial committee also visited factories where African American girls worked to ensure pressure was maintained on employers, and to recruit new members to the Patriotic Leagues.[69] National black YWCA workers also played an important role in gathering information about the existing conditions of black women workers. In June 1918 the National YWCA joined with the Women's Trade Union League, the Consumer's League, the New York Urban League, the Division of Industrial Studies of the Russell Sage Foundation, and the Committee on Colored Workers of the Manhattan Trade School to investigate conditions among black working females in industry in New York. To carry out the investigation they commissioned Gertrude Elise Johnson McDougald and Jessie Clark. McDougald had served as head of the Women's Department of the U.S. Employment Bureau from 1918 to 1919. She had previously worked for the New York branch of the U.S. Department of Labor and for the Henry Street Settlement House in New York.[70] For the survey, which was conducted in the summer of 1918, McDougald interviewed 175 African American women workers, while Jessie Clark, a white YWCA worker, interviewed the managers of 217 establishments who were responsible for the employment of 2,185 African American women.[71] The report, written up by Mary E. Jackson and published in March 1919, revealed that the majority of African American women workers entered unskilled and unorganized trades. The exception was their inroad into elevator-operator work, where African American women workers were included under state laws and benefited from union work. Overall, however, the report concluded that conditions for African American women workers were poor. They suffered discrimination on several counts: as black workers they were segregated in the workplace from white women, they were not allowed to compete on piecework, and they were paid significantly less than their white counterparts. The report attributed black women's acceptance of lower wages to a lack of union organization among them and to their segregation in the workplace, which made it difficult for them to know how much their white colleagues were earning. Undercutting white women's wages only served to intensify resentment on the part of white women toward the entry of black women into the workplace.[72]

The Joint Committee's report focused on the many obstacles black women faced once they had broken into the industrial workplace. But what is also striking about the report is its detailing of the ways in which African American women resisted their oppressive working conditions and how it was often the case that rather than resenting segregation, they resented, as did the black women members of the YWCA, being directed by white women. Apparently one of the causes of friction between white and African American women was overcome when an African American forewoman was put in charge of the work of black women. The authors of the report sympathized with this solution in their summation: "that a group which has always suffered from racial discrimination feels more comfortable and is better assured of fair play with supervision of its own race is easily understood."[73] However, the report also concluded that black women tended to be given jobs at the lowest end of the scale, allowing white women to take on more skilled work and taking the place of unskilled men.[74] In order to improve employment opportunities for African American women after the war, therefore, the report recommended that African American women receive training in specialized trades and in how to organize in the workplace. It also suggested that the public and employers needed to be educated to accept black women in industry.

Although the Joint Committee's survey highlighted some of the hurdles African American women workers had to overcome, it only covered those employers that already allowed black women to work for them. Many war industries refused to hire black women at all. Jackson's own independent study of wartime opportunities revealed that while some doors formerly closed to African American women and girls had been opened through the course of the war, little had been done to overcome the formidable obstacle of white America's unbending racism in many war industries. Cloaking her indignation in patriotic rhetoric, Jackson demanded to know why "even now the colored American woman who has given her brother, husband or lover, is denied the right to serve her country in many war activities."[75] As the war came to an end, Jackson became increasingly critical of the U.S. government for presenting the United States as a beacon for democracy while discriminating against its own citizens on the grounds of race. In the report she published in the *Association Monthly,* Jackson explained that "Until colored women have been accorded the right to compete in every line of endeavor for which training, capability and adaptability fit them we cannot hope to rank as an ideal for world-wide democracy."[76]

Mary Alden Hopkins, another black Y worker who contributed to the *Association Monthly*, testified to the discrimination black women workers faced, even at a time of national emergency. Emphasizing the contributions of black women through the course of the war, Hopkins charged that "at the same time that the colored women were giving both their money and their strength so lavishly, they were being in some places actually refused the right to work in ammunition factories." Women were being rejected for war work not only in the South, but even in the North, where "colored women are supposed to receive a fair deal." Hopkins recounted the story of one African American woman who was refused work at a grenade factory because of the difficulty of "cloakroom mixing." "Perhaps," Hopkins sarcastically remarked, "the soldier in the trenches would have felt the same way about the matter." She went on to report the reaction of the woman involved in the incident: "I am not wanted but my great grandfather was wanted when he marched in

1776 with two hundred others to fight for the independence of America."[77] The unnamed woman was, on the one hand, claiming the rights of American citizenship by highlighting African Americans' long history of defending and protecting the United States, while on the other hand, expressing disillusionment at the lack of progress on the race issue as demonstrated by her own exclusion. Her claim of citizenship rights as evidenced by service in the army was a much-used tactic on the part of African Americans who had supported involvement in all American wars, and particularly in World War I on this basis. Like many black Americans she had believed that rights could no longer be denied to a group who had loyally supported the United States in its professed crusade to save the world for democracy.[78]

At the end of the war Eva Bowles predicted that changes in labor patterns and advances into the industrial sector by African American women workers would be permanent.[79] In the immediate post-war period, there is evidence to support her claim, as from January to June of 1919 demand for African American workers in Harlem remained high.[80] The Colored Branch's Employment Bureau had been reorganized at the end of the war and placed under the leadership of Josephine Pinyon. In her report for the first sixth months of 1919 Pinyon recorded twice as many demands from employers as in the same six months of 1918, and the Employment Bureau secured nearly three times as many placements for its girls in the same period in 1919 as in 1918. If anything, in the first year following the end of the war, the problem was not too few job openings, but too few trained women to fill the openings that were available.[81] However negative many of the experiences of African Americans in industry during the war years, their very entrance into a previously closed sector had created an expectation that more opportunities would now be available to them. Black women's experience of long hours and grueling factory work also encouraged them to look for openings in more amenable professions so that, by 1919, the Colored Branch of the YWCA was receiving many more requests for openings in office and clerical work.[82] Many agreed with Addie Hunton when she wrote in May 1918 that the war had brought "a new era of industrial opportunity for the colored woman."[83]

However, as Hunton knew only too well, the optimism felt by black YWCA workers at home would not be shared by those who had contributed to the American war effort overseas. Black women's participation in war relief work overseas told a very different story. The hopes of many black women that they could expect real change in the way their white sisters viewed their status in America were crushed by their experiences as war workers in France, as well as the racist suffrage campaign that followed. Their misplaced optimism would lead to bitter disappointments in the post-war years, an intensified distrust of white women, and a desire on the part of black women to work for and with other black women. President Wilson's failure to apply his principled belief in self-determination to Germany's former African colonies, added to this disillusionment, and made pan-Africanism seem not only attractive, but increasingly the only solution to the race problem.

"Local Conditions, Racial Antipathies, Ancient Prejudices Militated Sadly against Her Usefulness in This Work": Black Women's War Work Overseas

Black women suffered discrimination, rejection, and disillusionment in their efforts to contribute to the war effort overseas. Black women offered their services in great numbers as nurses to the Red Cross, although they had experienced discrimination at the hands of white American nurses in the past. Their exclusion from the American Nurses Association had prompted them to form their own National Association of Colored Graduate Nurses in 1908.[84] The war changed the situation little. Black nurses were largely rejected by the Red Cross, and on the few occasions they were accepted, they were required, like their male counterparts, to do the most unskilled jobs. The Red Cross attempted to pass the blame onto the surgeon general's office. According to the Red Cross it was simply an administrative problem: white women could not be expected to sleep in the same quarters as black nurses, and since the surgeon general's office had failed to provide adequate housing to hold the two groups separately, there was no space for black nurses. In her patriotic account of black women's involvement in the war, Alice Dunbar-Nelson admitted that black women's contributions to the Red Cross were "considerably curtailed in many localities."[85] Not only were her services as a nurse rejected, but even as canteen workers, "there were other sections of the country in which canteen service was so manned as to be canteen service in name only. Local conditions, racial antipathies, ancient prejudices militated sadly against her usefulness in this work."[86] Refusing to be put off and following the example of the YWCA, many African American women, especially in the South, formed their own independent units of the Red Cross, which were "auxiliaries to the local branches presided over by the women of the other race." As the war came to an end, black women were finally given the go-ahead to serve as nurses in U.S. Army camps. Although 24 black nurses were finally enrolled (compared with 21,000 white nurses), one month later the armistice was signed. However, other black nurses served as Red Cross nurses by passing for white. Dunbar-Nelson records that as many as 300 black women may have served as Red Cross nurses in this way.[87]

Other leaders were more outspoken than Dunbar-Nelson in their criticism of the racism of the Red Cross and refused to accept its embarrassing justification of racial discrimination. In a speech delivered in 1920, Mary Church Terrell decried Red Cross hypocrisy: "How," she demanded to know, "can a white nurse so full of race prejudice that in time of war she is unwilling even to remain under the same roof with a colored woman overcome her innate revulsion to representatives of that race sufficiently to perform the many duties, some of which are as repulsive, when she is forced to nurse a helpless black man?"[88] Like many other black clubwomen, Terrell had considerable experience in interracial work and held white women particularly responsible for their failure to cooperate with their black sisters.[89] In 1919 Terrell traveled to Zurich to address the International Committee of Women for Permanent Peace. Although Terrell discovered that as the only official delegate with "a drop of colored blood" she must represent "the women of all the non-white countries in the world," she was favorably impressed by the attitude of the white American delegates who requested that she represent the American delegation in a speech to the Congress.[90] However, fellow clubwoman Mary Talbert's experiences of traveling with white Americans in postwar Europe served as a shocking reminder of the limits of interracial cooperation among American women. The first accredited African American delegate to the International Council of Women, Talbert traveled with Mary Waring and the white American women delegates through Europe to attend the Council's meeting in Christiana, Norway. Talbert later recounted for readers of *The Crisis* how throughout the journey the southern women had "made the life of the colored delegates as uncomfortable as possible." Constantly trying to segregate the black women in Italy and Switzerland, things came to a head at the American branch of the YWCA in Paris when, after journeying all night, the "white delegates were welcomed and accommodated while the colored delegates were even refused breakfast."[91] This incident, which was splashed across the pages of *The Crisis*, provoked public debate in black communities about the racial politics of the YWCA and highlighted to all African Americans the overt racism of the organization.[92]

The capacity of white Americans to export racism abroad, even into the theater of war, was also demonstrated by black women's involvement as canteen workers for the Young Men's Christian Association. Addie Hunton was a victim of, and a witness to, the untiring racism of white women when she was sent to France along with Kathryn Johnson and Helen Curtis (also YWCA workers), to serve African American troops under the auspices of the YMCA. In their published account of their experiences in France, Johnson and Hunton detail the many daily humiliations and petty prejudices to which they were subjected and which prevented them from fulfilling their role.[93] Alongside sixteen other black women workers, Hunton, Johnson, and Curtis worked in YMCA huts where they provided canteen services equipped with meals, chocolate, ice cream, and doughnuts, as well as library facilities. They taught soldiers to read and write home and counseled them through their homesickness.[94] As Melinda Plastas points out, the reluctance of biracial organizations like the YMCA to employ African American women resonated with the history of slavery: preventing black women from looking after their own family members while, on the other hand, allowing and even encouraging white women to come over and provide a homelike environment for their boys on the battlefield, thus helping to ensure support for the war at home. The denial or attempt to deny black women the right to look after their own was an uncomfortable and embittering reminder of worse times.[95] Hunton drew attention to the limitations placed on black women's ability to care for their boys in her comparison of the duties and conditions of black women workers with those of white women YMCA workers. While Hunton was one woman in a canteen that served nine thousand African American soldiers at Camp Lusitania, St. Nazaire, "In a hut of similar size among white soldiers, there would have been at least six women, and perhaps eight men. Here the only woman had from two to five male associates. Colored workers everywhere were so limited that one person found it necessary to do the work of three of four."[96] Hunton and Johnson also compared the attitudes of other welfare agencies engaged in war field activities, including the Knights of Columbus as well as the hospitals, which also discriminated against black soldiers. As frustrated as Hunton was with the YMCA she recognized that they were the only organization to employ black women workers in the war effort overseas. The YWCA, who assisted women welfare workers of other organizations as well as the French war brides waiting to come to the United States, rejected black women for overseas work, and, as Hunton explains, ignored those black women serving the YMCA in France: "few, if any YWCA workers gave any attention to this little colored group, not withstanding the fact that they were women, and Americans, just like the others."[97]

It is clear from Hunton and Johnson's account that even before the war was over, many white women were determined to make African American women realize that any seeming acceptance of them as equals during the war was only temporary, a consequence of the more tolerant attitude toward racial mixing on the part of the French, rather than an experience that would be transmitted home. In an account of her passage back to the United States, Hunton describes the growing frustration she and other black women felt at the persistent discrimination on the part of white women. On the ship home,

Hunton recalled how "all the women were placed on a floor below the white women."[98] It is interesting here how Hunton juxtaposes "the women," meaning the nineteen African American women welfare workers, with the other "white women." Black women may be placed below white women on the ship, but here, in Hunton's narrative, they are the normative, and the white women, other. The black YWCA women were also segregated in the dining room. When Hunton complained, she was informed that "southern white women workers on board the ship would be insulted if the colored workers ate in the same section of the dining-room with them, and, at any rate, the colored people need not expect any such treatment as had been given them by the French."[99] As a result of such instances of discrimination, by the end of her account, Hunton realizes that the shared struggle for democracy in Europe had not changed the relationship between blacks and whites one iota.

Their account also testifies to the conditions and prejudice which black soldiers were forced to endure. Hunton relates how black soldiers told them of the YMCA huts outside of which hung signs stating "No Negroes Allowed."[100] She also records the way in which black soldiers stood up to this discrimination, in ways they might not have risked at home for fear of lynching. One incident stands out when the white YMCA secretary insisted that all African American men sail in the steerage of the ship that was transporting them back to the United States. The African American soldiers refused and left the ship. They were then given equal accommodation.[101] Traditionally it is the war experiences of black men that have been viewed as playing an important role in the race movements of the 1920s. Women's racial uplift was apparently pushed into a secondary role as the masculinized New Negro took center stage. The 1920s has been seen as a decade where women stopped working in women's organizations and looked to men for leadership.[102] Yet Hunton and Johnson's account is significant in recording the war experiences of black women. Their war had highlighted for them the international nature of the race problem, and on their return, they became increasingly committed to the pan-African movement.[103] After the war African American Y women not only continued to work in women's organizations through which they asserted their right to race leadership, but also reinvigorated old organizations and created new institutions with pan-African agendas. Hunton was at the center of much of this development. While relinquishing her work as a field secretary for the NAACP in 1924, she continued her work as a clubwoman through her presidency of the North-eastern Federation of Women's Clubs, and as demonstrated in the previous chapter, increasingly focused her attentions on pan-African endeavors such as the ICWDR and the Circle for Peace and Foreign Relations. The activities of Hunton and other black Y workers after the war demonstrate that they remained committed first and foremost to the promotion and protection of black womanhood.

"They Fought and Died for a Lie": The Post-War Settlement

In addition to experiencing the many disappointments that arose out of working with white women, black women also felt let down by their statesmen's diplomacy on the international stage at the conclusion of World War I. Even before the United States entered the war, there had been an angry and bitter debate within the black press about whether blacks "should fight and die for a lie."[104] However, it was really only the more radical black groups—the socialists and the Garveyites—that continued to object strongly to the involvement of black soldiers in the war once black soldiers were actually "over there."[105] Although a high degree of ambivalence persisted, many African Americans followed Du Bois's advice to "close ranks" and looked to the war for opportunities to advance the status of all peoples of African descent.[106] By the war's close, however, many of these hopes were dashed; American institutions ranging from the Red Cross, to the government, to the YWCA and other welfare agencies had shown their willingness to continue Jim Crow practices even at a time of national emergency. In a speech delivered in 1920, Terrell articulated the frustration of many African American women and men in the immediate aftermath of the war:

> The Colored people of the United States are more restless, dissatisfied and unhappy to day than they have been since they were bound head, hand and foot as slaves. And they are growing more discontented with their status in their country every day. The reason is not far to seek. They staked all their hopes of bettering their condition upon the outcome of the World War and they feel that they have lost out.[107]

Terrell went on to outline the position of African Americans in relation to the American government since the end of the war. Critical of the way in which blacks were encouraged to help "make the world safe for democracy," Terrell was incensed that since the end of the war all mention of democracy had been dropped, both for African Americans in the United States and for the oppressed peoples of African descent across the rest of the world.[108] In reality, the conclusion of this war would be much like the conclusion of any other war: not, as Terrell had hoped, the first war for freedom rather than conquest, but one in which Germany's former African colonies would be divided up between Britain and France.[109] The consequence of such abuse of their trust had been that "colored people have lost faith in the white man. The majority now believe that race prejudice is so innate in the white United Statesian, that even though he promises to eradicate it, he is mentally, morally and spiritually incapacitated to do it."[110]

Terrell was keen to emphasize that African Americans had not been foolish to hope that the war might alter their status in America. On the contrary, never had the future seemed so bright for African Americans since they had first come to American shores. Their hope stemmed from the supposed "Wilsonian" purpose of the war, fighting for freedom and democracy rather than conquest. As Terrell pointed out, the establishment of a people's government in Russia which held out the promise of life and liberty to Russian Jews, the short-lived hope that the Irish and Indians had grasped from the British, and the winning of the suffrage by women in Britain had all inspired universal feelings of hope and attainable freedom. These feelings of optimism had made the racist incidents that marked the conduct of the war and the subsequent peace all the more disheartening. For Terrell, the growing ferocity of American racism during the war was symbolized by the lynching of African American soldiers as well as the discrimination of the Red Cross against black nurses. These incidents meant that many African Americans had "lost faith" not just in the white man, but also in the white woman.

Winning the Suffrage at the Cost of Sisterhood: White Women's Tactical Racism

Perhaps the most significant and symbolic betrayal after the war by white women was their treatment of African American women during the suffrage campaign.[111] While the disagreements between white and black women had originated with the passage of the Fourteenth Amendment after the Civil War, the divide grew as segregation became more rigid and the white suffrage movement increasingly relied on racist tactics to gain support for women's suffrage in the South.[112] The psychological impact of white women aligning with white male southerners after the war to win the vote for themselves whatever the cost could not have struck more forcefully or at a more inauspicious time. It revealed the weakness of the bonds of sisterhood across race lines and damaged the morale of black women war workers, and particularly YWCA workers who were trying to envisage a way for black and white women to work together.

Under the leadership of Susan B. Anthony, the National American Women's Suffrage Association (NAWSA) had established the precedent of using the race card to forward the interests of white women. For example in 1893 NAWSA passed a resolution arguing for white women's votes on the basis that there were "more white women who can read and write than all negro voters." By moving away from arguments that centered on the inalienable rights of all men and women and toward the rights of white Americans, white women had helped push black women toward the formation of the separate NACW in 1896.[113] When NAWSA was working to get the Nineteenth Amendment accepted by the southern states at the end of the war, they again demonstrated their willingness to sacrifice their black sisters on the altar of expediency. The black North-eastern Federation of Women's Clubs' application for membership was rejected by the NAWSA leadership, who informed them that "if the news is flashed throughout the Southern states at this most critical moment that the National American Association has just admitted an organization of 6,000 colored women, the enemies can cease from further effort—the defeat of the amendment will be assured."[114] While black women continued to support the suffrage amendment, the impact of white women's racism in the suffrage campaign had not been forgotten, and would continue even after the amendment had been passed.[115]

The skepticism with which black women regarded white women's tactics during the push for the suffrage amendment was not misplaced. Even after they had secured the vote, neither the League of Women Voters (formerly NAWSA) nor the more radical National Woman's Party made efforts to include black women or address the issue of racism.[116] When Hunton and a group of black women delegates attempted to have their controversial resolution read at the Woman's Party convention in 1921, the party's leader, veteran suffragette Alice Paul, tried to stop it. Hunton's resolution would ask the convention to appoint a Special Committee of the Woman's Party to demand that Congress appoint a special investigation committee to look into violations of the Nineteenth Amendment designed to deny black women the vote. In spite of Paul's opposition, Hunton insisted on putting her resolution before the convention. It was a source of embarrassment to the Woman's Party that the convention went on record as being against the resolution, but a source of satisfaction to Hunton "in having a large deputation of colored women prove that they were alert to the situation."[117]

White women's tactical racism was a serious obstacle to cooperation between white and black women. White supremacy was a difficult ideology from which to pick and choose, if you were a feminist, since it was constructed upon the restriction of white women to a domestic pedestal, as much as it relied on the oppression of all African Americans.[118] In using the race card, white women distanced themselves from black women not only in terms of race but also in terms of gendered roles. In doing so, white women became vulnerable to the sexist implications of white supremacy. Angela Davis suggests that we see this at work in the early twentieth century in the promotion of white women as mother figures whose primary responsibility was the production of the male species.

> As racism developed more durable roots within white women's organizations, so too did the sexist cult of motherhood creep into the very movement whose announced aim was the elimination of male supremacy. This coupling of sexism and racism was mutually strengthening; having opened its doors to the prevailing racist ideology more widely than ever before, the suffrage movement had opted for an obstacle course which placed its own goal of women suffrage in continuous jeopardy.[119]

If black women were becoming increasingly distanced from interracial work with white women, did this mean they now understood race to be deeper than sex? Some historians have suggested the racism of white women during the passage of the Nineteenth Amendment led black women to abandon any lingering trust in white women, and instead prioritize race issues, which meant male issues.[120] According to this view, since World War I, "most initiatives had been spearheaded by men—and women welcomed the development."[121] However, as we have seen, race women, like "New Negro" men, were also responding to change. For black women recognizing the interconnections between race and gender oppression, it was not only impossible to focus on racism and suspend their feminism but imperative to develop a strategy that took account of both race and gender as well. Working within an interracial organization like the YWCA, which pursued segregationist policies and practices at conferences, only served to heighten the race consciousness of black YWCA women, many of whom had been involved through the black clubwomen's network in the disappointing suffrage campaign.[122] At the same time, black Y women also had experiences of working with black men in race organizations that expected them to focus solely on race, but this in fact often encouraged their feminist development.[123] In the 1920s the continued intransigence of the national Y leadership as well as pressure from the YMCA to merge its race work with that of the YWCA meant black women would have to defend their Colored Branches not only from white women but also from black men.

Postwar Race Relations in the YWCA: Pressure from the YMCA

Both the YMCA and YWCA had provided some programs for men and women during the war, as the national emergency had made cooperation essential. Yet the YMCA would continue throughout the 1920s to offer programs to women and would try to usurp the role of the YWCA.[124] As an organization built on a different philosophy and history which appealed to different segments of society, the YWCA was sure to resist any attempt to wrest control over its programs for women, white and black.

For its part, the American YMCA, was always more strictly segregated than the YWCA, holding separate conferences for African American associations. Founded in 1853, the YMCA did not allow black men to join until after the Civil War, and then only on a segregated basis. However, it was not until the end of the nineteenth century that YMCA work among African Americans took off, when William A. Hunton (husband of Addie Hunton) and Jesse E. Moorland were taken on to promote association work among African Americans.[125] Nina Mjagkij has traced the development of African American branches of the YMCA at the turn of the century. Arguing that the search for a meaningful masculine identity was crucial to the black YMCA leaders' approach to advancing the race, Mjagkij saw the YMCA's construction of black masculinity as distinct from either Du Bois's Talented Tenth or Washington's individualistic accommodationist philosophies, yet as combining elements of both. According to Mjagkij, Christian black manhood represented

> an ideal of manhood that combined the virtues of traditional Victorian gentility with the manly display of muscular prowess: men who were industrious, thrifty, self-reliant, honest, pious, and culturally refined Christian gentlemen, as well as physically fit and healthy, individually ready to face the demands of a rapidly industrializing society.[126]

This vision of the physically and mentally strong gentleman who would be able to protect and provide for his family as husband and father sounded strikingly similar to the black masculinity represented on the pages of Garvey's *Negro World*. In common with female Garveyites and clubwomen like Nannie Burroughs, black YWCA workers were prepared to share in this discourse of black masculinity in order to justify their own leadership.[127] For example, in a speech reported in the Brooklyn Eagle, Addie Hunton criticized black men, declaring that "While white men have been preserving the sanctity of white woman, the colored woman has had to preserve her own sanctity."[128] At the same time, black women were determined to resist the attempts of black men who used this discourse to construct an oppositional image of black womanhood in which women required protection from the public sphere. Rather, black women used this "failure" of black masculinity as a platform from which to build their own organizations. Their war work had demonstrated their capacity to lead organizations and participate in the industrial world. This was an opportunity on which black women could build.

Through the 1920s the YMCA exerted growing pressure on the YWCA toward greater cooperation and possible merger between the two organizations.[129] The history of the possible merger between the YWCA and YMCA has to be understood within the context of developments in women's organizing which impacted on white and black women differently. Studies of white women's organizations have suggested that the 1920s saw a move away from women acting in single-sex groups and toward coeducational programs in many areas. Nancy Cott's study of the feminist movement suggested that women who continued to organize together in women-only groups in the 1920s did so more "by habit and expedience than commitment."[130] Yet black women not only continued to organize independently but were also increasingly committed to forming new alliances with other women of African descent through their involvement in pan-African organizations such as the ICWDR and the Circle for Peace and Foreign Relations. Black women were being pushed together not only by their difficult experiences of interracial work with white women, but also by their experiences with black men. The repositioning of black masculinity after World War I encouraged black men to assert their right to lead the race, as symbolized by the military parades of Garveyites and the masculinized spirit of the New Negro. As the discussion of women Garveyites in Chapter 4 will reveal, black women used a variety of methods to deal with those black men who believed they had the exclusive right to race leadership. In terms of its impact on YWCA women, the assertion of black masculinity after the war played a role in encouraging black women to work more, rather than less, with other black women who understood the connection between race and gender oppression. Some black women even used the threat posed by the immense popularity of Garvey's black nationalist UNIA to pressure the white leadership of the YWCA into granting extra resources to Colored Branches. For example, in 1920, Eva Bowles talked to the white leadership of the YWCA about the growing support for Marcus Garvey and the UNIA before asking for more money for black women's programs to reduce "the unrest among the colored people."[131]

The differences between the YMCA and the YWCA worried black and white women alike and led to a series of debates and disputes between the two organizations. Black and white women within the YWCA resisted the pressure of the YMCA for a multiplicity of reasons. Not only did the two organizations have different philosophies but the role of black men within the YMCA gave them far less access to white power structures within the organization. The assertion of an exclusive right to leadership on the part of black men may have enhanced women's awareness of the importance of cooperation with each other and increased their determination to defend the programs of the Colored Branches from YMCA encroachment. As Bowles pointed out, the pressure to merge from the YMCA was highly racialized. Many of the YMCA men proposing merger still wanted racially segregated branches. Negotiations between the YMCA and YWCA suggested that black women be used as guinea pigs for mixed-sex experiments not deemed appropriate for white women.[132] This caused concern among white YWCA women that this would encourage race solidarity rather than sex solidarity and undermine the achievements of the YWCA.[133] For black women, the maneuverings of the YMCA appeared strikingly similar to white women's attempts to take over black branches rather than integrate them on equal terms. Bowles reminded black women that "Thus far we have had no instance where our colored women have asked to be part of a men's movement, but in several instances the men have attempted to absorb the work of the women."[134] Lucy Slowe, dean of Howard University and member of the YWCA's Colored Work Committee, agreed "there is nothing to be gained by the women working in cooperation with the men and it seems regrettable that the women do not seem to object to the subjugation of their thinking to the men's."[135]

Although black women resisted the efforts of the YMCA to merge race work with the YWCA, this did not reflect an increased enthusiasm for interracial work with white women. The post-war years saw the YWCA move toward the more permanent separation of white and black women, rather than toward integration as recognition of the service of black women during the war. Bowles's powerful Colored Work Committee was made into a permanent institution and renamed the Bureau of Colored Work. The bureau was warmly welcomed by Colored Branches that preferred to deal directly with the National Board through the bureau, rather than with local white committees.[136] Moreover, the racist suffrage campaign and incidents of racial discrimination within the Y itself, as well as raised job expectations and the disappointing peace, all encouraged black separatist tendencies on the part of black Y workers. The necessity of building separate black power bases to negotiate with whites was one lesson that local African American YWCA branches had learned from the war. In the post-war years, black YWCA workers worked together to demand their rights as separate but equal associations.

"It Is Unpracticable and Unwise for Our White Women to Select Our Leaders"

Shortly before the YWCA's Cleveland Convention in May 1920, black Y workers met at Lugenia Burns Hope's home to "discuss and seek a remedy for the troubles existing in the work of the YWCA among the Colored Women of the

South."[137] Hope was a firm believer in interracial work and had a long history of working for racial equality within the YWCA. When she returned from her position as director of training for Hostess Houses at Camp Upton, Hope had tried to establish a black branch of the YWCA in Atlanta. Although she had secured the support of the central association and had on her side the National Board's 1910 resolution that had seemed to endorse the formation of Colored Branches in the South, she encountered outright obstruction from the white field supervisor for "colored work" in the South, Adella Ruffin.[138] It was in the context of this battle between black southern members and the white regional leadership that Hope and southern black Y women produced a position paper which summarized their demands for changes to the structure of the YWCA. In the position paper she presented to the YWCA Convention, Hope explained why black women wanted elected representation on the National Board: "the time has come," she said, "when no person can interpret the needs and desires of Colored people as well as a Colored person." She argued that the YWCA was the only purportedly interracial organization that did not recognize the need to have elected black officials on its national board, unlike for example, the International Committee of the YMCA. For Hope it was important that leadership opportunities be given to African American women in the YWCA, because they needed to develop "leadership in our own group."[139]

The main demand of the black YWCA women was simply that YWCA work for African American women be directed from national headquarters. This would mean the elimination of supervision of Colored Work from local or regional field committees in favor of supervision from the New York–based Colored Bureau for all Colored Branches, including student associations. Acknowledging that some white women were trying to work toward a more equal relationship between white and colored women, Hope nevertheless refused to accept this in place of a genuinely equal relationship, and demanded that black women be accorded the resources they needed to direct things themselves rather than struggle with intransigent white women:

> we desire this interracial relationship to grow normally and not to be forced. For while we believe in cooperation between the races we do know that it is impracticable and unwise for our white women to select our leaders or direct our activities. For they know only the individual Colored woman and must depend absolutely on her to do the thinking and directing.[140]

Recognizing that African American women's place in the YWCA was not simply as a "group among groups" (such as international students and recent immigrants), and that African American women were forced to stand together as a separate group within the YWCA, Hope added that "the Colored women know that our group is much more skeptical about white women than the world knows anything about." Hope was representing the views of members of local Colored Branches who during the war had seen the benefits of working with national boards where Bowles and the Bureau of Colored Work exercised formal control, rather than with local white committees. It was not the one-sided relationship that white women imagined. Rather than trying to persuade white women to work interracially with them, black women demanded that in an organization based on Christian ideals, and supposedly embracing all womanhood, black women should have equal access to opportunities and not have to endure the supervision of prejudiced white women like Adella Ruffin.

The other key demand of African American YWCA workers, as articulated by Hope, was the reversal of the practice established at the Asheville Conference in 1907 which prevented black women in a community from forming an association unless white women had first formed a central association to which the African American branch could then attach itself. Apart from the patronizing assumption that African American women were incapable of organizing without the direction of white women, it took control away from black women even before they had begun to associate. It told black women, as Hope put it, that "you can have no association but you may become a branch if the white women in your community will permit." The position paper recommended that this principle be abolished and black women be permitted to form their own association "whenever the branch relationship is not desirable for any reason whatever."[141] Hope argued that colored committees of local branches must appoint their own officers and representatives, since white women were incapable of understanding black women and their problems. Significantly, they demanded that in each locality the central association's responsibility for the secretary of Colored Work's salary be optional, thus encouraging a more healthy and "lasting relationship." Here we see this group of African American women determined to assert their independence from the white women's central associations, even at the risk of financial loss. If, however, this separate-but-equal solution was not acceptable to the National Board of the YWCA, then the women demanded a complete overhaul of the structures of the association at regional level, which would mean representation of African American women on all local, regional, and field committees, and complete control to the colored committees to choose their own black secretaries. The conclusion to the position paper revealed black women's frustrations and impatience at recent disappointments, insisting that "We see nothing for the YWCA as a Christian organization in this age of progress to do but to accept either one of these two policies."[142] In her address to the convention, Hope underlined the seriousness of the complaints drawn up in the position paper by suggesting that southern black women "would rather go back to [their] church organizations than have a special policy for colored women under the direction of a Southern white woman who knows absolutely nothing about us."[143]

The black members of the Y could see only two possible paths for the YWCA: to support Colored Branches as separate but truly equal, or to integrate African American women into the association at every level. The National Board, however, could see a third option, namely, procrastination. The board suggested the southern black women's demands should be dealt with by the regional South Atlantic Field Committee—the very group that had caused the complaints to arise in the first place. Following up on the suggestions, the National Board convened a meeting of representatives of local Southern Associations in Richmond, Virginia, and called on Bowles, who had traveled down from New York City, to mediate. To their disappointment black Y workers discovered that little progress could be achieved with intransigent regional associations when the National Board continued to deny racial discrimination in its treatment of local associations. African American Y workers responded by calling on their black club networks to put pressure on the Y. The NACW refused for the first time to endorse the YWCA, and after considerable and sustained pressure from black clubwomen, another conference on Colored Work was called. The one concession made on this occasion was the appointment of a single black woman, Charlotte Hawkins Brown, as member-at-large of the South Atlantic Field Committee.[144] The National Board's response fell precisely in between the two solutions acceptable to black women. It was neither meaningful integration nor separate but equal, but the continuance of a grudging and token inclusion of individual black women. However, the pressure applied by black Y workers and their club networks appears not to have been entirely in vain. In 1922 the National Board changed its policy, and agreed that the National Office rather than central or regional supervisors would thereafter handle colored work.

Although the relationship between black and white YWCA workers improved little in the immediate aftermath of the war, the Colored Branch in New York emerged from the war with more to celebrate. Two important reasons for this were the newly equipped building at 179 West 137th Street, "the best equipped colored YWCA in the country," and Emma Ransom's appointment as representative of the Colored Branch to the Metropolitan Board of the New York YWCA.[145] Ransom and the Colored Branch had been struggling for representation on the Metropolitan Board for a long time, and in December 1919 the Metropolitan Board finally voted to appoint Ransom, "to fill a vacancy made by a recent resignation."[146] Ransom's election to the Metropolitan Board was welcomed by the members of the Colored Branch, since it showed that working within an interracial organization was not completely futile. Yet it came at a time when the Colored Branch had already shaped its identity as a distinct and independent branch.

The second positive outcome of the war for the New York City Colored Branch was the money it was given by the Metropolitan Board to construct a new building to try and cope with the huge influx of black women to Harlem during the war years. During the war the Colored Work Committee had helped to develop a Rooms Registry in the Colored Branch. The Rooms Registry placed YWCA-vetted lodgings on a list of suitable residences for black girls. But it was the purchase and remodeling of their own building to be used solely as a residence center, next door to the new administration building on West 137th Street, that added greatly to its profile as it approached the new decade.[147] Opened in 1920, the Emma Ransom House contained fifty-one rooms, and could accommodate eighty-six people, many of them regular residents who contributed to community life at the Y. Though it was a residence hall for African Americans and was directed by a black woman, African American women nevertheless had to fight to secure equal representation on its board of directors.[148] Although the Metropolitan Board's financial input still allowed it a voice in the running of the black branch's programs, slowly but surely the Colored Branch was becoming a community center run by and for the people of Harlem.

For the women of the Colored Branch it was the transformation of their branch into a community center that was the most important by-product of their war work. The Employment Bureau, Rooms Registry, War Service Recreation Center, and later the Emma Ransom House increased the black community's involvement in the branch and placed the branch at the center of black cultural and political life. Cecelia Cabaniss Saunders, the executive director of the branch in the inter-war years, recalled in her history of the branch that in the first year after the war, fifty clubs and organizations met at the Colored Y, including the Circle for Negro War Relief; the Howard University, Fisk, and Morehouse Alumni Clubs; the Spelman Alumni Players' Guild; Delta Sigma Fraternity; Columbia University Students; the Foreign-Born Citizen's League; the Women's Non-Partisan Political League; the Dramatic Club; the Debutantes' Social Club; and the Knights and Daughters of Honor Lodge.[149] To accommodate the regular flow of visitors the building was open from seven a.m. until ten p.m., with parties ending at midnight. The front desk of the Colored Branch was not simply there to serve the women and girls who used the YWCA, but, as Saunders explained, to provide for the whole community:

> It has to be ready to give election returns; to locate some chance visitor to the Cafeteria; it had to know where the principal characters in "Shuffle Along" reside in Harlem. In addition, the all-knowing guardian of the Desk must be prepared to furnish names and addresses of all social welfare agencies and workers; hospitals and sanatoriums, Negro newspapers, summer boarding places, music schools, express companies, taxicab companies, theaters and moving picture houses, public stenographers, churches and address of prominent colored New Yorkers. There was recognition of neither race nor age, sex nor creed, in giving information to applicants in distress.[150]

Saunders's report described how the relationship between the branch and the community was a two-way process. The branch offered the community a variety of services, and "In response, the community—regarding the Association as its very own—rallied to its support." In 1921, the branch was able to meet 97 percent of its operating expense itself, raising more than $6,000 from the local community.[151] Saunders's report is notable for its persistent emphasis on the Colored Branch's attempts to achieve self-sufficiency. The report is full of detailed statistics of how close to self-sufficiency the branch had become in any given year. Significantly, Saunders saw 1926 as the most successful year for the Colored Branch, for black women and for racial advancement in general, because it saw the opening to the public of the first YWCA residence hotel operated by and for black women. Rightly attributing historic significance to this event, Saunders claimed:

> When the time comes to compile the history of the West 137th Street Branch, of the YWCA of the City of New York, or for that matter when the time comes to compile the history of Association work among colored women of this country, the year 1926 will mark one of the mile stones of Association and racial progress in that the year (1926) saw the completion and official opening to the public of the first YWCA residence hotel for colored women and girls.[152]

Saunders's view that a de facto segregated hotel was a milestone achievement is significant in terms of what it tells us about her attitudes toward interracial cooperation in the 1920s YWCA. In heralding the hotel as a triumph of what black women could do when they worked together, Saunders focused on race solidarity rather than on the benefits of working within an interracial organization. For Saunders, it was an achievement for the race, rather than for the YWCA.

Other YWCA workers also testified to the quality of service and facilities available to the black community from the Colored Branch in New York City. Anna Arnold Hedgeman, a black YWCA worker who had worked in Colored YWCA Branches in Ohio and New Jersey, described it as "the best-equipped facility available to Negroes in the United States" that "had an impact on the entire nation."[153] Hedgeman was so impressed with what she saw that she moved to Harlem and became the membership secretary of the West 137th Branch of the New York YWCA. As membership secretary of the Colored Branch, Hedgeman met women and girls from across the African Diaspora—the West Indies, Puerto Rico, Cuba, Panama, and South America—and from Africa itself.[154] Hedgeman saw the Colored Branch in Harlem as necessary, because "Negro women and girls from all over the City of New York traveled to our building for service, for even white branches of the YWCA were not open to them." Hedgeman also saw the Colored Branch in New York City as highly desirable because it was a space free from white interference: "I would have equipment with which to work and the challenge of the Largest Negro community in the nation. The wall of separation had done its work, I was completely free of and through with white people."[155] This was not entirely the case, since in the 1930s the branch also became the focal point for political and economic protest in the early 1930s. Responsible for training women in a variety of professions from nursing to bookkeeping, as well as in dressmaking and operating machinery, Hedgeman told how the branch "battled the garment industry, the trade union movement, the employment services, the department stores and other private industries to produce openings for the people we were training and for the already trained."[156] Under the leadership of Saunders, the branch cooperated with other community leaders to form the Advisory Committee on Negro Problems, whose work included pressuring City Hall to open up opportunities to African Americans in the civil service, and encouraging the hiring of more black teachers, police, and political representatives. Having "learned the value of political power" the branch also helped the campaign of a local black Harlem man to the candidacy of city councilman.[157]

The Colored Branch remembered by both Hedgeman and Saunders offered a space where women could come together to meet and form bonds with other women, protected from the discrimination they faced on the outside on account of their race and sex. At the same time it was a place where women could come together to organize resistance and gather strength to fight that discrimination. One of the programs put on by the branch that demonstrated both these goals featured African American women role models as guest speakers, "because we knew that Negro women shared with all women a kind of second-class citizenship in American culture."[158] Speakers included Maggie Walker, president of a black-owned bank in Richmond, Virginia. She spoke to the women of the YWCA about the importance of business training and the opportunities available to young black women. This, Hedgeman remarked, was particularly important in New York, because of the lack of jobs available to black women in the city outside of Harlem. Other speakers representing a range of clubs and organizations included Charlotte Hawkins Brown, Nannie Helen Burroughs, who "expressed her interest in the masses of Negro women who must be taught to read and write even though they might not have an opportunity for formal schooling," and Mary McLeod Bethune, who inspired the young women of the New York YWCA by reminding them that "You can do and be anything you wish if you are willing to sacrifice to achieve. Always remember that you are what you believe you are." The branch featured speakers on a variety of other topics: Madam Walker spoke about the hair and beauty industry, and Helen Curtis, veteran canteen worker for the YMCA in France and widow of the first American minister to Liberia, gave a talk to the women on "the beauty of Africa and the hunger of the young Africans for education." In her talk she emphasized "the variety of color among Negroes," and how to choose clothes to suit one's skin tones.[159] The Colored Branch would continue to play an important role in the history of Harlem and in the development of black women's feminist nationalism in the 1930s. It served as a meeting place for many black women activists and artists from and beyond Harlem and was the natural meeting place for the women who came together under the direction of Mary McLeod Bethune to form the new National Council of Negro Women in 1935. It would remain the NCNW's headquarters until 1940.

Black women were heavily invested in Colored Branches that afforded them a space where black women could offer leadership of their communities. When the YMCA came knocking on the door of the YWCA for talks about merging its race work, black women were just as keen to defend their branches from the encroachments of men as they had been determined to resist the control of white women. Nancy Robertson argues that white Y women were equally opposed to abandoning the gendered identity of their work, even to the extent that some of them were prepared to accept racial integration. When YWCA and YMCA benefactors like the Rockefellers suggested that savings could be made by having services for black men and women alike provided under one roof, white women pointed to their special interracial programs for black and white women in an effort to justify their continued separate-sex work.[160] Robertson argues that the debates about the place of the YWCA vis-à-vis the YMCA may have encouraged some white members to link race and gender and move toward a genuine desire for interracial programs. Whether the motivation was ideological or purely strategic, Robertson argues that it was the threat of merger with the YMCA in the 1920s that was the crucial motivating factor in pushing white women toward the disbandment of Colored Work Committees in favor of national committees of white and black women on interracial work.[161]

Black women, however, remained unpersuaded that the disbandment of powerful committees like the CWC really constituted a genuine move toward integrating the YWCA. Eva Bowles resigned when national committees were integrated in 1931 precisely because she saw it as the kind of integration she had fought against: the elimination of black women's power bases that made their viewpoint harder to hear and easier to ignore. As her niece Clarice Winn Davis explained, Bowles believed that the new integration "would diminish participation of Negroes in the policymaking of the organization."[162] Moreover, at the local level there was no abandonment of the YWCA's segregated structure. Local branches of the YWCA continued to be segregated for many years. Seventy percent of African Americans in the YWCA were in segregated branches in the 1940s, and the Colored Branch in Harlem continued to thrive on its separate identity, as the adoption of the name the "Harlem Branch" in 1941 and Saunders's account reveal.[163] It would take fifteen years after the disbandment of separate national committees before the Interracial Charter would be adopted in 1946 and another thirty years before the elimination of local segregated YWCAs. Throughout the 1950s, 1960s, and 1970s local black associations continued to struggle to integrate, and at other times resist integration, especially when it meant sacrificing the achievements built on years of black women working together, to those of far-less-inclusive white associations. In 1970, Dorothy Height and five hundred black delegates had to threaten a walk out before the YWCA convention (meeting in a southern city, Houston, for the first time since 1922) would adopt a resolution stating that the elimination of racism was to be the organization's one imperative.[164] When most YWCAs were finally integrated in the 1970s, it was far from satisfactory to many African American women. The maintenance of one, integrated YWCA in an exclusive white suburb did not constitute anything approaching meaningful integration. Worse still, black women had lost their separate voice and organization.[165]

Bowles, Hunton, Ransom, Saunders, and other Y workers used multiple strategies to achieve greater opportunities for black women. Black women's public acceptance of the Y made them vulnerable to charges that they accommodated white racism. Yet their public declaration of the YWCA's commitment to racial equality made it more difficult for white YWCA leaders to deny African American women and girls equal resources and put more pressure on them to live up to the expectations created by Bowles and others. Many black Y leaders did not believe in integration, regardless of the circumstances or cost, but rather supported biracial policies and devoted their efforts toward ensuring they were truly equal. These women recognized that separation, albeit enforced, provided numerous leadership opportunities for black women that they might not have otherwise had. Working to ensure that black branches would be run by black women for black women, these race women found an alternative power base to mixed-gender race organizations. In the process they developed networks of black women activists who had been exposed to the possibilities of black separatism. The significance of this for a generation of black women activists cannot be overestimated. For example, Dorothy Height, the president of the National Council of Negro Women from 1957 onwards, worked at the Colored Branch in Harlem under Cecelia Cabaniss Saunders in the 1930s, and was the assistant director of the Emma Ransom House. It was here that she met Mary McLeod Bethune when Bethune visited the branch, and through her first became involved in the NCNW. Height was also a professional staff member of the National Board of the YWCA for twenty-nine years until she retired in 1976. Anna Arnold Hedgeman also carried on working in separate YWCA branches when she left the Harlem Branch. She was the executive secretary of the black YWCAs in Philadelphia and Brooklyn, and later went on to become dean of women at Howard University. She would also serve in Mayor of New York Robert F. Wagner's cabinet and was on the organizing committee of the 1963 civil rights march on Washington.[166] Georgia Myrtle Teale, a former director of the Emma Ransom House, would become the dean of women at Wilberforce University. Many YWCA leaders had daughters who would become prominent feminist activists, including Addie Hunton, who had worked for both the Colored Branch of the New York City YWCA as well as the National Board. Hunton's daughter, Eunice Hunton Carter, would become Mary McLeod Bethune's right-hand woman as a charter member of the NCNW as well as the organization's legal counsel. An attendee of the founding conference of the United Nations in San Francisco, Carter would serve as a consultant for the Economic and Social Council of the United Nations for the International Council of Women in 1947.[167] Ultimately, black women were able to thrive and build on a long tradition of black women working with and for each other within white organizations. A whole generation of black women who had been connected with or worked for the YWCA in the 1910s and 1920s had learned how to use both separatism and integrationism. Bowles, Hunton, Ransom, and Saunders benefited from the resources of whites, while demanding independent branches for black women to work together for the benefit of the black community. In doing so they helped train other black women in the skills needed to progress in an America where blacks were neither integrated nor truly separate, and certainly not equal.

3

Luxuriant Growth

The Walkers and Black Economic Nationalism

Madam Walker is thoroughly a Race woman, and her every thought seems to be as to how best she can advance her Race. . . . Every age has its great men or women, and this is true of every people. No unbiased historian can chronicle the history of the Negro without weaving the name of Madam C J Walker into the warp and woof of his life and institutions here in America. Not only is Madam Walker first to dignify her profession as hair culturalist, but she is easily one of the first among the foremost citizens of her Race.[1]

Mythologized as the first black female millionaire, Madam C. J. Walker was a businesswoman, beautician, philanthropist, and political activist who came to prominence as the "inventor" of the Walker hair-growing treatment and beauty schools in the 1910s. Viewed by her detractors as a method of straightening hair, Walker claimed her products alleviated scalp conditions and other symptoms of poor diet and hygiene that prevented black women growing healthy hair. The essential elements of the Madam Walker "system" included a shampoo, a pomade (the hair "grower"), and the use of a specially designed heated hair comb.[2] These products would make Madam Walker one of the wealthiest—as well as the most widely known—black women in the early decades of the twentieth century. Central to Walker's success as a seller of hair and beauty products for black women was her ability to control her image. Not only did she issue helpful statements to the press detailing her latest miscellaneous charitable acts, but she also gave clear instruction to the "unbiased historian" on what should be her legacy. We see Walker's skills as a publicist on the pages of *The Crisis*, the *Negro World*, the *New York Age*, and the *Messenger*. Du Bois, Garvey, Booker T. Washington, and George Schuyler were persuaded that her hair product was no shameful hair straightener but concerned with improving the appearance and economic opportunities of the women of the race, and they celebrated her achievement on the pages of their publications. Embracing the new consumer age, Walker grasped quickly the importance of selling an image, a vision, a lifestyle, rather than simply a hair product. Walker promoted an image of black womanhood that appealed to the thousands of black women who would become both her consumers as well as her employees, when they trained to become Madam Walker agents. But in the process of developing what would become a very successful business, Walker also projected a vision of dignified black womanhood that reached far beyond her consumers and launched her career as a black political activist. These developments were not unconnected; rather, her promotion of respectable black womanhood in her company advertisements had relied from the very beginning on her own example of upward mobility.

This chapter examines how Madam Walker and her daughter A'Lelia Walker found a place for themselves at the center of black organizational life and political leadership. It was their economic empire that allowed them unusual access as race women into male political and cultural circles. In creating a black-owned business, run by and for black people, the Walkers fulfilled the visions of Washington, Du Bois, and Garvey and made allies of them all. At the same time, it was the Walkers' positive vision of black womanhood that had helped them sell their product and build their empire in the first place. For example, Madam Walker's promotion of respectable women's labor enabled her to forge important relationships with prominent clubwomen such as Mary Talbert, Nannie Helen Burroughs, Margaret Murray Washington, and Mary McLeod Bethune. Like these clubwomen, Madam Walker was able to recognize approaches to the race problem as alternatives that were ever in flux, rather than fixed and oppositional. Using the networks she built up with black women from a range of organizations and clubs, Walker was able to connect individual economic improvement with the promotion of black womanhood. This ability to remove the distinction between individual economic incentive and community building has been described by Nicole Biggart as "charismatic capitalism," that is, a company led by a dynamic figure that "combined the profit motive with the qualities of a social or religious movement." Using the concept of charismatic capitalism, Kathy Peiss suggests that both Walker and her competitor, Annie Turnbo Malone, were early exponents of this business method. Both companies prospered because of the powerful leadership of their indomitable founders and their ability to link together different strands of their employees' and consumers' lives. Charismatic capitalism provides a useful framework for understanding how Walker was able to position her own progress as crucial to the uplift of black women.[3]

"Rags-to-Riches": Becoming Madam C. J. Walker

Although Walker was not the first to dignify her profession as a hair culturalist, she was one of the foremost race women of her time. As such, Walker has been the subject of several biographical studies in recent years, yet she has had little impact on narratives of black leadership, black women's organizations, and the development of black feminist thought in the early twentieth century. Often mentioned, but infrequently debated, both Walker and her daughter are referred to in accounts of the Harlem Renaissance and histories of black women, usually as atypical women who overcame innumerable obstacles.[4] Moreover, as Charles Latham points out, there is far more speculation than accurate information in circulation on the Walkers, even in standard sources like the *Dictionary of American Biography*.[5] Walker undoubtedly contributed to some of this misinformation, since she was not afraid of embellishing her past to help sell her product. Aware of how little control black women had traditionally held over how they were represented, Madam C. J. Walker was determined to construct her own image from the very beginning. When Walker first launched her product, her advertising strategy relied on the retelling of her life story. Throughout her career she reproduced versions of this story in newspaper advertisements, in company brochures, and in her many speeches before groups of prospective sales agents. In the most frequently retold version, Walker narrated her rise from "the cotton fields of the South" to a job as a washerwoman in St. Louis. Concerned about her own hair loss, she had a divinely inspired dream that revealed the secret ingredients that would become the Madam Walker hair grower. Walker traveled the United States recruiting agents to sell her product and training hairdressers to perform the treatment. By 1918 she was making more than $250,000 a year through sales of the product and had a sales force of 20,000 agents.[6] Central to the appeal of this version of Walker's story was the narration of a recognizable rags-to-riches story, which demonstrated her honest hard toil as well as God's support for her business venture. As an early press release explained, "in the early stages of her remarkable business, [Madam Walker] thought nothing of working eighteen hours at a stretch, in order to make her business a success."[7]

While there were several variations on this story, most of them incorporated these essential if not entirely accurate details. The more accurate version was not entirely without drama and helps us to understand how Walker's company developed. She was born to Owen and Minerva Breedlove on a former slave plantation in Delta, Louisiana, on December 23, 1867. Orphaned at the age of seven, Walker moved to Vicksburg, Mississippi, with her sister Louvenia when she was ten. At fourteen Walker married Moses Jeff McWilliams, with whom she had a daughter, Lelia, in 1885. However, Moses died in 1887. To support herself and her young daughter, she moved to St. Louis and became a laundress, while also attending night schools. Her early widowhood and subsequent choice of career as a washerwoman, rather than a domestic servant, suggests that like many black women she was only too aware of her vulnerable sexual status. Walker's claim that divine intervention had inspired her to dream up the hair grower glosses over the fact that while in St. Louis she had worked as an agent for another black hairdresser, Annie Turnbo Malone, known as Madam Poro, and had been experimenting with her hair products to stimulate her own hair growth. This was no accidental omission, since Walker appeared to model her own business on the extremely successful company of the woman who would later become her chief competitor. How much of Walker's knowledge of the special ingredient was taken from her rival and competitor Malone may never be known. Both women probably took a basic product and altered it to suit black women's hair. It may have been this St. Louis rivalry that prompted Walker in 1905 to move to Denver, where she started selling her product and recruiting agents through door-to-door sales. Here, in 1906, Walker met and married Charles J. Walker, a newspaperman who helped her with publicity for the company. By the time his business incompetence and marital infidelities caused her to divorce him in 1912, Walker had taken his name and added the title "Madam," by which she would thereafter be known. At a time when white men and women routinely addressed black women by their first names, or as "girl," or with the disrespectful familiarity suggested by "Auntie," it is not surprising that many black women kept their married names and titles after their divorce. The title "Madam," however, redirected the emphasis away from Walker's marital status and focused on her professional status as a beautician and businesswoman.[8]

After several years in Denver, Walker was keen to establish a permanent headquarters for her business. Such a headquarters would allow her to travel around the United States to recruit new agents and network with race leaders who might endorse her product and invest in her business. She already had one base in Pittsburgh, where in 1908 she had set up Lelia College and a correspondence course under the management of A'Lelia. In 1910, Walker decided to move the company headquarters to Indianapolis. Anxious to find investors in her laboratory and beauty school, Walker wrote to Booker T. Washington in January 1910, asking him to throw his weight behind her company and to encourage others to invest in it. Washington replied that he was far too busy with the industrial school he had founded at Tuskegee to take on any further commitments.[9] Having failed to persuade any businessmen to invest, she incorporated the Madam Walker Manufacturing Company in 1911, naming herself as sole owner of all the stock. It was at this stage that Walker found Freeman B. Ransom, who would become the company lawyer and business manager for the next thirty-six years. The establishment of her factory and headquarters in Indianapolis under Ransom's management and of a college under A'Lelia in Pittsburgh gave Walker the freedom to travel around American towns and cities to find new agents. Holding a meeting at the local black church or YWCA, Walker would give a slide show entitled "The Negro Woman in Business," before training a few local women in hairdressing techniques. Agents were also recruited through local newspaper publicity drives, which informed black women that they could learn the Walker method through the Lelia College in Pittsburgh, and later through other colleges opened in Harlem and Chicago or via the correspondence course.[10] Walker's recruitment trips also took her to other parts of the world where black women could benefit from her business expertise. In November 1913 Walker set out on a tour of the Caribbean and Central America, recruiting agents in Jamaica, Haiti, Cuba, Panama, and Costa Rica.[11] It was during the course of these recruitment trips that Walker began to make connections between her business interests and her growing interest in political affairs. Her contacts with clubwomen and school founders taught her that she needed to get the black business establishment on her side, and that in order to do this, she needed to present herself as a committed race woman.

Although there are differences between Madam Walker's public version of her story and the historical record, any examination of Walker needs to appreciate the importance of both versions. Walker's version is significant in terms of its wide distribution, acceptance, and appeal to black women. Walker used her "life-story" both to market her product to individual purchasers and to encourage black women who were interested in becoming Walker agents.[12] But she also used it as a way of positioning herself within the complex world of American race politics. A typical American rags-to-riches tale, on the one hand, Walker's life story seemed to fulfill Booker T. Washington's prediction that only hard work, vocational training, and economic achievement could effectively challenge white supremacy. Yet Walker was selling a product traditionally associated with white manufacturers. For years white pharmaceuticals had sold hair straighteners which promised to take the "kink" out of the hair, a process of which Washington was known to disapprove.[13] In constructing an alternative vision of black beauty, work, and consumption, Walker challenged not only the monopoly of white pharmaceuticals who had for so long kept blacks out of the industry, but also white constructions of black women as unattractive and undeserving of respect. Walker's story, then, was about her ability to transform her product into something that was respectable and compatible with racial pride. Not only would her product relieve dry scalps and promote healthy hair growth, but in improving the appearance of black women, Walker argued she was also helping black women access better jobs. Rather than selling a cheap hair product, she was offering a lifestyle to anyone who was willing to work for it. A Madam Walker agent could become respectable through honest hard work, race proud because free from dependence on whites, and glamorous because mobile, creative, and financially independent. Ultimately, an inspiring rags-to-riches story was not sufficient to transform the image of the black hair industry. In order to present herself as a woman engaged in a reputable business, Walker needed to demonstrate that she was concerned with the uplift of the race. To do this, Walker needed the backing of black business and political leaders. The rest of this chapter will examine how Walker and her daughter combined the roles of race woman and businesswoman, and how in the process they contributed to debates about respectability, racial pride, women's leadership, and economic nationalism.

"Not Merely Satisfied in Making Money for Myself": Becoming a Race Woman

Topping Walker's list of leaders to win over was Booker T. Washington. The self-appointed leader of black business through his foundation of the National Negro Business League, Washington was viewed, at least by white Americans, as the spokesman for his race, and as such held immense powers of patronage in both black and white political circles. Although Walker was not interested in securing introductions to his white philanthropist friends, she was clearly aware that his disapproval could be fatal to a project's success, while his enmity could lead to economic ruin or worse, as many of those with whom Walker associated had discovered.[14] Unperturbed by Washington's earlier rebuff, Walker tried again in 1911, this time requesting permission to speak at his forthcoming Tuskegee Negro Conference. Washington wrote her a stern refusal, insisting that his convention would not be suitable for Walker's purposes: "I fear you misunderstand the kind of meeting our Tuskegee Negro Conference will be. . . . I am well acquainted with the business in which you are engaged, but somehow I do not feel that a visit to our Conference would offer the opportunity which you seem to desire."[15] It seems that Washington had his doubts about Madam Walker's business plans, since he equated all black hair treatment with hair straightening and skin whitening, which he disdained as imitative of whites.[16] However, Washington's rejection of Walker also owed something to his views concerning women's proper sphere. His earlier reluctance to include women speakers at the Tuskegee Negro Conference had prompted Margaret Murray Washington to set up a separate women's organization in the form of the Tuskegee Town Women's Club and Night School because she felt women's voices were ignored at her husband's Negro Conference.[17]

Although the Tuskegee Negro Conference was a meeting of farmers, Walker believed they would appreciate her story and that her successful large-scale enterprise might inspire them and help her publicize her product. Although Washington had denied her an audience at the Tuskegee Conference, Walker refused to be put off. In her efforts to be heard, she arrived at Tuskegee with a letter of introduction from Thomas Taylor, the executive secretary of Indianapolis's Colored YMCA. Her perseverance was rewarded, as she was finally given permission to speak for ten minutes in the chapel. Perhaps Washington felt the religious sphere a more appropriate one for women, and was prepared to listen to Walker in what he considered an unbusiness-like environment. According to Washington's biographer Louis Harlan, Walker won Washington's sympathy by demonstrating her hair-care products on female members of the Washington family.[18] Whether it was through actions or words, Walker had wedged her foot in the Tuskegee door.

Walker next attempted to find an opening for herself within the National Negro Business League (NNBL). She arrived in Chicago in August 1912, keen to attend the NNBL's thirteenth annual convention and to promote her product.[19] The convention was a particularly appropriate venue for Walker to introduce the new Madam Walker Manufacturing Company, since there were other manufacturers of hair-care products scheduled to address the meeting, including Mrs. Julia H. P. Coleman, a licensed pharmacist from Washington, D.C., and Anthony Overton of Overton Hygienic Manufacturing Company, who sold Hygienic Pet Baking Powder as well as cosmetics for black women.[20] When Washington, in his role as president of the NNBL, invited comments from the audience in response to Overton's presentation, George Knox, the publisher of the *Indianapolis Freeman* and a close friend of Walker, asked that she be given a platform to address the conference. Washington quashed the request, and instead gave the platform to another manufacturer from Indianapolis. But on the final day of the convention, in an act of resistance that showed her determination not to be silenced by male business leaders, Walker demanded the floor from Washington. In a manner that was reminiscent of Sojourner Truth's legendary intervention at the Women's Rights Convention in Akron, Walker launched a passionate defense of her right to be heard.[21] She argued that an organization interested in promoting black economic self-sufficiency should not be blinded by prejudice against successful black women like her who were doing just that:

> Surely you are not going to shut the door in my face. I feel that I am in a business that is a credit to the womanhood of our race. . . . I went into a business that is despised, that is criticized and talked about by everybody—the business of growing hair. . . . I am a woman that came from the cotton fields of the South. I was promoted from there to the wash-tub . . . and from there I promoted myself into the business of manufacturing hair goods and preparations. I have built my own factory on my own ground, 38 by 209 feet. I employ in that factory seven people, including a book keeper, a stenographer, a cook and a house girl. . . . I own my own automobile and runabout. . . . I am not ashamed of my humble beginning. Don't think because you have to go down in the wash-tub that you are any less a lady![22]

Walker challenged her audience to reject the cult of true womanhood that positioned respectable white women within the domestic sphere, on the back of exploited black women's labor. Evoking the American dream, Walker linked the formerly despised images of black womanhood during slavery to her own humble beginnings. Central to Walker's vision of respectable black womanhood here is the dignity of work, as expressed through her confident managerial language. Three times in this short extract she uses the word "business," while all the time emphasizing the things she does to and for others: *I employ, I promoted, I own,* and *I have built.* Contrary to the views of some of her audience, black pride for women, as well as men, lay in their ability to earn a decent wage, particularly when black men were excluded from the right to earn a family wage. Walker uses the language of hard work and production, but she also refers unashamedly to herself as a consumer, the proud owner of an automobile and a runabout. As a commodity, a car was not simply a symbol of wealth. At a time when black Americans were constantly being ejected from white-only carriages on the railroads, car ownership was, as Du Bois put it, "to a considerable extent personal investments designed to counteract the insult of the Jim Crow [system of transportation]."[23] Moreover, in the Jim Crow South any display of conspicuous consumption on the part of black Americans could be seen as a threat to white supremacy, since it suggested that African Americans might be on an equal footing with whites in the marketplace.[24] As a woman who traveled extensively around the South on recruitment trips, Walker needed a convertible car for more than just convenience;

Figure 4. Madam Walker driving her Model T Ford outside her home in Indianapolis. 1912. Madam C. J. Walker Collection, Indiana Historical Society.

Figure 5. A typical Madam Walker advertisement. Madam C. J. Walker Collection, Indiana Historical Society.

A Real Opportunity for Women who wish to become Independent

Mme WALKER'S SYSTEM

of Scientific Scalp Treatment and Sales of her Hair Preparations are giving support to more than 100,000 people in this Industry. Come in and learn how.

it suggested she maintained a superior position in the marketplace, thereby challenging white notions of black inferiority. The rags-to-riches story Walker represented in her speech to the NNBL furnished evidence that black women could work hard for themselves and the race, and could become economically independent. In outlining to the male delegates her vision of dignified black womanhood, Walker also demonstrated her belief in the importance of self-definition. Her astonishing repetition of the first person pronoun underlies this belief that it is her right as a black woman (rather than Washington's or that of the convention) to define images of black womanhood.

The importance of the dignity of work for black women would become a recurrent theme of Walker's speeches, and she took particular pride in the fact that she had enabled hundreds of other black women to gain economic independence through a "more pleasant and profitable occupation."[25] When she was invited back to the NNBL convention as a guest speaker in 1914, Walker told the delegates: "I am not merely satisfied in making money for myself, for I am endeavoring to provide employment for hundreds of women of my race." In the same speech she also emphasized the importance of black women seizing opportunities to secure their independence before asking the delegates to pass a resolution endorsing her work, because "it will help me to be of more practical service to the several worthy causes in which I am particularly interested" and "because it will help me in the struggle I am making to build up Negro womanhood."[26] Walker's triumph at the 1912 and subsequent NNBL conventions enabled her to find a place for herself as a black businesswoman in a decidedly male world. Right from the beginning when Walker had first gained hard-won access to male audiences, she used her platform to articulate her vision for black women. She continued to promote this vision as her relationship with Washington and the predominantly male NNBL evolved. Walker became a major donor to Washington's school, and in return, the 1914 NNBL conference passed a resolution endorsing her as "the foremost business woman of our race."[27] Walker continued to emphasize the close relationship between dignified women's work and race pride in her speeches to the male-dominated NNBL convention. She urged the "girls and women of the race" not to be afraid to tackle any business, however modest their background, and recounted her story of success "in order that other women of my race may take hold of similar work and make good."[28]

While Walker's initial difficulty in obtaining recognition at NNBL conventions was due in no small measure to the fact that her work focused exclusively on women, she may also have been regarded as a threat because the success of her business far exceeded that of the average male delegate,

Figure 6. Madam Walker with Booker T. Washington (*center*) and others at the dedication of the Senate Avenue YMCA in Indianapolis. Madam C. J. Walker Collection, Indiana Historical Society.

many of whom were professionals or clergymen rather than businessmen.[29] Walker's real achievement exposed those men who used their platform at the NNBL to overstate their case, or as Nannie Burroughs put it: "men [who] come to the league with their stock considerably watered."[30] By contrast, Walker's stock was undiluted: by 1916 Walker's annual sales had reached the $100,000 mark, and the *New York Age* reported that Walker had as many as 10,000 Walker agents. By the time of her death the Madam Walker Manufacturing Company had well in excess of 20,000 agents.[31] Certainly Washington's public response to Walker indicated his gendered consciousness of Walker's success as a woman: "You talk about what the men are doing in a business way; why if we don't watch out the women will excel us."[32] While this was said in a jocular way, Washington clearly did not want his Business League to be overshadowed by a woman. Even so, for Walker it was important that she had enlisted Washington as a firm ally, and she was devastated by his premature death in 1915.[33] But Walker's connection with Tuskegee continued. She kept up her regular donations to the school, and in 1916 was invited by Margaret

Murray Washington to return to Tuskegee and address the institute as part of her lecture tour. As usual, she was favorably received.[34] Ultimately Walker had managed to overcome the skepticism with which Booker T. Washington viewed both her enterprise and her ability to conduct it as a black woman. Acceptance by Washington and the NNBL, as well as her growing financial resources, transformed Walker into a serious race woman and allowed her to become more daring in her choice of support for organizations devoted to improving the condition of African Americans. Confident of her financial independence, Walker began to exert her political influence by both supporting and helping to create new and often radical organizations. The two most palpable examples of this were her support for and active involvement in the National Equal Rights League (NERL) and the International League of Peoples of the Darker Races (ILPDR), two organizations whose political focus and global ambitions contrasted sharply with the business concerns of the NNBL.

Promoting New Growth: Madam Walker's Pan-African Vision

As with many other African American leaders, U.S. involvement in World War I pushed Walker in an increasingly militant direction in her efforts to secure the rights of African Americans. By 1918 the debate within the black press as to how far, if at all, African American soldiers should be involved in a white man's war had become increasingly divisive. Du Bois risked his reputation on it, controversially encouraging black Americans to take their part in the struggle for democracy in Europe and urging them to "forget our special grievances and close our ranks shoulder to shoulder with our own white fellow citizens and the allied nations that are fighting for democracy."[35] However, other race leaders, including Marcus Garvey and the editors of the socialist magazine *The Messenger*, Chandler Owen and A. Philip Randolph, railed against the hypocrisy of white America and accused Du Bois of a failure of leadership for suggesting that the involvement of black soldiers in the war would help erase race prejudice: "Since when has the subject race come out of a war with its rights and privileges accorded for such participation," wondered Owen.[36] The astute Walker, however, understood the need to demonstrate her loyalty to the war effort. Constantly warned by Ransom, Walker realized that her business empire and the influence it bought her could be destroyed if she provoked the U.S. government. Walker was not about to risk the business that had carried her onto the political scene in the first place, and so she ostentatiously displayed her support for the war, through her purchase of Liberty Loan bonds, which she also urged Walker agents to buy. Madam

Walker was also on the Advisory Committee for the Circle for Negro War Relief, alongside other prominent race women, including Margaret Murray Washington and Addie Hunton. The Circle was designed to look after the general welfare of black soldiers while in service as well as their dependent families, by acting as a clearinghouse for donations.[37] As Walker traveled around the United States promoting her product and visiting Walker agents, she claimed America as her own, urging black Americans to recognize the importance of black soldiers' contribution to the war effort: "When the war begun it was thought that 'our boys' would not be needed but we see that they are needed and victory shall not have been won until the black boys of America shed their blood on the battlefield. This is your country, your home. What you have suffered in the past should not deter you from going forth to protect the homes and lives of your women and children."[38]

However, Walker was not afraid of expressing her conviction that the conditions endured by black men, especially in the South, would have to change when they returned from France. As soldiers abroad, black men had been treated, at least by the French, as equals, and had surely earned the right to respect at home. This view came across clearly in a letter Walker addressed to Colonel William Jay Schieffelin, a wealthy white reformer and president of Schieffelin Drugs. Admonishing him for misrepresenting her position on the war as unjustifiably militant, Walker defended her viewpoint and the right of African Americans to protest their disgraceful treatment at the hands of white Americans:

> their country called them to defend its honor on the battlefields of Europe and they have bravely, fearlessly bled and died, that that honor might be maintained. And now they will soon be returning. To what? Does any reasonable person imagine to the old order of things? To submit to being strung up, riddled with bullets, burned at the stake etc? No! A thousand times no. . . . They will come back to face like men, whatever is in store for them and like men defend themselves, their families, their homes . . . and if death be the result—so be it. An honorable death is far better than the miserable existence imposed upon most of our people in the South.[39]

In advocating armed resistance to the white mobs that had turned the summer of 1919 into one which would be remembered for its bloody race riots, Walker was distancing herself from the accommodationism associated with the Tuskegee camp and aligning herself with the spirit of the New Negro.[40] Echoing Garvey and Chandler Owen, Walker urged black Americans to defend themselves with force if necessary. Walker's language reflected the fact that the war had helped move her away from a narrowly American to a pan-African understanding of blacks' oppression in America. While the victorious allies gathered in Paris in 1919 to ensure Germany was punished and to take control of Germany's former African colonies, President Wilson presented the peace conference to the American public as an opportunity to impose his blueprint for a more equitable future on America's quarrelsome European allies. Walker too was keen to introduce a fairer balance of power between the oppressed and the oppressors of the world, and saw the peace conference as an opportunity to liberate Germany's former colonies in Africa. This developing interest in the post-war settlement led Walker toward association with William Monroe Trotter and his National Equal Rights League (NERL).

Walker had long been receptive to the ideas of William Monroe Trotter, the uncompromising editor of the *Boston Guardian* and founder of the NERL. Deeply opposed to any accommodation with white racism, Trotter was ostracized by Booker T. Washington and supporters of the Tuskegee Machine. In 1903 he had heckled Washington at a meeting in Boston and had been arrested and imprisoned. Even more famously, in 1912, he was dismissed from the Oval Office by Woodrow Wilson for challenging him on his civil rights record.[41] Despite these controversies, Walker was not put off, and in 1915 had Ransom invite Trotter to Indianapolis to speak at the Bethel African Methodist Episcopal Church, where he again attacked President Wilson's poor record on race matters.[42] In September 1917 Walker renewed the acquaintance when she joined two hundred other delegates at the Mother Zion African Methodist Episcopal Zion Church in New York City for the tenth annual convention of the NERL. Between 1917 and 1919, black organizations across the United States were meeting to discuss the outcome of the war. The NERL was no exception. At the 1917 NERL convention, delegates agreed to send representatives to the Colored Representative Congress for World Democracy to be held the following year in Washington, D.C. Elected vice-president-at-large by the local New York branch of the NERL, Walker was included in the delegation that was to represent New York at the 1918 Washington congress.[43] Following the equal rights convention in New York, Walker welcomed all the delegates to a reception at her home, and it was here that she renewed her acquaintance with Ida B. Wells-Barnett, the radical antilynching journalist and women's rights crusader based in Chicago.[44]

Wells-Barnett had met Walker many years before her trip to New York. She recalled how during a previous encounter she had been skeptical of Walker's plans and "paid very little heed to her predictions as to what she [Walker] was going to do. She had little or no education, and was never ashamed of having been a washerwoman earning a dollar and a half a day." When Wells-Barnett encountered Walker many years later as a delegate to the NERL convention, she was inspired by her achievement:

> She was a woman who by hard work and persistent effort had succeeded in establishing herself and her business in New York City. She had already had a town house, beautifully furnished, and had established beauty parlors and agents in and around New York City, thus giving demonstration of what a black woman who has vision and ambition can really do.[45]

Having spent time at the Walkers' townhouse, Wells-Barnett appeared struck and inspired not simply by Walker's business success but by her seemingly effortless translation of persistent hard work into gracious consumption too. As we will see later, it was A'Lelia Walker who would perfect this skill.

Walker and Wells-Barnett met again the following year in Washington, D.C., at the Race Congress for World Democracy. The delegates to the Congress petitioned President Wilson to abolish segregation in federal offices and interstate travel and to end the disfranchisement of black voters. They also demanded the passage of a federal antilynching bill. It was here that Walker was elected as one of only two female delegates to the Paris Peace Conference in an election in which, as she boasted in a letter to Ransom, "I am told that I ran ahead of all the names submitted, even to the Bishops."[46] However, as in her earlier encounters with Booker T. Washington and the NNBL, Walker again came up against men who sought to preclude women's involvement at the front line of black politics. Although elected along with Ida Wells-Barnett, "the committee decided that no women be sent except as alternatives and five men were nominated as delegates and Mrs Ida Wells-Barnett and myself as alternatives. Mrs B registered a strong protest and declined the empty honours, which resulted in us being elected from the floor, as full and legal delegates."[47] Walker made up her mind to go to Paris as a delegate of the Congress and a spokesperson for black women, though she thought it unlikely that the Congress would be able to fund any of the delegates. Cautious as ever and unhappy about Walker's close association with the belligerent Trotter, Ransom warned her against going to France and suggested she would be unlikely to get a passport in any case.[48] Ransom was extremely concerned about the impact that Walker's association with radicals might have both on the company and on those associated with it. Business manager and attorney for the company since its incorporation in 1911, Ransom had impressed Walker with his formidable organizational skills and solid counsel when it came to business affairs.[49] Ransom also had his own career outside the Walker Company as a distinguished civic leader. He sat on the board of many local organizations including the local YMCA and NAACP, and was himself in high demand as a speaker. It appeared that he too had political ambitions (with the Republican Party) that coincided with his boss's entrance into radical politics.[50] Ransom also maintained important contacts with Tuskegee, and in particular Emmet J. Scott, whom he appears to have consulted as to the likelihood of any African Americans reaching the Paris Peace Conference. Using Scott to support his argument that Walker should not go to France, Ransom informed Walker that "I talked with Emmet Scott and he is in perfect accord with my opinion that there is no way that this can really be done."[51] Walker held a genuine admiration and respect for her lawyer and took his advice seriously. She was, however, capable of distinguishing her political views from those of her business advisor, and continued to pursue her new interest in pan-African affairs.

The NERL was only one of many black factions meeting in conferences across the country to elect delegates to represent their interests at the Paris Peace Conference. Garvey's UNIA also chose Ida B. Wells-Barnett as well as the socialist A. Philip Randolph to speak on its behalf, and the Hamitic League nominated two of its members, Arthur A. Schomburg, collector of Africana, and Garveyite John Bruce.[52] In an attempt to unite these disparate forces, Madam Walker joined with the Reverend Adam Clayton Powell Sr., the Reverend Frederick Cullen, Randolph, and Garvey to form the International League of Peoples of the Darker Races (ILPDR). Walker's association with Randolph and Garvey preceded their cooperation in the ILPDR. She had helped both men set up their respective publications through the advertisements she placed in Randolph's *Messenger* and Garvey's *Negro World*. Walker also employed Randolph's wife, Lucille Green Randolph, who was a friend of A'Lelia's and whose financial resources garnered from her success as one of the most profitable Walker agents in Harlem had been critical in allowing Randolph and Owen to publish the *Messenger*.[53] As with Trotter, Walker's association with two leading black socialists was risky. While the State Department kept close surveillance on Du Bois's *Crisis* and Garvey's *Negro World*, it was Randolph and Owen whom the young J. Edgar Hoover viewed as particularly dangerous in his first report on African American sedition, and their *Messenger*, which he considered "the most able and the most dangerous of all negro publications."[54]

In many ways Walker's involvement with the Garvey movement was unsurprising, since her black nationalist sympathies as expressed through her letters and business initiatives brought her very close to the ideas being espoused by Marcus Garvey. Like Garvey, Walker had also been inspired by Washington's industrial school at Tuskegee. Whereas Garvey had thought of replicating Washington's experiment in Jamaica, Walker had a burning ambition to establish an industrial and mission school in Africa. To this end she put aside a share of her annual earnings and in her will pledged $10,000 to the project.[55] But Garvey's militant opposition to the war made him a risky ally in 1919. While it took the Department of Justice until 1923 to find their excuse to indict Garvey, others, including Chandler Owen and Du Bois, began much earlier in publicly expressing their doubts about his separatist program and collecting evidence for their successful "Garvey Must Go" campaign.[56] Walker, however, clearly empathized with the newcomer who had, like herself, built up an empire from nothing. She helped Garvey's movement take off early on by making direct financial contributions toward the purchase in 1919 of the UNIA's permanent meeting place, the Harlem Liberty Hall, as well as interacting with Garvey himself through her involvement in the ILPDR.[57]

Gathering together this group of male leaders at Villa Lewaro, her newly constructed mansion on the Hudson, Walker helped to launch the new league in January 1919 and played a leading role in its development. According to the *World Forum*, the bimonthly organ of the organization, the ILPDR aimed to organize all delegates intending to represent race organizations into one unit, "so that the race may present a front of solidarity and unity, in aims, methods, and action." Toward this end they planned on establishing a headquarters in Paris where all race representatives to the Paris Peace Conference could meet, as well as arranging accommodations and interpreters to aid delegates once in France. The ILPDR produced a memorandum of peace proposals which outlined the main concerns they intended to pursue at the peace conference. This included the demand for an international agreement to forbid "all economic, political and social discriminations in all countries based upon color," and planned for a "supernational" commission, composed of the world's "educated classes of Negroes" to govern Germany's former African colonies.[58] Beyond the Paris Peace Conference, the ILPDR looked to establish itself as a permanent international council, which would negotiate with other international bodies on behalf of peoples of the "darker races." Unlike the UNIA, but in common with the ICWDR, the ILPDR saw the race problem as extending to all "non-white" peoples, or "people of the darker races." Applicants for ILPDR membership were required to express their commitment to "aid the struggles of darker peoples, in all lands, for social, economic and political justice."[59] The league's program would be concerned with the progress and struggles for self-determination of peoples from Africa, India, Persia, China, Japan, South America, and the Pacific Islands. Madam Walker played a leading role in outlining the permanent program of the ILPDR, and was praised by the other officers for her "breadth of vision, her unselfish and generous interest in and devotion to the larger methods and measures for race freedom and justice."[60] While Adam Clayton Powell Sr. would serve as president, Walker, the business success, was elected treasurer and was to lead the $100,000 campaign to develop the league's work.

Ransom, however, was concerned about Walker's involvement in the ILPDR and warned her that "you will have to watch your league for I very much suspect that they will want you to finance most of their little projects. It seems strange to me that so few prominent New Yorkers are connected with it, in fact, there seems to be practically none."[61] Ransom in fact meant there were few prominent conservative New Yorkers associated with the league, as Garvey and the popular Reverend Adam Clayton Powell Sr. were two of the most well known black men in the United States at the end of the 1910s. Ransom did not share Walker's willingness to become involved in new radical race organizations, believing rather that Walker owed it to her race to pursue the more cautious approach he favored: "People who have developed great businesses, attained great wealth and influence, no longer belong to themselves but to the people and to posterity and they cannot be too careful as to entangling alliances, such as may bring them in ill-repute or in a way affect their business standing and integrity."[62] The records of the Military Intelligence Division reveal that Ransom had cause for concern. The ILPDR's connection with prominent Japanese figures including S. Kuvoiwa, the "William Randolph Hearst" of the Japanese newspaper industry, had made the organization the subject of heavy surveillance and vulnerable to charges of espionage.[63]

Like many of the other delegates chosen at various black conventions across the country, Trotter, Randolph, and Walker never made it to France. When Walker applied for a commercial business visa, her connection with Trotter's NERL, Garvey's UNIA, and Randolph's *Messenger*, and her own role in the ILPDR, made her an object of suspicion in the eyes of the State Department. The Bureau of Investigation advised the State Department to refuse passports for all National Race Congress delegates in order to avoid them mentioning the so-called Negro question at the Peace Conference.[64] Jessie Fauset, who was acting editor-in-chief of *The Crisis* in Du Bois's absence, editorialized that Walker's passport had been denied "because she was a woman."[65] In fact, Walker was refused a passport because, like Wells-Barnett, she was seen as a powerful organizer and dangerous critic of white supremacy. In the end the only African American delegate to reach Paris in time for the peace conference was Du Bois, who represented the NAACP, though Trotter (who was refused a passport and smuggled himself on to a ship as a cook) eventually arrived in Paris after the first draft of the Paris Peace Treaty had been signed.[66] Whether it was the advice from Ransom, the State Department's refusal to issue her passport, her increasingly frequent bouts of ill health, or simply her good business instincts that alerted her to the risky course she was pursuing, Walker resigned her membership of the ILPDR in February 1919.[67]

Nonetheless, Walker's willingness to become personally involved in new and risky projects with black leaders like Garvey and Trotter, who were scorned by much of the conservative black press, showed her desire to project herself as an independent race representative, a race woman with her own thoughts and ideas who was anchored in neither the integrationist nor black nationalist camp. With the ILPDR, Walker had envisaged an organization that transcended traditional race divisions in the United States by bringing race leaders into contact with leaders of other oppressed peoples around the world. African Americans might learn more by concentrating on what they had in common with other oppressed peoples of color, rather than on what divided them at home. Although Walker was well aware that to be seen interacting with prominent race leaders could help her promote her business interests, she was not content to sit back and be merely a financial supporter of the visions of others. Rather she wanted to be taken seriously as a thinker in her own right. Walker's involvement in many of the most influential race movements of her day allowed her to project her vision of black womanhood into debates about women's role in business and in global affairs. Although Walker owed much of her reputation to her work for race organizations and contacts with male leaders, she always maintained a steady focus on black women's groups. Through her association with black women's organizations, her cultivation of important feminist pan-African thinkers and activists, and her organization of thousands of Walker company employees into a women's benevolent association, Walker herself came to represent a feminist and often black nationalist agenda which she articulated through her speeches and company propaganda.

"Woman's Duty to Woman": Madam Walker as Clubwoman and Role Model

Walker maintained close contacts with some of the leading women activists and thinkers of her day, who in turn were connected to important women's organizations. For example, Walker was personally close to clubwomen, including Mary Church Terrell, Margaret Murray Washington, Mary Talbert, and Mary McLeod Bethune, and had business relationships with Charlotte Hawkins Brown and Nannie Helen Burroughs. Walker shared platforms and correspondence with the leaders of the 137th Street Colored Branch of the YWCA, Cecelia Cabaniss Saunders and Eva Bowles, and had a direct impact on some of the leading feminist pan-African thinkers associated with the Harlem Renaissance.[68] Her recruitment trips around the United States enabled her to meet a wide spectrum of black women's groups and engage with a variety of ideas and experiences. It also meant that her own political activism had an impact on the many groups with whom she met. By the mid-1910s Walker was greeted as a celebrity wherever she went, hosted by local dignitaries and given a platform at the local Y or black church.[69]

One important feminist pan-Africanist who endorsed Walker's approach was Amy Jacques Garvey, a leading figure in the UNIA and the second wife of Marcus Garvey. In her women's page in the *Negro World*, the official publication of the UNIA, Amy Jacques Garvey held Walker up as an example to women of the race. Amy Jacques Garvey frequently used her editorials to express disapproval of women who spent too much time on their appearance and in particular those who tried to imitate white standards of beauty by straightening their hair or trying to whiten their skins.[70] However, she saw Madam Walker as a credit to the race, as someone who celebrated black beauty rather than copied white ideals of beauty, and who was concerned, as Walker herself maintained, to increase black women's awareness of hygiene and self-presentation. More importantly, however, Jacques Garvey applauded Walker because she had achieved economic success through a black-run business: "So many of our women think they need Mme. Walker's wealth to start, but she started with but little money. She had a will and found a way. You can do so . . . Could we offer a better suggestion than that the women of the Universal Negro Improvement Association consider the business phase of their lives and take steps to improve it?"[71] Walker's business philosophy was held up as an example of black economic nationalism; indeed, Jacques Garvey could see no better way of serving the womanhood of the race than to follow the example set by Madam Walker. An editorial endorsement by Jacques Garvey could significantly increase the Walker Company's public standing; with its weekly circulation of between 60,000 and 200,000 the *Negro World* was one of the most widely read black newspapers of its day.[72] Likewise, the influence of Jacques Garvey and other black nationalists was evidenced on the pages of the Walker Manufacturing Company's magazine a few years later. Just as Jacques Garvey would use her women's page to urge black women to boycott white stores and patronize black-owned businesses, a *Walker News* editorial sternly reminded black Americans to "keep the money that comes to you within the group as long as possible." The editor went on to issue a special message to Walker agents: "We urge every Walker agent to make sure that everyday she buys from Negroes everything that she needs if Negroes have it. Follow the slogan 'Every day in every way we spend our money with Negroes—do you?'"[73]

Walker and her legacy had a pervasive influence on intellectual circles well into the 1920s as evidenced by the endorsement of another leading feminist writer in the New Negro movement. Jessie Fauset, who was a key novelist of the Harlem Renaissance, often depicted heroines who were sympathetic to black nationalism. In her first novel, *There Is Confusion,* Fauset acknowledged Walker's significance as a role model for young working women. Maggie, a young black working-class woman who has tried to escape poverty through marriage, eventually establishes her independence when she escapes from a gambling husband and finds a career as a fictionalized Madame Walker agent. Fauset uses this plot line to praise by implication the opportunities Walker created for young black women, when Maggie tells us: "You know there's a Madame Harkness who's invented a method of softening hair, and of taking the harshness out of your folk's locks. . . . I think there is a big future in it. It ought to mean a lot to us. Everybody wants to be beautiful, and every woman looks better if her hair is soft and manageable."[74] Maggie admires Walker as a woman who opened an avenue for women to economic independence. Maggie has developed from being a marriage-oriented social climber to an independent race woman through her association with the hair company. Fauset's image of the New Negro woman as depicted in her novels is fiercely independent and race proud; it is a testament to Walker's impact on women in different spheres that Fauset used one of her novels to praise her contribution to the race. Like Walker, Fauset had a significant impact on the thinking of the women around her through her role at *The Crisis*. As literary editor of *The Crisis*, the official journal of the NAACP, Fauset represented an organization that was, in theory, diametrically opposed to the philosophy articulated by Marcus Garvey and his UNIA. That Fauset and Jacques Garvey could both agree on Walker's importance as a feminist role model illustrates the way in which black women were able to bring together apparently oppositional ideologies.

Walker was also prominently involved in two of the most important women's groups for African Americans in the early part of the twentieth century, the Young Women's Christian Association, particularly the Colored Branch of the Y in Harlem, and the National Association of Colored Women (NACW). Walker's close relationship with the Colored Branches of the YWCA further demonstrated her deep commitment to advancing the position of African American women. Walker first took an interest in the Y movement when she moved to Indianapolis in 1911 and made headlines as the first black donor to pledge one thousand dollars to the black Young Men's Christian Association in that city. When making her pledge she had declared "If the association can save our boys, our girls will be saved, and that's what I'm interested in. . . . Some day I would like to see a colored girls' association started."[75] When Walker moved to Harlem she was quick to realize the importance of the Colored Branch of the YWCA as a cultural and political center, and soon became one of its most regular donors. She also became a member of the board of the Management Committee of the Colored YWCA and later the second vice-president. A popular speaker at the YWCA's training evenings on business opportunities for black women, Walker would deliver a rousing address to a crowded audience on "How I Succeeded in Business."[76] Eva Bowles remembered Walker's service to the community and the YWCA in her report to the National YWCA: "One of the Committee of Managers of the Colored Women's Branch of the New York City Y.W.C.A., Mrs Walker . . . was extraordinarily generous, spending a large sum of money every year upon the education of young men and women, and in assisting in all movements which tended toward the advancement of her race."[77] As seen in Chapter 2, the YWCA was an important base for cultural, social, and political activities during the Harlem Renaissance. That Walker was a member of the Committee of Management of the YWCA therefore enhanced her profile as a leading race woman in Harlem, and given her business expertise and the lectures she delivered at the YWCA it is likely that her story inspired many a young woman who resided at or visited the YWCA.

Although Walker contributed her money and prestige to interracial groups such as the NAACP and YWCA, she was committed to working in African American groups.[78] Early on Walker had seen the importance of connecting herself and her company with the leading black clubwomen around the country. In 1904 she had attended the St. Louis convention of the fledgling NACW. However, it was not until the 1912 convention at Hampton Institute that she addressed the convention herself, choosing as her theme "business opportunities for women." On that occasion Walker demonstrated her commitment to the NACW by paying the expenses of an NACW delegation that was to travel to Richmond to petition the governor of Virginia to grant clemency in the case of the death sentence pronounced on a young black woman.[79] In

1918, Walker was welcomed back by the NACW as a guest speaker to the Denver convention. Addressing the women delegates gathered in the city where she had first established her business, Walker spoke on women's important role in business. Believing that the NACW should embrace women from all backgrounds, including the women she employed, Walker used her platform to appeal to the clubwomen to "get closer in touch with our women in the factory."[80] Walker had used her own meteoric rise to transform the beauty industry into a respectable profession. With the increased incomes made available to thousands of women who became her agents, the NACW should reach out to women from working-class backgrounds who were now able to afford the NACW subscriptions, donate money to NACW campaigns, and have a say in the NACW's agenda.[81]

Walker urged the convention to broaden its agenda so that it would attract more women from lower-class backgrounds. It was also at the Denver convention that Walker's contribution to the NACW was publicly acknowledged. She was invited to preside over a mortgage-burning ceremony to celebrate the successful end of the NACW's two-year campaign to purchase Cedar Hill, the Washington, D.C., home of Frederick Douglass. As the largest single donor, contributing five hundred dollars to the campaign, Walker had been chosen to strike the match that burned the mortgage.[82] This was a symbolic moment acknowledging Walker's important place on the clubwomen's circuit. From then on, in subsequent conventions and in the NACW's *National Notes*, Walker's legacy would be held up to clubwomen as an example of what a great race woman could achieve.[83] Walker's acceptance by the NACW offers evidence of the evolving nature of the clubwomen's movement in the 1910s. That a divorced, dark-skinned hairdresser could be held up as a role model for other NACW members suggests that the organization was not constrained by white notions of what constituted respectable womanhood, but able to adapt with the times.

Walker's involvement with the women leaders of black political and social reform also brought her immense benefits. Not only did the NACW's celebration of her enhance her image as a race woman, it also provided her with valuable contacts that she exploited to the benefit of her business and employees. Walker used her contacts with the NACW leadership to professionalize her trade by expanding the Walker system into their schools and institutes. For example, she installed a Walker hair treatment course at Mary McLeod Bethune's Daytona Normal and Industrial School.[84] Walker also borrowed the structure and conventions of the NACW to organize her agents into a national federation of black women who were brought together not just by race pride and a desire to lift as they climbed, but also by economic incentive. Previously she had kept in touch with her agents through personally appointed local trainers and the Indianapolis Headquarters, but as the numbers of agents passed the 10,000 figure, Walker felt a more organized approach was needed. There was a clear economic incentive to organize, as with an ever-expanding workforce it became important to keep in close touch with agents in order to prevent others from adulterating her goods by repackaging and selling them as their own. However, Walker was also motivated by her involvement in numerous women's club movements and other political groups that had taught her the political and economic value to the community of black women acting together.

Walker first outlined her vision for the Madam Walker Benevolent Association to Ransom in April 1916, after her permanent move from Indianapolis to Harlem. Explaining how she would first organize local clubs across the United States, Walker then planned to call a meeting of all Walker agents to form a national federation similar to the NACW, but without a central bureaucracy to handle the money, which could be done at a local level.[85] The Madam Walker Benevolent Association was imitative of the NACW structure insofar as it produced a national newsletter and held national and regional conventions designed to bring agents together to discuss their common problems and ideas for the future and to reward clubs that had done most in the way of philanthropic work. Chapters of the Madam Walker Benevolent Association were affiliated with the NACW, and used the National as a forum for their charity work. In a letter to her agents, Walker emphasized how the aims of the new organization were designed to help them and black womanhood more generally:

> The purpose of this organization is; first, to have a National Body of Workers, with a common intent and purpose; second to know who the agents of Madam C J Walker Mfg Company are; third to protect all such agents against misrepresentations and false statements of fakes and impostors, and last, to have this organization, its rules and regulations so strict, and perfect, until it will be utterly impossible for any one to handle our goods, unless such a one is a regular agent of the Company, and is a member of the National Organization.[86]

Committed to having a workforce that was concerned not just with making money, but desirous of helping the race as a whole, and particularly other black women, Walker instructed Ransom to "Address them as Dear Friend" and "make a special appeal to them for one dollar each for the Memorial Fund." The fund was in memory of Booker T. Washington, who had recently died and whose widow Walker now counted as a friend. Her respect for Margaret Washington partly explained Walker's personal wish to raise money for the memorial fund, but she had another motive, as she explained to Ransom: "It will show to the world that the Walker Agents are doing something else other than just making money for themselves."[87] Ever mindful of her company's image, Walker's strategy was justified by the national publicity given the new Benevolent Association. The *New York Age* led with the headline "Organization Has Attracted National Attention Since Its Large Subscription to Washington Memorial Fund." It went on to describe the initial meeting of the New York Benevolent Association, which had formed at Lelia College in Harlem. At this meeting both Walker and her daughter were elected officers of the local organization, and pledges to the fund of over one hundred dollars were made.[88] Walker also introduced many economic incentives to encourage agents not only to join the Benevolent Association but also to increase their sales. These included five hundred dollars in prizes to the agents selling the largest number of boxes of Walker goods and returning the largest number of empty boxes and to the agent responsible for recruiting the largest number of delegates to the national organization. To help facilitate these initiatives, new agents could be brought on board for only ten dollars rather than the usual twenty-five dollars.[89]

The Madam Walker Benevolent Association, unlike the NACW, attracted many members from working-class backgrounds. Yet its rhetoric seems to have been strongly influenced by that of the clubwomen. For example, the language of the guidelines drawn up for agents, which was issued with the first call for membership, is strikingly similar to the tone of NACW publications. There is an overwhelming emphasis on cleanliness, neatness, preparation, and hard work. Personal hygiene as well as professionalism at all times is emphasized.[90] For example, number seven on the list of guidelines advised agents: "See that your hair always looks well in order to interest others you must first make the impression by keeping your hair in first class condition."[91] Walker believed that beautifully washed and styled hair was a standard that any professional agent should meet. But she also believed it should be available to all. Rather than trying to distance Walker agents from their poorer sisters, Walker saw her product as something inclusive that could liberate all women, no matter what their background and irrespective of whether they could afford to go to a beauty salon.[92] Ideally, women would buy their treatments from and have their hair done by a Walker agent, but Walker agents also sold the hair preparation direct to women who could not afford to have it done in a salon. Walker explained that these women should be helped as sisters:

> Do not be narrow and selfish to the extent that you would not sell goods to anyone because they do not take the treatment from you. We are anxious to help all humanity, the poor as well as the rich, especially those of our race. There are thousands who would buy and use the goods who are not able to pay the extra cost of having it done for them. The hair may not grow as rapidly nor look as beautiful, but they will get results and as long as they are satisfied and you have made your profit from the sale, all is well.[93]

Certainly by helping poorer women, Walker was also boosting her profit margins. But Walker's evangelism was rooted in her firm belief that the cause of the Madam Walker Manufacturing Company was the cause of black women. She frequently dropped the price of becoming an accredited Walker agent along with the starter pack of hair products from $25 to $10 for the poorer women she met on her travels in the South. For those that could not afford even the cut price, Walker "put them on their honor to pay whenever they can."[94] But Walker's appeal to her agents to think of those less fortunate than themselves also made good business sense, especially as Walker agents were becoming increasingly perturbed that they could be bypassed and that products could be sold directly to pharmacies and other outlets, which could potentially undercut agents' client bases by adulterating the Walker formula. In an attempt to safeguard the agents and her profits from competitors' adulteration of her products, Walker introduced a specially designed Walker seal to distinguish official products.[95]

The first national meeting of Walker agents, the Madam Walker Beauty Culturists Union Convention, took place in Philadelphia in 1917. Held at the Philadelphia Union Baptist Church, home of the Reverend Wesley G. Parks, the vice-president of the National Baptist Convention, Walker delivered her keynote speech on one of her favorite themes, "Woman's Duty to Woman."[96] She also used this platform to speak of the war, advising her people to remain loyal to their homes, country, and flag, but warning that while America was the greatest country under the sun, "we must not let our love of our country, our patriotic loyalty cause us to abate one whit in our protest against wrong and injustice. We should protest until the American sense of justice is so aroused that such affairs as the East St. Louis Riot be forever impossible."[97] Like many race leaders, Walker was indignant at the treatment of black soldiers by white racist mobs, and disturbed by the growth of racial tensions that frequently spilled into race riots in the Midwest and North. Inspired by Walker's address, the convention delegates voted to send a protest to President Wilson expressing their feelings about the war and the race riots:

> We the representatives of the National Convention of the Madam C J Walker Agents in convention assembled and in a larger sense representing twelve million Negroes have keenly felt the injustice done our race and country through the recent lynching at Memphis, Tenn. and horrible race riot at East St. Louis and knowing that no people in all the world are more loyal and patriotic than the colored people of America, respectfully submit to you this our protest against the continuation of such wrongs and injustice in this land of the free and home of the brave, and we further respectfully urge that you as President of these United States use your great influence that Congress enact the necessary laws to prevent a recurrence of such disgraceful affairs.[98]

On the one hand, the Walker agents positioned themselves as Americans with rights under the Constitution, while on the other, they also saw themselves as united with the twelve million black Americans who shared their indignation at the treatment of returning black soldiers. Like the NACW, the NCNW, and other black women's groups, Walker agents were not only concerned with the issues immediately affecting their own female attendees, but also concerned with wider racial justice. Understanding that for black Americans "politics was not separate from lived experience or the imagined world of what is possible," Madam Walker and her agents related their own economic struggles to the wider racial problems of black America.[99] At subsequent Walker agent conventions, Walker continued to inspire her agents to connect their business interests with the interests of the race. In her speeches, Walker retained much of the same force she had always projected when she was trying to promote herself, her product, and her race: they always began with her own example. For instance, at a regional meeting of Walker agents at Watt Street School in Philadelphia in April 1918 she told them that "What I have done you can do. I am here to interest and inspire you if possible. If I am not successful in helping you, remember I did the best I could. I want to meet every agent personally before I leave the city."[100]

Walker's success in recruiting new sales agents rested not only on her public image as a race woman and philanthropist, but also on her reputation as a good employer. Indeed the *Chicago Defender* suggested that Walker's greatest achievement lay in her efforts to promote the general welfare of her employees. Distinguishing her from other philanthropists, the paper explained that unlike other do-gooders, "She did not gain a pharisaic reputation with the public of being a bountiful giver for the uplift of the unfortunate, while her employees toiled day after day for petty wages upon which they could not possibly live."[101] Her agents echoed these sentiments in a set of resolutions they passed following Madam Walker's death in which they testified that "[Walker] did not gain her wealth by overworking or underpaying her employees. On the contrary, they were among the most humanely treated and the best paid of the country."[102] Walker repeatedly expressed her pride that through her business she had created not just a hair product, but jobs for thousands of black women, enabling them to experience economic independence for the first time. Walker's creation of a network of agents who bought her products and practiced in beauty parlors or door to door was not new; other companies such as Avon, as well as her main competitor and former employer Annie Turnbo Malone, had pioneered door-to-door commission sales. However, Walker's innovation lay in her ability to combine individual economic incentive with concern for racial uplift to create a politically focused benevolent association: "I want my agents to feel that their first duty is to humanity . . . to do their bit to help and advance the best interests of the race."[103]

Monuments to the Race: A'Lelia Walker and the New Promotion of the Walker Brand

As we have seen, Madam Walker was keen to create a new and positive image of black womanhood, and the way in which she marketed herself and her company played a large role in the construction of this image. Walker's strategy for projecting this image was to use her company literature and advertising to present herself as a race-proud woman from a humble background who had overcome many obstacles. However, her daughter, A'Lelia Walker, recognized the need to adapt to the new spirit of post-war America. A'Lelia promoted her own image as an alternative vision of black womanhood. Her image was modern and sexy and tapped into an evolving market. Rather than emphasizing the long hours and hard work involved in becoming a successful Walker sales agent, A'Lelia chose instead to emphasize the glamorous life of the beauty expert and the lifestyle the good wages provided. Although the image A'Lelia projected differed from her mother's, her method for marketing that image was important in the Madam Walker Manufacturing Company's marketing strategy in the late 1910s and beyond. Between them the Walkers played an important role in transforming the image of black womanhood and opening up opportunities to black women in the first half of the twentieth century.

For Walker and her daughter, the private—or at least a version of it—very early on became the public. Both women constructed an image of themselves and used the machinery of their business to project it. Walker's promotional literature demonstrated how her race pride extended to all aspects of her life, as she practiced her message of black economic nationalism. For example, an early press release described how "Every flat, and apartment house, erected here in Indianapolis or elsewhere, by Madam Walker, was done by a colored contractor. Her attorney, physician, and business manager are all members of her race."[104] All the major black journals and newspapers carried advertisements for the Walker Company that featured prominent images of the Walker women. Many black newspapers and journals often carried separate feature articles on Madam Walker, with copy often provided by Ransom. In these articles, the writers took pride in retelling Walker's rags-to-riches story, insisting that her product was not a hair-straightener and praising her contribution to the race. W. E. B. Du Bois wrote that Walker had transformed a generation through her teaching of hygiene and hair care. He challenged her detractors who accused her of trying to straighten hair and make African Americans look more like whites, arguing rather that Walker had "revolutionized the personal habits and appearance of millions of human beings." George Schuyler devoted an eleven-page story in *The Messenger* recounting her contribution to black womanhood.[105]

Whereas Madam Walker issued a series of press releases listing her charitable contributions, A'Lelia's exotic lifestyle and glamorous salons generated their own publicity for the company. Both black and white newspapers gave her free copy, which not only helped her to sell her product, but offered to black women an image of a black woman who celebrated consumption as well as hard work. A'Lelia deliberately styled her image in keeping with that of the New, as opposed to the "Old," Negro; that is, just as her mother had displayed her hard work, her production, A'Lelia suggested that consumption was similar proof of race progress, a progress no longer inhibited by the conservative, uplift rhetoric of the first post-Reconstruction generation. Black women could, if they chose, identify more with the fruits of their work, with consumption, rather than with physical action of the work itself. For A'Lelia it was the social context of a job that should be emphasized rather than the routine nature of the work.[106] Her elaborate costumes and sumptuous parties reflected this attitude to work and celebrated her body as "an instrument of pleasure rather than an instrument of labor." As Paul Gilroy, Tera Hunter, and others have noted, for formerly enslaved peoples, the freedom to celebrate leisure time might be more important than the "freedom" to work.[107]

A'Lelia Walker's attitude to work certainly appears less self-conscious than her mother's in its disregard both for white stereotypes of blacks as lazy indolent children and for black men's notions of what constituted appropriate women's work, yet A'Lelia worked hard at constructing this image of herself as carefree and glamorous. A'Lelia's life has come to symbolize a trouble-free period before the Crash and the Great Depression. Yet like this image of the twenties, A'Lelia's life was much more complicated; the obstacles of race, gender, and class with which she had to contend have been glossed over, because she herself worked hard to deflect attention from them. A'Lelia played a prominent role in projecting this image of herself as carefree and extravagant, especially to white audiences. Indeed for many whites, A'Lelia came to embody the glamour and exoticism of uptown Manhattan in the 1920s. Carl Van Vechten, the well-known negrophile, immortalized A'Lelia as Adora Boniface in *Nigger Heaven*, the novel that scandalized the Harlem literati.[108] He later remarked, "You should have known A'Lelia Walker. . . . Nothing in this age is quite as good as THAT."[109] While many of A'Lelia's friends confirmed this image of A'Lelia the good-time girl, others recognized her complexity. In his oft-quoted description of A'Lelia in his memoir, *The Big Sea*, Langston Hughes pictured her as the "joy-goddess of Harlem's 1920s," "a gorgeous dark Amazon, in a silver turban." Her funeral, which swelled with family, friends, and Walker agents, was apparently more of a party than a funeral, and marked for Hughes "the end of the gay times of the New Negro era in Harlem."[110] Yet even as he recalled A'Lelia the good-time girl, Hughes also celebrated a woman free of slavery:

> She died as she had lived
> With no wearying pain
> Binding her to life
> Like a hateful chain[111]

Written on the occasion of A'Lelia's funeral, Hughes's poem recognizes A'Lelia's New Negro spirit: unlike her mother, and many other race leaders of that generation, A'Lelia had freed herself of the chains of the "old Negro." Race progress as defined by building up black communities through hard work, thrift, and production was a philosophy that would be replaced, at least in the Walker Company's marketing strategy, by that of conspicuous consumption, when A'Lelia took charge in 1919.

A'Lelia's role in the Walker Company has not been taken seriously by recent commentators. This is partly due to the focus on her industrious mother, and in part because of this image of her as the party queen of Harlem. Madam Walker's great-great-granddaughter and biographer A'Lelia Bundles views A'Lelia Walker through the lens of her mother's achievements: "clearly Lelia lacked her mother's fortitude and perseverance. Nevertheless, she had inherited her flair for the dramatic."[112] There have been several fictional accounts of both Madam Walker and A'Lelia that have also helped contribute to this image of A'Lelia. In her tale of *The Rise and Triumph of Madam C. J. Walker*, Beverly Lowry creates an A'Lelia who squandered her mother's inheritance and cared little about the business.[113] In the 1920s and '30s, however, the black press recognized and celebrated A'Lelia and her role within the Madam Walker Manufacturing Company. For example, the *Inter-State Tattler* recognized that A'Lelia was not the consummate spoiled heiress, but rather had infused the company with her business techniques and marketing strategies and had played a crucial role in the business while her mother was alive:

> A'Lelia comes in for her share of credit. She spent a lot of money on a lot of things her mother thought foolish, but had it not been for A'Lelia the Indianapolis concern might not have become the gold mine it was reputed to be in 1915. It was A'Lelia with her college education, her ideas of system, and her ideas of business promotion and business technique that brought it about.[114]

As Edkins and Marks later noted, A'Lelia was actually over twenty years old when the Walker Company was first started and thirty-four when she became an heiress; she had, in fact, spent the major part of her life sharing her mother's struggles and working hard for the success of the company.[115] In 1916, the *Colored American Review* recognized the shared work that had brought about the success of the Madam Walker Manufacturing Company. When Walker set up and took charge of the Indianapolis Headquarters, it was A'Lelia in Pittsburgh who took the business forward to the East:

> She like her mother, had no predecessor in the business of this kind on such a large scale. It was her clear vision and ability to adjust herself to new conditions and new fields of labor, as well as to seize opportunities when they presented themselves that directed her attention to the East and to the Great Metropolis, New York City.

The article goes on to describe the important, if different roles of Madam and A'Lelia Walker: while her mother projected the image of respectable hard work, A'Lelia showed that the Walkers could conquer the cultural capital of America as well.[116]

Although both Walkers could consume magnificently as well as work industriously, it was A'Lelia who grasped much more quickly than her mother that their marketing strategy should reflect this new consumerism. Especially after the war, customers did not want to hear about the virtue of struggle and hard work, themes that had previously been reflected in the Walker Company's marketing strategy. It was A'Lelia's initiative after the war and following her mother's death that helped the Walker Company develop a successful marketing strategy in the new consumer age. While their different styles at times came into conflict when both women were running the company, Madam Walker came to accept that A'Lelia's celebration of consumption not only offered a challenging alternative to white constructions of black womanhood, but also helped to sell their product. One example that illustrates how Madam Walker learned from her daughter concerned their disagreement over the refurbishment of the 136th Street salon run by A'Lelia, which would become the most famous Walker beauty salon in the country. The correspondence between A'Lelia, her mother, and Ransom indicates that the project became a growing source of friction as costs mounted. However, while initially reluctant to commit resources to it, by 1916 Madam Walker was brimming

Figure 7. Walker agents and beauty culturists at Villa Lewaro in 1924. Madam C. J. Walker Collection, Indiana Historical Society.

Figure 8. A'Lelia Walker's 136th Street Beauty Parlor. (Mrs. Robinson's Beauty Parlor, Interior View, circa 1915–16.) Byron Collection, 93.1.1.10840, Museum of the City of New York.

Figure 9. One of two music rooms at the 108 West 136th Street Walker home. (Mrs. Robinson's Beauty Parlor, clients in waiting room, circa 1915–16.) Byron Collection, 93.1.1.10836, Museum of the City of New York.

Figure 10. Lelia College, New York. A'Lelia Walker *(left)* receiving a treatment. Her adopted daughter, May Walker *(third from left, in background)*, is treating a customer. (Mrs. Robinson's Beauty Parlor, circa 1915–16.) Byron Collection, 93.1.1.10837, Museum of the City of New York.

with enthusiasm at her daughter's foresight in her description of the parlor to Ransom:

> you will agree with Lelia when she said that it would be a monument for us both. It is just impossible for me to describe it to you. The Hair Parlor beats anything I have seen anywhere even in the best Hair Parlors of the whites. The decorators said that of all the work they had done here in that line there is nothing to equal it not even on Fifth Avenue, so you know it must be wonderful. It was a surprise and I haven't a word to say against it. . . . Lelia's business is bringing her close to two thousand a month and the business has picked up wonderfully since she opened up.[117]

Madam Walker's enthusiasm for the 136th Street salon was soon translated into a new venture of her own. Whereas A'Lelia had constructed a monument to the Walker Company, Madam Walker embarked on an enormous project to build a mansion that would be a "monument to the race." Officially opened in August 1918, Walker's $300,000 house was, according to one of many newspaper accounts, "so splendid and so perfectly appointed that it would serve not alone as a source of pride to her and others of her race, but compel the respect and admiration of scoffing whites."[118] Hiring the black architect Vertnor Tandy, Walker had built a home which "attracted the attention of the entire country."[119] Villa Lewaro, named after the first two letters of A'Lelia's married name (Lelia Walker Robinson) by her friend the opera singer Enrico Caruso, had thirty rooms, including ten bathrooms, ten bedrooms, a pool room, a library, a dining room, a music room, a swimming pool, and a gymnasium, and furniture made to order. Walker's achievement in building Villa Lewaro was the race's achievement. It compelled the attention, if not the admiration and respect, of white Americans who could not imagine a racial order where a black former washerwoman might live in upstate New York, a neighbor of the rich and powerful. It was also A'Lelia's achievement, as it was her vision that had paved the way for Villa Lewaro. Understanding this two-way influence—mother to daughter and back again—allows us to see A'Lelia not as a spoiled heiress, but rather, in her own way, a race leader.

To mark the villa's opening in the summer of 1918, the Walker women held their first "race conference." Mother and daughter disagreed about precisely who should be invited. Madam Walker, who as we have seen put little store by factional quarrels, invited all the most prominent race men and women of the day, including Emmet J. Scott as guest speaker. Booker T. Washington's former secretary and now the special assistant to the secretary of war for Negro affairs, Scott was a controversial choice. Although Washington had died three years before, the animosity that existed between the accommodationists who had supported Washington and the more militant civil rights activists who had gone on to form the NAACP had not entirely dissipated. Furthermore, Scott's post in the War Department positioned him uncomfortably close to the Military Intelligence Division, and he would play a key role in persuading the State Department to deny passports to Walker, Randolph, Wells-Barnett, and the rest of what he called the "Trotter Bunch."[120] A'Lelia was dismayed by what she regarded as her mother's disregard for social etiquette, complaining to Ransom that her mother had invited enemies as well as supporters of Scott and fearing that Scott would snub her mother as a result. Moreover, A'Lelia considered it poor etiquette to combine social and political events and bad business to combine work and politics.[121] Nor was she alone in her concern that it was a dangerous time to be hosting a race conference given the current war. Earlier in the year Ransom had warned Madam Walker that her involvement in race politics, particularly at a time of war, might compromise her ability to conduct her business.[122] Emmet J. Scott certainly knew this to be the truth, since he had seen Walker's name in surveillance reports of black radical organizations such as the ILPDR. Moreover, he had warned black editors just a few months previously that "This is not the time to discuss race problems."[123]

While A'Lelia was deeply concerned that Scott would forfeit the conference because of the other people on the guest list, she believed that her mother saw it as an opportunity to "bring these different factions together after they have scrapped all of these years." A'Lelia doubted her mother's ability to bridge the longstanding divisions between representatives of Tuskegee and the NAACP, but she was proved wrong. Newspaper accounts of the conference reveal both that Scott and many rival NAACP leaders did attend Walker's conference and that African Americans' involvement in the war was discussed. Attendees included Mary Talbert, Mary White Ovington, James Weldon Johnson, and John H. Shillady of the NAACP; clubwomen Elizabeth Carter, Addie Dickerson, and Charlotte Hawkins Brown; Harlem YWCA secretary Cecelia Cabaniss Saunders; and Lester Walton of the *New York Age*.[124] The *Pittsburgh Courier* reported the speech delivered by Madam Walker to welcome her guests and explain why she had called a meeting of race leaders. Walker felt African American leaders of all political persuasions should have a chance to put their concerns to the War Secretary, as well as share with each other their unease over African American involvement in the war. Walker used the occasion to argue for greater race solidarity between leaders of opposing factions, suggesting that "this was the time when members of the race should forget all their differences; stand together for the higher principles involved in this war."[125] However, while Walker saw the war as an opportunity to bring about race solidarity, A'Lelia on the other hand felt embarrassed that their housewarming party had been transformed into a serious race conference which might give offense to race leaders. Yet it was testament to Madam Walker's influence that these divided factions did respond to her call for a race conference in 1918. A'Lelia learned from her mother's example and would also demonstrate an ability to maintain relationships with race leaders at either end of the political spectrum. Villa Lewaro meanwhile became a monument to the Walkers' economic success and race activism. While Madam Walker stipulated in her will that the house be given to the NAACP following her daughter's death, during the 1920s Villa Lewaro became the venue for A'Lelia's sumptuous house parties at which up and coming young artists hoped to be presented.[126]

Figure 11. The picture of A'Lelia Walker that appeared on the front page of the *Messenger*, October 1926. A'Lelia Bundles/Walker Family Collection/madamcjwalker.com.

Following her mother's death A'Lelia continued to modernize the business, while still focusing on the company's commitment to helping the race, and particularly black women. One of A'Lelia's greatest marketing successes was her "Trip Around the World" campaign, an idea she had after returning from a trip to Europe, Africa, and the Holy Land. Beginning as a letter-writing campaign to prominent race men and women, it was a contest through which nominated candidates could receive votes by sending in tokens which could be collected from various Walker hair and beauty preparations. Each package of shampoo, hair grower, face cream, and perfume had a special voting coupon entitling the purchaser to cast a designated number of votes for their preferred candidate.[127] The four highest-polled candidates would win an all-expenses-paid trip around the world, taking them to thirty-five cities in fifteen countries. The educational benefits of travel were emphasized and, demonstrating her mother's tuition, the trip was promoted as being beneficial to the race as a whole. A'Lelia Walker is quoted in the advertisements as desiring "more of our Race to visit foreign countries, to see the world, and to know personally of its people." Moreover, the runner-up prizes included educational scholarships of $250 and $500.[128]

As contestants took out advertisements to attract votes, the Walker Company received considerable free publicity as a result of this campaign. One contestant, Percival A. Burrows, an assistant general secretary to the Universal Negro Improvement Association, put out an advertisement citing a letter of endorsement for his entry into the contest from Marcus Garvey himself. Presenting himself as the candidate of the UNIA, Burrows described how "Almost Every Negro Organization is represented in this contest, and I am sure that it is your desire that we should win."[129] Another candidate, A. W. Lloyd from St. Louis, Missouri, used his advertisement to explain why his voters should buy Madam Walker preparations; he cited the Walkers' many philanthropic acts, including donations to the YWCA and endowment of NAACP and NACW scholarships, as well as the employment of many men and women of the race.[130] George Schuyler advertised the campaign in a complimentary article in the *Messenger*, in which he praised A'Lelia's vision, claiming that "no other firm, white or black, ever thought up a project of more educational and inspirational value." Schuyler argued that the Walker business empire served as a corrective to "that small minority of men who are still wont to claim superiority over the female."[131] The *Messenger* continued to promote A'Lelia's image throughout the 1920s, and it is on the front cover of the October 1926 *Messenger* that the most well known image of A'Lelia appeared. This image is A'Lelia at her most graceful: her hair piled up on her head, wearing sables and elegant jewelry, she gazes directly and proudly at the camera.[132]

This image of elegant ease, however, relied upon a business sense that was often mercenary in its exploitation of every social occasion as a marketing opportunity. A'Lelia even arranged her adopted daughter's wedding in order to focus publicity on the company. A'Lelia had adopted Mae Walker Robinson in Indianapolis in 1912. Mae Walker Robinson had long flowing locks and dark skin and served as an excellent advertisement for the company's hair products.[133] Late in 1923, A'Lelia seems to have decided it was time that Mae was married to a Dr. Gordon Jackson from Chicago, who was thirteen years older than Mae. The couple was given the most spectacular wedding Harlem had ever seen. A'Lelia herself made little effort to disguise the fact that the wedding was a marketing ploy, reporting to Ransom: "Yes I noticed the article in the *Crisis* this month. It is very good. Well the wedding served for one purpose if no other;—it let the people know we are still on the map."[134]

A'Lelia continued to use her mother's contacts to promote the business.

She invited race women and men such as Robert R. Moton, Washington's successor at Tuskegee, to serve as guest speakers at the annual convention of Walker agents.[135] A'Lelia's involvement in charitable causes, while given less emphasis in the company's literature, was scarcely less noteworthy. Besides continuing endowments started by her mother and giving regular sums to important race organizations like the NAACP, A'Lelia became personally involved in charitable work. A member of the Women's Auxiliary to the NAACP, A'Lelia forged partnerships with the auxiliary members who had known her mother, including Addie Hunton and Helen Curtis; with wives of senior NAACP officials, including Mrs. Grace Nail Johnson, Mrs. William Pickens, and Mrs. Du Bois; and with singer Revella Hughes, actress Rose McClendon, and Jessie Fauset.[136] A'Lelia's wealth and the organizational experience of auxiliary members led to the development of joint fund-raising ideas. In 1924, the auxiliary's first year, the Walker Company awarded the Women's Auxiliary the first-prize scholarship of one hundred dollars to go toward the education of "some worthy student." The Women's Auxiliary won the right to give the scholarship to a student of its choice because it had achieved the largest increases in contributions to the NAACP during that year.[137] Meetings of the Women's Auxiliary were usually held at the 137th Street Colored Branch of the YWCA, but on occasion A'Lelia opened up the nearby stylish Walker studio to host these meetings. There could be no role more suitable for the hostess extraordinaire.[138] The auxiliary also raised money for the NAACP through putting on benefit concerts. These concerts were held at popular uptown venues such as the Manhattan Casino, and by attracting famous performers such as Sissle and Blake managed to raise in one sitting as much as one thousand dollars for the NAACP.[139]

A'Lelia's support for the integrationist NAACP did not prevent her from offering support to Marcus Garvey and his black nationalist organization, the UNIA. Like her mother, A'Lelia was learning to straddle the organizational divides created by black male leaders. A'Lelia fulfilled her mother's deathbed pledge of $5,000 to the NAACP Anti-Lynching Crusaders. Marcus Garvey had also relied on the support of A'Lelia's mother, who had been a regular advertiser and contributor to the UNIA, and he was clearly worried that A'Lelia's NAACP donation indicated a permanent shift toward exclusive support for the rival organization. In an editorial for the *Negro World* in June 1919, Garvey criticized A'Lelia, arguing that she should contribute her money to a UNIA fund "for the purpose of purchasing a house in which poor colored persons about to be evicted by autocratic landlords might receive shelter."[140] However, Garvey's attack clearly did not deter A'Lelia's support for the UNIA. Her company's advertisements continued to appear in the *Negro World*, and in 1924 she collaborated for a time with Lawrence Chenault, a black actor who had appeared on Broadway and in Oscar Micheaux's films, as well as at the UNIA Liberty Hall in Harlem. Together A'Lelia and Chenault staged a musical extravaganza, which, at the suggestion of W. C. Handy, included a tribute to the old cakewalk, a dance which A'Lelia herself apparently performed for the audience. Both A'Lelia and Chenault expressed their desire put on regular musical performances at Liberty Hall, though their initial enthusiasm appeared to have waned by the end of the month.[141] As her musical experiments suggest, A'Lelia was searching for a role to which she would be more naturally suited than that of conventional race activist and clubwoman; she would have a more dramatic impact on the generation of artists, writers, and political activists that were flowering in Harlem in the 1920s.

Until recently, women were seen as having limited promotional and financial roles in the Harlem Renaissance. A'Lelia's role as a promoter in this cultural movement has similarly been dismissed. David Levering Lewis disparaged her contribution to the Harlem Renaissance, because she did not offer financial assistance to individual artists: "to the intellectuals and artists of the Harlem Renaissance she opened her houses and almost never her purse."[142] But in opening up her homes, A'Lelia did support Harlem's artists: her weekend parties at Villa Lewaro served to showcase new and unknown artists and she later established the Dark Tower as a kind of salon in October 1927. Although originally conceived as a tea club that would provide a job for her adopted daughter Mae Walker, the Dark Tower provided a space for writers and artists to come together, share ideas, and meet important figures in the publishing world. Situated at the center of Harlem's community life, A'Lelia's 136th Street apartment was a stone's throw from the 135th Street library and the 137th Street YWCA. Selling sandwiches and soft drinks, the club carried a membership fee of one dollar. Although whites were allowed to become members, as A'Lelia explained to Ransom, "I let it be known that it is opened for the new Negro writers and the younger group such as Countee Cullen and a number of others in the same field."[143] The Dark Tower derived its name from Cullen's poem of the same name, which was written on the wall alongside Langston Hughes's "Weary Blues." A crowded opening night was well received, although some writers balked at paying for drinks at a home where they had been so used to receiving free hospitality.[144]

While the Dark Tower was unable to make enough money to support itself in the long term and under pressure from Ransom was officially closed down in December 1928, it had provided, at least for a short while, a formal salon for the writers and artists of Harlem. During this time the Dark Tower quickly became the gathering place for black artists. Harold Jackman, writer and friend of Countee Cullen, frequented the Tower on a regular basis, and his correspondence reveals the continuing importance of the Tower in late 1929, as a meeting place for poor artists who could not afford to attend NAACP benefits.[145] Countee Cullen's second wife, Ida Cullen, remembered A'Lelia's Dark Tower: "she had this beautiful brownstone home, that was a meeting place for all of these people ... writers, musician, and painters."[146] The many artists who frequented the Dark Tower testify to the important function it had served. As A'Lelia herself put it, "Having no talent or gift, but a love and keen appreciation for art, The Dark Tower was my contribution."[147] In sponsoring a salon, albeit one that charged for drinks and entry, A'Lelia was again demonstrating her wealth through her consumption of art. She could afford to invest time and money in a venture that was, almost by definition, short-lived and financially unrewarding.

It is important to measure A'Lelia's legacy in terms of its impact on those women who valued her image of black womanhood. In a society that deemed black skin unattractive, and conspicuous consumption as something that was only fit for and attainable by whites, A'Lelia's defiant glamour showed that a black woman could be as powerful, confident, and trend-setting as any society hostess white Manhattan had to offer. At a time when black women seldom traveled outside the United States except to perform for whites, the Walkers' publicity-raising tours around the world earned them numerous notices in foreign newspapers. A friend would later remember how A'Lelia once made an entrance at Covent Garden on one of her European tours: "Her appearance was so spectacular that the singers were put completely out of countenance."[148] Remembered as she was captured in the 1926 photograph that adorned the front page of the October *Messenger*—dressed in furs and bedecked with jewels—A'Lelia projected an image of effortless fun and opulence that was in the end an illusion. Her three unhappy marriages and lack of self-confidence, which she revealed only in her letters to Ransom, suggest a woman who had realized that image was perhaps more important than reality, but who still dreaded facing that reality. Forever comparing herself to her determined and ambitious mother, A'Lelia would always fall short in her own estimation, not to mention that of most others.[149]

The careers of the Walkers serve to highlight the many ways in which black women were able to circumvent the factional nature of black politics, and link the everyday ordinary politics and the "imagined world of what is possible" with participation in formal politics. They did this not only through finding a place for themselves in black women's organizations and male-dominated race organizations but also by creating new organizations, images, and dreams. Madam Walker's understanding of the international nature of racial oppression as well as her ability to straddle organizational divisions and work with politically diverse male race leaders shows how some women were able to surmount the obstacles that made it difficult for black women to shape black political debates. The 1910s and 1920s witnessed the development of an increasingly coherent black feminist agenda: black women, both individually, and through race and women's organizations, were coming together to challenge old images of black womanhood and assert their own. The right to define yourself, as well as the close link between intellectual thought and practice—themes which were evident in Walker's actions and own intellectual development—would become key strands of black feminist thought in the late 1970s and early 1980s.

Madam Walker was commemorated as the twenty-first African American to be included as part of the U.S. Postal Service's Black Heritage Series commemorative stamps, yet this wrongly presents her as an aberration. It is wrong to record simply that she overcame the obstacles of gender and race and fulfilled the American dream. Her success did not lie in the fact that she owned a home next to the Rockefellers and was widely regarded as "the first black female millionaire." Her contribution was far more sophisticated and significant than that, for, over a lifetime and in cooperation with other black women, Walker sought to change the way in which black womanhood was marketed and received, not only by black men and white society but by black women themselves. Walker's legacy is not a fulfillment of the American dream, but rather a demonstration of how black Americans could work together to overcome their differences, could protest the wrongs inflicted on them by white Americans, while coming together in economic, political, and cultural ways to improve their own lives. While Madam Walker's legacy has been revived recently, A'Lelia's reputation for glamor continues to be the subject of storytelling. Yet A'Lelia's career as a businesswoman, marketing strategist, and cultural sponsor revealed that she was also capable of adopting multiple strategies in her struggle to find a space where her voice could be heard. Reliant on neither white patrons nor black men, A'Lelia was a savvy businesswoman who challenged white and black stereotypes of black women. Walker and her daughter improved the lives of many black women through their ability to breach a predominantly male, and a predominantly white, business world. As the *Colored American Review* put it in 1916:

These two women, mother and daughter, have done, in the age of their day and generation, work that will be a light of everlasting good to beckon their sisters onward and upward. Their success as business women has moved back the clouds of prejudice, and lessened the narrow conception as well as the insignificant regard men hold for women in the business and professional world of to-day. . . . It is well for the woman of to-day who is contemplating business, to take note of . . . the qualities that led these two noble women of industry to renowned success.[150]

4

Amy Jacques Garvey, Jessie Fauset, and Pan-African Feminist Thought

Amy Jacques Garvey and Jessie Fauset were writers and activists at the heart of the New Negro movement in Harlem in the 1920s. As representatives of Garveyism and the Harlem Renaissance, these women are usually seen as belonging to separate camps with conflicting ideologies: one a black nationalist movement, the other a cultural civil rights movement. Both women were emotionally involved with, and have had much of the credit due them passed onto, the men for whom they worked. Neglect of them is attributable, at least in part, to the legendary press battle between Marcus Garvey and W. E. B. Du Bois, which has come to define the way in which we interpret this period as one of deep division. Garvey, the founder of the UNIA, the first black mass movement in American history, was viewed by the Harlem intelligentsia as a dangerous rival whose influence had to be curtailed. Du Bois, as editor of *The Crisis*, the journal of the NAACP, was often viewed as the representative of an organization whose goals were diametrically opposed to that of the black nationalist Garvey. Du Bois was an early contributor to the "Garvey Must Go Campaign," which culminated in a letter to the Department of Justice denouncing Garvey's business leadership.[1] While Tony Martin sought to integrate the histories of the Harlem Renaissance and the Garvey movement, many accounts focused on either the Harlem Renaissance or Garveyism.[2] However, an analysis of Jessie Fauset and Amy Jacques Garvey as spokeswomen for these supposedly separate movements reveals the ways in which New Negro women overcame the ideological and organizational boundaries that have sometimes been used to separate the Harlem Renaissance and Garveyism. This chapter will show how through intellectual and practical endeavor these two women contributed to the increasingly internationalist black feminist tradition that was being developed by black women involved in club life, the pan-African movement, and interracial movements for racial uplift. In order to understand how both women operated, this chapter will look first at the position of women within the UNIA, and then at how Amy Jacques Garvey carved a place for herself within the movement. I will argue that she used her leadership role within the UNIA, and particularly the *Negro World*, to shape a feminist black nationalism. I then explore the often similar ideas advanced by Jessie Fauset, both in her work for and writings in *The Crisis*, and in her novels, *There Is Confusion* (1924) and *The Chinaberry Tree* (1931). This detailed analysis will reveal that for these two women, there was no insuperable division between integration and black nationalism.

Gender Roles in the Universal Negro Improvement Association

Founded in Kingston, Jamaica, in 1914 by Marcus Garvey, the UNIA was a pan-African organization that sought the liberation and unity of all peoples of African descent. By 1923, it claimed to have attracted over six million members in nine hundred branches across North, South, and Central America, the Caribbean, Africa, Europe, and Australia. While visiting New York City on a fund-raising tour in 1916, Garvey decided to transfer his headquarters to Harlem, the "Negro Mecca" of the United States. As with many nationalist movements, Garvey used the printed word as well as the spectacle of flags, rituals, and uniforms to construct a common history that would inspire and unite all peoples of African descent. The UNIA's newspaper, the *Negro World*, played a key role in creating that unity. Launched in 1918 with the help of his first wife, Amy Ashwood, the *Negro World* became one of the most widely read black newspapers of its day. Estimates for the circulation of the Garvey newspaper vary: Garvey claimed it had a weekly circulation of 200,000, while Department of Justice estimates suggest a number closer to 60,000. Accepting that both figures might be exaggerations, the *Negro World's* weekly readership still surpassed the readership of the monthly *Crisis* and *Messenger*. With the introduction of Spanish and French pages into the *Negro World* and the multiple readership of single copies, the newspaper reached an audience of tens of thousands across the Caribbean, Central America, and parts of Africa. So widespread was Garvey's pan-African readership that Britain, France, Italy, Portugal, and Belgium were frightened into banning the newspaper in their African colonies, while in the French colony of Dahomey, possession of the *Negro World* carried the death sentence.[3]

The UNIA could boast considerable success in its first decade: by the time Garvey was arrested on dubious charges of mail fraud in 1923, he had created the first black mass movement in the United States, inspired millions of followers from all around the world, and brought employment and race pride to thousands of people of African descent. At a time when most African Americans had to work either for or with whites, and many race leaders were fighting for the right to work and live with white Americans, the UNIA was busy building up a black economic empire, including a weekly newspaper, a publishing house, the Black Star Line Shipping Company, and black-owned grocery stores.[4] For all his achievements Garvey was not without his critics. Members of the UNIA often appeared to their detractors to be copying the costumes of empire when they donned their gold sashes, plumed hats, and white gloves for parades and conventions. Du Bois mocked the "fancy costumes" as well as the "new songs and ceremonies" Garveyites displayed at their annual conventions, while Claude McKay viewed UNIA conventions as "stupendous vaudeville." The *New York Age*, a more consistent critic of Garvey, claimed to speak for the people when it suggested that the "great majority of colored persons of New York look upon Garvey [as] putting on a big show to amuse them."[5] A *Negro World* reporter, however, described with pride the magnificent costume Garvey favored in 1921:

> The Provisional President of Africa wore a military hat, very pointed, tipped with white feathers, broadcloth trousers with gold stripe down the side, a Sam Browne belt crossing the shoulder and around the waist, gold epaulets, gold and red trimmings on the sleeves, gold sword and white gloves.[6]

Garvey's showmanship was a central feature not only of contemporary criticism; it was also at the forefront of early historical appraisals.[7] However, rather than simply criticizing Garvey, later studies tried to understand his appeal. For example, Garveyism's appeal has been reassessed through the lens of the Harlem Renaissance. The work of Tony Martin and Ted Vincent, and more recently, David Krasner suggests that the UNIA played a central role in the Harlem Renaissance.[8] Theirs has been a useful contribution, because by repositioning the Garvey movement at the center of the Harlem Renaissance we redefine not only Garveyism, but also the Harlem Renaissance itself. Rather than being an elitist movement that was focused on a few poets in Harlem, the Harlem Renaissance appears instead to have engaged a far wider cross section of participants and audience than has often been imagined, not least of all black women.

Another burgeoning field has been the study of gender roles within the movement. The earliest "gender" scholarship focused on women in the Garvey movement, and stressed their importance as participants, demonstrating that they were "there."[9] Indeed, almost half the members of the original executive in Kingston were women, a figure which compares favorably with the Niagara movement and the later formation of the NAACP.[10] Women were written in to the UNIA's constitution: the Declaration of the Rights of the Negro Peoples of the World, drawn up at the first UNIA convention held in New

York City in 1920, asserted that all Negro men, women, and children were free citizens of Africa, the "Motherland of all Negroes."[11] Women held both national and local offices and produced much of the organization's propagandist literature and art. Each local division had a "Lady President." Women also made up large numbers of the rank and file through participation in female-run women's auxiliaries such as the Black Cross Nurses, who served as health-care providers and launched community social welfare projects, as well as in the first black women's military unit, the Universal African Motor Corps.[12] It is, then, generally accepted that women played an important role within the UNIA. What is the subject of debate, however, is what agency women had in constructing their roles and what scope they had to alter the gender hierarchies created by male leaders of the UNIA.

A survey of the *Negro World* and UNIA papers reveals that the performance of manliness, or what Garvey called "true manhood," was important for black men in constructing gender roles within the movement. For Garveyites black manhood was free, productive, and racially separate. They dismissed as weak and effeminate those leaders like Du Bois, who through his involvement with integrationist movements such as the NAACP, was dependent on cooperation with whites. One Garveyite supporter explained the difference between the two organizations: "[the NAACP] appeals to the Beau Brummel, Lord Chesterfield, kid-glover, silk-stocking, creased-trousered, patent leather shoe element, while the UNIA appeals to the sober, sane, serious, earnest, hard-working man, who earns his living by the sweat of his brow."[13] Garvey also drew on this image of free labor to distinguish his men from those who worked for whites. It was, for Garvey, "the age of men, not pygmies, not of serfs and peons and dogs, but men and we who make up the membership of the UNIA reflect the new manhood of the Negro."[14] Although Garvey's image of black womanhood also relied on keeping black women away from contact with white men, he looked back to an imagined past where women had not had to work because their men had been able to protect them: "Let's go back to the days of true manhood when women truly reverenced us. . . . let us again place our women upon the pedestal from whence they have been forced into the vortex of the seething world of business. . . . We would have . . . more mothers, many more virtuous wives, many more amiable and lovable daughters if man would play his part as he should."[15] If black men were allowed to be "true" men and earn a decent wage, then they could protect their wives, who would be "free" to stay at home.[16]

Much of the new work on Garveyism has examined how men within the UNIA constructed these gender roles. This exciting new work has interrogated the structures, language, and spectacles of the UNIA and shown how they relied upon a highly masculinized rhetoric, which often sought to preclude the power and influence of high-ranking women members. For example, Michelle Ann Stephens argues that Garvey promoted a fictional black empire through what she calls the "commodity spectacle," the performance of "civilized" black manhood as represented by the plumes and feathers of Garveyism. However, she also argues that Garvey's appeal lay precisely in his embrace of a new masculinized racial empire where diasporic race united all peoples of African descent.[17] In upholding this diasporic vision of nation Garvey rejected European notions of nationalism as the basis for black identity in the West. This has enabled Stephens to move beyond failure narratives and go some way to understanding Garvey's appeal.[18] Martin Summers's study of masculinity has also tried to understand the gender politics of Garveyism by comparing Garveyites with the Prince Hall Masons. Summers suggests that male Garveyites used the paradigms of production and patriarchy to construct black "manliness" against a "Victorian" view of women's gendered roles.[19] Other work has explored the sexual politics of Garveyism, and suggested that women as well as men used the rhetoric of racial destiny to police women's sexuality and to promote a separate realm of "mother work" for women within the movement.[20]

My reading builds on previous studies that seek to understand the appeal of Garveyism and the construction of gender roles by men. This study, however, is interested in why the movement appealed to women, and how women constructed gender roles within the UNIA. If Garveyism embodied an aggressive masculinized racial consciousness, why did so many women join the movement, and why did they stay to try and shape it differently? This chapter suggests that black women's understanding of black nationalism and pan-Africanism derived not only from their experiences within the UNIA, but also from their shared experiences as black women and a belief that pan-Africanism had to play a central role within a feminist agenda. This meant that while they might engage in the discourse of masculinized Garveyism, they put it to different ends. Women leaders within the UNIA sought to define a gender identity, status, and role that reflected their reality as wage workers and race workers, rather than as the idealized woman imagined by black men. However, they often used the language of black masculinity to help them defend their own roles. Just as black men constructed masculinity against an oppositional view of black femininity and white dandyism, so black women of the UNIA, like women in the NBC, used a critique of men's roles as the base from which to construct their own gender roles. Frequently exposed to the Garveyite rhetoric of "true manhood," high-ranking women officials within the UNIA changed and appropriated this gendered language, using it as a stepping-stone for promoting feminist black nationalism. By engaging in the discourse of "true manhood," female Garveyites were able to hold to account those men who failed to live up to expected standards of black masculinity. They imagined male Garveyites as too concerned with effeminate bickering and as lacking the courage necessary for strong leadership. This created a space in which black women must come to the forefront and provide the strong leadership black men had failed to deliver.

Fighting for Leadership Roles: Black Women in the UNIA

Women within the UNIA did not rely exclusively on the language of black masculinity to carve a space for themselves; they also struggled to create their own vision of black womanhood. They organized both as a group, to challenge the structural gendered hierarchies of the organization, and also as individuals to promote their alternative vision through public speeches, performances, and publication in the UNIA's main organ, the *Negro World*. One occasion which offered UNIA women a chance to come together and discuss their role within the movement was the annual summer convention. The UNIA Convention was an occasion to showcase the organization's achievements, meet international delegates, and parade uniformed members down Fifth Avenue. Conventions also provided opportunities to discuss policy and leadership, and to produce resolutions designed to "mobilize the masses."[21] Held in New York City beginning in the summer of 1920, the UNIA Convention provided a forum for women members to meet and network with other Garveyite women from around the world. At the 1922 convention, a group of UNIA women grasped the opportunity to challenge the male leadership publicly. Led by Victoria Turner, a delegate from St. Louis, a group of UNIA women demanded that the convention listen to what women had to say about their gender roles and accept women's right to lead. Introducing a set of resolutions signed by the majority of women delegates to the convention and drawn up by Turner, the women demanded greater recognition and authority as delegates, officers, field representatives, and policy makers.[22] The resolutions specifically demanded that women's units like the Black Cross Nurses and the Motor Corps be headed by women and that women be placed on every committee and given important office and fieldwork assignments. Their demands also included a specific reference to women being put in "initiative positions" so that they would have a real impact on policy making. Finally, the women demanded that Henrietta Vinton Davis be given a special policy-making and coordinating role so that black women all over the world "can function without restriction from the men." A debate on the resolutions followed in which the majority agreed that women were "curbed to a great extent in the exercise of their initiative powers in formulating plans which would make for the good of the organization."[23] At this point, Garvey, who had remained conspicuously absent throughout the debate, entered the convention and dismissed the women's complaints. Garvey argued that women were already recognized in the UNIA Constitution and that if there were any inconsistencies in the treatment of women the fault lay with the local chapters rather than the national organization.[24] He put forward his own compromise that "the women be encouraged to formulate plans" as it would do "no harm." Garvey's compromise resolution was adopted.[25]

This bruising encounter forced UNIA women to recognize the power of Garveyite rhetoric. Their public demand for equal roles was easily dismantled by a masculinized language which encouraged their efforts as long as they caused the leadership "no harm." Certainly Turner understood how important control of language was if women were to achieve their goals. She had told the convention that "We need women in the important place of the organization to help refine and mold public sentiment, realizing the colossal program of this great organization, and as we are determined to reclaim our own land, Africa."[26] If women were in a position to influence language and policy making within the movement, then they would be able to shape black nationalism and challenge the discourse of "true manhood" which pervaded much Garveyite thought and practice and which had allowed Garvey to question the validity of their complaint. Although male leadership and Garvey's own enactment of masculinity would remain important, in the mid-1920s women played increasingly important roles within the UNIA from which they challenged gender constructions and provoked conflict with the male leadership.

Even before the 1922 convention showdown, there had been women members of the UNIA who had refused to accept subordinate roles in the organization. Amy Ashwood and her mother were active participants in the UNIA's foundation in Kingston, Jamaica.[27] According to her biographer, Lionel Yard, Amy Ashwood shared at least equal responsibility with Garvey for the founding of the UNIA. Coming to the United States in 1918, Ashwood found Garvey and the UNIA in a precarious financial position, but worked hard to ensure that the fledgling organization survived. She succeeded in negotiating the purchase of the first Liberty Hall in Harlem, and ensured the continuance of the *Negro World* by continually managing to persuade its printer to extend credit.[28] According to Ula Taylor, Ashwood's position became increasingly vulnerable following her marriage to Garvey on Christmas Day, 1919. Ashwood apparently refused to conform to her husband's expectations of an ideal wife through her public smoking, drinking, and forthright expression of her opinions. Garvey divorced her in June 1922.[29] Even after Ashwood's fall from grace, there were other individuals who offered alternative role models for women in the UNIA. Henrietta Vinton Davis and Madame De Mena both served the UNIA as international officers. Davis had been appointed director of the UNIA Black Star Shipping Company in June 1919, and was also one of the signers of the Declaration of Rights for Negroes in 1920. In the following decade Davis would serve as an assistant president general. A commanding orator, she was popular with grassroots workers, and could rely on an enthusiastic audience to greet her on her speaking tours. After her return from a trip to Cuba, the UNIA convention voted to pay her an annual salary of $6,000, and Garvey bestowed on her the order of Lady Commander of the Sublime Order of the Nile.[30] As a high-ranking UNIA official, Davis played an important role in constructing an alternative vision of women's role within the movement. Hinting at her own skepticism when it came to black men's leadership, she declared in an article for the *Negro World*: "if our men hesitate to follow our leader, Marcus Garvey, who dares to do all, then the women of the race must come forward, they must join the great army of Amazons and follow a Joan of Arc who is willing to be burned at the stake to save her country. Africa must be saved!"[31] Here Davis juxtaposes two very different images of female leadership. On the one hand she uses an image of female sacrifice, a Joan of Arc, who will be forced to lead the struggle if the men (figured as potential Dauphin) do not act. On the other hand she conjures up the legendary nation of female warriors, thereby asserting women's strength to lead. In contrasting these images, Davis adapts the language used by male Garveyites to attack the Beau Brummels that made up the NAACP. If male Garveyites prove not to be sober and hardworking men (Garvey, locked away in an Atlanta prison had already proved his willingness to risk all), then black women will have no choice but to take up the challenge and assert their masculine, warrior-type qualities.

Maymie L. T. De Mena, another influential female voice within the UNIA, seemed prepared to answer Davis's call for an army of Amazons to lead the race. Born in Nicaragua, De Mena became widely known within the UNIA not least for leading a UNIA parade in Kingston, Jamaica, on horseback, brandishing a sword. An international organizer for the UNIA, in 1929 she took over from Davis as fourth assistant president. Like Davis, De Mena also criticized the black male leadership, but she disentangled their fantasies of ideal womanhood from women's actual work within the UNIA.

> Very little if anything is said of the women who form such a large percentage of the membership of this great movement. For seven years we have been lauding our men through the press, on the platform, and,

in fact, from every angle, while in reality the backbone and sinew of the UNIA has been and is the real women of the organization, who are laboring incessantly for the freedom of Negroes the world over. Until recently women of the organization have been given to understand that they must remain in their places—which place constituted nothing more than a Black Cross Nurse or a general secretary of the division.[32]

Acknowledging that women members had challenged men's constructions of their roles in recent years, De Mena went on to issue a rallying call for women to work together to reshape the UNIA, in spite of the opposition they faced from black men: "We are sounding the call to all the women in the UNIA to line up for women's rights in this great organization of our choice, for we know our cause is just, and right must win."[33]

Black women were aware that black men's attempts to position them within the domestic sphere presented a powerful obstacle to securing leadership positions. But as De Mena pointed out, black men's imagining of ideal black womanhood distorted the social reality of black women's position within the UNIA. As in many other civil rights movements, women in the UNIA played important organizing roles which required them to practice different kinds of leadership.[34] Examining Garveyism through the eyes of black women, whose influence on gender relations became increasingly important in the 1920s, allows us to make connections with other important black feminists who were articulating similar visions of black womanhood in the 1920s. As we have seen in Chapter 1, Nannie Helen Burroughs similarly pictured black men as lacking in manhood when defending the space she had created for black women's leadership.[35] It is hardly surprising that black women shared much of the language and engaged in the same discourse about black masculinity. What is more interesting is how they used that language to imagine black women as leaders. The speeches and writings of Amy Jacques Garvey, the most vocal spokesperson for black women's interests within the movement, offered one such vision of leadership.

Amy Jacques Garvey: Black Nationalist and Feminist

In April 1917 Amy Jacques Garvey left Jamaica for New York City, where she would remain for the next ten years. Within two years of arriving in New York, she secured a central role in the UNIA, possibly due to her earlier acquaintance in Kingston with Amy Ashwood.[36] From 1919 onwards Jacques Garvey would serve the UNIA as secretary, legal advisor, journalist, and associate editor of the organization's weekly newspaper the *Negro World*, to which she contributed the women's page. She continued to perform these roles after her marriage to Garvey in July 1922, but was careful about how and when she chose to promote her own, feminist agenda. For example, the record of the August 1922 convention at which the women delegates demanded a greater role for women offers no evidence that Jacques Garvey was involved. In the early years of her marriage she styled herself as merely representing her husband's views, as she told one newspaper: "I only live to perpetuate the ideas of my husband just as thousands of other Negroes."[37] When Garvey was arrested for mail fraud in 1923 by the U.S. government and finally imprisoned in 1925, she took charge of his legal defense campaign and the management of the UNIA Headquarters in Harlem. Often regarded as the unofficial leader of the movement, Jacques Garvey took care to point out that she held no official elected position, but rather styled herself as Garvey's wife and representative. Like many other male leaders, including Booker T. Washington, Garvey expected his wife's unquestioning support and did not like the idea of a woman, let alone his wife, assuming control of the movement. While in prison Garvey wrote to UNIA members through the *Negro World*, asking them to look after his wife, whom he referred to as his "helpmate."[38] Later historians of the Garvey movement have perpetuated this image of Jacques Garvey as the "helpmate" of Garvey rather than studying her own intellectual contribution to black nationalism. For example, Tony Martin depicted Jacques Garvey as "the perfect spouse" who "tried her hand" at prose. This is something of an understatement for a woman who edited and wrote many of Garvey's speeches, which she also compiled in two published volumes, who penned countless editorials for the women's page in the *Negro World*, as well as her memoir, *Garvey and Garveyism* (1963), and who later contributed articles to *The African: Journal of African Affairs* and the Nigerian-based *West African Pilot*.[39] But there is a paradox: according to Judith Stein, Jacques Garvey made more of a success of her marriage to Garvey than Amy Ashwood had because she "chose to invest her strength and talents in her husband's career. She defined her role as Garvey's comforter and surrogate, whereas Amy Ashwood had viewed herself more as an equal."[40] Ashwood paid for this apparent equality. After just a few months of marriage, Garvey separated from her, thereby depriving her of the platform from which she might articulate her pan-African feminism. Recognizing this, Ashwood refused to accept the legality of Garvey's divorce, and continued to call herself Mrs. Garvey. Meanwhile, Jacques Garvey, who had been intimate with both Amy Ashwood and Garvey in the months of their short marriage—she had even accompanied them on their honeymoon—learned firsthand how not to handle the egotistical man. As his secretary, Jacques Garvey was a skillful helpmate, and she adapted this role when she became the wife of Marcus Garvey. Unlike her predecessor, Jacques Garvey was able to keep open her access to the stage of black politics, while at the same time maintaining some control over her own "private" performance.

Negotiating the Public and the Private as an "Able Wife"

Jacques Garvey's strategic negotiation between her "private" and "public" roles has long gone unrecognized. In 1971 an article in *Ebony* magazine still described Jacques Garvey as doing "Marcus' work."[41] Honor Ford Smith sees Jacques Garvey as typifying the "ideal image" of the UNIA woman because "she did not question her role as wife . . . combining these duties with her responsibilities as a tireless supporter of Garvey."[42] One of the reasons Jacques Garvey has been viewed through this lens of supportive helpmate, the ideal UNIA wife, rather than in terms of her own intellectual contribution is because Jacques Garvey was at times complicit in the construction of this image. Another explanation can be found in feminists' concern with the relationship between the private and the public. The importance in feminist studies of the dictum that the personal is political cannot disguise the fact that the idea—in intellectual terms or in praxis—has not always assisted feminist causes. This desire to link private behavior with a public figure's overall assessment has inadvertently victimized women more often than men, owing to a perceived need to explain, and sometimes exploit, the apparent contradiction between a woman's "unfeminist" private life and articulation of a feminist agenda in public.[43] I suggest that as part of the move away from an essentialist feminist viewpoint, we should make greater efforts to contextualize black women's personal lives and work, and to recognize the strategic negotiations that many black women had to make between their domestic and public lives in the early twentieth century. By examining Jacques Garvey's contributions to black feminist thought as expressed through her women's page in the *Negro World* alongside both her private and public utterances on her relationship with Garvey, it becomes clear that Jacques Garvey was fully aware that her ability to present black feminism on a public stage was inextricably linked to her capacity to perform the helpmate for her husband both in public and in private, as and when required.

Certainly Jacques Garvey's later recollections support the view that she understood her marriage to Garvey as a role to be performed. Recalling her marriage to Garvey many years later, Jacques Garvey suggested she had chosen to invest her strength in Garveyism the movement, rather than in Garvey the man; in the pan-African movement; and in her own career. In the interview Jacques Garvey gave *Ebony* in 1971, she denied that Garvey had dominated or overshadowed her, claimed legitimacy as Garvey's successor, and made clear that theirs was a political marriage:

> Hell no man, never! Marcus Garvey never married me for love. No sir, that was not the proposal. He needed me that was all. He needed someone he could trust, it wasn't a personal matter. He knew that the life of the organization [UNIA] was at stake. He said to me, "the lives and opportunity of all those people will be in your hands if I am imprisoned or assassinated. I want to know that there will be someone who will carry the message when I'm gone—someone who cannot be bought—at any price."[44]

Similarly, Jacques Garvey's 1963 memoir *Garvey and Garveyism* is a calculated account in which she grants herself much of the credit for sustaining Garveyism through Garvey's years in prison and for perpetuating the legacy of both Garvey and the movement for much of the twentieth century. Here we are given to understand that marriage to an overbearing, egocentric man who offered little emotional support required Jacques Garvey to spend much of her private life dissembling. She devotes considerable space in her memoir to explaining her reasons for staying with Garvey through such difficult circumstances and hints at her complicity in the construction of the image of herself as Garvey's helpmate.[45] It has to be accepted that Jacques Garvey's recollections of her difficult personal relationship with Marcus Garvey may well have been affected by the context in which they were published. In the 1960s and '70s, black feminists in the United States were challenging men's leadership roles within the civil rights and black power movements as well as those who sought to disconnect personal behavior from political acts. While Jacques Garvey may have chosen to emphasize her own agency in choosing the role of helpmate in the 1960s, there is plenty of evidence to suggest that her experiences with Garvey and other UNIA men in the 1920s made her cautious about how she expressed herself earlier in her career. Jacques Garvey's understanding of gender politics both in Jamaica and in the United States enabled her to present her role as one of assistant to her husband.

Jacques Garvey's need and willingness to perform the helpmate changed over time and depended on the fortunes of the UNIA and her husband. In March 1923, eight months after the couple married and just two months before she would take the stand as a defense witness in Garvey's fraud trial, the "new wife of Marcus Garvey" was interviewed by a reporter for the *Negro World*. The interviewer, J.A.G. (whose initials are, intriguingly, a rearrangement of Jacques Garvey's own), introduced himself by explaining why he liked interviewing "the ladies." He went on to ask the "new wife" what she was thinking about. Jacques Garvey, we are told, replied "roguishly": "'About my husband.' Of 'his' work she states, it is his, 'whole existence. Take away his work and you take away his life. Knowing this, I endeavor to be conversant with subjects that would help in his career, and try to make home a haven of rest and comfort for him.'"[46] Clearly Jacques Garvey was somewhat more than "conversant" on topics that might interest her husband. She was at this point heavily involved with the running of the *Negro World* and delivered speeches regularly on behalf of the UNIA. The month before, she had published a collection of Garvey's philosophy and opinions over which she had full editorial control and copyright.[47] It is conceivable that here, as in her relations with her husband, Jacques Garvey was dissembling; expressing "roguishly" her submission to her husband, performing the domestic homemaker; underplaying her role in the UNIA, but overplaying the role of wife. Certainly the meek woman interviewed here sounds nothing like the radical who began to articulate a feminist black nationalism just a year later on the pages of the *Negro World*. By the time Jacques Garvey launched her women's page in the *Negro World*, however, she had already had more than one run-in with the male leadership of the UNIA. It was clear that they regarded her as a threat. Jacques Garvey had to find a means of defending her position if she wanted to avoid having her influence curtailed.

When Garvey had first been incarcerated following his 1923 trial, Jacques Garvey had immediately been spotlighted in the press as an "able wife," who might be fit to take his place. According to the *Pittsburgh American*, "the conviction appears to be growing, that Mrs. Garvey is an able, strong-minded woman equipped in every way to do good work for the nationalist movement, by sweeping the dust of misunderstanding from the minds of some, by strengthening the bonds of unity between the members of the UNIA, by making new friends for the cause and converting some of its enemies."[48] So great was this "growing conviction," that the *Crusader*, a rival publication, had accused Garvey of "turning the UNIA over to his wife." The editors of the *Negro World* claimed to be defending Jacques Garvey when they reported the attack on her in the July 14, 1923, issue of the paper. Having denied her influence within the organization, they piously concluded that "It is beneath the dignity of common decency to attempt to drag the name of an innocent and helpless woman into an arena where she cannot properly defend herself."[49] Rejecting this image of women as helpless and unused to participating in the public sphere, Jacques Garvey was vigorous in defending herself against the male editors of the *Negro World* who tried to belittle her involvement in the UNIA in gendered terms, and who tried to disconnect feminist struggle from the nationalist cause. As an assistant editor of the *Negro World* Jacques Garvey was more than capable of defending herself. In a letter sent to the editor, which was published the following week, Jacques Garvey asserted her right to define and defend for herself those arenas she had chosen to enter.

> You have characterized me as "innocent and helpless." I am innocent of the honor of having the UNIA "turned over" to me by my husband, but I am not innocent of the depths to which colored men can stoop to further their petty personal schemes.... My four and a half years of active service in the UNIA under the personal direction of Marcus Garvey has given me a fair knowledge of men and the methods they employ in the organization and out of it.... With my unusual general knowledge and experiences for a young woman, may I not ask if the word "helpless" is not misapplied?[50]

While keen to refute charges that her husband had unconstitutionally handed her control of the UNIA, Jacques Garvey at the same time puts forward her qualifications for leadership in terms of her personal relationship with Garvey. Her four years of training and experience at the top of the organization put her in a better position than most to understand the workings of the UNIA and learn how to deal with disputes. The men within the organization should know that she understood their "methods," their attempt to prescribe gender roles that limited women's opportunities for leadership. But had they forgotten who they were dealing with? Jacques Garvey went on, in a sarcastic vein, to thank the editors of the *Negro World* for their chivalrous defense and display of "manhood": "If the editorial was written in my defense, I have to thank you for same, and hope that if ever I am in need of a protector (not to draw his sword in my defense, but to flash his quill) you, sir, will as on this occasion, unsolicited, spill as much ink as will prove my 'innocence' and protect me as a 'helpless' woman."[51] Here Jacques Garvey uses sexual innuendo to demonstrate her awareness of the hypocrisy of "true manhood"; an ideology that demanded men protect their apparently helpless women, was the same ideology that insisted on women's purity, while allowing men greater sexual freedom.

As she was only too well aware, Jacques Garvey's early role within the Garvey movement lay precisely in her personal relationship with Garvey, first as his secretary and then, more informally, as his wife. It was this relationship which allowed her to act in a public space and to construct her own private-public boundaries, and it was this relationship she took pains not to jeopardize as her predecessor had done. As her memoir and later interviews suggest, Jacques Garvey's loyalty was to the "ism" rather than the man.[52] But the two were so closely linked that it was impossible to harm one without damaging the other. Aware that her private world was inextricably linked to her public one, Jacques Garvey took care to ensure that her marriage was not detrimental to the feminist cause she advocated, refusing to discuss publicly the emotional abuse she endured from Marcus until the publication of her memoir in 1963.[53] In the 1960s, Jacques Garvey would position their relationship as a practical, political one, but in the early 1920s she was prepared to perform, albeit "roguishly," the ideal supportive wife who created a haven for her weary husband. While her husband was incarcerated Jacques Garvey frequently blurred the boundaries between her helpmate and leadership roles. In doing so, she was able to maintain her influence within the movement and promote her vision of black womanhood to the readers of the *Negro World*.

The question of who constructs the boundaries between the "private" and the "public," and how, is part of wider feminist debate. How far did Jacques Garvey's "private" affect her ability to promote a feminist agenda to her female readers and supporters in the UNIA? What is the significance of the fact that in 1923 we see the newlywed Jacques Garvey talking "roguishly" in an interview about keeping her home clean and peaceful for her husband yet in 1925 insisting (perhaps with reference to her own financial predicament following her husband's imprisonment earlier that year) that "the modern woman . . . prefers to be a bread-winner than a half-starved wife?"[54] In the first case we see Jacques Garvey the young wife, choosing to make public her "private" obedience to the husband, but with a wink and a nod in which her modest efforts to be "conversant" with her husband's interests (in line with the advice of most women's magazines) are so exaggerated as to draw attention to her high-profile role. By contrast, in 1925, when her husband is in prison, we see Jacques Garvey defending women's right to economic independence, particularly when the alternative is dependence on black men who lack the means to financially support women. In both cases Jacques Garvey is discussing the boundaries of the private and the public and demonstrating women's agency in defining these boundaries.

In her biography of Amy Jacques Garvey, Taylor highlights what she sees as the contradiction between Jacques Garvey's advocacy of women's equality in print and her own "male-dominated marriage." Viewing it as one of the most significant aspects of her editorial writing for the *Negro World*, Taylor suggests that rather than making judgments about what this says about her views of patriarchy we should recognize her skillful maneuvering between the family and the public world.[55] Taylor offers a useful framework for understanding Jacques Garvey's strategic performance of private and public, using the term "community feminism" to describe Jacques Garvey's negotiation of her "helpmate" and leadership roles. Community feminism rejects essentialist understandings of feminism and acknowledges the "multiple identities of black women" and the importance of their uplift work to black communities. For Taylor, it was Jacques Garvey's community feminism that "empowered her to establish personal parameters regarding her public and private roles, and only her husband had the right to question her decisions." According to Taylor, Jacques Garvey accepted male Garveyites' belief that women should be self-sacrificing wives, but also believed that women could simultaneously play a leadership role within the movement.[56] But perhaps Taylor's community feminism relies too much on women accepting, rather than performing, the role of self-sacrificing wife. As with Margaret Murray Washington and other black women leaders before her, Jacques Garvey's careful adoption of the language of black masculinity suggests she did not necessarily accept the gender role she was prepared to perform in order to gain access to that public space from which she might articulate her feminist agenda. She certainly had reason to dissemble, having witnessed the removal from power and access to public spaces of her rival, Amy Ashwood, precisely because of her failure to live up to Marcus Garvey's expectations of the "modest" wife. Jacques Garvey later recalled her husband saying that he "must have her [Ashwood's] sympathy and understanding of every action of mine."[57] As Taylor points out, Ashwood, unlike Jacques Garvey, had frequently spoken at UNIA conventions. Although Jacques Garvey also became a powerful orator, she relied, as had many black women before her, on the printed word to put across her feminist agenda and was prepared to make strategic compromises in her family life to enable this to happen.

In her memoir, Jacques Garvey recalled with some relish one occasion in which she had successfully handled the balancing act between helpmate and leader. Called upon to address the audience at a mass meeting of the UNIA in New York City, she remembered how "The audience clapped and called out, We want Mrs. Garvey. . . . their cheering had died down, I had caught the infectious spirit and responded with a speech, that came to its climax in a call to rededicate their lives for service to all." Significantly, Jacques Garvey also recorded the reaction of her husband, who, she informs us, responded "smilingly": "Now I have a rival, but I am glad she is my wife."[58] The work of black clubwomen and other race leaders suggest that Jacques Garvey was by no means alone in her understanding that her ability to articulate her feminism in a public space depended on her finding ways to keep her husband "smiling."

Feminist social theorists have also recognized the difficulties of accepting a private-public divide. The private-versus-public debate in feminist studies has moved beyond explaining "contradictions" between a woman's "private" and "public" behavior and toward trying to understand the ways in which the boundaries between private and public have been constantly repositioned by men and women, and changed over time. Feminist theorists such as Nira Yuval-Davis and Sylvia Walby have informed my reading of Jacques Garvey in their recognition that "power relations operate within primary social relations as well as within the more impersonal secondary social relations of the civil and political domains." Understanding that different power dynamics are operative in the "private" and public sphere, the private becomes not simply a woman's or "domestic" domain but rather another arena in which power hierarchies are constructed.[59] Defining certain acts and relationship as "private," or "domestic," might simply put them beyond the purview of state interference or protection (although it is usually the state that has defined the boundaries of where it should not intervene), rather than granting women any more autonomy. At the same time women have used the same notion of women's private sphere to protect themselves in a hostile male public sphere. For example, to defend herself from public criticism, Jacques Garvey put certain criticisms of her "private life" off-limits. Choosing when to separate her private from her public, and when to integrate them, she was able to use her personal relationship with Garvey to protect her public career.

As a public advocate of equality between men and women in marriage, Jacques Garvey did not draw attention to her own private marital difficulties. Yet when her public leadership was questioned she was prepared to draw on her private role as Garvey's wife to defend her public persona. Rather than being circumscribed by male-defined boundaries of what was appropriate behavior for women in public and private, Jacques Garvey turned these prescriptions on their head by choosing her own boundaries and using them to protect herself from those who would silence her public voice. While a strategic and sometimes defensive act, it also allowed her some agency. Her earlier confrontations with black male leaders within the UNIA suggest Jacques Garvey was right to try and find a way to negotiate with men who tried to prescribe a separate women's sphere. What is perhaps more interesting than the unsurprising fact that Jacques Garvey had a "conventional" 1920s male-dominated marriage which failed to live up to her publicly expressed feminist writings is that she understood the construction of boundaries between the private and the public as a political act. This is not to accept Jacques Garvey's later implication that she calculatingly accepted an emotionally unsatisfactory marriage as a reasonable sacrifice for the cause, but rather that she believed women must learn how to use and redefine the parameters of the public-private spheres that men had created to control women. Throughout her editorials Jacques Garvey would encourage black women to do just this.

"Our Women and What They Think": An Alternative Vision of Black Womanhood

Beginning in February 1924, Jacques Garvey's women's page provided a public space in which black women could participate in political debate. Her title, "Our Women and What They Think," reflected this intent. The women's page ran from 1924 to 1927, the most productive years of the Harlem Renaissance, and, perhaps not coincidentally, the period when Garvey was tried, imprisoned, and later exiled. During Garvey's imprisonment Jacques Garvey continued to perform the services of a "helpmate": she campaigned tirelessly for his release, raised funds for legal appeals, and made regular trips south to visit her not always appreciative husband. But she also took the opportunity to define her own role, and to shape a feminist black nationalism.[60] While there is no evidence to suggest that Garvey censored Jacques Garvey's editorials from his prison cell, he clearly believed he had a right to do so. In a letter to Jacques Garvey marked by its grudging praise, her husband explained his previous failure to comment on her editorials: "Your editorials are all good Miss Vanity, that's why I have said nothing, otherwise you would have heard from me on the subject. I am glad you [are] reading heavier literature, you should go over some of the sciences."[61] Throughout his time in prison, Garvey repeatedly attempted to assert his authority over his wife as well as to demonstrate that he could, as a "true man," continue to protect his wife. Accepting that his role was perhaps restricted by his imprisonment, he spoke directly to the male members of the UNIA: "I commend to your care and attention, my wife who has been my helpmate and inspiration for years."[62] Yet this was a man who relied on his wife for everything, from bringing him new underwear to organizing the campaign for his release. Garvey's tone reflected more his ideal of the virtuous woman on the pedestal than the reality of his busy wife who was keeping not only his affairs but the affairs of the organization in order. In this context, Garvey's appeal to his readers to "look after" his "helpmate" is evidence not so much of his continued power to promote the ideology of the "true man" but his increasing need to persuade others that this was not pure fiction. It also hints at a shift in Jacques Garvey's position from "helpmate" to rival.

Certainly in her editorials, Jacques Garvey made clear she did not require looking after. In an early editorial Jacques Garvey explained the goal of her page:

> Usually a Woman's Page in any journal is devoted solely to dress, home hints, and love topics, but our Page is unique, in that it seeks to give out thoughts of our women on all subjects affecting them in particular and others in general. This pleases the modern Negro woman, who believes that God Almighty has not limited her intellect because of her sex, and that the helpful and instructive thoughts expressed by her in her home, with the aid of this page, could be read in thousands of other homes and influence the lives of untold numbers.[63]

Here Jacques Garvey establishes her page as a black feminist platform upon which the "modern" black woman can voice her thoughts uninhibited, and around which a network of "untold numbers" of like-minded women could be formed. Articulating her vision of how a feminist philosophy could in practice affect the lives of thousands of black women, Jacques Garvey again emphasized the close relationship between intellectual endeavor and activism. Jacques Garvey wanted her page to be used as a forum to generate discussion among women of African descent from various backgrounds. She often stressed the importance of building cross-class feminist networks, particularly urging her readers to "Help your less-informed sisters. Mix among them a little more, hear their woes and sufferings."[64] The numerous badly written contributions Jacques Garvey received suggest that her page had a readership of women from a variety of educational and ethnic backgrounds. They also suggest that she was inundated with contributions, but also frustrated with how few were printworthy: "persons who have not a common school education and who have not studied the rules of composition of prose or verse, should not send contributions in prose or verse."[65]

In her women's page Amy Jacques Garvey built on the tradition of black clubwomen who had been developing strategies for negotiating the private-public "divide" and justifying their involvement in public life for many years. Some scholars have viewed Jacques Garvey's writings as continuing the philosophies of social reformers like Jane Addams and Anna Julia Cooper, who believed that women's distinct virtues in the domestic sphere would humanize politics. This tradition believed that the purity of black women made them the natural leaders of the race, and that the race could rise no higher than its women.[66] Others have seen Jacques Garvey's writings as extremely modern and shocking to traditional black clubwomen: "Hers was a different voice . . . and [her] ideas were far too radical for many black middle-class women."[67] Jacques Garvey's philosophy did take from the tradition of women's humanizing influence on politics. At the same time hers was a voice that, though new, was not "too radical" for black "middle-class" women. For example, in line with Cooper (and male Garveyites) she believed that women have special roles as mothers and nurturers, but she argued that women's experiences in motherhood enabled them to bring more to politics. At the same time, she insisted that no one had the right to determine the balance between women's domestic and public roles other than individual women themselves. Understanding the central importance of women being able to balance their domestic life with their public careers, Jacques Garvey brought up time and again in her women's page the debate on the role of women at home and in the workplace. For example, in "Will the entrance of Woman in Politics Affect Home Life?" she is adamant that women have the right to work outside the home if they so choose, and that they would in fact improve both the private and the public sphere: "Despite opposition women are in politics and are influencing and making humane legislations that only the detailed and fine minds of the female sex can conceive. Such legislations uplift the homes, communities and nation; therefore the home has not been neglected but benefited." Jacques Garvey argued that women should not need to choose between the private and public spheres, or between their feminism first and their nationalism second. Instead, she believed that "The only question is how much time a woman should spend in her home and how much should be devoted to politics. We unhesitatingly say that this is a matter for the individual, and women are rational and reasonable enough to give as much time to the home as the exigencies of the hour demand."[68] Here Jacques Garvey articulates what would become for her a key theme: women must struggle to define gender roles for themselves.

In her women's page Jacques Garvey saw no conflict between expressing her interest in the plight of all women across the globe, while at the same time admitting that women of African descent were her first concern. Her sympathies were "as comprehensive as the Negro race," and while they extended to other races, black women came first, for "Negro Women have a more urgent necessity to have an interest in and sympathy for their own than have the women of other race groups."[69] At a time when Marcus Garvey had recently banned joint membership of the UNIA and NAACP, Jacques Garvey refused to limit her appeal strictly to UNIA women, but encouraged all black women to send in contributions to the page. Jacques Garvey's pan-African interests encouraged an internationalist approach to women's rights, and through her editorials she showed a keen interest in the progress made by women throughout the world. Seldom did a week pass in which she did not applaud the success of a breakthrough for women in Turkey or under the new Soviet regime, whilst lamenting regressions elsewhere. For example, in an article provocatively entitled "Shall We Obey?" she applauded the attempt of women in England to eliminate the word "obey" from the marriage ceremony: "Their objection is well founded not merely on the ground that no woman should have to pledge herself to obey a husband as her lord and master, but because it no longer means anything. No man, of course, has the right to demand abject obedience from his wife and no woman in these days would give it if he did."[70] Jacques Garvey is deliberately distinguishing between her vision of womanhood—the modern woman—and the more conventional gender roles imagined by leading male Garveyites, including her husband. The traditional gendered language of the Christian wedding ceremony in which a bride promises to obey her husband seems inappropriate for Jacques Garvey, because it does not reflect women's real attitudes toward relationships: "it no longer means anything," she writes. Jacques Garvey argued that changes in marriage laws in the English-speaking world since the mid-nineteenth century were among some of the most important developments for women, particularly regarding married women's winning of property rights. Stressing that women everywhere were agitating for an equal share of power, Jacques Garvey argued that black women should not be left behind. Welcoming the advent of the New Negro woman, Jacques Garvey proclaimed:

> No line of endeavour remains closed for long to the modern woman. She agitates for equal opportunities and gets them; she makes good on the job and gains the respect of men who heretofore opposed her; she prefers to be a bread-winner than a half-starved wife. She is not afraid of hard work, and by being independent she gets more out of the present day husband than her grandmother did in the good old days.[71]

As this passage makes clear, Jacques Garvey's feminism developed between her earlier helpmate role in 1922 and the mid-twenties, when her women's page was at its peak. She continued to negotiate the boundaries between the public and the private, but she appeared to invoke the helpmate role less often. Rather, she argued that women should be allowed to perform the same tasks as men and suggested they would fight for the right to do so.

Jacques Garvey believed that women should play a leading role in the development of black nationalist thought and practical pan-African endeavor. Specifically, she believed that her women's page could and should be used as an active tool in the pan-African feminist struggle, a belief she stressed repeatedly in her editorials. The purpose of the women's page was "the unification and cooperation of the women of the race for the betterment of the race."[72] In her efforts to position black nationalism within a feminist framework, Jacques Garvey increasingly understood the interdependence of race and gender oppression in global terms. Just as the clubwomen who made up the ICWDR were using their organizational network to make connections with other women across the Diaspora, Jacques Garvey believed that women of African descent could use the apparatus of the UNIA to bring about the betterment of the race. Jacques Garvey's concern for black women around the globe is evident in her criticism of U.S. foreign policy. In tones similar to those of Jessie Fauset and Addie Hunton, Jacques Garvey voiced her dissatisfaction with the unjust system of international relations embodied in the newly formed League of Nations. In "What Has the League of Nations Accomplished?" Jacques Garvey argued that Africa, with no representation in the league, was still ravished at the whim of the colonial powers. "When selfish, inhuman nations sit in judgment on themselves, what can one expect? The unorganized and oppressed peoples have no voice at the League of Nations. They must make their complaints through their oppressors."[73] Just a few months earlier Jacques Garvey had made a speech on behalf of the UNIA at the African Methodist Episcopal Church in Washington, D.C., in which she strongly denounced the occupation of Haiti by U.S. forces, a view she shared with many black clubwomen and particularly the newly formed pan-African women's group the ICWDR.[74]

Jacques Garvey exhorted black women both to redeem Africa and to engage in racial-uplift work, so that peoples of African descent would have the respect of the world. Central to her vision of racial uplift was her belief in black economic nationalism. She was an early advocate of the "don't shop where you can't work" policy, a form of economic boycott that would later be adopted in Harlem and other U.S. cities in the 1930s. Jacques Garvey scolded women for handing their money over to white businesses in Harlem rather than setting up their own stores.[75] While she saw black nationalist feminism as a modern movement, she was keen to show an awareness of and appreciation for the legacy of earlier black women's struggles. In "What Some Great Women of the Race Have Accomplished," she argued that most men and women of African descent needed to learn more of their cultural heritage and noble past. Jacques Garvey focused specifically on black American women, whose cultural and political endeavors had too long gone unnoticed even by descendants of the race. She stressed the importance of celebrating a collective knowledge of and pride in noble black women in America's past, holding up as race women literary figures Phyllis Wheatley and Frances Ellen Watkins Harper, and social reformer Victoria Earle Matthews. She applauded those "many women of the race now living, . . . who are making a place for themselves in the history of the race. . . . in all activities of life our women are measuring up to the highest standard of service, of accomplishment, and always leading our men in sacrifice and service."[76]

"Strengthen Your Shaking Knees and Move Forward or We Will Displace You": Creating a Space for the New Vision

Jacques Garvey's desire to shape black nationalism within a feminist framework saw her celebrate strong black women; it also accounts for her increasingly uncompromising critique of those men within the movement who failed to accept women as leaders. Given her earlier struggles with men who had used gendered language to silence her, it is perhaps unsurprising that Jacques Garvey appropriated that language to attack black men whose divisive behavior had, in her view, undermined the race struggle. In a 1925 editorial, which appeared just one week after Henrietta Vinton Davis had conjured up her own army of amazons, Jacques Garvey also called on the power of legendary African womanhood to challenge the roles of black men: "Africa must be for Africans, and Negroes everywhere must be independent, God being our helper and guide. Mr Black Man, watch your step! Ethiopia's Queens will reign again, and her Amazons protect her shores and people. Strengthen your shaking knees and move forward, or we will displace you and lead on to victory and to glory."[77] Rather than helpmates, women are positioned as ready to take the place of cowardly men. They did not need protection, they were capable of protecting their own and leading the race just as they had in the past. In the same editorial Jacques Garvey criticized black men for their procrastination and demanded immediate action: "We are tired of hearing Negro men say, 'There is a better day coming' while they do nothing to usher in the day." She warned black men that they would be brushed aside by the determined and ready army of black women who were prepared to lead the fight.[78]

By 1925, Jacques Garvey was also prepared to make these criticisms at public meetings. In a speech delivered to a UNIA women's meeting at Liberty Hall in Harlem, Jacques Garvey reiterated this call for black women to take the place of black men who had failed to lead. According to a report in the *Negro World*, Jacques Garvey "received enthusiastic applause as she spurred the women of the race to greater efforts, scored the men who had failed the cause and broken their vows, and told of her distinguished husband's unmeasurable devotion to the cause of African Redemption." Excluding as ever her distinguished husband, and ticket to power, Jacques Garvey castigated men who failed to live up to their grand claims and called on women who were prepared to dedicate themselves to the cause:

> Men must understand that when they essay to lead and serve us they must give all or we will take all from them, and if the men do not realize their responsibilities we women must make up our minds to assume the responsibility, if it takes our lives.... I hope that when the time comes for a call for women to serve this race, there will be no hesitancy. Fine furs will not redeem Africa, and the time will surely come when the women will be called upon to make a special sacrifice in answer to Africa's call.[79]

Although Jacques Garvey sometimes editorialized about women who paid too much attention to their clothes and appearance, it is not inconceivable that here she is also referencing the fine feathers and plumes adopted by male Garveyites. In another editorial Jacques Garvey again contrasts the energy and resolve of black women with the fickleness and apathy of black men: "our women will endure untold hardships for any period, so as to achieve their goal, while the men lack perseverance and expect heaven on earth without working to bring such things to pass." She goes on to apologize to black men, in terms that emphasize a concern to protect them, thereby underlining their effeminacy:

> We will not further relate the many deficiencies of Negro men that contribute to the backwardness of the race, as we do not want them to feel that we are exposing them to the ridicule of others; but suffice it to say that if they were as energetic and unselfish as we women, the race would have a decent rating among the races of the world.[80]

Jacques Garvey does, however, go on in later editorials to recount the inadequacies of male Garveyites. This has caused some commentators to dismiss Jacques Garvey's attacks in equally gendered terms. For example, Winston James has characterized Jacques Garvey's editorial criticisms of black men as a "fountain of rage, contempt, even hatred" which is "difficult to fathom."[81] In doing so he situates Jacques Garvey's critique in the world of private, feminized emotions, which have no political significance. Taylor is more sympathetic toward Jacques Garvey, suggesting her "anger" was due to her feelings that the male leadership did not appreciate her work for the organization. She also draws on Anne Garland's work to demonstrate how anger can play an important role in transforming private concerns into a coherent worldview.[82] I would argue that rather than expressing pent-up feminine frustration, Jacques Garvey uses the same gendered language of male Garveyites to criticize those men who have failed to live up to the standards of true manhood they set themselves. If these standards of true manhood cannot be met, she suggests that an alternative view of gender relations is required, one where women are empowered to lead.

Following the stream of criticism that she addressed to black male Garveyites through 1925 and 1926, Jacques Garvey used the election of a woman as president of another nationalist movement to challenge black men publicly to accept women's leadership within the UNIA. Applauding the election of Mrs. Sarojini Naidu as president of the Hindu Indian National Congress in 1926, Jacques Garvey demanded to know if the black race had not similarly capable women. Given Garvey's imprisonment and widely circulating rumors that Jacques Garvey was herself running the organization in the interim, she clearly had herself in mind when she suggested that "black men would be highly indignant if a Negro woman was proposed to reside over our National Convention; small minded Negro men would object vociferously if the able wife of a deceased executive was slated to fill his position."[83] Jacques Garvey went on to point out that male Garveyites' attempts to subordinate women even compared unfavorably to the white-male-dominated U.S. government:

> If the United States Senate and Congress can open their doors to white women, we serve notice on our men that Negro women will demand equal opportunity to fill any position in the Universal Negro Improvement Association or anywhere else without discrimination because of sex. We are very sorry if it hurts your old fashioned tyrannical feelings, and we not only make the demand, but we intend to enforce it.[84]

While not exactly anticipating Garvey's early demise, Jacques Garvey's reference to her husband (not yet a deceased executive, but still an incapacitated one) served to underscore her own potency as the "able wife," "slated to fill his position." Jacques Garvey appears to be fascinated with wives who succeed to leadership positions because of slain or otherwise incapacitated husbands and frequently wrote about the wives of famous world leaders, who "if hubby dies or becomes incapacitated, [they] can fit in his place and save a situation."[85] Similarly, the juxtaposition of "small-minded Negro men" with the apparent tolerance of the U.S. Senate for white women challenged their stature as "manly" men: white men and the men of the Indian National Congress, unlike men of the UNIA, did not feel threatened by their women in positions of authority.

In the context of the power struggle taking place in Garvey's absence, Jacques Garvey grasped this opportunity to assert black women's right to shape the direction of black nationalism. Jacques Garvey did not believe that nationalism should be directed only by black women. Rather, she understood nationalism and feminism as compatible and saw nationalist ideology as the product of interactions between men and women (rather than solely between men). She believed that "their [women's] place is alongside of the men, in the thick of the battle."[86] No one was in a better position than Jacques Garvey to know the difficulties of advocating a radical feminism within a black nationalist organization. Yet far from viewing the two as incompatible she constructed a framework in which nationalism and feminism were both part of the same struggle, a struggle shaped, at least in part, by the gendered discourse of the Garvey movement. That she worked and lived within a black nationalist organization, which in her view failed to live up to its liberation motif, contributed in some respects toward this realization. Like contemporary feminists, Jacques Garvey understood that race and gender were interlinked, and in her editorials she showed that she recognized race itself as a gendered concept. Linking race and gender oppression with worldwide gender and race liberation struggles in Europe, Africa, and the Caribbean helped Jacques Garvey express her pan-African consciousness. When she arrived in the United States and took up the mantle of spokeswoman for the UNIA, Jacques Garvey had to work within and build upon traditions of integrationist and black nationalist civil rights protest in which women had always been told that they had to wait, that the race struggle must come before women's rights.[87] In this context her insistence that the two issues were part of the same struggle, that one could not be prioritized above the other, was a significant step forward in developing a black feminist tradition. Jacques Garvey would continue to support pan-African struggles throughout her life. Her belief in the futility of institutional factionalism would allow her to work with her husband's former enemies, including Du Bois, with whom she collaborated in 1944 as a convener of the Fifth Pan-African Congress.[88] Her commitment to the idea that black nationalism and feminism could not only exist together, but were part of the same struggle, continued after she left the United States in 1927 to forward the struggle in Jamaica.[89]

Jessie Redmon Fauset: Feminist and Pan-Africanist

The woman who had helped W. E. B. Du Bois to plan the Second and Fourth Pan-African Congresses also advocated a feminist and black nationalist philosophy to her readers. Jessie Redmon Fauset was the most published black female novelist of the Harlem Renaissance and was literary editor of *The Crisis*, the movement's foremost journal. Although Fauset worked for the NAACP, an interracial organization, she articulated in her fiction and essays many of the same ideas and themes as Jacques Garvey. Like Jacques Garvey, Fauset worked within an organization dominated by a charismatic male leader. Fauset's professional and emotional relationship with sociologist, novelist, and *Crisis* editor W. E. B. Du Bois was in many ways similar to the relationship of Jacques Garvey and Marcus Garvey. Both women carried out much of the day-to-day work of the famous men for whom they worked, and both were overshadowed and subsequently ignored by historians in favor of the men they cared for. In common with Jacques Garvey, Fauset had a powerful feminist and often black nationalist critique of the society that surrounded her and has often been misunderstood. Her novels have been dubbed assimilationist and bourgeois, and it is this low esteem for Fauset's skills as a novelist that has been partially responsible for the neglect of her role as a promoter during the Harlem Renaissance. This criticism has often relied on the false premise that Fauset and her novels are interchangeable: Fauset is portrayed as a snobbish individual and artist, supposedly evidenced by the elitism of the middle-class characters who people her books and who, like Fauset herself, are assimilationist in their desires and ambitions. By comparing Fauset with Jacques Garvey, this chapter will demonstrate that Fauset interrogated the idea of race, class, and gender as stable categories, while simultaneously positing race as a useful tool for organizing resistance.

Born in 1882 and raised in Philadelphia, Fauset's background has often been taken as the starting point for understanding her subsequent career as a writer. Assuming she came from a very comfortable middle-class background due to her father's profession as an African Methodist Episcopal minister as well as her family's long ancestry in Philadelphia, historians and literary critics have been quick to suggest that these supposedly elite roots formed the background for her "bourgeois" and "conventional" novels. In an early examination of black literature, Robert Bone proclaimed that "undoubtedly the most formative influence on Miss Fauset's work was her family background. An authentic old Philadelphian, she was never able to transcend the limits of this sheltered world."[90] However, Carolyn Sylvander's biographical research suggests that Fauset's early years were far from being as sheltered and secure as Bone and other critics have assumed.[91] Fauset bitterly recalled the difficulties of being the only black girl at a white school and how race discrimination prevented her from gaining a higher education in turn-of-the-century Philadelphia. Bryn Mawr, her preferred choice of university, would not accept a black woman in their teacher-training program, but instead shipped her out on a scholarship to Cornell University. In 1905 Fauset became the first woman to graduate from Cornell with a Phi Beta Kappa key and the first black American woman to become a member of the Greek letter society. She would also gain a master's in French at the University of Pennsylvania in 1919 and would later go on to study at the Sorbonne.[92] Despite her impressive qualifications, no school in the Philadelphia school district would employ Fauset. She would spend the next fourteen years as a French teacher at the M Street High School in Washington, D.C., the most famous black high school in the country, which would become the Dunbar High School in 1917.[93] Her appointment to the post of literary editor of *The Crisis* from 1919 to 1926 was the result of her long years of involvement with the NAACP in Washington, D.C. During her time in the segregated capital, Fauset helped fight discrimination suits, contributed frequently to *The Crisis*, and from 1903 onward maintained a correspondence with the editor, Du Bois.[94] Although Fauset could not claim to be of the "folk" and failed to produce parents who had been formerly enslaved, her experiences represent a more complicated picture of relative privilege and denial, struggle and opportunity, than her critics would have us believe.

The focus of historical interest on Du Bois meant that for a long time Fauset and her role at *The Crisis* were neglected. While there have been attempts to reassess Fauset's significance during the Harlem Renaissance, many accounts persist in their consideration of Fauset only in relation to Du Bois. She is commonly viewed as his "right-hand woman at *The Crisis*, the skillfully genteel novelist of black manners."[95] Yet Fauset by no means shared all the views of her boss. While Fauset's approach to the race problem was guided by her understanding of the connections between race and gender as categories constructed for oppression as well as resistance, Du Bois's analysis of the problems of African Americans was undoubtedly narrowed by the male-dominated discourse upon which his assumptions were built. As Hazel Carby has pointed out, it is not enough that Du Bois politically supported women's equal rights if an understanding of gender structures did not permeate his own work: "There is unfortunately, no simple correspondence between anyone's support for female equality and the ideological effect of the gendered structures of thought and feeling at work in any text one might write and publish."[96] Furthermore, Du Bois's support for women's suffrage seems to have made his own gender politics immune from close scrutiny. His marital infidelity, his penchant for choosing young, attractive women to work with him (including Fauset), and his sacrifice of his daughter on the altar of art through his orchestration of her marriage to the gay black poet Countee Cullen have done little to undermine his reputation as the leading black thinker of the twentieth century.[97] More often Du Bois's gendered assumptions impacted on the lives and careers of the women who worked with him and with whom he had sexual relationships, possibly including Fauset herself.[98] Fauset's emotional ties to Du Bois led her to make him a sizable loan at considerable cost to her physical health, which he was extremely slow to pay back and which may well have been the reason she left *The Crisis* in 1926.[99]

Fauset also distinguished herself from Du Bois in her handling of authors and editorship of *The Crisis*. A survey of the correspondence between Fauset and many of the contributors to the journal reveals her role in encouraging then-unknown writers Langston Hughes, Countee Cullen, and Claude McKay to send their work to *The Crisis*.[100] Du Bois on the other hand managed to alienate many contributors through his roughshod handling of, and only intermittent respect for, writers' ownership of their work. After Fauset left *The Crisis* in 1926, these same writers were shocked by Du Bois's editorial decisions, such as publishing their earlier work without their permission.[101] Du Bois cast his disapproval over those contributors to *The Crisis* who dared to publish their work elsewhere. He was particularly censorious of *Fire!!*, the licentious one-issue publication produced by Wallace Thurman, Langston Hughes, Gwendolyn Bennett, and others in November 1926, because of its themes of intrarace racism, self-hatred, and incestuous relations. Ann Douglas assumes Fauset was also opposed to *Fire!!* because she would naturally side with the "Talented Tenther" Du Bois. Yet Fauset was responsible for recruiting these same writers to *The Crisis*, and frequently used the very themes that disgusted her boss, such as intrarace prejudice and incest, in her own fiction.[102]

While Fauset promoted the careers of male poets, her greatest contribution to *The Crisis* was the exposure she gave to large numbers of women writers.[103] Fauset used her editorial power within *The Crisis* to counterbalance the gender bias that supported artistic production by men. This manifested itself in fewer funds being made available for women in terms of grants and private philanthropy, negative reviews, and the scanty coverage awarded women by male editors or publishers, as well as the less obvious slights that made it much harder for women to obtain critical success in this period, and with which Fauset was only too familiar.[104] While there were some supporters of Fauset's work who offered encouragement—Du Bois and Alain Locke both greeted the publication of Fauset's first novel, *There Is Confusion,* as a literary landmark—for the most part even the positive assessments missed the point of Fauset's novels or attempted to pigeonhole her as "the potential Jane Austen of Negro literature."[105] A comparison with Austen might be viewed as extremely complimentary by some writers in certain contexts, but it served to distance Fauset from the exciting writing of the New Negro. During the Harlem Renaissance, black literature addressed and frequently politicized debates about racial identity and miscegenation. Although Fauset's novels engaged with these discussions, her critics understood her domestic settings as disconnecting her from these debates. For example, Alain Locke praised Fauset's novel for its "quiet pool of material" which was "too often disregarded for the swift and muddy waters of the Negro underworld." Others made clear their disregard for the novel of manners: George Schuyler described *There Is Confusion* as "not very engrossing as a work of fiction," but added that at least he was "never bored."[106]

Many male reviewers often missed the irony and masked criticism that lay behind women's work and instead offered judgments on what constituted authentic black literature as defined by their own work.[107] In Fauset's case, these criticisms often included a reference to her supposed sexual inexperience (she did not marry until 1929), which was designed to undermine her "authenticity" further. For example, in a private letter to Fauset's friend Countee Cullen, the writer Eric Walrond criticized Fauset's novels, complaining that "her outlook on life is too glaringly that of the school marm, the range of her experience is too petty and bourgeois."[108] In a published review of her work in the *New Republic*, Walrond's criticism of Fauset went beyond the bounds of the usual critical review, describing her work as "mediocre": "a work of puny painstaking labor, *There Is Confusion*, is not meant for people who know anything about the Negro and his problems. It is aimed with unpardonable naïveté at the very young or the pertinently old."[109] The personal language used by Walrond and others to review the work of women was seldom found in reference to a male writer. Walrond questions Fauset's authenticity as an African American writer. In his view, her experiences are so unrepresentative and middle class that she is unqualified to represent the black experience.

The Jamaican poet Claude McKay, who willingly accepted Fauset's patronage, also merged his critique of Fauset's personality and work into one. In his autobiography *A Long Way from Home*, McKay wrote that "Miss Fauset is dainty as a primrose, and her novels are quite as fastidious and precious." He too used Fauset's work as a negative against which he might validate his own authenticity as a writer. In a letter written from France to the historian and collector Arthur Schomburg, McKay boasted that his novels would prove unpopular because they would offend what he called "[the] hypocritical Negro literati," but, he added, "I think I'm nearer the truth and tragedy and gaiety of Negro Life than Miss Jessie Fauset."[110] There was irony in McKay's suggestion that Fauset was the one selling out. Whereas there was a wide market for novels of Harlem nightlife such as Carl Van Vechten's *Nigger Heaven* and McKay's own *Home to Harlem*, Fauset struggled to find publishers for her work. As Fauset explained in a 1932 interview, the first publisher to see the manuscript of *There Is Confusion* confessed as he rejected it: "White readers just don't expect Negroes to be like this."[111] Nor did black readers expect

Fauset's depictions of black men. Harold Jackman, a schoolteacher in New York and "friend" of Fauset, described Fauset's second book, *Plum Bun*, as "lousy, absolutely terrible. Really, I don't see how the publishers could take it. Jessie doesn't know men, she doesn't write prose well; it is bad, bad, bad. . . . it is one of the worst books I have read in a long time."[112] It is curious that so many writer-critics were unable to distinguish their feelings about Fauset from their "professional" judgments of her work. Perhaps it was professional jealousy: as literary editor of *The Crisis* and a published author, Fauset held a position of influence and seniority over many of her critics. But perhaps it was the themes of Fauset's novels that most irritated her contemporaries. Novels about black women who questioned constructions of "authentic" racial identity by middle-class black men might have struck a little too close to home.

Fauset's first novel, *There Is Confusion*, was hailed as the first New Negro novel.[113] To celebrate this achievement a gathering of publishers and New Negro writers was held at the Civic Club in downtown Manhattan on March 21, 1924. It included a special dinner arranged by Fauset's friends and fellow writers, Harlem librarian Regina Andrews and the artist and writer Gwendolyn Bennett. Although the occasion had started off as a celebration of Fauset's first novel, the gathering was hijacked by the Howard University philosopher Alain Locke, who was toastmaster for the night. Fauset recalled the occasion in a letter she wrote Locke nine years later:

> I have always disliked your attitude toward my work dating from the time years ago when you went out of your way to tell my brother that the dinner given at the civic club for "There is Confusion" wasn't for me. Incidentally I may tell you now that that idea originated with Regina Anderson and Gwendolyn Bennett, both members of a little library club with which I was associated. How you and one or two others sought to distort the idea and veil its original graciousness . . . I have known for years. And I still remember the consummate skill with which you that night as toast-master strove to keep speech and comment away from the person for whom the occasion was meant.[114]

Locke was described by historian David Levering Lewis as a "certified misogynist . . . [who] dismissed female students on the first class day with the promise of an automatic grade of C." The impact of Locke's aversion to women was compounded by his preference for handsome young men, since he was in a position to promote the careers of those men he favored.[115] To be sure, Locke was an important figure in the 1920s. A professor at Howard University in Washington, D.C., Locke was situated away from the heart of the Harlem Renaissance. Nevertheless it was he who edited the landmark collection *The New Negro* (1925) and acted as a go-between for Zora Neale Hurston, Langston Hughes, and Aaron Douglas, and the white patron of black art Charlotte Mason.[116] Because of his position and connections, most of the younger Harlem literati kowtowed to Locke, but Fauset's indignation at Locke's superior attitude and disparagement of her work in several reviews forced her to confront him. Nor was the Civic Club dinner the only occasion on which Locke had attempted to silence Fauset's voice. Locke would also try to exclude Fauset from his New Negro anthology in spite of Du Bois's insistence that to do so would mean leaving out one of the most important writers of the period.[117] The Virginia-based poet Anne Spencer confirmed Locke's reluctance to promote women when she later suggested that she had been held back by Locke because he had wanted to promote his favorites, such as Countee Cullen and other young men he liked to have around him.[118]

Fauset seldom complained about the sometimes vicious reviews she received from colleagues, and even friends, while she was in a position of some authority. Much later, however, when her career as a novelist had ended, but her reputation was still being debated, she did attempt to assert control over how the young men she had once helped now chose to represent her. For example, in Arna Bontemps's introduction to his anthology, he belittled her teaching career, speaking of her "only" teaching at Dunbar, and omitting to mention the years after her resignation from *The Crisis* when she had taught at De Witt Clinton, which was then the largest high school in the United States. In a letter to Langston Hughes written in 1949, Fauset complained about Bontemps's attitude: "I've suffered a good deal from colored men writers from Locke down to Bontemps—you know the sort of thing, 'Without sneering, teach the rest to sneer.'"[119] Bontemps's description was particularly ungracious as it had been Fauset who had encouraged Bontemps to leave his job as a postman in California and move to New York City, by publishing one of his poems in *The Crisis*, and Fauset who continued to encourage him to write. Those whom Fauset helped early in their careers seldom reciprocated; nor were they able or willing to imagine the additional obstacles that black woman writers must overcome. Responding to a letter from Hughes in which he had complained of the difficulties of life, the usually sympathetic Fauset felt compelled to point out: "you think life is hard and complicated! It is, it is! But when one adds to that being a woman!"[120]

Editor and Essayist: *The Crisis* and *The Brownies' Book*

Fauset's experience and understanding of the particular difficulties facing black women led her to use her role as literary editor of *The Crisis*, and as managing editor of the children's magazine *The Brownies' Book*, to showcase the talent of black women of all ages from all over the United States. *The Brownies' Book* was a children's magazine that Fauset published with Du Bois and Augustus Dill from January 1920 to December 1921. *The Brownies' Book* was intended to promote race pride at an early age in African American children. In the very first issue Fauset staked this claim:

> To children, who with eager look
> Scanned vainly library shelf and nook,
> For History or Song or Story
> That told of Colored Peoples' glory,-
> We dedicate THE BROWNIES' BOOK.[121]

In her weekly column, "The Judge," in which she advised (imaginary) children on the hardships of growing up, Fauset told a fifteen-year-old girl: "This world has long been unfair to women and girls. It is doing a little better now, but it is not yet doing well."[122] To see how Fauset was playing her part in making it a "little better," one need only look at the list of contributors to the magazine; it reads like a who's who of women who would become prominent in the 1920s as writers and women's rights activists, including Effie Lee Newsome, Eulalie Spence, Nella Larsen, Georgia Douglas Johnson, Madeline Allison, Elizabeth Ross Haynes, and Crystal Bird. The young artist Laura Wheeling was the regular illustrator for the magazine. These women form the backbone of *The Brownies' Book*, and as regular contributors they constituted a literary network of their own. They used the magazine to discuss issues that concerned women and girls and recounted the stories of heroic African Americans of the past. For example, Haynes wrote an article on Benjamin Banneker, eighteenth-century mathematician and astronomer, while Fauset contributed an article about Sojourner Truth as a pioneer suffragette.[123] Although it lasted only two years, the production of a magazine for African American children in the 1920s was a bold step, and Fauset's central role in its publication has only recently been acknowledged.[124]

As well as publishing other women's work, Fauset used her regular column in *The Crisis* to review women's work published elsewhere. For example, in 1919 she reviewed a "Negro number" of *Birth Control Review*, in which she discussed a play by Mary Burill and a short story by Angelina Weld Grimke, which she described as being "in exquisite vein" and "very readable indeed."[125] Many of the prominent women writers and artists of the Harlem Renaissance that Fauset would later publish in *The Crisis* were already known to her from her days as a schoolteacher at the M Street High School in Washington, D.C. Among others, the poet and playwright Angelina Grimke had been her colleague, and it was here that she met and became friends with the women who dominated Washington's literary scene, including Georgia Douglas Johnson, Mary Burill, and Effie Lee Newsome. The poet and playwright Johnson remembered how Fauset "very generously helped her to gather together material for her first book." For her part Fauset would later quote Johnson's poem "The Supplicant" in her second novel, *Plum Bun*.[126] Gwendolyn Bennett, whose poetry Fauset had published in *The Crisis*, dedicated her poem "To Usward" to Fauset in celebration of the publication of *There Is Confusion*.[127] Also part of the female literary network was Alice Dunbar-Nelson, widow of black poet Paul Dunbar. A poet in her own right and a women's rights activist, Dunbar-Nelson wrote of Fauset in her diary and admired her poetry.[128] YWCA leaders, including Juliette Derricotte and Addie Hunton, were also part of Fauset's network. Fauset spoke on black literature at YWCA conferences and worked with the clubwoman and pan-Africanist Addie Hunton in organizing the Fourth Pan-African Congress in New York City.[129] Fauset also reviewed Hunton and Johnson's *Two Colored Women with the American Expeditionary Forces* in *The Crisis*, and the account clearly served as the basis for her description of Maggie's experiences as a YMCA nurse in France during World War I in *There Is Confusion*.[130] Outside of her official *Crisis* work, Fauset encouraged women writers through her weekly literary salon. Held at her Harlem apartment, Fauset's gatherings provided a space for black women to discuss their work, free from the voyeurism of white onlookers from downtown. Unlike many of her male contemporaries Fauset was ambivalent about white sponsors of black art who came uptown to gather "black" material for use in their own books. As Langston Hughes explained in his memoir *The Big Sea*, "Jessie Fauset did not feel like opening her home to mere sightseers, or faddists momentarily in love with Negro life."[131]

Fauset's connections with black women writers and activists who were involved in pan-African organizations were also reflected in the essays and articles she wrote for *The Crisis* between 1919 and 1926. Besides her regular column, Fauset also acted as managing editor when Du Bois was away. For example, Fauset ran the magazine from December 1918 to June 1919 while Du Bois attended the Paris Peace Conference. In her internal letters and published reports for *The Crisis* in these months, Fauset kept pan-African issues at the forefront: she frequently criticized the Paris Peace Treaty, and linked it to the United States' treatment of returning black soldiers.[132] When Du Bois returned from Paris, Fauset continued to use her influence to highlight pan-African concerns. She was particularly interested in the role that the League of Nations might play in helping the cause of African freedom. Like Amy Jacques Garvey, she frequently avowed her belief in a free Africa. In "Nationalism and Egypt" Fauset denounced the takeover of Egypt as a "protectorate" by the British and the failure of the United States and Britain to recognize the "evil" of their foreign policy. She stressed the hypocrisy of fighting for liberty in World War I while repudiating African claims to liberty. Fauset argued that in refusing to recognize the Egyptian delegation, the Paris Peace Conference had proved that the Wilsonian rhetoric of freedom and self-determination was all hypocritical cant. Fauset saw the unjust Paris Peace Treaty and League of Nations as a cause around which all peoples of African descent should unite. Supporting Egypt's protest to the league, Fauset concluded that "Egypt is really speaking for the whole dark world. Thus is the scene being staged for the greatest and most lasting conflict of peoples?"[133] Fauset was also interested in how other nations perceived America's handling of race issues. In one article she remarked on how the Japanese press viewed America's treatment of "darker races" and how they made links between America's oppression of blacks at home and its treatment of nonwhite peoples abroad.[134]

There are remarkable similarities in the language and topics discussed by Fauset and Jacques Garvey in *The Crisis* and the *Negro World*. Although Jacques Garvey did not begin her women's page until 1924, she often referred to the Versailles Treaty and criticized the League of Nations as a white man's club. Furthermore, Jacques Garvey was also well-informed about developments in other parts of the world relating to women and all pan-African issues, and similarly quoted snippets from foreign newspapers and magazines. Fauset sounds as though she were writing the headline for the *Negro World* rather than an article for the integrationist *Crisis* when she dramatically prophesies the "greatest and most lasting conflict of peoples." Jessie Fauset also shared with Jacques Garvey a commitment to practical as well as intellectual support for the pan-African movement. One of the few black American women to take part in the Second Pan-African Congress that convened under Du Bois's leadership in London, Brussels, and Paris, Fauset delivered an address in which she "told of the colored graduates in the United States and showed the pictures of the first women who had obtained the degree in Doctor of Philosophy." She also sent a greeting from the black women of America to the women of Africa.[135] In her report for *The Crisis* on her impressions of the Congress, Fauset stressed the unity of people of African descent, describing how "we clasped hands with our newly found brethren and departed, feeling that it was good to be alive and most wonderful to be colored. Not one of us but envisaged in his heart the dawn of a day of new and perfect brotherhood."[136]

Between 1919 and 1924, Du Bois and Marcus Garvey increasingly devoted the front pages of their publications to denouncing each other and asserting the clear ideological ground between the two organizations and approaches they represented. If we look beyond the front-page posturing of these two men, however, we find there is often much that the two publications agree on. Both publications had women writers who articulated a feminist pan-Africanism, both advertised the activities of the black clubwomen's movement, and both celebrated the achievements of black women writers and entrepreneurs such as Madam Walker. Fauset in particular often reported on the events connected with the women's club movement. In October 1922 she covered the Thirteenth Biennial of the National Association of Colored Women (NACW). Fauset was invited to attend the Richmond convention as a guest speaker because of her recent involvement in the Second Pan-African Congress. Fauset spoke to the clubwomen on "the development of Negro poetry" as well as offering her interpretation of the Pan-African Congress. In her address on the importance of the liberation of all peoples of African descent, Fauset demonstrated that black women had a role to play in this process. She was keen to relay this in her account of the convention which she published in *The Crisis*. In her report Fauset stressed the NACW's essentially political nature and described the attendees as "remarkable women who are engaged in every conceivable movement destined to benefit womanhood and childhood." A member of the NACW through her involvement with the Delta Sigma Theta Sorority, Fauset saw the NACW's potential as a "great and far reaching organization with far reaching possibilities."[137] The 1922 Richmond convention paid particular attention to making contacts with women from other parts of the Diaspora and was the occasion for the founding of the ICWDR by Margaret Murray Washington. Many of the themes Fauset addressed on the pages of *The Crisis*, such as black American involvement in World War I and race solidarity, reemerge in the novels she published in the 1920s and 1930s. In her fiction, Fauset brought into a coherent framework her concern with race and gender equality through a critique of men who imposed conventional gender roles on women, and her characterization of strong, race-proud women.

Race Pride and Black Womanhood in Fauset's *There Is Confusion* and *The Chinaberry Tree*

Fauset's novels examine the intersection of class, gender, and racial identity in early-twentieth-century America. Her female protagonists question the restrictions placed on black women by white society, but they also challenge the way black men use racialized arguments to justify women's subordination. Her male characters often make prescriptive judgments on what constitutes "authentic" black identity, and question the race credentials of women who challenge them. Critical of the pretensions of middle-class men, Fauset creates female characters who express their racial pride and feminist consciousness through cultural, political, and economic means. Through the course of Fauset's novels, many characters gain knowledge of the cultural pride that racial separatism has helped create. Fauset's depictions of middle-class women expressing their race pride and articulating their black nationalist sympathies are striking given the black nationalist–versus–integrationist framework which has dominated both contemporary debate and much later literary criticism. At the same time, she insists on the cultural and economic investment that African Americans have made in the United States, and argues that they should not give up on it. In the immediate future Fauset believed that African Americans should work toward greater *intra*racial cooperation and toward a black cultural nationalism, both because this is good for individuals and the black community, and because it might at the same time pave a pathway toward possible and eventual integration.

Along with many other female authors of the Harlem Renaissance, Fauset was neglected until the 1960s and 1970s. When critics began to look at her work again she was criticized on two counts: form and content. Quite simply, Fauset was regarded as lacking the skill to construct a workable narrative, falling back on the conventional romance because this was the best she could do. The other criticism was directed at the content of her work. Fauset was accused of being an assimilationist, trying to show that the black middle classes were no different from whites. One of the first to look again at Fauset was Robert Bone. Labeling her "Victorian" and "Rear Guard," Bone in his scathing judgment in 1958 would set the tone for later critics.[138] In the 1960s and 1970s, as the black nationalist critique of the African American middle classes became more militant, post-war judgments of Fauset would be reinforced. Amiri Baraka railed against those writers who identified with the black middle class and claimed that their desire to be white had hindered the emergence of a black American literature.[139] For Arthur Davis, Fauset's prominence and productivity meant that she should be singled out as "the most prolific, and in many ways the most representative, of [the] glorifiers of the Negro middle class."[140] Association with this static middle-class identity apparently disqualified Fauset from exhibiting black pride and made it impossible that she might be sympathetic toward black nationalism. Lumped together with other middle-class authors, Fauset was viewed as a representative of this class, rather than a novelist, female role model, and promoter of feminist pan-Africanism.[141] This interpretation was encouraged by the developing body of work which claimed black blues singers as the more "authentic" spokespersons for black culture.[142] Recent feminist critics have responded to these criticisms, both by presenting alternative interpretations of Fauset's form and by questioning the essentializing of the folk and working-class experience which, through the study of folk forms, was coming to define an "authentic" black culture.[143] For example, Deborah McDowell has examined Fauset's parody of the fairy tale and the conventional women's romance. Others have called for a greater contextualization of the work and life of women writers, in particular the recognition that in the early twentieth century "gender assumptions, and oppositions between public and private spheres, were still very much intact."[144] Contextualizing black women's work also means avoiding the temptation of imposing on early-twentieth-century women an ahistorical and essentialist definition of what constitutes "authentic" black identity. While the shift in African American literary studies away from privileging elite voices and toward a recovery of the voiceless working class has produced some excellent work, there is also danger in constructing a new essentialism in which the "folk" and the blues come to define authentic blackness.[145]

Fauset was interested in working out the tensions between African Americans' integrationist impulses and their black cultural nationalism. Rather than "glorifying" the black middle classes, Fauset explores the ways in which gender and class are often used to validate or question racial integrity. Carol Batker's comparative study of Native American, Jewish, and African American women's writers in the Progressive Era supports the view that women often negotiated between integrationism and nationalism. She is critical of literary critics who "elide assimilationism and middle-class politics in their readings because they assume a cause and effect relationship among acculturation, middle-class status, and integration." On the other hand, Batker also sees Fauset as making "only a passing nod to black nationalism," and as dismissing the influence of Africa as too distant in time from 1920s America. So while Batker sees Fauset's positioning within this debate as more nuanced and complex than many previous critics, she underplays the increasing importance of pan-Africanism in Fauset's worldview and is reluctant to move away from the accepted image of Fauset the integrationist.[146] Building on previous literary criticism and taking into consideration Fauset's political pan-Africanism, activism in the club movement, and feminist outlook as expressed in her extensive correspondence, the rest of this chapter situates Fauset's novels within the black nationalist–integrationist debate. The focus will rest primarily on *There Is Confusion* and *The Chinaberry Tree*, because it is in these works that Fauset most clearly addresses the apparent conflict between separatism and integration. It will be suggested that it is possible to see Fauset as both American and pan-Africanist, as both integrationist and black cultural nationalist.[147]

Fauset's novels are full of strong, independent women who address the concerns of New Negro women. In *There Is Confusion* we see the development of female characters who have romantic interests, but who are also concerned with their careers. Joanna Marshall is a New Negro woman, whose race pride spurs her to success as a dancer and singer in a white world that has limited opportunities for black artists. The other important female character is working-class Maggie Ellersley, a family friend of the educated and financially secure Marshall family. Joanna and Maggie develop in relation to each other: at different stages of their lives, both women challenge the restrictions placed on them and the men who question their authenticity as New Negro women. What is revealed is that those characters who, like Fauset, express a feminist outlook in their private and public lives, find that their race loyalty and authenticity is questioned. An examination of the feminist expression of Fauset's characters, therefore, is essential for a closer study of these links between feminism, middle-class status, and questioned authenticity.

The way in which racialized gender roles impact on black men and women is a central theme of *There Is Confusion*. Fauset's protagonists are a mixture of those who accept and then reject, and those who have always rejected the constructions of race and gender that keep African Americans, and black women in particular, in a restricted space. Early on in *There Is Confusion*, Fauset is describing the unmarried aunt of Peter Bye, the would-be suitor of the ambitious Joanna, whose own ambitions for a medical career are inspired by his greater ambition to win Joanna. The narrator steps in to inform us that this particular spinster aunt was not one to be pitied, as conventional romance would have us do: "In those days the position of old maid had its decided advantages—few people if any gave her the benefit of the doubt that she might have remained single from choice."[148] But Fauset has set out to subvert the conventional romance, and it is women who have both careers and romantic relationships who are the focus of the novel.

Joanna, who is struggling with her career as a black woman because of racial discrimination in the theater, also has to contend with the obstacles placed in her way due to her gender. She tries to find employment in the theater, but is constantly rejected because she is black and a woman. We are told, "The big theatrical trusts refused her absolutely—one had even said frankly: 'We'll try a colored man in a white company but we won't have any colored woman.'"[149] When Joanna does begin to find stage success in spite of her color, she feels compelled to give up her boyfriend, Peter Bye, who feels threatened by her independence. He tells Joanna, "your life seems so full. Sometimes I think there is nothing I can bring you."[150] Joanna breaks her engagement with Peter because he has, in her view, failed to live up to his potential as a "race man." Peter appears weak. He does not share Joanna's lofty ideals. He believes "the world owes me a living."[151] There is too much discrimination against black medical students; he would rather learn jazz piano and play in cabarets. Joanna berates him with language similar to that used by Jacques Garvey to challenge the failings of male Garveyites: Joanna declares, "I don't want a coward and a shirker for a husband. Buck up, Peter, be a man. You've got to be one if you're going to marry me."[152] While Peter spends much of his time predicting that he will never get ahead because of racial discrimination, Joanna reflects on how fortunate she is to have a career:

> Very often she found herself glad that she had her work. Without it, what would she have done? What did girls do when they waited for their young men? Heavens, how awful to be sitting around listlessly from day to day, waiting, waiting.... it was this lack of interest and purpose on the part of girls which brought about so many hasty marriages which terminated in—no, not poverty—mediocrity.[153]

Just as Joanna tries to hold Peter up to an almost Garveyite ideal of black masculinity, black men try to impose their standards of black femininity on their women. While these standards are voiced by black men, they are frequently performed by other black women within the novel. For example, Joanna's character is often juxtaposed not only with that of her domesticated sister Sylvia, but also with that of the family friend, working-class Maggie Ellersley, both of whom are apparently more concerned with finding marital bliss than with their careers. Sylvia, who is engaged to marry Brian Spencer, works at home as a dressmaker. Sylvia's is an acceptable occupation to New Negro men: she is insulated not only from the racial discrimination that working for whites could bring (and from which black men could do little to protect their women), but also from the public sphere. Joanna, on the other hand, not only exposes herself to frequent racial insults through her ambition to get on stage, but refuses to allow her boyfriend to protect her. Joanna is discussing her career with Sylvia's husband-to-be. Brian compares Joanna's relationship with Peter with his own treatment at the hands of Joanna's sister: "'She [Sylvia] kept me in the back of her head I'll swear, while you with your singing and dancing and your wildcat schemes of getting on the stage! Better stick to your own Janna, and build up colored art.'"[154] Here, in contrast to Sylvia, Joanna's failure to limit her ambitions to the domestic sphere is used as a basis from which to question her race pride and loyalty and to imply that she wants to be with whites, rather than with "her own." Joanna is amazed by this connection: "'Why, I am,' cried Joanna, astonished. 'You don't think I want to forsake—*us*. Not at all. But I want to show *us* to the world. I am colored, of course, but American first. Why shouldn't I speak to all America?'"[155] In Joanna's response we see her struggling between her black cultural pride and her desire to display her skill on a white stage, to assert her American identity.

Throughout the novel, women who challenge their conventional status and question the notion of separate spheres are in turn liable to have their loyalty to the race questioned. Fauset's female characters are not simply questioning the restrictions placed on them as women, but also what constitutes racial pride. While Fauset sometimes makes this link explicit, as in the conversation between Joanna and Brian, at other times she does it more subtly, by placing the two debates next to each other in the narrative. For example, what begins as a conversation between Peter and Joanna about his belief in the central importance of love above all else—a premise about which Joanna is scornful—ends in a discussion about integration, separatism, and racial pride. Peter has just told Joanna that "Love is the most natural and ordinary thing in the world," but Joanna responds by pointing out how love means something very different for men and women: "Don't talk like a silly, Peter. You know perfectly well that for a woman love usually means a household of children, the getting of a thousand meals, picking up laundry, no time for herself for meditation, or reading or ____."[156] The couple move directly from Joanna's challenge to a discussion of Joanna's decision to take dancing instruction from a French teacher, Bertully. Although he is prepared to teach black women, Bertully accepts the demands of his white clients and will not give lessons to Joanna with the rest of the group. However, when Joanna asks if he will instruct her if she gets up enough numbers for a separate group of black girls, he agrees. Peter questions her willingness "to be set apart like that"; for Peter, segregation is a terrible insult, integration an absolute goal, but Joanna disagrees. "'What do I care?' asked Joanna the practical, 'You've got to take life as you find it Peter. The way I figure it is this. If all I needed to get on the stage was the mastery of a difficult step, I'd get there, wouldn't I? For somehow, sometime, I'd learn how to overcome that difficulty.'"[157] Like clubwomen and YWCA women, Joanna is prepared to use strategies of separatism to get what she wants and believes that in the long run this might lead to an integrated society. But in the meantime the question of integration is neither her concern nor her aim: "'Now my problem is how to master, how to get around prejudice. It is an awful nuisance; in some parts of this country it is more than a nuisance, it's a veritable menace. Philip says he's going to change all that some day.'"[158]

We see Joanna trying to work out how to overcome prejudice in her dancing career. Engaged as a dancer in the pageant "Dance of the Nations," Joanna performs the role of the "Negro" and the Native American. When the company loses the white woman who usually plays the role of "America," Joanna is asked to dance "America" in her place. Joanna learns that white America refuses to recognize her unless she appears white. She must wear a white mask to perform "America." At the end of the performance, however, Joanna takes off her mask, reveals her black skin, and stakes her claim as an American: "there is no one in the audience more American than I am. My great grandfather fought in the Revolution, my uncle fought in the Civil war, and my brother is 'over there' now."[159] Just as African American men had used their participation in World War I and previous wars to argue for equal citizenship, we see Joanna claiming her rights as an American during a time of war. The Greenwich Village audience is persuaded; they applaud Joanna's emotional plea, and when the production moves to Broadway she is crowned a star. The narrator, however, points out that Joanna's acceptance in New York was not representative of the reception she might receive elsewhere in America; in fact, it could not have happened in any other part of America.[160] During the Harlem Renaissance, white New Yorkers were fascinated by the exotic black performer, but they still required African Americans to perform in blackface, to perform a version of the stereotypes created by white Americans. Fauset drew attention to the minstrel mask black performers had to wear for whites in a moving article she wrote for *The Crisis* on the minstrel Bert Williams. Fauset praised his ability to perform one role for whites while communicating a different message to his black audience. But she also condemned white America for refusing to accept his talent unless he wore blackface.[161] Similarly, in *There Is Confusion*, Fauset suggests that black performers are always required to wear a mask when they perform for white audiences. Joanna can only perform as a serious dancer if she assimilates whiteness, if she denies her cultural heritage. Joanna had believed she could master any step, adopt any strategy that would help her find a way around racial prejudice. By the end of the novel Joanna has come to realize that if performing whiteness is the price to pay for acceptance, then it is a price too high.[162]

Joanna's repeated expressions of race pride and professed ambivalence toward white society make clear that her growing sympathy for separatism is not simply an accommodation to segregation, but rather an expression of her developing black nationalism and feminism. Joanna's growing artistic success as a performer means that she is obliged to attend parties frequented by artistic whites and patronizing philanthropists. Joanna is not a "good mixer": "Following the natural reaction at this time of her racial group, she had tended to seek all her ideals among colored people and where these were lacking to create them for herself. Between them and herself the barrier was too impassable. Besides, it was women who had the real difficulties to overcome, disabilities of sex and of tradition."[163] Joanna's reaction to racially mixed parties draws parallels with Fauset's own well-known dislike for the parties hosted by Carl Van Vechten, the white critic and sponsor of black art. Fauset found him "very dull; it is amazing to me that he is able to draw about him the kind of people that he does."[164]

By the end of the novel, Joanna's experience of discrimination on account of her race and gender has extinguished her desire to perform for white Americans; she no longer believes in the possibility of bridging divisions between black and white Americans. When Peter, now her fiancé, asks her to give up her dancing career, Joanna responds immediately: "Of course, of course, I know it." While Joanna's decision has been read as an abandonment of her independence, a feminist betrayal, the narrator makes it clear that her decision is more complicated than that, and that we should view her decision within the context of her growing separation from white culture and a desire to work within and for the race.[165] Joanna will instead take up composition, thereby making an artistic contribution to black culture in which she will not have to perform on a minstrel stage for white audiences.[166] The passage immediately preceding this discussion about her career choice suggests that this is how we should see Joanna's decision: not a capitulation to her future husband, but the abandonment of any thought of integration into white America. Peter is telling Joanna of his friend who wants to leave America for France, but whose sister does not see why she should give up her home. The sister wants to believe that "It *is* my country even if my skin is black?" Responding to the story, Joanna declares: "If you're black in America, you have to renounce. But that's life too, Peter. You've got to renounce something—always." Peter agrees that you have to "make renunciations which life demands and you've got to make those involved in the clash of color."[167] And so *There Is Confusion* ends with the recapitulation of the struggle between the impulse to integrate and the need to renounce that impulse in favor of working within the race. For Joanna, the very act of pursuing or accepting separatist strategies dissolves her desire for integration into white American society altogether.

Joanna gives up her preferred career as a performer for white audiences in favor of making a contribution to black art. She is also able to spend time ensuring that her children grow up protected in a race-proud family. By contrast, Maggie is no longer dependent on a husband or marriage for her happiness or financial security. The unsung heroine of the novel, Maggie has been ignored in many feminist readings of Fauset, which have tended to focus only on the middle-class Joanna. In fact, in many ways Maggie is the more interesting female character in this story: she finds a way to race pride through her ambitious career. Unlike Joanna, however, Maggie's career is not concerned with performing for whites: she is a budding Madam Walker who aspires to create beautiful race-proud women in a manner consistent with black economic nationalist principles. Maggie, who starts off as Joanna's complete opposite (her ambition is a socially mobile marriage) ends up seeing success in terms of self-fulfillment, economic security, and a definite place in the black community. Maggie is frequently juxtaposed with Joanna, particularly by Peter, who at one point in the middle of the novel breaks with Joanna and becomes engaged to Maggie:

> She [Maggie] had a very charming, flattering air of deference, of dependence when she was out. It was singularly pleasing and yet puzzling to Peter. Joanna now was just as likely to cross the street as not, without waiting for a guiding hand, a protecting arm. If she had once visited a locality she knew quite as much about getting away from it as her escort. But Maggie was helpless, dependent.

Fauset takes pains to show us that Maggie was performing a version of black womanhood that she thought would please Peter. Although puzzled, Peter is far from displeased with the performance: "Strange when they were all growing up together he would have said she was quite as independent in her way as Joanna." Peter notes her successful hairdressing business which has brought her economic independence. But unlike Joanna, Maggie appears to be dependent on him. Although Peter is aware that he is watching and participating in a performance, it suits him to go along with it, and have Maggie cook, sew, and wait on him.[168]

Unlike Joanna, whose family can support her, Maggie's economic security, and that of her family, depends on her fulfillment of her latterly realized ambition as a hairdresser and businesswoman. It is working-class Maggie who is allowed to combine feminist goals with aspiring middle-class status and racial pride. Indeed, as Ann Ducille has pointed out, for all the criticism of Fauset and her bourgeois pretensions, working-class women are consistently drawn in sympathetic ways and are among the few characters to have happily-ever-after endings.[169] Motivated by the desire to look after her poor mother, who was left penniless when her husband died, Maggie takes a part-time course in hairdressing with a Madam Harkness. Maggie finds racial pride in black beauty and working for an astute, race-conscious black woman.[170] Having shaken off the fairy-tale belief that she could find happiness simply through a good marriage, Maggie discovers that "new-found independence was a source of the greatest joy. . . . She would stand on her own two feet, Maggie Ellersley, serene, independent, self-reliant."[171] Fauset does not privilege Maggie's experiences over that of the middle-class Marshall girls. But she is aware of and frequently alludes to the different circumstances within which Maggie has to operate, such as her exposure to the sexually threatening behavior of white men on the subway, as well as the violence of her former black husband (a "type" of man she meets only through her mother's need to take in lodgers to raise Maggie), experiences which the middle-class car-owning Marshall girls are not exposed to.[172] Maggie's race pride is also linked to her service as a canteen worker for the YMCA during World War I. Maggie's experiences serving the black soldiers stationed in France exposes her to American racism abroad. It also brings her into contact with Joanna's brother, who is serving as a soldier, and who is equally disillusioned with the idea of integration. Up until World War I, Philip has believed in the integrationist dream. His ambition had been to build an NAACP-type organization which would improve race relations. Having witnessed American racism during the war, however, he abandons his dream, and before he dies, marries the new serene Maggie.[173]

Many of the themes in *There Is Confusion* are echoed in Fauset's third novel, *The Chinaberry Tree* (1931). Again we see the interlinking of Fauset's central concerns: feminism, middle-class identity, and black cultural nationalism. In this novel, however, Fauset seems unconcerned with white society. The characters live in a predominantly black world, albeit one in which intrarace racism and concern for skin color and racial pride cause conflict. In *The Chinaberry Tree*, Fauset exposes the hypocrisy and double standards of black middle-class communities, particularly when it comes to their attitudes to women. The two central characters are Laurentine Strange and her cousin Melissa Paul. Laurentine is the product of a loving and lifelong, but illicit, relationship between her black mother, Sarah Strange, and a wealthy white local landowner, Colonel Halloway. Laurentine is not only "illegitimate" but "the child of a connection that all America frowns on" as well.[174] As such she sees herself as an "unauthentic" member of the race, and a bearer of her mother's "bad blood."[175] To make up for the bad blood she has inherited, Laurentine maintains an ultravirtuous reputation. She is "the epitome of all those virtues and restraints which colored men so arrogantly demand in the women they make their wives."[176] A beautiful, economically independent, and successful dressmaker who employs other women, Laurentine has her confidence undermined by a belief that she will never fall in love and get married, because no race-proud man would want to marry the daughter of "illegitimate" miscegenation. Her fears appear to be realized when she is let down by her first suitor, Phil Hackett. Phil drops his suit because he believes Laurentine's reputation is blemished by her mother's long affair with a white man, even though Laurentine herself has a reputation for being "as pure as snow, chaste as a nun."[177] She recognizes that Phil has behaved shabbily and that her heart will mend; nevertheless Laurentine is bitterly disappointed at his rejection:

> She was sick . . . for what could she expect? She would live like this always, seeing herself ripen, ripen—she was twenty-four, there were many years of cruel burning, unsatisfied life still before her. Yes she would ripen—some poet had said it— "ripen, fall and cease." It would be exactly as though she had never been; like a leaf, that had fallen too early; like a flower that some one had picked and deliberately thrown away, —no worse, had carelessly dropped to be trampled on, withered.[178]

Her disappointment owes more to the fact that she has recently become aware of her own sexuality. Rejected as an authentic African American, she begins to question her eligibility for womanhood. Laurentine eventually meets a race-proud doctor, Dr. Stephen Denleigh. Stephen is a "real" man who does not question her authenticity and is unconcerned with the circumstances of her birth. He believes that "biology transcends society" and rejects the local black community's obsession with heredity that serves to create race divisions.[179]

Providing a contrast to Laurentine's struggle for respectability is the mistakenly assured respectability of her cousin Melissa and her "pure" relationship with her secret suitor, Malory Forten. Melissa prides herself on her own legitimate birth and her relationship with Malory who she believes comes from a respectable family. In fact, Melissa is the product of an affair between her mother and Malory's father. Whereas Laurentine's mother pursued a relationship outside the race, Melissa finds one not only within the race, but in the family. Unaware of the brewing tragedy, Melissa also provides a contrast to Laurentine in her disregard for the past and embrace of the present. Melissa is presented as young and brimming with confidence. Whereas Laurentine, who is still only twenty-four, is worrying that she will soon "ripen, cease and fall," Melissa "had the modern girl's own clear ideas on birth control."[180] As her relationship with Malory develops, however, Melissa becomes increasingly concerned with Malory's restrictive views about women's proper sphere. Malory's views about women are revealed when he sees Melissa dancing with a male friend at a Christmas party.[181] Malory's reaction is part jealousy and part disapproval that his girl would express her sexuality through her dancing: "I'm telling you again, I didn't like your dancing that vulgar dance. That sort of thing isn't er—well, Melissa it just isn't the kind of thing I like from a girl whom I'm expecting to be my wife." The narrator is critical of Malory's expectations of how women he would marry should behave. Melissa is stunned by his reaction.[182] Malory tries to explain his feelings to Melissa: "there's just a streak in me that makes me want my girl to be super—that's all there is to it. It's not jealousy exactly. I don't seem to want her to be looked at, or talked about—I guess in my mind I sort of want her to be quiet, almost mousy."[183] Melissa is beginning to realize she might not share the same vision of black womanhood as her suitor; she thought Malory loved her because of her liveliness, not in spite of it.

In *The Chinaberry Tree* Fauset also contrasts the standards that black men apply to the idolized domestic woman, with their own sexual behavior toward women they could access outside marriage. Fauset compares Melissa's behavior with that of Gertrude Brown, a sophisticated Brown University freshman, straight out of flapper school, who has come home for the Christmas holiday. With a boldness that Malory would deplore in a woman whom he would be prepared to make his wife, Gertrude makes a direct play for Malory, inviting him around for dinner at the family home. After dinner Gertrude smokes a cigarette, and Malory, who "was not quite sure that he liked to see women smoke," soon realizes that "Gertrude did her smoking as she seemed to do everything, easily, naturally."[184] Malory, it seems, has different expectations of the woman he would be prepared to marry. Although sexually attracted to the confident and sophisticated Gertrude, Malory guiltily runs off to visit Melissa and is comforted by what he regards as her dependence. Malory is reassured when he compares Melissa to Gertrude, "Melissa, now . . . gave no promise of possessing or ever succeeding to a similar development. She would never be a finished product he would always have to mould her and shape her. Not that that in the deeper inner consciousness of the true male was so undesirable. After all she was really very dear." Melissa's "dearness" is compounded by her lack of worldly knowledge, and this apparent helplessness overwhelms Malory in his desire to protect and shape her.[185]

Melissa's concern grows with her increasing understanding of how Malory's gender politics informs his ideas about race respectability, authenticity, and legitimacy. Having made up her mind to tell Malory about Laurentine's "illegitimacy," Melissa sees, in a critical way, Malory's views on women and race: "it [her confession] might bring with it an enveloping tarnish—she might not appear so *white,* so desirable in her lover's eyes. Malory, she knew, wanted his roses dewy, his woman's reputation, not to say her virtue, unblemished and undiscussed" (emphasis added).[186] Fauset's connection of race and womanhood here is significant. By her membership in a family whose name is tarnished with illicit sexual affairs with a white man, Melissa's capacity to correspond to Malory's image of true (white) womanhood is diminished. One of the essentials of the true woman was her virtue, which should indeed be "unblemished" (uncolored) and "undiscussed."[187] When Malory discovers the truth of Laurentine's birth, his reaction reminds us of Marcus Garvey's idealization of black women: "Every fellow does want his wife to be on a pedestal; he'd like to think of her as a little inviolate shrine that isn't ever touched by the things in the world that are ugly and sordid."[188] No longer on a pedestal, untouched by worldly matters, Melissa no longer appears so "white." Here Fauset shows the relationship among gender roles, race, and respectability. As in *There Is Confusion*, Fauset demonstrates how those who challenged gendered expectations have their racialized identity questioned.

Whereas Malory questions the virtue and racial identity of women who express their sexuality in ways he disapproves of, Fauset turns this link on its head. Her characterization of Malory explicitly challenges his right to decide for anyone what constitutes authentic race pride and behavior. He is depicted as lacking in race pride and manliness. The narrator tells us that Malory "had absolutely no feeling about color." Malory is presented as individualistic and selfish. He does not suffer from racial discrimination, since "Of his own racial group he belonged to the cream." While he is not rich, he is of the right "birth, gentility, decency," that is, light-skinned. Fauset is critical of his complacency; his light skin creates a lack of awareness of what it means to be African American in a racist white American society. His lack of race pride is underscored by his effeminacy and his attitude toward women.[189] In Malory, Fauset constructs an image of the dandy, reminding us of the *Negro World* reporter's characterization of the NAACP worker as a Beau Brummel. Just as Jacques Garvey effeminized those male Garveyites whose fitness for race leadership she doubted, Fauset often effeminizes Malory, whom she describes as having a "slight, rather delicate figure," a "low voice," "unobtrusive, perfect manners," and "neat, inconspicuous clothes."[190] At the age of twenty he lives in a household of withered old women who try to smother him. He is contrasted with Melissa's other, more "manly" suitor, Asshur. Dark-skinned Asshur wants to be a scientific farmer, farming being "an essential industry" that requires an outdoor relationship with nature. While Melissa favors Malory, she cannot help but admire Asshur's manliness: "an effect of daring and more important still the promise of great loyalty." Malory, on the other hand, "was not especially daring or breezy."[191] Ultimately those men, Steven and Asshur, who accept black women as they are, and do not try to impose their own standards on them, are presented as the most racially proud and manly. In contrast, men who question the authenticity and racial pride of black women are presented by Fauset as being effeminate and lacking in pride themselves.

Throughout Fauset's novels there is a high tension between trying to work within white America and with white Americans, and remaining true to an "authentic" racial identity, whether on the stage, or even in the theater of war. Gender often plays a key role in determining how racial identity is performed and understood. Ultimately, Fauset's characters are scarred by their experiences of working with whites, and the novels carry a warning about close association with white Americans. Yet it is not surprising that critics have read integrationist messages in Fauset's work, since their assessments have so often rested on their understanding of Fauset as an integrationist herself. Fauset worked for many years for the NAACP, an organization committed to improving race relations in the United States. But she was also committed to the pan-African movement, believing in the common plight and shared heritage of peoples of African descent. Like many of the African American women with whom she networked, Fauset was aware of the possible tensions between her American identity and an international, pan-African identity. Both Fauset's pan-African political activities and her work for interracial groups need to be integrated into readings of her work to allow us to see that Fauset does not have to be either an integrationist or a black nationalist; both exist as workable strategies for Fauset and her characters.

Fauset's novels explore the connections between gender, race, and class. Within these often unstable categories, Fauset's characters in *There Is Confusion* and *The Chinaberry Tree* endeavor to build self-respect and an assured sense of themselves as independent black women away from the white world. Fauset herself had long believed in the importance of doing just this. In a letter she wrote to Du Bois in 1905, she argued that it was crucial for African Americans to have "race pride, self-pride and self-sufficiency." For Fauset, these were important values for African Americans not because they were white standards, but because they were the best criteria by which black Americans should measure themselves. Fauset believed that African Americans should understand "the necessity of living our lives as nearly as possible, absolutely, instead of comparing them always with white standards." In this early letter Fauset expressed her dual belief in racial separatism and ultimate integration. In the immediate future, African Americans should rely on themselves and other peoples of African descent; they should be self-sufficient, and serve both the cause of black nationalist pride and ultimate integration. Building communities based on the values of African Americans rather than whites "would in the end breed self-dependence and self-respect, and subjective respect means always sooner or later an outcome of objective respect."[192]

There is no evidence that Fauset and Jacques Garvey knew each other personally, but as the right-hand women of Harlem's most notorious rivals they undoubtedly knew of each other, and likely read each other's work. Both used their position as editors of widely circulating black publications to promote their own brand of a feminist-based pan-Africanism. While Jacques Garvey relied mainly on her weekly editorials to promulgate her views, Fauset used her novels as well as her power to put other women into print. In the mid-1920s Jessie Fauset and Amy Jacques Garvey were developing the black feminist thought of earlier clubwomen and race activists and expressing in a written form their consciousness of the need to find a way of working in and beyond a racial framework that seemed to demand loyalty either to integrationism or black nationalism. Nor were they alone; other black women played prominent roles in both the Harlem Renaissance and the UNIA. For example, the sculptress Augusta Savage, who was married to Robert Poston, a prominent Garveyite, carved busts of both Marcus Garvey and W. E. B. Du Bois, while Zora Neale Hurston started her career writing for the *Negro World*.[193]

Like Fauset, Amy Jacques Garvey was well aware that black separatism could not exist alone as a viable strategy for dealing with American racism. Indeed, the Garvey movement's "Back to Africa" rhetoric was, in part, a strategy to achieve civil rights for black Americans at home. The Declaration of the Rights of Negroes of 1920, which sets out the tenets and philosophies of the UNIA, included a demand that all forms of segregation against men and women of African descent be ended, including in housing, transport, education, and voting privileges.[194] This did not mean that Garveyites did not support voluntary black separatism and pan-African race solidarity, but that they recognized that these two strategies were dependent on each other for their success. As Jacques Garvey later explained:

> Interaction of the minority race group into all phases of the life of the nation will be a national victory, hastened to its climax by international opinion regarding the treatment accorded Negroes as the barometer of American democracy; but in the years to come, the practical realization will be absorption. Lacking the prestige of a Greater Liberia nation of their own in the motherland, it will turn out to be a hollow victory. Garveyism planned that the units should complement each other and demonstrate to a skeptical world the ability of colored Americans not only to fight for their rights in the land of their birth but also to venture forth to Africa and build and man their own democratic nation.[195]

Epilogue

In December 1921 Alice Woodby McKane, M.D., wrote a letter to Herbert J. Seligmann, the Jewish author and journalist who worked on publicity for the NAACP. McKane was writing in protest against Seligmann's article for the *New York Age* in which he had criticized Marcus Garvey. At the heart of McKane's complaint lay a frustration with those who tried to insist that there was only one solution, approach, or organization that could solve America's race problem. For McKane, it was imperative that black Americans adopt the best of several strategies rather than limiting themselves to the ideas of one group:

> In the first place I claim membership in the Boston Branch of the N.A.A.C.P., the National Equal Rights League, and the U.N.I.A. A queer mixture you will no doubt say, but the contention to myself is that in each I see some good for the betterment of the race with which I am identified; and I therefore wish to add my small quota to each for not one alone of all three, to my way of thinking, cover the need.

McKane believed that African Americans' desire to work both independently of and at other times in cooperation with whites reflected their dual heritage:

> Many of us think in black of the black because that ancestral blood is in our veins. I am one of those, and I desire to see Africa preserved for Africans. . . . I therefore welcome Mr Garvey and what I call his constructive endeavour to better the black man's conditions here and there. I have also another racial blood in me, the American Indian, and that coupled with the fact that I was born here and that my ancestors both red and black have fought for all that American Civilization holds dear, makes me feel that no one has a better right to enjoy the rights and privileges here than I and my kind; therefore, I contend for all the rights and privileges on that ground.[1]

Although the civil rights movement might provide a salary and career for some, McKane pointed out that many civil rights activists worked as volunteers, in low-status positions because they believed in a cause. This letter from a grass-roots activist reveals what race leaders and salaried officers of national organizations were inclined to forget: that it was not a choice between working independently of whites or working with whites, but rather that both strategies were part of the solution to the race problem. Leaders and officers of the NAACP and UNIA, however, often believed that their membership should pledge themselves to only one approach. Garvey recognized and condemned this overlap in organizational membership when he banned joint membership of the UNIA and NAACP amidst the height of *The Crisis*' campaign against his organization.[2]

By contrast, black women's organizations relied on crossover and joint membership of the numerous organizations which they created. Black women's networks were incredibly important in sustaining individuals and organizations through years of change in the early twentieth century. At a time when many hotels and accommodations across the United States were segregated, the homes and workplaces of these women served as meeting places and havens from discrimination. These networks encouraged women who were acquaintances or colleagues to become friends and allies, and they supported each other's projects when times were hard. Many of these networks were sustained through involvement with umbrella organizations such as the NACW and the YWCA as well as the literary networks that formed around publications such as *The Crisis* and the *Negro World*. The Colored Branch of the YWCA in New York City, though an affiliated branch of an interracial organization, became the central meeting place for black women looking to promote new ideas, organizations, and survival strategies in the early years of the Depression. These organizations facilitated a mentoring system that functioned across generational networks. For example, when the uninitiated Bethune first came to the 1912 NACW convention, Addie Hunton, who had been present at the founding of the NACW, took Bethune under her wing and became her mentor. In return, Bethune later guided Hunton's daughter, Eunice Hunton Carter, whom she had picked out while working for the Colored Branch in New York. Carter went on to become a founding member of Bethune's NCNW, for which she later acted as legal advisor, chair of the board of trustees, and accredited observer at the United Nations.[3] Dorothy Height was also selected by Bethune while working for the Colored Branch of the YWCA in Harlem.[4] These networks also responded to change and encouraged the creation of new organizations as older, established ones became defunct. The new organizations increasingly reflected the diversity of women's experiences. While the NACW continued to exert an important presence on black women's organizational life up until the early 1930s, other black women's organizations were able to respond more quickly to the economic and political changes that had transformed black communities by that time: the migration of African Americans to the North and to urban centers, women's suffrage and the increased political involvement of African Americans in electoral politics in the North, the relentlessness of southern segregation, and the flowering of the Harlem Renaissance. These developments meant that by the 1930s, new black women's organizations increasingly based themselves in formal headquarters in New York City or Washington, D.C., rather than in the hometown or school base of their leader.

Besides providing practical support for each other, black women activists supported each other intellectually. While many of them might not have described themselves as feminists, this book has demonstrated that much of what they did would later come to be accepted as characteristic of black feminist thought. This is evident in the organizational networks and cultural productions of these race women which stressed the importance of self-definition, the interconnectedness of race, gender, and class as sources of oppression, the close connections between intellectual and practical endeavors, and an awareness of the legacy of past struggle.[5] Black clubwomen in the early twentieth century recognized that they had both a right and an obligation to define black womanhood for themselves. Indeed it had been the attacks of white men on the reputation of black womanhood that had prompted black women to form the NACW.[6] At the same time, black women had to contend with black men who tried to keep them from leadership within race organizations. Resisting, on the one hand, white images of black women as sexually immoral, and on the other, black men's positioning of their women on the domestic pedestal, black women both engaged in the discourse of respectability and used the language of black masculinity in order to find a space for their own voice. Working with white women and at other times with black men meant that black women had to learn how to speak their languages. This does not mean they accepted their values. Using the discourse of respectability and masculinity to address their different audiences, black women were able to articulate an alternative vision of black womanhood, in which black women were race proud, race workers, and above all, race leaders. At the same time they used a variety of other mechanisms—journals, parades, conventions, literature, grand buildings, the black body itself—to create and disseminate positive images of black women.

Black women leaders were aware of the multiple jeopardy that confronted early-twentieth-century black women. Although the failure of whites to differentiate among African Americans caused some black women to emphasize class differentiation, many black women reformers believed in the NACW's motto of "lifting as we climb." Few black women leaders had climbed so far that they were unfamiliar with what it felt like at the bottom. Furthermore the resoluteness of white racism in the early twentieth century meant that the black middle classes became increasingly reliant on and closer to their poorer sisters.[7] As Margaret Washington explained, "We cannot separate ourselves from our people, no matter how much we try; for one, I have no desire to do so."[8] As Linda Gordon argues, black women, in comparison to white women, "were more focused on their own kind. . . . there was less chronological distance, for all their privileges were so recent and so tenuous."[9] The unstable nature of middle-class status among black Americans meant they were only too aware of class as a source of oppression. The diaries of Alice Dunbar-Nelson and letters of Georgia Douglas Johnson reveal how their desperate need to find money to cover even basic household expenses played no small part in motivating them to write plays and poetry.[10] Jessie Fauset's correspondence is also marked by an awareness of her financial vulnerability, not least because she frequently could not afford vital medical treatment.[11] As Chapter 4 shows, Fauset explored the interconnectedness of race, gender, and class through her depiction of the working women in her novels. In her portrayal of Maggie Ellersley as a Madam Walker agent and hairdresser, Fauset suggests that for Maggie a career was not simply an answer to feminist ambition or race pride, but an economic necessity. The social reformers who worked within the YWCA were more than aware that many of the young women and girls who flocked to the 137th Street Y came for jobs, food, and shelter, rather than spiritual uplift, and so they offered employment bureaus, adult education, and a community.[12]

As we have seen, the notion of a black middle-class in this period is problematic, since the nature of jobs available to most African Americans means that a Marxist understanding of class that relates to control of the means of production reveals little about African American class differences. Moreover, the class status of black American women frequently changed through their lifetime. The daughters of slaves, Mary McLeod Bethune and Madam Walker came to be the most powerful black women of their generation. Meanwhile, Madam Walker and Nannie Helen Burroughs worked hard to improve the status of those occupations available to black women, such as hairdressing and domestic service. Those histories of black leadership that have sought to redress this problem have attempted to define middle-class in relation to an "ideology of racial uplift" or a "politics of respectability" rather than to occupational status.[13] Yet this study has demonstrated that black men and women attached diverse and complex meanings to respectability and racial uplift, according to their gender, education, and ethnic background. What is more, definitions of class based on values need to take account of the fact that middle-class ideologies were not formed in a vacuum and sometimes were endorsed by men and women from all socio-economic groups.[14] This is not to say that class divisions among African American women in the early twentieth century did not exist, or were not important, but rather that class definitions and boundaries were fluid. They were also connected to constructions of gender and racial identity, as well as attitudes to work. While class itself could not be defined by traditional occupational status, work was an important definer of racial pride, and therefore status. One measure of the status of an African American woman's job was its distance from direct supervision by whites, and the extent to which she was working for herself and for black Americans.[15] Walker and her daughter A'Lelia encouraged black women to reject the role assigned them by whites and assert their own image of black women workers. By taking pride in work that was done for other African Americans—be it hairdressing, small businesses that employed a handful of blacks, or schools that turned our thousands of black Americans with a knowledge of their past—women like Madam Walker blurred the lines between working for yourself and working for the race.

Black women leaders promoted race pride by celebrating their collective past. Their race pride was most often displayed through their awareness of the achievements of African Americans, particularly women, who had come before them. Fauset and Jacques Garvey also used their editorial positions to promote race pride through reviewing black historical works, writing articles about famous black women, and highlighting the work of their contemporaries. NACW conventions also devoted considerable time, energy, and financial resources to memorializing the achievements of African Americans. Many of their campaigns centered on the raising of funds to restore some of the most important sites in black historical memory. The successful campaign to purchase and restore Frederick Douglass's home in Anacostia was one of their proudest achievements, and fulfilled many of the goals of the NACW: black women working together to celebrate their past and have control over their future. Similarly, the NACW devoted considerable energy toward a memorial fund for Booker T. Washington. Reflecting a belief in the importance of culture, and particularly oral history, the NACW also celebrated the history of black Americans through regular performances of historical pageants.[16] Many of these same clubwomen brought their enthusiasm and pride in black history into the ICWDR. Members of the ICWDR insisted on the importance of collective and shared knowledge of Diasporic Africans, so they not only studied the conditions of women in the developing world and women of African descent, but promoted black studies in public schools and became members of Carter G. Woodson's Association for the Study of Negro Life and History.[17]

Another core belief shared by these activists is that they all presumed a connection between their intellectual development and their practical activism. Jacques Garvey urged black women to promote black women's rights in both literary and practical endeavor so that they would be able to make the world listen and understand that "Negro women are great thinkers as well as doers."[18] While later black twentieth-century feminists have taken pains to point out the importance of black feminist academics being doers as well as thinkers, this book has demonstrated that black women thinkers in the early twentieth century were, with few exceptions, also activists. Fauset and Jacques Garvey played practical roles in pan-African and black nationalist movements, and many activists also wrote fiction, poetry, journalism, and plays in which they outlined their views on women's rights and the race struggle. Margaret Murray Washington, Alice Dunbar-Nelson, Addie Hunton, Mary Church Terrell, Georgia Douglas Johnson, Augusta Savage, and Marita Bonner, all combined careers as race and women's activists with careers in journalism, playwriting, and other cultural media. Similarly, Madam Walker used the speeches she delivered at churches, to clubwomen conventions, and before race organizations and Walker agents to delineate her feminist and economic nationalist viewpoint. Her advertisements demonstrate her clear understanding of the link between her feminist outlook and business interests. Contemporary black feminism is indebted to the insights, organizational activities, successes, and failures of black feminist activists in the early twentieth century. The importance of self-definition, the interconnectedness of gender, race, and class, the link between intellectual and practical endeavor, and an awareness of the legacy of past struggle were later articulated by scholars such as Patricia Hill Collins and bell hooks as the central tenets of a black feminist theoretical framework.[19] Like their forebears, black feminists have continued to form new and separate black women's organizations, including the National Black Feminist Organization founded in 1973 and the Association of Black Women Historians, while also trying to influence the agendas of organizations like the National Organization for Women and the National Women's Studies Association.

By focusing on the careers and organizational activities of race women, this study demonstrates the variety and complexity of strategies used to tackle race and gender discrimination in the first four decades of the twentieth century. Although black women worked in both interracial and black women's organizations, by the 1930s their experiences of interracial work caused many to question the desirability of integration, since the world envisioned by white feminists, and indeed some black men, was not necessarily one they wanted to share. By the time the National YWCA signed the Interracial Charter in 1946, many stalwarts of the black YWCA movement, including Eva Bowles, Addie Hunton, Cecelia Cabaniss Saunders, and Anna Hedgeman, had resigned because they felt there was no role for them within an integrated YWCA.[20] While many black Y workers recognized that integration was unlikely to be implemented in a way that brought real benefits to African Americans, and would diminish African American women's leadership opportunities, some believed that this was nevertheless a price worth paying. Fannie Pitt Byrd, a staff member of the Harlem YWCA, believed that "[Principle] rather than expediency must be [the] golden rule. . . . We must give up what may be some 'advantages' of segregation for the slower process of integration."[21] But the process of integration was too slow. Although the YWCA finally adopted the Interracial Charter in 1946, its impact in the South was to allow black branches to be formed in areas where white women had previously opposed their presence. Born of the Interracial Charter, these black branches ironically became important power bases for black women in the 1940s and 1950s. They would be made obsolete when another move toward integration occurred in the 1970s.[22] Other black women continued to see the expediency in working within separate units in interracial organizations. This ability to work with whites in order to take advantage of the greater resources at their disposal would be adapted when traditional voluntary sector work fell increasingly under the auspices of the federal government. In the New Deal era, black women like Bethune tolerated segregation, insisted on black direction of black programs, and fought for equal resources for black men and women. They drew on their years of experiences in interracial organizations and on their club networks to find ways in which to influence white American politics.

Black women also continued to organize with black men and to play a role in contesting and shaping black nationalism. Although black women experienced gender oppression within black separatist movements, they persisted in their promotion of a feminist agenda within these movements. Jacques Garvey promoted feminist black nationalism both in the United States and, from 1928 onwards, in her homeland, Jamaica. She produced numerous new editions of Garvey's *Philosophies and Opinions,* and published and distributed her memoir, *Garvey and Garveyism.* She also encouraged study of the Garvey movement by availing herself and her collections to a new wave of Garvey scholars from the 1960s onwards.[23] Jacques Garvey's continued practical involvement in the Pan-African Congress movement, and her publication of feminist articles in the United States and Jamaica until her death, also testified to her indefatigable commitment to feminist black nationalism.[24] Along with Nannie Burroughs and Jessie Fauset, Jacques Garvey contributed toward a feminist vision of black nationalism. As this study has shown, Burroughs, Jacques Garvey, and Fauset employed the language of black masculinity in ways which helped them to assert their own vision of black women as leaders. Through finding a place for feminism within black nationalism, they helped other black women to understand and define their black feminist nationalist consciousness. For example, Anna Arnold Hedgeman, the black YWCA worker who joined the Colored Branch in Harlem to escape whites, was initially unable to name her separatist leanings. It was only later that she realized they were akin to what she would later call nationalism: "although the word 'nationalism' was not in my vocabulary, I knew that somehow the great talent and spirit of Negroes must be developed into a unified voice to demand not alms, but its birthright."[25]

Black women questioned whether integration was a desirable end in itself. Addie Hunton, who left the YWCA but continued to work for the NAACP, warned the latter organization that "unless we speedily build a bridge of justice and cooperation the chasm of misunderstanding and distrust may become too wide to be spanned, thus making possible terrible cataclysms."[26] Burroughs, who had always argued that integration for its own sake was meaningless, explained that African Americans had to ask themselves "Where is the Negro going and what is he going to do when he gets there?" Was integration a feasible option if, like Burroughs, you believed that the materialism of the United States was such that "America will destroy herself and revert to barbarism if she continues to cultivate the things of the flesh and neglect the higher virtues"?[27] While some black women questioned integration on ideological grounds, others saw the strategic value of black separatism. Whether black nationalism was primarily of strategic or ideological importance is, however, a difficult question. In a segregated society, where black men and women had to mask their motives and understood race as a double-voiced discourse, it is difficult to ascertain where their ideal lay.[28] It is not all that easy to separate strategic from ideological black nationalism, since this group of black women could only work within the segregated American society which they knew, and it is possible that many African American leaders pursued whichever strategy worked best at the time. That is not to say that strategic maneuvering always or even predominately overrode the ideological beliefs of these women. Indeed, for some, the process of using black nationalist strategies and working together as black women in separate organizations made ideological converts of them. As Anna Hedgeman explained, after years of working with other black women and at other times with racist white women, it was natural to put up "a wall of separation. . . . I was . . . through with white people." Fauset's heroines also construct a wall of separation between themselves and white people. They ultimately become more interested in bridging divisions within the race rather than between blacks and whites. In *There Is Confusion*, Joanna Marshall wants ideally to be part of a fully integrated white America. Through the process of working with racist whites, however, Joanna realizes that the world is far from ideal, and comes to believe that a separatist strategy offers the best means of solving the race problem. But in the process of pursuing a separatist strategy Joanna comes to believe in separatism for ideological reasons too; the integration she has experienced requires a loss of identity and an assimilation of whiteness, a price too high to pay.

African Americans continued to interrogate the meaning and importance of integration when the Supreme Court handed down its *Brown v. Board of Education* ruling compelling the integration of public-school education in 1954. As Zora Neale Hurston explained, it was not so much a question of eschewing integrationism, since she could not as an African American be in favor of enforced segregation. Rather, it was difficult to want to be with whites who did not want to be with her, since "physical contact means nothing unless the spirit is there."[29] Neither could she entirely welcome the implications for race pride that the acceptance of integration seemed to carry: "It is a contradiction in terms to scream race pride and equality while at the same time spurning Negro teachers and self-association."[30] For Hurston, integration was all very well if it improved the schooling of African American children and the wages of African American teachers and encouraged race pride. The jury was divided on whether this would be the case. Hurston's skepticism was both in keeping with ideas of an earlier generation of black women and prescient of future disillusionment on the part of African American leaders following the civil rights movement, as to whether integration was really the panacea to America's race problem.

Notes

Introduction

1. *Pittsburgh Courier,* January 13, 1943. Rogers's own journalistic career belies the notion of a dichotomous opposition between integrationism and black nationalism. He contributed articles to both the *Negro World* and *The Crisis*. Turner, "Joel Augustus Rogers," 35–38; Boyd, *Wrapped in Rainbows,* 366.

2. Alice Dunbar-Nelson wrote a women's column for the *Pittsburgh Courier* in 1926 and 1930; Jessie Fauset was literary editor of *The Crisis* from 1919 to 1926.

3. Madam Walker to F. B. Ransom, March 20, 1919, box 1, MWC-IHS.

4. *Walker News,* September 1931; Codicil to the Last Will and Testament of Sarah Walker and the Court's Construction Thereof, item 4, p.3, box 3, MWC-IHS.

5. Wolcott, *Remaking Respectability*; Mitchell, *Righteous Propaganda*.

6. John Cell and Adam Fairclough actually have three camps: separatism, accommodationism, and militant confrontation. See Cell, *The Highest Stage of White Supremacy,* 257–62, and Fairclough, *Better Day Coming,* xiii.

7. Adeleke, *Without Regard to Race*; Vela, "The Washington–Du Bois Controversy." For a critique of historians who stuck to this integrationist narrative, see Marable, *Race, Reform, Rebellion,* 59–63. For an account that revises the Washington-versus-Du Bois dichotomy, see Meier and Rudwick, "The Boycott Movement against Jim Crow Streetcars," 756–63. See Tyson, "Robert F. Williams," for revision of black power versus civil rights.

8. Du Bois, *Souls of Black Folk,* 615.

9. Du Bois, *Dusk of Dawn,* 199

10. Johnson, *Negro Americans, What Now?* 12.

11. Cruse, *Crisis of the Negro Intellectual,* 564.

12. Gayle, "Black Aesthetic," 1870–1877; Jones, "Myth of a Negro Literature," 293–301.

13. See, for example, Bone, *Negro Novel in America,* 102; Davis, *From the Dark Tower,* 90; Cash, *African American Women and Social Action,* 9–10.

14. Moses, *Golden Age of Black Nationalism,* 10; Stuckey, *Slave Culture,* 225.

15. Stuckey, *Slave Culture*; Moses, *Golden Age of Black Nationalism*; Adeleke, *UnAfrican Americans* and *Without Regard to Race*.

16. Hobsbawm, "Ethnicity and Nationalism in Europe Today," 3.

17. Anderson, *Imagined Communities*; Lemelle and Kelley, "Introduction: Imagining Home"; Tate, "Prophesy and Transformation," 211–12; Adeleke, *UnAfrican Americans*.

18. Hobsbawm, *Nations and Nationalism since 1870*, 130; Sluga, "Female and National Self-Determination," 495–521. See also Jayawardena, *Feminism and Nationalism in the Third World*.

19. Rhodes, *Mary Ann Shadd Cary*, 87

20. Ibid., 217–218.

21. See, for example, Marable, "Groundings with My Sisters," 19–20.

22. Pateman, *The Sexual Contract*, 4; Yuval-Davis, *Gender and Nation*, 2.

23. Gilroy, *Black Atlantic*, 25.

24. Molefi Kete Asante views Delaney as a founding father of Africological thought. See Gilroy, *Black Atlantic*, 20, and Asante, *Kernet, Afrocentricity, and Knowledge*, 112.

25. Carby, *Race Men*, 13.

26. Hobsbawm, *Nations and Nationalism since 1870*; Smith, *Ethnic Origins of Nations*; Bracey, Meier, and Rudwick, eds., *Black Nationalism in America*; Gilroy, *Black Atlantic*. For more recent accounts, see Adeleke, *UnAfrican Americans*, and Lawrence, *Nationalism: History and Theory*.

27. Mitchell, *Righteous Propaganda*; Taylor, *Veiled Garvey*. Also see Stephens, *Black Empire*.

28. Woolf, *Three Guineas*, 107–9.

29. West, "Introduction: Feminism Constructs Nationalism," xiii.

30. Enloe, *Bananas, Beaches, and Bases*, 42, 44. See also Yuval-Davis, *Gender and Nation*, 117–18; Jayawardena, *Feminism and Nationalism in the Third World*.

31. West, "Introduction: Feminism Constructs Nationalism," xxx.

32. For women in the Nation of Islam, see Taylor, "As-Salaam Alaikum," 177–96; West, "Nation Builders." For the sexual politics of the Garvey movement, see Mitchell, *Righteous Propaganda*; for feminist nationalism in India, see Sarkar, *Hindu Wife, Hindu Nation*, and in former nation-states, see Mexnaric, "Gender as an Ethno-Marker," 76–97; for the developing world, see Jayawardena, *Feminism and Nationalism in the Third World*; for collections that compare feminist nationalism around the world, see West, ed., *Feminist Nationalism*. See also the special issue on "Gender and Nationalism," in *Nations and Nationalism* 6 (4) 2000: 491–638.

33. Collins, *Black Feminist Thought*, 22–33.

34. Hewitt, "Beyond the Search for Sisterhood."

35. Hunter, *To Joy My Freedom*; Davis, *Blues Legacies and Black Feminism*.

36. Baker, *Blues, Ideology, and Afro-American Literature*.

37. Ducille, "Blues Notes on Black Sexuality," 194.

38. Wall, "Passing for What?" 87–103; Carby, *Reconstructing Womanhood*, 163–75; Jones, "Myth of a Negro Literature," 294.

39. For an example of this broad use of the term *middle class*, see Lemke, introduction to *Lifting As They Climb*.

40. Gilmore, *Gender and Jim Crow*, xviii; Gaines, *Uplifting the Race*, 246, 259; Mitchell, *Righteous Propaganda*; Carby, *Race Men*.

41. Harley, "When Your Work Is Not Who You Are," 25; Gaines, *Uplifting the Race*, 13–17; Summers, *Manliness and Its Discontents*, 6–7.

42. Wolcott, "Bible, Bath, and Broom," 105. See also Shaw, *What a Woman Ought to Be and Do,* 13–103. See Chapter 1 for further discussion.

43. Wolcott, *Remaking Respectability,* 7. For the view that black clubwomen imposed "middle-class" notions of respectability on their less fortunate sisters, see White, "The Cost of Club Work." Davis, though sympathetic to clubwomen's defense of their sexual respectability argues that this strategy denied black women sexual agency. Davis, *Blues Legacies,* 43–44. Also see Higginbotham, "African-American Women's History and the Metalanguage of Race," 272.

44. For a discussion of the term *race woman,* see Higginbotham, "African-American Women's History and the Metalanguage of Race," 267.

45. West, *Caring for Justice,* 88–93; Foreman, "Looking Back from Zora"; Evans, "Women's History and Political Theory," 119–39.

46. See Chapter 4 for a more detailed discussion on feminists and their private lives.

47. Walby, "Is Citizenship Gendered?" 383; Yuval-Davis, *Gender and Nation,* 80.

48. Collins, *Black Feminist Thought,* 31.

Chapter 1. Laying the Groundwork: Washington, Burroughs, Bethune, and the Clubwomen's Movement

1. Giddings, *When and Where I Enter,* 95. For the history of the founding of the NACW, see Shaw, "Black Club Women and the Creation of the National Association of Club Women."

2. *National Notes,* January 1899.

3. Smith, "The Larger Life for the Woman," *National Notes,* May-June 1915.

4. Kay, "A Woman in a New World," *National Notes,* May-June 1915

5. Hanson, *Mary McLeod Bethune,* 100. For other historians who subscribe to this view, see Lemke, introduction to *Lifting As They Climb;* White, *Too Heavy a Load;* Cash, *African American Women and Social Action,* 8.

6. Cash, *African American Women and Social Action,* 9–10.

7. Wall, "Passing for What?" 87–103, and Christian, *Black Feminist Criticism,* 173. For a challenge to the middle-class clubwomen versus sexually liberated blues woman dichotomy, see Batker, "Love Me Like I Like to Be," 199–213.

8. See, for example, White, *Too Heavy a Load,* especially Chapters 1 and 3.

9. For use of the term *mistrissism,* see White, *Too Heavy a Load.* For excellent accounts of individual clubwomen, see Harley, "Nannie Helen Burroughs," 62–71; Rouse, "Out of the Shadow of Tuskegee," 31–46; Rouse, *Lugenia Burns Hope.* Accounts that place clubwomen within the context of social welfare activism include Gordon, "Black and White Visions of Welfare"; Wolcott, *Remaking Respectability;* Smith, *Sick and Tired of Being Sick and Tired;* Shaw, *What a Woman Ought to Be and to Do;* Lasch-Quinn, *Black Neighbors.*

10. Wolcott, *Remaking Respectability;* Shaw, *What a Woman Ought to Be and to Do.*

11. Rouse, "Out of the Shadow of Tuskegee," 42. Scholars who take Washington's marriage to Booker as a starting point for her inevitable conservatism include White, *Too Heavy a Load,* 50; Giddings, *When and Where I Enter,* 104, 111; Guy-Sheftall, *Daughters*

of Sorrow, 57. Many accounts have indexed under Margaret Washington, "conservatism." See White, *Too Heavy a Load*, and Bair, "Pan Africanism as Process," 121–44.

12. Lane, *A Documentary History of Mrs. Booker T. Washington*, 95–96, 99–100. The Washington–Du Bois conflict continues to fascinate scholars. See, for example, Moore, *Booker T. Washington, W. E. B. Du Bois, and the Struggle for Racial Uplift*.

13. Emmet J. Scott, "Margaret Murray Washington," *Ladies Home Journal*, May 1907, in *BTW Papers*, 9:289–90; Rouse, "Out of the Shadow of Tuskegee," 31. For more biographical information on Washington, see Lane, *Documentary History of Mrs. Booker T. Washington*, 19–33.

14. Scott, "Margaret Murray Washington," in *Ladies Home Journal*, May 1907, in *BTW Papers*, 9:289–90; Rouse, "Out of the Shadow of Tuskegee," 31.

15. Neverdon-Morton, "Self-Help Programs," 210.

16. Margaret James Murray to Booker T. Washington, July 1892, *BTW Papers*, 3:254.

17. See, for example, William G. Willcox to Julius Rosenwald, October 30, 1915, *BTW Papers*, 13:418.

18. *New York Age*, June 8, 1899, from Paris, *BTW Papers*, 5:132.

19. Margaret Murray Washington, "Club Work among Negro Women," reprinted in *Black Women in White America*, ed. Lerner, 447.

20. Margaret Murray Washington to Ednah Dow Littlehale Cheney, November 23, 1896, *BTW Papers*, 4:237.

21. Ibid., 4:238.

22. Davis, *Lifting As They Climb*, 15–20.

23. Lane, *Documentary History of Mrs. Booker T. Washington*, 169.

24. *St. Louis Palladium*, July 16, 1904, reel 6, NACWC Papers; *Boston Guardian*, July 23, 1904, reel 8, NACWC Papers.

25. Washington, *Up from Slavery*, 130.

26. Scott, "Margaret Murray Washington," in *Ladies Home Journal*, May 1907, in *BTW Papers*, 9:289–90.

27. "An Account of Addresses by Washington and Mrs Washington," September 12, 1898, *BTW papers*, 4:461.

28. Ibid., 4:463.

29. Ibid., 4:465.

30. Margaret Murray Washington to Booker T. Washington October 26, 1891, *BTW Papers*, 3:175, and July 17, 1892, *BTW Papers*, 3:248.

31. Margaret Murray Washington, *National Notes*, June 1913.

32. White, *Too Heavy a Load*, 48, and Davis, *Women, Race, and Class*, 144. See also Neverdon-Morton, "Black Woman's Struggle for Equality in the South," 53.

33. Lucy Brown Johnston to Booker T. Washington, May 11, 1912, *BTW Papers*, 2:457.

34. White, *Too Heavy a Load*, 48; Davis, *Women, Race, and Class*, 144.

35. Margaret Murray Washington, "Club Work among Negro Women," 444–47.

36. Du Bois to N. B. Morston, March 11, 1907, reel 2, *Du Bois Papers*.

37. Lane, *Documentary History of Mrs. Booker T. Washington*, 66–67; *National Notes*, November-December 1914, 6; Margaret Murray Washington, "Club Work among Negro Women," 446.

38. Margaret Murray Washington, *National Notes*, June 1913.

39. Washington organized the Tuskegee Town Women's Club because her husband had excluded women from the Tuskegee Negro Conference. Scott, "Margaret Murray Washington," *Ladies Home Journal*, May 1907, in *BTW Papers*, 9:291–93. For Washington's role as a local club organizer, see "Synopsis of the Lecture by Mrs. Booker T. Washington on the Organizing of Women's Clubs on the Evening of June 22, 1910," reel 10, NACWC Papers; see also "Tenth Annual Report of the Tuskegee Woman's Club 1905," *BTW Papers*, 8:476–77; Rouse, "Out of the Shadow of Tuskegee," 33–34.

40. Margaret Murray Washington, *National Notes*, June 1913.

41. Minutes of the First meeting at Lincoln Heights, MCT-LOC, reel 5; *New York Age*, August 19, 1923.

42. *New York Age*, July 19, 1906.

43. Minutes of the 1906 NACW Detroit Convention, reel 1, NACWC Papers.

44. *New York Age*, July 19, 1906.

45. Scott, "Margaret Murray Washington," *Ladies Home Journal*, May 1907, in *BTW Papers*, 9:291–93; Neverdon-Morton, "Self-Help Programs," 211–12.

46. Rouse, "Out of the Shadow of Tuskegee," 40.

47. Minutes of the 1920 NACW Tuskegee Convention, June 20, 1920, reel 1, NACWC Papers.

48. Hayford was married to Joseph Casely Hayford, a well-known leader in the early Pan-African movement from Ghana. For more on Hayford, see Bair, "Pan Africanism as Process," 121–44.

49. Minutes of the 1922 NACW Richmond Convention, reel 1, NACWC Papers.

50. Ibid.

51. *Chicago Defender*, August 26, 1922.

52. Margaret Murray Washington to Lugenia Burns Hope, September 15, 1922, Box 102-12, MCT-MSRC. See also Margaret Murray Washington to Mary Church Terrell, September 20, 1922, reel 5, MCT-LOC.

53. Margaret Murray Washington to coworkers of the ICWDR, September 6, 1922, reel 5, MCT-LOC.

54. Margaret Murray Washington to coworkers of the ICWDR, September 6, 1922, and Margaret Murray Washington to Mary Church Terrell, October 16, 1922, reel 5, MCT-LOC. See also Margaret Murray Washington to Lugenia Burns Hope, September 15, 1922, Box 102-12, MCT-MSRC.

55. Minutes of the First Meeting at Lincoln Heights, reel 5, MCT-LOC; *New York Age*, August 19, 1923.

56. Minutes of the First Meeting at Lincoln Heights, reel 5, MCT-LOC.

57. Ibid.; *New York Age*, August 19, 1923.

58. For details of the French reaction to the export of American racism to Paris during and after World War I, see Levenstein, *Seductive Journey*, 39–41, 187–95, 263–66.

59. Minutes of the Third Annual Meeting of the ICWDR included in a letter from Margaret Murray Washington to Mary Church Terrell, October 4, 1924, reel 5, MCT-LOC.

60. Ibid.

61. Ibid.

62. Margaret Murray Washington to Mary Church Terrell, December 19, 1924, reel 5, MCT-LOC.

63. "International Council Holds Public Meeting," *Chicago Defender*, August 16, 1924, cited in Rouse, "Out of the Shadow of Tuskegee," 31–46.

64. Ula Taylor suggests Jacques Garvey would not have been welcome in the ICWDR because of the "unquestionably elite pedigree of ICWDR women." See Taylor, *Veiled Garvey*, 70. An opposite view, however, sees the ICWDR as breaking radically from the NACW in terms of its international focus. See White, *Too Heavy a Load*, 146.

65. *National Notes*, January 1925.

66. Lutz, "Dizzy Steps to Heaven," 221.

67. Higginbotham, *Righteous Discontent*, 225–26.

68. Lutz, "Dizzy Steps to Heaven," 223.

69. *Tuskegee Messenger*, August 30, 1930.

70. *Afro-American Ledger*, August 3, 1935.

71. Lutz, "Dizzy Steps to Heaven," 228.

72. "Statement of the Aims and Purposes of the Circle for Peace and Foreign Relations and Explanation of Its Methods and Statement of Work Planned for 1927," reel 21, *Du Bois Papers*; Lutz, "Dizzy Steps to Heaven," 230.

73. Du Bois admitted in a *Crisis* editorial that he was pushed into it. See *The Crisis*, October 1926.

74. See Addie Waites Hunton to W. E. B. Du Bois, March 10, July 2, 1927, and "Statement of the Circle for Peace and Foreign Relations," June 21, 1927, reel 21, *Du Bois Papers*.

75. The list of organizers included Dorothy Peterson, Jessie Fauset, Nina Du Bois, Helen Curtis, Ida Gibbs-Hunt, Helen Fauset Lanning (Fauset's sister), Lillian Alexander (NAACP worker), Eunice Hunton Carter, Addie Dickerson, Regina Andrews, Elizabeth Davis, and Layle Lane. Delegates included Maggie L. Walker, Mary Talbert, Nannie Burroughs, Mary McLeod Bethune, Alice Dunbar-Nelson, and Charlotte Hawkins Brown. Program of the Fourth Pan-African Congress, 1927, reel 22, *Du Bois Papers*.

76. See "Mayor Walker and Governor Smith Greet Pan-African Congress," NAACP press release, August 18, 1927, and *New York Times*, August 14, 1927, reel 5, Gumby Papers.

77. Program of the Fourth Pan-African Congress, 1927, reel 22, *Du Bois Papers*.

78. "Fourth Pan-African Congress Ends Session: Issues Manifesto," NAACP press release, August 26, 1927, reel 5, Gumby Papers.

79. Davies, *Black Women, Writing, and Identity*, 49–50. See also White, "Africa on My Mind," 117–50.

80. Program of the Fourth Pan-African Congress, 1927, reel 22, *Du Bois Papers*.

81. Melvin Jack Chisum to Booker T. Washington, February 20, 1906, *BTW Papers*, 8: 530.

82. See Nannie Helen Burroughs to Booker T. Washington, July 8, 1914, *BTW Papers*, 13:82; Nannie Helen Burroughs to Emmet J. Scott, June 29, 1915, *BTW Papers*, 13:333.

83. See Harley, "Nannie Helen Burroughs," 67, and Wolcott, "Bible, Bath, and Broom," 88–110.

84. Higginbotham, *Righteous Discontent*, 203.

85. Burroughs is either not mentioned or mentioned only very briefly in accounts of the NACW. See, for example, White, "Cost of Club Work," 247–69; White, *Too Heavy a Load*; Neverdon-Morton, *Afro-American Women of the South*. Although there have been plenty of articles, there have been few book-length studies on Burroughs. Harley, "Nannie Helen Burroughs," 62.

86. Higginbotham, *Righteous Discontent*; Johnson, *Uplifting the Women and the Race*.

87. Washington, *Frustrated Fellowship*.

88. Higginbotham, *Righteous Discontent*, 50.

89. Washington, *Frustrated Fellowship*, 160, Higginbotham, *Righteous Discontent*, 66–67, 153–54.

90. Higginbotham, *Righteous Discontent*, 50.

91. Constitution of the Woman's Convention, Auxiliary to the National Baptist Convention U.S.A., Inc. In "Manuscript for Handbook for Woman's Convention," n.d., box 46, NHB-LOC.

92. Sernett, ed., *African American Religious History*, 376.

93. Burroughs, "Report of the Work of Baptist Women: Twentieth Annual Report," in *African American Religious History*, ed. Sernett, 382.

94. Higginbotham, *Righteous Discontent*, 169–70.

95. Ibid., 187.

96. Ibid.

97. Ibid., 195–96.

98. Ibid., 187–88.

99. Wolcott, "Bath, Bible, and Broom," 91.

100. This was the official motto of the National Training School, cited in Harley, "Nannie Helen Burroughs," 65

101. Wolcott, "Bath, Bible, and Broom," 89.

102. "Circular of Information for the Seventeenth Annual Session of the National Training School for Women and Girls Incorporated, 1925–1926," p. 13, box 310, NHB-LOC.

103. Burroughs faced down many challenges from the male leadership of the NBC, including serious attempts in 1909, 1928, and 1938. See, for example, Burroughs, "You Can't Have My Baby," *Black Dispatch*, January 22, 1928, box 46, NHB-LOC.

104. Higginbotham, *Righteous Discontent*, 213; Johnson, *Uplifting the Women and the Race*; Wolcott, "Bible, Bath, and Broom"; Burroughs, cited in Johnson, *Uplifting the Women and the Race*, 367.

105. Circular of Information for the Nineteenth Annual Session, 1928, p. 4, box 309, NHB-LOC.

106. Higginbotham, *Righteous Discontent*, 159; Hunter, "Correct Thing," 696–98.

107. Calvin, "That's Nannie Burroughs' Job, and She Does It," *Pittsburgh Courier*, June 8, 1929, reprinted in *Black Women in White America*, ed. Lerner, 132–34.

108. Untitled newspaper editorial, August 21, 1924, box 318, NHB-LOC.

109. "Negroes Who Have Helped Themselves," 1930, box 309, NHB-LOC.

110. Untitled newspaper editorial, August 21, 1924, box 318, NHB-LOC.

111. "Negroes Who Have Helped Themselves," 1930, box 309, NHB-LOC.

112. Marable, "Groundings with My Sisters," 12. For more on domestic workers, see Haynes, "Negroes in Domestic Service in the United States," 384–442.

113. Jones, *Labor of Love, Labor of Sorrow,* 256.

114. "Circular of Information for the Seventeenth Annual Session of the National Training School for Women and Girls Incorporated, 1925–1926," pp. 11, 13, box 310, NHB-LOC.

115. Higginbotham, *Righteous Discontent,* 187. See also Gaines, *Uplifting the Race*; Carby, "Policing the Black Woman's Body in an Urban Context," 738–55; White, "Cost of Club Work," 247–69.

116. Wolcott, "Bible, Bath, and Broom," 94, 98–99.

117. Ibid., 89

118. For example, Bethune insisted on being called Mrs. Bethune, and never divorced her husband although they had separated in 1907, while Madam Walker kept her husband's name but added a dignified title. It is interesting, and perhaps not coincidental, that the overwhelming majority of women included in this study did not have husbands in close proximity at the height of their careers, whether due to the husband's death, imprisonment, or separation.

119. Burroughs, "You Can't Have My Baby," *Black Dispatch,* January 22, 1928, box 46, NHB-LOC; "Burroughs' School Fills a Real Need Says Dr. Woodson," *Afro American,* n.d., box 318, NHB-LOC.

120. Walker spoke to the NBC in September 1916. See Bundles, *On Her Own Ground,* 192. Burroughs and Walker were correspondents. In 1919 they arranged to discuss a "reconstruction program for colored women." See Madam Walker to Nannie H. Burroughs, March 26, 1919, box 1, MWC-IHS.

121. Barnett, "Nannie Burroughs and the Education of Black Women," 107.

122. Wolcott, "Bible, Bath, and Broom," 98–100.

123. Former student questionnaires, box 310, NHB-LOC.

124. Taylor, "Womanhood Glorified," 397.

125. Wolcott, "Bible, Bath, and Broom," 91.

126. *Topeka Plaindealer,* February 7, 1902, in Gatewood, *Aristocrats of Color,* 142.

127. Barnett, "Nannie Burroughs and the Education of Black Women," 101.

128. *Afro-American Ledger,* July 21, 1906, reel 5, NACWC Papers.

129. See Burroughs's papers for her correspondence with Bethune and Waring, particularly Burroughs to Mary F. Waring, February 5, 1934, box 31, NHB-LOC.

130. Easter, *Nannie Helen Burroughs,* 130.

131. *Afro-American Ledger,* July 21, 1906, reel 5, NACWC Papers.

132. Burroughs, "Unload the Leeches and Parasitic 'Toms' and Take Promise Land."

133. See Terborg-Penn, "Discrimination against Afro-American Women in the Woman's Movement," 17–27, and Barnett, "Nannie Burroughs and the Education of Black Women," 97–109.

134. Burroughs, "Report of the Work of Baptist Women," 390.

135. Burroughs, "Black Women and Reform," *The Crisis*, August 1915.
136. Burroughs, "Report of the Work of Baptist Women," 390.
137. Ibid.
138. Ibid., 393.
139. Brown, *National Notes*, December 1924.
140. *Chicago Defender*, August 16, 1924.
141. Davis, *National Notes*, January 1925.
142. NACW members of the NLRCW included Mary Church Terrell, Maggie Lena Walker, and Elizabeth Ross Haynes. See "Minutes of the Temporary Organization of the NLRCW," box 309, NHB-LOC. For more on the NLRCW, see Higginbotham, "Clubwomen and Electoral Politics in the 1920s," 145.
143. For more on black women's political affiliations throughout the 1930s, see Higginbotham, "Clubwomen and Electoral Politics in the 1920s," 134–56, and Terborg-Penn, "African American Women and the Vote," 10–24.
144. See *The Crisis*, May 1924; *Opportunity*, December 1924.
145. "NAWE, a Labor Organization with a Constructive Program," box 308, NHB-LOC.
146. Ibid.
147. Barnett, "Nannie Burroughs and the Education of Black Women," 101–2.
148. Burroughs, "Report of the Work of Baptist Women," 390.
149. Barnett, "Religion, Politics, and Gender," 166.
150. NBC, Eighteenth Annual Session of the WC, 1918, cited in Higginbotham, *Righteous Discontent*, 225; *The Crisis*, December 1919.
151. Gordon, "Black and White Visions of Welfare," 581.
152. Higginbotham, *Righteous Discontent*, 223.
153. Burroughs, "Unload the Leeches and Parasitic 'Toms' and Take Promise Land."
154. Burroughs, "Up from the Depth," 50–51.
155. Ibid.
156. Jacques Garvey, "A Great Woman of the Race Who Works," *Negro World*, December 6, 1924.
157. Burroughs, "With All Thy Getting."
158. Bethune, "A College on a Garbage Dump," reprinted in *Black Women in White America*, ed. Lerner, 136.
159. Ibid., 139–40.
160. Ibid., 143.
161. Audrey Thomas McCluskey, introduction to *Mary McLeod Bethune*, ed. McCluskey and Smith, 67.
162. "Autobiographical Statement: A Yearning and Longing Appeased," p. 8, part 1, reel 1, MMB-LOC.
163. Ibid.
164. For more information about the Daytona school, see McCluskey, introduction to *Mary McLeod Bethune*, 68.
165. Perkins, "Pragmatic Idealism of Mary McLeod Bethune," 30–36. See also Hanson, *Mary McLeod Bethune*, 61.

166. Hanson, *Mary McLeod Bethune*, 138.

167. Smith, "Mary McLeod Bethune's 'Last Will and Testament,'" 113–15.

168. Bethune, "My Last Will and Testament," *Ebony*, August 10, 1955.

169. Holt, *Mary McLeod Bethune*, 206.

170. Hanson, *Mary McLeod Bethune*, 207.

171. For an account of Bethune as the pragmatic educator, see Perkins "Pragmatic Idealism of Mary McLeod Bethune," 30–36. For an account that stresses Bethune's pragmatic political activism, see Hanson, *Mary McLeod Bethune*, 3.

172. Davis, *Lifting As They Climb*, 177–79.

173. Mary McLeod Bethune to Margaret Murray Washington, March 20, 1923, in *Mary McLeod Bethune*, ed. McCluskey and Smith, 83.

174. See "Letter to the Florida Federation of Colored Women's Clubs 1917" and "Southern Negro Women and Race Cooperation," in *Mary McLeod Bethune*, ed. McCluskey and Smith, 139, 145.

175. Davis, *Lifting As They Climb*, 54.

176. Bundles, *On Her Own Ground*, 128; Giddings, *When and Where I Enter*, 200.

177. Mary McLeod Bethune to Madam Walker, April 5, 1917, box 1, MWC-IHS.

178. All presidents of the NACW had previously served as vice-president-at-large for at least one two-year administration term, if not more. See Davis, *Lifting As We Climb*, 32–40.

179. *National Notes*, December 1926.

180. Elaine Smith suggests that Bethune, along with other clubwomen leaders, inflated the membership figures to enhance their political leverage. See McCluskey and Smith, eds., *Mary McLeod Bethune*, 138 n. 7; Davis, *Lifting As We Climb*, 67–71.

181. "President's Address to the Fifteenth Biennial Convention of the National Association of Colored Women, Oakland, California," August 2, 1926, reprinted in *Mary McLeod Bethune*, ed. McCluskey and Smith, 156–57; Davis, *Lifting As We Climb*, 83–84.

182. Davis, *Lifting As We Climb*, 73.

183. For the revised constitution, see *National Notes*, January 1928. For the 1928 yearbook and official directory, see reel 20, NACWC Papers. See also McCluskey and Smith, eds., *Mary McLeod Bethune*, 165–67.

184. McCluskey and Smith, eds., *Mary McLeod Bethune*, 167.

185. Ibid., 166.

186. Ibid., 166.

187. Minutes of the 1926 Oakland Convention, p. 34, reel 1, NACWC Papers. For details of Bethune's early ambitions to become a missionary, see "Autobiographical Statement: A Yearning and Longing Appeased," part 1, reel 1, MMB-LOC.

188. See "President's Address to the Fifteenth Biennial Convention of the National Association of Colored Women Oakland, California," August 2, 1926, reprinted in *Mary McLeod Bethune*, ed. McCluskey and Smith, 161.

189. McCluskey and Smith, eds., *Mary McLeod Bethune*, 134; White, *Too Heavy a Load*, 40.

190. McCluskey and Smith, eds., *Mary McLeod Bethune*, 134; Hine and Thompson, *Shining Thread of Hope*, 251.

191. According to correspondence exchanged between Burroughs and then-president Mary W. Waring, the NCW went behind the formal NACW leadership and consulted only with former president Sallie W. Stewart, who was regarded by many of her colleagues as ineffective and untrustworthy. See Nannie H. Burroughs to Mary F. Waring, June 25, 1934, box 44, NHB-LOC.

192. Rouse, *Lugenia Burns Hope*, 118. For the history of the ASWPL, see Hall, *Revolt against Chivalry*.

193. Giddings, *When and Where I Enter*, 210.

194. Davis, *Lifting As We Climb*, 88.

195. President Sallie W. Stewart acknowledged as much in her presidential statement. See Davis, *Lifting As We Climb*, 88.

196. Davis, *Lifting As We Climb*, 102.

197. Mary McLeod Bethune to Sallie W. Stewart and Other Coworkers, January 29, 1930, reel 7, NACWC Papers.

198. Ibid. See also Giddings, *When and Where I Enter*, 203.

199. For this interpretation, see White, *Too Heavy a Load*, 156–57.

200. In fact, the NACW would never join the NCNW. See "NACW Declines to Join the NCNW," reel 2, NACWC Papers.

201. Giddings, *When and Where I Enter*, 212.

202. Those unable to attend but expressing "hearty approval" included Lucy Slowe, dean of Howard University and president of the National Association of College Women, Lugenia Burns Hope, and Washington, D.C., playwright and poet Georgia Douglas Johnson. See Minutes of the Organizational Meeting of the NCNW, December 5, 1935, box 1, Series 1, NCNW Papers.

203. Minutes of the Organizational Meeting of the NCNW, December 5, 1935, box 1, NCNW Papers.

204. Bethune, "My Last Will and Testament," 106

205. White, *Too Heavy a Load*, 150.

206. The NCNW's creation challenges what some historians had regarded as a decline in separate-sex organizing following the passage of the Nineteenth Amendment. See, for example, Cott, *Grounding of Modern Feminism*, 96, and Freedman, "Separatism as Strategy," 512–29.

207. Du Bois, "Separation and Self-Respect," *The Crisis*, March 1935.

208. Du Bois, "Segregation," *The Crisis*, January 1934.

209. For details of the White–Du Bois feud, see Lewis, *W. E. B. Du Bois*, 334–50.

210. Hanson, *Mary McLeod Bethune*, 138.

211. For the "rising tide of interracialism," see Giddings, *When and Where I Enter*, 207.

212. The other "woman of color" was Kamala Nehru, wife of Jawaharlal Nehru, leader of the Indian National Congress in 1945. Lewis, *W. E. B. Du Bois*, 505.

213. Minutes, NCNW Meeting, November 26, 1938, p. 13, box 1, Series 1, NCNW Papers.

214. Height, *Open Wide the Freedom Gates*, especially Chapter 9.

215. For discussion of the tensions between clubwomen and the masculine language

of self-determination in the 1920s and 1930s, see Victoria Wolcott, *Remaking Respectability*, especially Chapters 5 and 6. For the view that clubwomen were incapable of dealing with the challenges posed by the masculine discourse of the New Negro and of the Garvey movement, see White, *Too Heavy a Load*, 129.

Chapter 2. Black Nationalism and Interracialism in the Young Women's Christian Association

1. Lugenia Burns Hope et al., "What the Colored Women Are Asking of the Y.W.C.A.," reprinted in *Black Women in White America*, ed. Lerner, 480–82. Hope founded the Atlanta Neighborhood Union in 1908 to work for social reform with black women in Atlanta. They raised money for kindergartens and nurseries, and other Progressive Era concerns. See Rouse, *Lugenia Burns Hope*.

2. The Colored Branch changed its name to the Harlem Branch in 1941. Throughout the chapter I call it the Colored Branch because that is what its members called it during the period covered in this chapter. See BOD, October 20, 1941. NYCAA.

3. Spratt, "To Be Separate or One," in *Men and Women Adrift*, ed. Mjagkij and Spratt, 188–205. For studies that examine the YWCA in the South, see Rouse, *Lugenia Burns Hope*; Hall, *Revolt against Chivalry*.

4. Olcott, *Work of Colored Women*; Robertson, "Deeper Even Than Race?"; Jones, "Struggle among Saints," in *Men and Women Adrift*, ed. Mjagkij and Spratt, 160–87.

5. While much of Weisenfeld's local study of the Colored Branch in Harlem presents black women as pushing for greater integration, she does recognize that by the 1940s, when the Interracial Charter was signed, there were many black women who found this transition equally as hard as, if not harder than, white women found it. Weisenfeld, *African American Women and Christian Activism*, 198–202; Robertson, "Deeper Even Than Race?" 336. More understanding of the tension between strategies of separatism versus integration is Margaret Spratt's comparative study of the black Christian women's organizations in Pittsburgh and Cleveland from 1920 to 1946. See Spratt, "To Be Separate or One," 188–205.

6. Olcott, *Work of Colored Women*, 5. Eva Del Vakia Bowles became the first paid black staff worker for the YWCA in the United States. See *New York City Post*, March 1918. For biographical details, see Hine, Brown, and Terborg-Penn, *Black Women in America*, s.v "Eva Bowles."

7. Weisenfeld describes Bowles's statement as "a charitable interpretation of a segregated system." Weisenfeld, *African American Women and Christian Activism*, 149.

8. Hunton, *Beginnings among Colored Women*, 20

9. Margaret Murray Washington to Lugenia Burns Hope, February 6, 1920, cited in Jones, "Struggle among Saints," 160.

10. For the view that most black YWCA women favored integration, see Robertson, "Deeper Even Than Race?" 377–78.

11. Sims, *The First Twenty Five Years*, 17.

12. Mrs. Marshall Roberts's Union Prayer Circle, which formed in New York City in 1858, would rename itself the Ladies Christian Union in 1866, the same year that women

in Boston first organized a YWCA. Mjagkij and Spratt, introduction to *Men and Women Adrift*, ed. Mjagkij and Spratt, 6.

13. Sims, *An Unfolding Purpose*, 11.

14. Ibid., 71; Weisenfeld, *African American Women and Christian Activism*, 33–34. For a contemporary account of early association work among African American women, see Hunton, *Beginnings among Colored Women*.

15. Bowles, "Negro Women and the YWCA of the United States," series 3A, reel 107.8, NBA; Bell and Wilkins, *Interracial Practices in Community YWCAs*.

16. Gilbert, "Early Policies Regarding Branches: 1926–1940," from a report headed "Growth of Southern Work" compiled by Miss Annie Kate Gilbert, series 3A, reel 107.7, NBA.

17. Olcott, *The Work of Colored Women*, 6–7.

18. Ibid.

19. Weisenfeld, *African American Women and Christian Activism*, 37–62.

20. Ibid., 48.

21. ECM, January 12, 1905, NYCAA.

22. Ibid., February 2, 1905.

23. Ibid.

24. Weisenfeld, *African American Women and Christian Activism*, 53

25. ECM, February 9, 1905, NYCAA.

26. Ibid., October 26, 1905; BOD, December 8, 1919, NYCAA.

27. Weisenfeld, *African American Women and Christian Activism*, 54.

28. Ibid.

29. Ibid., 56.

30. This was the white Harlem Branch founded in 1891 and independent from the Central 15th Street Branch and its other affiliated branches: the West Side Settlement at 460 West 44th Street, the Margaret Louisa Home and Restaurant, and the Seaside Home in Asbury Park, New Jersey. The Harlem Branch is not to be confused with the Colored Branch, which was not renamed the Harlem Branch until 1941. ECM, February 17, 1911, NYCAA.

31. ECM, March 23, 1911, NYCAA.

32. BOD, p. 2, October 1, 1911, NYCAA. The Executive Committee became the Board of Directors of the New York City YWCA when the 15th Street and white Harlem YWCA merged in 1911.

33. See Saunders, *Half Century*. For the story of the growth of Harlem as a black community, see Johnson, *Black Manhattan*.

34. BOD, May 12, 1913, NYCAA.

35. Ibid.

36. Ransom, *Pilgrimage of Harriet Ransom's Son*, 203, cited in Weisenfeld, *African American Women and Christian Activism*, 103.

37. BOD, November 8, 1915, and December 8, 1919, NYCAA.

38. Rouse, *Lugenia Burns Hope*, 93.

39. Weisenfeld, *African American Women and Christian Activism*, 9–10.

40. "Colored Work 1907–1920: Preliminary City Work and Foundation of Student Work, Report Prepared for the National Board," p. 4, n.d., NBA.

41. Minutes of the 1908 NACW Brooklyn Biennial Convention, reel 1, NACWC Papers. See also Salem, *To Better Our World*, 47–48.

42. Minutes of the National Board Sub-Committee on Colored Work, December 10, 1913, NBA, cited in Jones, "Struggle among Saints," 169.

43. Rouse, *Lugenia Burns Hope*, 93.

44. Hopkins, "Square Deal for Colored Women," *Association Monthly*, April 1919, 152.

45. Mjagkij and Spratt, introduction to *Men and Women Adrift*; Robertson, "Deeper Even Than Race?" 116. This interpretation fits with other work that has emphasized the war's significance in nationalizing the race problem through, for example, the migration of blacks to the North and urban areas and the dramatic increase in lynching, often of black soldiers. See, for example, Lewis, *W. E. B. Du Bois*, 7–9

46. Weisenfeld, *African American Women and Christian Activism*, 121–43.

47. Jackson, "Colored Girls in the Second Line of Defense," *Association Monthly*, October 1918, 363.

48. Olcott, *Work of Colored Women*, 132.

49. Ibid., 82.

50. Ibid.

51. Council on Colored Work Minutes, 1907–1920; Colored Work Committee Summary of Minutes Compiled in 1931 from 1919–1931, NBA.

52. Weisenfeld, *African American Women and Christian Activism*, 133. Helen Curtis was the widow of the minister to Liberia, was a fashion designer, and had led the Hostess House at Camp Upton. She would later become a member of the ICWDR. Florida Ruffin Ridley was the daughter of Josephine St. Pierre Ruffin, a founder of the black women's club movement in the 1890s. Ridley was a journalist and YWCA worker. Marie Peek Johnson had been recruited earlier by the Colored Branch to run its Rooms Registry.

53. *New York City Post*, May 25, 1918, TICF.

54. Olcott, *Work of Colored Women*, 129.

55. See Marks, *We're Good and Gone*, and Barbeau and Henri, *Unknown Soldiers*.

56. Olcott, *Work of Colored Women*, 13.

57. Bowles, "Colored Girl in Our Midst," *Association Monthly*, December 1917, 492.

58. Olcott, "Growth of Colored Work," *Association Monthly*, November 1919, 432.

59. *New York Age*, January 19, 1918; Rouse, *Lugenia Burns Hope*, 95–96.

60. Olcott, *Work of Colored Women*, 17–18.

61. Saunders, *Half Century*, 5. Saunders became executive secretary of the Colored Branch in 1914 and remained at its head until 1947. Born in 1883, Saunders came from a family who had been free for generations. Having graduated from Fisk University in 1909, she worked for the National YWCA before taking up her position at the Colored Branch in Harlem. For more biographical information, see Hine, Brown, and Terborg-Penn, *Black Women in America*, s.v. "Cecelia Cabaniss Saunders."

62. Olcott, *Work of Colored Women*, 10.

63. Ibid., 79.

64. "Woman Sculptor's Work Reveals Interesting Study of Racial Characteristics," *New York City Post*, May 1, 1919, TICF.
65. Olcott, *Work of Colored Women*, 69.
66. Ibid.
67. Those who have dismissed the YWCA as a "swim and gym club" include Dodson, *Role of the YWCA in a Changing Era*, 97, and Zald, *Organizational Change*, xiii. Both are cited in Robertson, "Deeper Even Than Race?" 22.
68. Olcott, *Work of Colored Women*, 70.
69. Ibid., 69.
70. Roses and Randolph, eds., *Harlem Renaissance and Beyond*, 232.
71. Olcott, *Work of Colored Women*, 80–81.
72. Ibid.
73. Ibid.
74. Ibid.
75. Jackson, "Colored Girls in the Second Line of Defense," *Association Monthly*, October 1918, 363.
76. Ibid.
77. Hopkins, "Square Deal for Colored Women," *Association Monthly*, April 1919, 153.
78. There were other vocal black critics of the war who were quick to point out that African Americans had never had their rights properly respected in spite of their long history of fighting in American wars. See, for example, Owen, "Failure of Negro Leadership," *Messenger*, January 1918.
79. "War Opportunities for Colored Women," *New York City Post*, March 18, 1918, TICF.
80. Olcott, *Work of Colored Women*, 82.
81. Ibid.
82. Ibid.
83. Hunton, "Colored Women Sailed for France," *New York City Post*, May 25, 1918.
84. Hine and Thompson, *Shining Thread of Hope*, 223–24. For the history of black women's struggle to become nurses, see Hine, *Black Women in White*.
85. Dunbar-Nelson, "Negro Women in the War," at <http://www.lib.byu.edu/~rdh/wwi/comment/Scott/SCh27.htm> accessed on Sept 30, 2006.
86. Dunbar-Nelson "Negro Women in the War."
87. Ibid. See also Hine and Thompson, *Shining Thread of Hope*, 225, and Hine, *Black Women in White*.
88. Mary Church Terrell, "Racial Worm Turns," c. 1920, reel 21, MCT-LOC.
89. For biographical details of Terrell, see Giddings, *When and Where I Enter*, 18–19.
90. Terrell, *Colored Woman in a White World*, 332.
91. *The Crisis*, December 1920, 57.
92. *The Crisis*, December 1920, 57; Elizabeth Ross Haynes speech at the 1921 Louisville YWCA Conference, Council on Colored Work Minutes: Colored Work 1907–1920, NBA.
93. Hunton and Johnson, *Two Colored Women with the Expeditionary Forces*.
94. Ibid., 33–35.

95. Plastas, "Band of Noble Women," 76. On motherhood and race, see Collins, "Producing the Mothers of the Nation," 118–29.

96. Hunton and Johnson, *Two Colored Women with the Expeditionary Forces*, 34.

97. Ibid., 32.

98. Ibid.

99. Ibid., 29.

100. Ibid., 26.

101. Ibid., 28.

102. Giddings, *When and Where I Enter*, 183–85; Plastas, "Band of Noble Women," 77, 80; Freedman, "Separatism as Strategy," 512–29.

103. Hunton and Curtis both became members of the ICWDR and organized the Fourth Pan-African Congress in New York. See Chapter 1.

104. "Thousands Died for a Lie," *Brooklyn Eagle*, October 13, 1919, TICF.

105. See Chapter 3 for disputes in the black press over support for the war.

106. Du Bois, "Close Ranks," *The Crisis*, July 1918.

107. Terrell, "Racial Worm Turns," c. 1920, reel 21, MCT-LOC.

108. Ibid.

109. For a detailed discussion on African Americans' demands that self-determination be applied to Africa at the Paris Peace Treaty, see Chapter 3.

110. Terrell, "Racial Worm Turns," c. 1920, reel 21, MCT-LOC.

111. The story of the racist suffrage campaign has been well documented, most notably by Terborg-Penn, *African American Women in the Struggle for the Vote*.

112. Ibid., 8.

113. Anthony and Harper, eds., *History of Woman Suffrage*, 4:216; Davis, *Women, Race, and Class*, 115–16.

114. Cited in Davis, *Women, Race, and Class*, 145.

115. Ibid.

116. For details of the formation of the National Women's Party, see Smith, "New Paths to Power," 397.

117. Hunton, cited in Giddings, *When and Where I Enter*, 169.

118. Gilmore, *Gender and Jim Crow*, esp. Chapter 3.

119. Davis, *Women, Race, and Class*, 121–22.

120. Dorothy C. Salem, *To Better Our World*, 251, and Scharf and Jensen, eds., *Decades of Discontent*, 3–18; Plastas, "Band of Noble Women," 80–81; Giddings, *When and Where I Enter*, 183–84.

121. Giddings, *When and Where I Enter*, 184.

122. Saunders, *Half Century*, 2–6.

123. See Chapter 4 in this volume.

124. Vandenbueng-Daves, "Manly Pursuit of a Partnership between the Sexes," 1326–1327.

125. Mjagkij, *Light in the Darkness*, 3.

126. Mjagkij, "True Manhood," 141.

127. See Chapter 4 for a discussion of how Burroughs and Amy Jacques Garvey engaged with the discourse of black masculinity.

128. "Thousands Died for a Lie," *Brooklyn Eagle*, October 13, 1919, TICF.

129. For the history of the negotiations surrounding the projected merger, see Vandenbuerg-Daves, "Manly Pursuit of a Partnership between the Sexes," 1325, and Robertson, "Deeper Even Than Race?" 257.

130. Cott, *Grounding of Modern Feminism*, 96. See also Freedman, "Separatism as Strategy," 512–29.

131. See Council on Colored Work Minutes, September 24, 1920, pp. 3–4, NBA. See also Robertson, "Deeper Even Than Race?" 312.

132. Council on Colored Work Minutes, March 12, 1926, CWC, NBA.

133. Robertson, "Deeper Even Than Race?" 79, 241.

134. Ibid., 281.

135. Council on Colored Work Minutes, December 13, 1929, CWC, NBA.

136. Robertson, "Deeper Even Than Race," 124–25.

137. Jones, "Struggle among Saints," 180.

138. Rouse, *Lugenia Burns Hope*, 96–97. The 1910 resolution stated that black groups could form independent associations if they were able to support their own work, and if there was no central association, the association was weak, or conditions made branch affiliation "unfeasible." See Jones, "Struggle among Saints," 169. Hope had also been involved in the Commission on Interracial Cooperation (CIC). Founded by a white liberal Methodist minister, Will Alexander, in Atlanta in 1920, it at first sought to exclude women. However, white and black women were later included, and set up their own organization within the CIC. For more on the CIC, see Neverdon-Morton, "Advancement of the Race," 127–30.

139. Hope et al., "What the Colored Women Are Asking of the YWCA," reprinted in *Black Women in White America*, ed. Lerner, 481.

140. Ibid., 481–82.

141. Ibid., 480–82. Ironically, it was the Interracial Charter of 1936 that saw the implementation of black women's demands for the right to set up their own black branch. See the epilogue in this volume.

142. Hope et al., "What the Colored Women Are Asking of the YWCA," 480–82.

143. "Mrs. Hope on the Cleveland Meeting," May 30, 1920, YWCA folder, NUC. Cited in Rouse, *Lugenia Burns Hope*, 101.

144. For more on this conference, see Hall, *Revolt against Chivalry*, 83–86, and Salem, *To Better Our World*, 243–46.

145. Hedgeman, *Trumpet Sounds*, 45.

146. BOD, December 8, 1919, NYCAA.

147. *New York Age*, February 10, 1923.

148. Ibid.

149. Saunders, *Half Century*, 9.

150. Ibid.

151. Ibid.

152. Ibid., 13.

153. Hedgeman, *Trumpet Sounds*, 45.

154. Ibid.

155. Ibid.
156. Ibid., 50.
157. Ibid., 50–51, 55.
158. Ibid., 45.
159. Ibid., 49.
160. Robertson, "Deeper Even Than Race?" 273–90.
161. Ibid., 242.
162. Clarice Winn Davis, "Eva del Vakia Bowles," in *Dictionary of Negro Biography*, 54–55, cited in Robertson, "Deeper Even Than Race?" 327. Others, including Carter G. Woodson, thought that the white leadership had forced Bowles out: "And so Miss Bowles goes the Way of Moorland," *New York Age*, June 4, 1932, cited in Robertson, ibid., 327 n. 93.
163. Saunders, *Half Century*; BOD, p. 4, October 20, 1941, NYCAA.
164. Robertson, "Deeper Even Than Race?" 391. For Height's account, see Height, *Open Wide the Freedom Gates*, 128–29.
165. See, for example, Busby, "Price of Integration," in *Men and Women Adrift*, ed. Mjagkij and Spratt, 206–30.
166. See Hedgeman, *Trumpet Sounds*, for further details of her career.
167. Hine, Brown, and Terborg-Penn, *Black Women in America*, s.v. "Eunice Hunton Carter."

Chapter 3. Luxuriant Growth: The Walkers and Black Economic Nationalism

1. Fragment of press release re Madam Walker and charity, ca. 1918, box 2, MWC-IHS.
2. According to Kathy Peiss, women entrepreneurs took the language of industry and applied it to their beauty schools and products. For female beauticians, a system meant "a signature skin and hair treatment program around which entrepreneurs opened cosmetology schools and ran correspondence courses." Peiss, "Vital Industry," 232.
3. See Biggart, *Charismatic Capitalism*, cited in Peiss, "Vital Industry," 235.
4. Recent biographies of Walker include Bundles, *On Her Own Ground*, and Lowry's fictionalized account, *Her Dream of Dreams*. Many of the essays on Walker are also written by Bundles. See, for example, Bundles, "Madam C. J. Walker" and "Sharing the Wealth." The only other treatments are either fictional or heroine stories for children which tend to focus on retelling the rags-to-riches story, for example, McKissack and McKissack, *Madam C. J. Walker: Self-Made Millionaire*. For accounts of black women that mention Walker or her daughter, but only in passing, see, for example, White, *Too Heavy a Load*, 80, 215; Giddings, *When and Where I Enter*, 104, 138, 187–89, 200; Lewis, *When Harlem Was in Vogue*, 110, 165.
5. Latham, "Historical Sketch."
6. Madam Walker to F. B. Ransom, December 20, 1918, box 1, MWC-IHS. This was the account placed by the Walker Company in numerous newspapers. See, for example, Snelson, "Slave Cabin to a Queen's Palace: Mme C. J. Walker Company Pioneer in Negro Business," box 12, MWC-IHS. See also Schuyler, "Madam C. J. Walker," *Messenger*, August 1924.
7. Early press release on Madam Walker, n.d., box 12, MWC-IHS.

8. For further details of Madam Walker's early life, see Latham, "Historical Sketch," and Bundles, *On Her Own Ground*.

9. Madam Walker to Booker T. Washington, January 19, 1910, Booker T. Washington to Madam Walker, January 26, 1910, box 531, BTW-LOC.

10. See Latham, "Historical Sketch."

11. "Madam Walker Sails for Cuba," *Chicago Defender*, November 29, 1913.

12. For promotion of the story among Walker agents, see *Madam C. J. Walker Beauty Manual*, 15;

13. Bundles, *On Her Own Ground*, 66–67.

14. For example, Washington threatened to destroy Judge Robert Terrell's career if he did not rein in the views of his wife, Mary Church Terrell. Moore, *Leading the Race*, esp. 91–92, 204–5.

15. Booker T. Washington to Madam Walker, December 6, 1911, box 531, BTW-LOC.

16. Washington's biographer Louis Harlan notes that Washington "first opposed membership in the National Negro Business League for . . . cosmetics manufacturers on the ground that they fostered imitation of white beauty standards, but he later relented." Bundles argues that Washington purposefully excluded hair-care products manufacturers from his 1907 book *The Negro in Business* and that while he allowed two black women hairdressers to address the annual NNBL convention in 1901 and 1905, this was because they served white clients rather than black women. See *BTW Papers*, 3:385, and Bundles, *On Her Own Ground*, 122.

17. Synopsis of the Lecture by Mrs. Booker T. Washington on the Organizing of Womens' Clubs, June 22, 1910, reel 6, NACWC Papers.

18. Bundles, *On Her Own Ground*, 125.

19. The NNBL was founded in 1900 to celebrate African American entrepreneurship and encourage black economic independence. By 1912 it had attracted three thousand members. Bundles notes that the seeds of the NNBL actually lay in Du Bois's Atlanta conference the Negro in Business, held in May 1899. According to Ida B. Wells-Barnett, Washington stole the concept from Du Bois. See Bundles, *On Her Own Ground*, 131.

20. Bundles, *On Her Own Ground*, 133–34.

21. Report of the 13th Annual Convention of the NNBL August 21–23, 1912, reel 2, RNNBL.

22. Ibid.

23. Du Bois, "Negro and Communism," in *The Crisis*, cited in Wilson, "Race in Commodity Exchange and Consumption," 601.

24. Wilson, "Race in Commodity Exchange and Consumption," 595.

25. Report of the Fifteenth Annual Convention of the NNBL, August 20–22, 1914, reel 5, RNNBL.

26. Ibid.

27. Ibid.

28. Report of the Fourteenth Annual Convention of the NNBL August 20–22, 1913, reel 2, RNNBL.

29. For a discussion of the composition of the NNBL, see Frazier, *Black Bourgeoisie*, 135.

30. See Nannie Helen Burroughs to Booker T. Washington, July 8, 1914, *BTW Papers*, 13:82. In his reply, Washington agreed that there was a tendency to "overstatement in the matter of their wealth" among NNBL delegates. See Booker T. Washington to Nannie Helen Burroughs, July 13, 1914, *BTW Papers*, 13:87.

31. "Over 10,000 in Her Employ," *New York Age*, n.d. 1916, cited in Bundles, *On Her Own Ground*, 179. See also Madam Walker to F. B. Ransom, December 20, 1918, box 1, MWC-IHS.

32. Report of the Fourteenth Annual Convention of the NNBL August 20–22, 1913, reel 2, RNNBL.

33. Madam Walker to F. B. Ransom, November 15, 1915, box 1, MWC-IHS.

34. "Mme C. J. Walker's Lecture Tour," *Colored American Review*, July-August 1916.

35. Du Bois, "Close Ranks," *The Crisis*, July 1918.

36. Owen, "The Failure of Negro Leadership," *Messenger*, January 1918.

37. "Well Known Women Become Members of the Circle for Negro War Relief," *New York Age*, January 19, 1918. By 1918 the Circle for Negro War Relief had sixty-one units nationwide, covering thirty states with two thousand members, and had raised more than $50,000. See "The Call That Never Came," *The Crisis*, March 1919 and December 1919.

38. "Madam C. J. Walker Tells of Her Success," *Pittsburgh Courier* April 19, 1918.

39. Madam Walker to Colonel Schieffelin, January 13, 1919, box 1, MWC-IHS.

40. Lewis, *W. E. B. Du Bois*, 7–9.

41. For more biographical details of Trotter, see Fox, *Guardian of Boston*, and Bennett, *Pioneers in Protest*.

42. Bundles, *On Her Own Ground*, 162–63.

43. *New York Age*, September 27, 1917; New York Branch of the Equal Rights League to Madam Walker, December 12, 1918, box 1, MWC-IHS.

44. Duster, *Crusade for Justice*, 377–78. For biographical details of Wells-Barnett, see "Ida Wells Barnett," in *Harlem Renaissance and Beyond*, ed. Roses and Randolph, 339.

45. Duster, *Crusade for Justice*, 378.

46. Madam Walker to F. B. Ransom, December 19, 1918, box 1, MWC-IHS.

47. Ibid.

48. Madam Walker to F. B. Ransom, December 6, 1918, box 1, MWC-IHS.

49. Bundles, *On Her Own Ground*, 106.

50. *Cleveland Advocate*, p.1, March 6, 1920.

51. F. B. Ransom to Madam Walker, November 27, 1918, box 1, MWC-IHS.

52. Duster, *Crusade for Justice*, 378.

53. Lucille Randolph, a Howard graduate and former New York City schoolteacher, was also active in the women's and socialist movements, standing unsuccessfully in 1917 for New York State assembly alderman on the socialist ticket. See Anderson, *A. Philip Randolph*, 70, 77, 82.

54. J. Edgar Hoover, "Radicalism and Sedition Among Negroes," August 6, 1919, cited in Lewis, *W. E. B. Du Bois*, 6–7.

55. Fragment of press release re Madam Walker and charity, ca. 1918, box 2, MWC-IHS; Last Will and Testament of Sarah Walker and the Court's Construction Thereof, item

7, p.3, box 3, MWC-IHS. Bundles suggests that the demands of her business prevented her from taking personal direction of such an immense project. Instead, Walker offered $1,000 to one of the major black churches that was willing to start a Tuskegee in Africa. Walker also gave funds to existing mission schools, such as the Pondoland School in South Africa, and she paid for a young African boy to attend Tuskegee in the hope that he would be able to help develop an industrial school on the West Coast of Africa. Bundles, *On Her Own Ground*, 250.

56. Lewis, *When Harlem Was in Vogue*, 42; Ted Vincent, ed., *Voices of a Black Nation*, 93.

57. "Garvey Gains Confidence of Madam Walker," *New York Amsterdam News*, July 6, 1938. According to this newspaper account, Walker frequently gave money to Garvey and the UNIA. See also Bureau of Investigations Report on Various Supporters, December 5, 1918, cited in Lewis, *W. E. B. Du Bois*, 59.

58. "Memorandum of Peace Proposals of the International League of Darker Peoples," *World Forum*, January 1919, in M1440, reel 5: 3–4, File 10218–296, Correspondence of the Military Intelligence Division Relating to Negro Subversion, RG 165, Records of the War Department General and Special Staffs.

59. Ibid., 1.

60. Ibid., 2–3.

61. F. B. Ransom to Madam Walker, January 17, 1919, box 1, MWC-IHS.

62. Ibid., February 1, 1919.

63. R. W. Finch, "Japanese Intrigue With Negroes and Other Dark Skinned Radicals," March 5, 1919, 1. M1440 reel 5, File 10218–296, Correspondence of the Military Intelligence Division Relating to Negro Subversion, RG 165, Records of the War Department General and Special Staffs.

64. See Acting Chief to R. W. Flourney, Esq., Chief Bureau of Citizenship, State Department, January 4, 1919, reel 761 OG336880, RG 65 FBI M1085 761, Records of the FBI. See also J. M. Dunn to R. W. Flourney, January 16, 1919, in *Federal Surveillance of Afro-Americans*, ed. Kornweibel, reel 22.

65. Jessie Fauset, "Looking Glass," *The Crisis*, March 1919.

66. Lewis, *W. E. B. Du Bois*, 60.

67. F. B. Ransom to Madam Walker, February 3, 1919, box 1, MWC-IHS.

68. See List of correspondents, box 9, MWC-IHS.

69. For a report of just one of many such occasions, see Madam Walker to F. B. Ransom, September 1, 1915, box 1, MWC-IHS.

70. See, for example, Jacques Garvey, "Woman's Mode of Dress," *Negro World*, December 20, 1924.

71. Jacques Garvey, "Shopping at This Time of Year a Pleasure," *Negro World*, December 13, 1924.

72. "Report of Joseph G. Tucker, Department of Justice–Bureau of Investigation Surveillance of Black Americans," in *Federal Surveillance of Afro-Americans*, ed. Kornweibel, reel 1. For a fuller discussion of the *Negro World*'s circulation figures, see Chapter 4.

73. *Walker News*, August 1930.

74. Fauset, *There Is Confusion*, 83.

75. Bundles, *On Her Own Ground*, 117.

76. *New York Age*, February 8, 1919.

77. Bowles, "Negro Women and the YWCA of the United States," p. 3, series 3A, reel 107.8, NBA

78. The Walker Manufacturing Company had placed advertisements in *The Crisis* since 1912, and Walker frequently made donations, including a gift of $5,000, to the Anti-Lynching Campaign in 1919. See Mr. Storey's Secretary to Mrs. C. J. Walker, May 10, 1919, reel 1, Part 7: The Anti-Lynching Campaign, 1912–1955, Series B: Anti-Lynching Legislative and Publicity Files, 1916–1955, NAACP-LOC.

79. Minutes of the 1912 NACW Hampton Biennial Convention, reel 1, NACWC Papers.

80. Minutes of the 1918 NACW Denver Biennial Convention, reel 1, NACWC Papers.

81. The Madam Walker Benevolent Association would affiliate with both the NACW and later the NCNW. See Minutes of the 1918 NACW Denver Biennial Convention, reel 16, MCT-LOC.

82. "Mme C J Walker Delivers Address," *Chicago Defender*, July 12, 1918; Davis, *Lifting As They Climb*, 262–63.

83. See, for example, *National Notes*, June 1927, in which Walker is described as a "race genius," who "still lives, in the hearts of her daughters and men and women she grouped about her to carry on."

84. Mary McLeod Bethune to Madam Walker, April 5, 1917, box 1, MWC-IHS.

85. Madam Walker to F. B. Ransom, April 17, 1916, box 1, MWC-IHS.

86. Notice to the Agents of the Madam C. J. Walker Manufacturing Company, 1917, box 7, MWC-IHS.

87. Madam Walker to F. B. Ransom, April 17, 1916, box 1, MWC-IHS.

88. "Business Women Give to Memorial Fund," *New York Age*, April 13, 1918.

89. Notice to the Agents of the Madam C. J. Walker Manufacturing Company, 1917, box 7, MWC-IHS.

90. Hints to Agents, 1917, box 7, MWC-IHS.

91. Ibid.

92. Ibid.

93. Ibid.

94. Madam Walker to F. B. Ransom, September 16, 1916, box 1, MWC-IHS.

95. Hints to Agents, 1917, box 7, MWC-IHS.

96. *New York Age*, September 8, 1917. Walker agents used a variety of names for the local and regional chapters and conventions. While regional chapters were often called the Madam Walker Benevolent Association, in national convention, the organization was usually referred to as the Madam Walker Beauty Culturists Union. Delegates to the convention wore badges marked "Madam C. J. Walker National Association of Hair Growers."

97. Walker Company Press Release in "National and Regional Conventions," box 12, MWC-IHS. See also *The Crisis*, November 1917.

98. Walker Company Press Release in "National and Regional Conventions," box 12, MWC-IHS.

99. Kelley, "We Are Not What We Seem," 78.

100. "Madam Walker Tells of Her Success," *Pittsburgh Courier*, April 18, 1918.

101. *Chicago Defender*, August 9, 1919.

102. Resolution of Walker Employees at Madam Walker's Death, 1919, p. 1, box 3, MWC-IHS.

103. *Chicago Defender* August 10, 1918.

104. Early Press Release on Madam Walker, n.d., box 12, MWC-IHS.

105. Du Bois, "A Great Woman," *The Crisis*, July 1919; George Schuyler, "Madam Walker," *Messenger*, August 1924, 151–58, 264–66.

106. For the importance of the social context rather than physical nature of black women's work, see Jones, *American Work*, 17.

107. Gilroy, "One Nation under a Groove," 274; Hunter, *To Joy My Freedom*.

108. Van Vechten, *Nigger Heaven*. A'Lelia later wrote to Carl Van Vechten thanking him for his portrayal of her as the exotic society hostess. See A'Lelia Walker to Carl Van Vechten, August 8, 1926, in Carl Van Vechten Papers, Manuscripts Division, New York Public Library, New York.

109. Carl Van Vechten to Chester Himes, in *Keep a-Inchin' Along*, by Carl Van Vechten, 154.

110. Hughes, *Big Sea*, 247.

111. *Walker News*, September 1931, box 12, MWC-IHS.

112. Bundles, *On Her Own Ground*, 281.

113. Lowry, *Her Dream of Dreams*, 426–41. The novelist Ben Neihart's fictional account of A'Lelia, *Rough Amusements*, subtitled *The True Story of A'Lelia Walker, Patroness of the Harlem Renaissance's Down-Low Culture*, has also perpetuated the image of A'Lelia as nothing more than a party girl.

114. *Inter-State Tattler*, September 10, 1931, cited in *Power of Pride*, ed. Marks and Edkins, 66.

115. Marks and Edkins, eds., *Power of Pride*, 66.

116. *The Colored American Review*, March 1916.

117. Madam Walker to F. B. Ransom, February 22, 1916, box 1, MWC-IHS.

118. *Afro American Baltimore*, December 6, 1930, TICF.

119. Ibid.

120. J. M. Dunn to R. W. Flourney, January 16, 1919, in *Federal Surveillance of Afro-Americans*, ed. Kornweibel, reel 22.

121. A'Lelia Walker to F. B. Ransom, July 24, 1918, box 4, MWC-IHS.

122. See F. B. Ransom to Madam Walker, January 6, 1918, box 1, MWC-IHS.

123. *The Crisis*, May 1919; Moton, *Finding a Way Out*, 250–65.

124. *Pittsburgh Courier*, September 5, 1918; A'Lelia Walker to F. B. Ransom, July 24, 1918, box 4, MWC-IHS.

125. *Pittsburgh Courier*, September 5 1918.

126. Codicil to the Last Will and Testament of Sarah Walker and the Court's Construction Thereof, item 3, p.2, box 3. MWC-IHS; *New York Amsterdam News*, December 3, 1930. For an example of a Harlem Renaissance author hoping to be invited to Villa Lewaro see Jessie Fauset to Langston Hughes, box 61, Tues. 23, n.d., LHP; For details of A'Lelia's parties see Hughes, *Big Sea*, 244–46; Bundles, *On Her Own Ground*, 283.

127. Publicity file, box 12, MWC-IHS.

128. Ibid.

129. Ibid.

130. "Some of the Reasons Why You Should Buy Mme C J Walker Preparations," Publicity File, box 12, MWC-IHS.

131. Schuyler, "Madam Walker," *Messenger*, August 1924, 151–58, 264–66.

132. *Messenger*, October 1926.

133. Bundles, *On Her Own Ground*, 139–42.

134. A'Lelia Walker to F. B. Ransom, January 5, 1924, box 4, MWC-IHS. See also *The Crisis*, January 1924.

135. "Atlanta Ready for Walker Agents' Enthusiastic Convention August 12–14," *New York Amsterdam News*, August 5, 1925.

136. Grace Nail Johnson, memo to Women's Auxiliary (WA) members, February 5, 1925, series C, container 416, NAACP-LOC.

137. Bessie Olive Miller, President of the WA, to Members, January 20, 1925, series C, container 416, NAACP-LOC.

138. WA memo, April 1925, series C, container 417, NAACP-LOC.

139. Miss Randolph to Mrs. McClendon, June 15, 1925, series C, container 416, NAACP-LOC.

140. *Negro World*, June 7, 1919, cited in Vincent, *Keep Cool*, 120.

141. Vincent, *Keep Cool*, 120–21.

142. Lewis, *When Harlem Was in Vogue*, 167.

143. A'Lelia Walker to F. B. Ransom, October 18, 1927, box 4, MWC-IHS.

144. In his account of an evening at the Dark Tower, Harold Jackman told his friend Countee Cullen that one guest was so cross that A'Lelia wanted to charge fifty cents that A'Lelia struck him and was nearly embroiled in a physical fight. Harold Jackman to Countee Cullen, December 12, 1929, CCP.

145. Harold Jackman to Countee Cullen, April 26, December 12, 1929, CCP.

146. Ida Cullen, interviewed by Jim Hatch, December 15, 1971, Ida Cullen's apartment, New York City. Hatch-Billops Collection, Schomburg Center for Research in Black Culture, New York City.

147. A'Lelia Walker, cited in Marks and Edkins, eds., *Power of Pride*, 75.

148. For Madam Walker's foreign press notices, see Madam Walker to F. B. Ransom, September 9, 1915, box 1, MWC-IHS. For A'Lelia's Covent Garden entrance, see Van Vechten, *Keep a-Inchin' Along*, 282.

149. See A'Lelia Walker to F. B. Ransom, May 4, 1917, June 12, 1924, February 28, 1925, October 31, 1925, March 6, 1926, box 4, MWC-IHS.

150. *Colored American Review*, March 1916.

Chapter 4. Amy Jacques Garvey, Jessie Fauset, and Pan-African Feminist Thought

1. The campaign against Garvey among the black intelligentsia was led by the black socialist and *Messenger* editor Chandler Owen. Although Du Bois used the *Crisis* to launch his attacks on Garvey, he was not one of the many editors who signed the letter. See Letter to the U.S. Attorney General, January 15, 1923, series II, reel 35, *NAACP Papers*.

Other black newspapers that carried attacks on Garvey included the *New York Amsterdam News*, the *New York Age*, the *Pittsburgh Courier*, and the *Chicago Defender*.

2. See Martin, *Literary Garveyism*; Martin, ed., *African Fundamentalism*. See also Vincent, *Voices of a Black Nation*. For accounts which stress Garveyism's failure as a political movement and which overlook his literary contribution to the Harlem Renaissance, see Lewis, *When Harlem Was in Vogue*, and Anderson, *This Was Harlem*. More recent studies have analyzed Garveyism and the Harlem Renaissance together. See, for example, Stephens, *Black Empire*, and Turner, *Caribbean Crusaders*.

3. For Department of Justice estimates of black publication circulation figures, see "Report of Joseph G. Tucker," in *Federal Surveillance of Afro-Americans*, ed. Kornweibel, reel 1. For more details on circulation of the *Negro World*, see Lewis, *Marcus Garvey*, 81–82.

4. Jacques Garvey, *Garvey and Garveyism*, 25.

5. Du Bois citation in Hill, "Making Noise," 118; McKay "stupendous vaudeville" in *Harlem*, 9; *New York Age* 28 August, 1920, both cited in Krasner, *Beautiful Pageant*, 185.

6. *Negro World* cited in Hill, "Making Noise," 184.

7. For early critiques of Garvey, see, for example, Cronon, *Black Moses*; Draper, *Rediscovery of Black Nationalism*, 48–56; Franklin, *From Slavery to Freedom*, 489–92.

8. See Martin, *Literary Garveyism*; Martin, ed., *African Fundamentalism*; Krasner, *Beautiful Pageant*.

9. See, for example, Martin, "Women in the Garvey Movement," 67.

10. There were only two black women signatories to the call of 1908 which resulted in the Niagara Movement and later formation of the NAACP: Ida B. Wells and Mary Church Terrell. See Salem, "Black Women and the NAACP," 54–70.

11. "Declaration of the Rights of the Negro Peoples of the World. Article XII, Section 1," in *Philosophy and Opinions*, ed. Jacques Garvey, 136–37.

12. There is little scholarship on the Black Cross Nurses and the African Motor Corps. The Black Cross Nurses were constituted because African American women were not allowed to serve in the Red Cross. They had their own column on Jacques Garvey's Women's Page in the *Negro World* where they offered health advice. The African Motor Corps was a military unit that focused on car mechanic skills. See McDonnaugh, "Sister Samad," 80. For more information on both units, see Hill et al., eds., *Marcus Garvey and the UNIA Papers*, 3:766–72.

13. *Negro World*, January 1, 1921; reprinted in the Baltimore *Afro-American*, cited in Krasner, *Beautiful Pageant*, 170.

14. *Negro World*, June 23, 1923, cited in Bair, "True Women, Real Men," 156.

15. Ibid.

16. Ibid.

17. Stephens, *Black Empire*, 83.

18. Ibid., 101.

19. Summers, *Manliness and Its Discontents*, 134.

20. Mitchell, *Righteous Propaganda*, 228–29.

21. Lewis, *Marcus Garvey*, 85.

22. "Unity of Our Women," in Minutes of the Convention of the UNIA, August 31, 1922, in *Marcus Garvey and the UNIA Papers,* ed. Hill et al., 4:1037.

23. Ibid.

24. Ibid., 4:1038.

25. Ibid., 4:1037–38.

26. Ibid., 4:1037.

27. Martin, "Women in the Garvey Movement," 68.

28. Yard, *Biography of Amy Ashwood Garvey,* 67–69.

29. Taylor, *Veiled Garvey,* 30.

30. Seraille, "Henrietta Vinton Davis and the Garvey movement," 1073–91. The *Negro World* contains numerous articles describing the enthusiastic audiences that greeted Davis's speaking tours. See, for example, *Negro World,* February 26, December 10, 1921.

31. Davis, "Exigencies of Leadership: Women Determined to Measure Up If Negro Men Fail," *Negro World,* October 17, 1925.

32. De Mena, "To the Editor of the Women's Page: Part Women Must Play in the Organization," *Negro World,* January 23, 1926. For more on De Mena, see Hill et al., eds., *Marcus Garvey and UNIA Papers,* 1:376–77.

33. De Mena, "To the Editor of the Women's Page: Part Women Must Play in the Organization."

34. Robnett, *How Long, How Long?*; Summers, *Manliness and Its Discontents,* 133.

35. Burroughs, "Unload the Leeches and Parasitic 'Toms.'"

36. For details of the relationship between Amy Ashwood and Amy Jacques Garvey, see Taylor, *Veiled Garvey,* 23–28.

37. *Commercial Fortune Cincinnati,* May 21, 1923, cited in Taylor, *Veiled Garvey,* 51.

38. Jacques Garvey, *Garvey and Garveyism,* 117.

39. See Martin, *Marcus Garvey, Hero,* cited in Adler, "Always Leading Our Men," 348.

40. Stein, *World of Marcus Garvey,* 151, cited in Adler, "Always Leading Our Men," 348.

41. Reed, "Amy Jacques Garvey," *Ebony,* June 1971.

42. Smith, "Women and the Garvey Movement in Jamaica," 78.

43. Throughout the history of feminism, women have frequently been attacked for their private conduct, especially in terms of their relationships with men. See, for example, Chilton, *Billie's Blues,* 68–69. For work that corrects this, see Davis, *Blues Legacies and Black Feminism,* 94.

44. Reed, "Amy Jacques Garvey," *Ebony,* June 1971, 2.

45. Jacques Garvey, *Garvey and Garveyism,* 218–19, 244–52.

46. *Negro World,* March 17, 1923.

47. Jacques Garvey, ed., *Philosophy and Opinions.*

48. *Pittsburgh American,* July 20, 1923, cited in Taylor, *Veiled Garvey,* 50.

49. *Negro World,* July 14, 1923.

50. Ibid., July 21, 1923.

51. Ibid.

52. Reed, "Amy Jacques Garvey," *Ebony*, June 1971, 2; Jacques Garvey, *Garvey and Garveyism*, 196–97, 219, 244–52.

53. Jacques Garvey, *Garvey and Garveyism*, 196–97, 219.

54. *Negro World*, October 24, 1925.

55. Taylor, *Veiled Garvey*, 87.

56. Ibid., 64, 67, 1.

57. Jacques Garvey, *Garvey and Garveyism*, 43.

58. Ibid., 164.

59. Yuval-Davis, *Gender and Nation*, 80. See also Walby, "Is Citizenship Gendered?" 397–95.

60. Jacques Garvey, *Garvey and Garveyism*, 117.

61. Marcus Garvey to Amy Jacques Garvey, June 9, 1926, Marcus Garvey Memorial Collection, Fisk University Special Collections.

62. *Negro World*, June 30, 1923; Jacques Garvey, *Garvey and Garveyism*, 117.

63. *Negro World*, April 11, 1925.

64. Ibid., August 2, 1924.

65. Ibid., June 7, 1924.

66. Adler, "Always Leading Our Men," 361–62, and White, *Too Heavy a Load*, 138–40.

67. James, *Holding Aloft the Banner of Ethiopia*, 148.

68. *Negro World*, June 14, 1924.

69. Ibid., June 7, 1925.

70. Ibid., October 18, 1924.

71. Ibid., October 24, 1925.

72. Ibid., June 7, 1925.

73. Ibid., October 3, 1925.

74. Ibid., August 22, 1925.

75. Ibid., December 13, 1924.

76. Ibid., June 7, 1925.

77. Ibid., October 24, 1925.

78. Ibid.

79. Report of Jacques Garvey's June 29 speech in the *Negro World*, July 4, 1925, 3.

80. *Negro World*, January 19, 1926.

81. James, *Holding Aloft the Banner of Ethiopia*, 154.

82. Taylor, *Veiled Garvey*, 84; Garland, *Women Activists*.

83. *Negro World*, January 19, 1926.

84. Ibid.

85. Ibid., October 24, 1925.

86. Ibid., December 19, 1925.

87. The origins of the women's movement in the abolitionist struggles of the antebellum period are well known. After the Fourteenth Amendment, with the first reference to citizens being male, the two movements split as white women leaders tired of being made to wait while black men were enfranchised. See Davis, *Women, Race, and Class*, 30–46.

88. The congress aimed to bring together people of African descent to discuss the means of bringing about an Africa free from white rule. In 1944 Du Bois and Amy Jacques Garvey began to collaborate to organize a Fifth Pan-African Congress which would be held in Manchester in October 1945. See W. E. B. Du Bois to Amy Jacques Garvey, April 7, 1944, in the Amy Jacques Garvey Papers, Marcus Garvey Memorial Collection, Fisk University Archives. For more on the Pan-African Congress, see Adi and Sherwood, eds., *The 1945 Manchester Pan-African Congress Revisited.*

89. Jacques Garvey, "Role of Women in Liberation Struggles," 109–12.

90. Bone, *Negro Novel in America*, 102.

91. Sylvander, *Jessie Redmon Fauset*, 25–26.

92. Starkey, "Jessie Fauset," *Southern Workman*, May 1932, 217–20.

93. Sylvander, *Jessie Redmon Fauset*, 33. Although Fauset refers to her teaching at Dunbar, which she did from 1917 to 1919, I usually use its earlier name, the M Street High School, as this was the name of the school Fauset taught at for twelve of her fourteen years as a Washington schoolteacher.

94. Du Bois, *Correspondence of W. E. B. Du Bois*, 143.

95. Douglas, *Terrible Honesty*, 83.

96. Carby, *Race Men*, 12.

97. Yolande Du Bois to W. E. B. Du Bois, May 23, 1929, reel 28, *Du Bois Papers*.

98. Correspondence between Fauset and Du Bois hints at a relationship more intimate than friendship. For example, on her way to France in 1914, Fauset writes to Du Bois of how she tucked his letter under her pillow all night. Jessie Fauset to W. E. B. Du Bois, June 24, 1914, reel 4, *Du Bois Papers*. Lewis is convinced that the pair had been lovers for some time prior to the Pan-African Congress of 1922; his case seems to rest on their absence from the office as well as Fauset's poems about heartbreak. See Lewis, *W. E. B. Du Bois*, 49–50, 188–90, 215, 267, 272, 274.

99. Publicly, Fauset always professed her loyalty to Du Bois, but in correspondence with close friends, Fauset revealed her frustration that Du Bois took her support for granted. See Jessie Fauset, letter to Joel Spingarn, January, 17 1926, box 4. Joel Spingarn Papers, Manuscript Division, New York Public Library.

100. See, for example, Fauset's letters to Langston Hughes: November 10, December 7, 1920, January 18, 1921, May 6, 1924, box 61, LHP.

101. See, for example, Langston Hughes's letter to Claude McKay, September 13, 1928, in which Hughes responds to McKay's complaints about Du Bois's editorship of *The Crisis*. Box 2, Claude McKay Collection, Yale Collection of American Literature, Beinecke Rare Books and Manuscript Library.

102. Douglas, *Terrible Honesty*, 83. On Fauset's role as a promoter during the Harlem Renaissance, see Johnson, "Literary Midwife," 143–53.

103. Maureen Honey estimates that from 1918 to 1927, excluding those names whose gender is not obvious, there are a total of 347 poems by men in *The Crisis* and *Opportunity*, and 277 by women. She also estimates that the numbers for *The Crisis* were more or less even. See Honey, *Shadowed Dreams*, 2, n. 5.

104. Hull, *Color, Sex, and Poetry*, 10–13.

105. William Stanley Braithwaite, cited in Johnson, "Literary Midwife," 143–53.

106. Locke, cited in Sylvander, *Jessie Redmon Fauset*, 73–75; Schuyler, *Messenger*, May 1924, 145.

107. Other women writers who experienced similarly personal attacks on their work include Zora Neale Hurston. See, for example, Richard Wright on Hurston's *Their Eyes Were Watching God* in *Zora Neale Hurston*, ed. Gates and Appiah, 17.

108. Eric Walrond to Countee Cullen, October 1925, reel 1, CCP.

109. Walrond, "Review of Jessie Fauset's *There Is Confusion*," in *New Republic*, July 9, 1924, 192.

110. McKay, *A Long Way from Home*, 112. Claude McKay to Arthur Schomburg, April 28, 1925, Arthur Schomburg Papers, SC.

111. Starkey, "Jessie Fauset," *Southern Workman*, May 1932, 219.

112. Harold Jackman to Countee Cullen, January 31, 1929, reel 1, CCP.

113. Thaddious M. Davis, foreword to *There Is Confusion*, by Fauset, vi.

114. Regina Andrews becomes Regina Anderson after her marriage. Jessie Fauset to Alain Locke, January 9, 1933, box 164–28, Alain Locke Collection, Moorland-Spingarn Research Center. Locke wrote a patronizing article about Fauset's book *The Chinaberry Tree*. See Locke, "We Turn to Prose," *Opportunity*, February 1932.

115. Lewis, *When Harlem Was in Vogue*, 96.

116. Locke, *New Negro*. See Scruggs, "Alain Locke and Walter White," 91–99.

117. Du Bois even suggested he would have to withdraw his own contribution unless Fauset's was also accepted. W. E. B. Du Bois to Alain Locke, May 13, 1925, reel 15, *Du Bois Papers*.

118. Green, *Time's Unfading Garden*, 140.

119. Jessie Fauset to Langston Hughes, June 9, 1949, box 61, LHP.

120. Jessie Fauset to Langston Hughes, April 23, n.y., box 61, LHP.

121. Fauset, *Brownies' Book*, January 1920. Fauset also regularly published the poet Lucian B. Watkins, the most prolific *Negro World* poet.

122. Fauset, "The Judge," *Brownies' Book*, February 1920.

123. Haynes, "Benjamin Banneker," *Brownies' Book*, June 1920; Fauset, *Brownies' Book*, April 1920.

124. Like *The Crisis*, *The Brownies' Book* has long been attributed to Du Bois. However, as the correspondence and issues reveal, Fauset did much of the work for this publication. See Sinnette, "The Brownies' Book," 137.

125. Fauset, "Thru the Looking Glass," *The Crisis*, November 1919.

126. Johnson, autobiographical introduction, in *Caroling Dusk*, ed. Cullen, 74; Fauset, *Plum Bun*.

127. Gwendolyn Bennett, "To Usward," *The Crisis*, May 1924.

128. Hull, ed., *Give Us Each Day*, 21, 45, 367, 428.

129. Juliette Dericotte, "Reference for Jessie Fauset," box 51, Harmon Foundation Files, Manuscript Division, LOC. Derricotte was a leading YWCA student worker. In her reference for Fauset she describes how Fauset led discussion groups and interpreted black thought for the YWCA. See also correspondence between Jessie Fauset and Addie Hunton, *Crisis* File, March 11, 1921 series F, container 1, NAACP-LOC.

130. Fauset, "On the Bookshelf," *Crisis*, June 1921.

131. Hughes, *Big Sea*, 247.

132. Fauset, *Crisis* report, April 1919, reel 8, *Du Bois Papers*.

133. Fauset, "Nationalism and Egypt," *The Crisis*, April 1920, 310–16.

134. Fauset, *The Crisis*, November 1919.

135. The other women taking part in the Second Pan-African Congress were Addie Hunton and Mary Talbert. See Plastas, "Band of Noble Women," 56–139; Fauset, "Impressions of the Second Pan-African Congress," *The Crisis*, November 1921, 12.

136. Fauset, "Impressions of the Second Pan-African Congress," 12.

137. Fauset, *The Crisis*, October 1922. Fauset belonged to several clubwomen's organizations, including the Anti-Lynching Crusaders and the NAACP's Women's Auxiliary.

138. Bone, *Negro Novel in America*, 99, 101.

139. Jones, "Myth of a Negro Literature," 294.

140. Davis, *From the Dark Tower*, 90.

141. Wall, "Passing for What?" 87–103.

142. Baker, *Blues, Ideology, and Afro-American Literature*; Carby, "It Jus Be's Dat Way Sometime."

143. For critiques of Baker, see Ducille, "Blues Notes on Black Sexuality," 193–97. See also Ducille's book-length study *Coupling Convention*, esp. Chapter 5, and McClendon, *Politics of Color*.

144. McDowell, "Introduction: Regulating Midwives," xxii. See also McDowell, "Neglected Dimension of Jessie Redmon Fauset," 879–95; Foreman, "Looking Back from Zora," 655.

145. For examples of this excellent work, see Hunter, *To Joy My Freedom*; Davis, *Blues Legacies and Black Feminism*.

146. Batker, *Reforming Fictions*, 7, 64, 71–72.

147. *There Is Confusion* has been the least understood of Fauset's novels, while *The Chinaberry Tree* has received relatively little critical attention. *Plum Bun* has generally been considered Fauset's best novel. Her final novel, *Comedy: American Style*, has recently become a more popular text for critical review.

148. Fauset, *There Is Confusion*, 37.

149. Ibid., 275.

150. Ibid., 160–61.

151. Ibid., 157.

152. Ibid.

153. Ibid., 146.

154. Ibid., 76.

155. Ibid.

156. Ibid., 95.

157. Ibid., 98.

158. Ibid.

159. Ibid., 232.

160. Ibid.

161. Fauset, "Symbolism of Bert Williams," *The Crisis*, May 1922.

162. Fauset, *There Is Confusion*, 292.

163. Ibid., 234.
164. See Jessie Fauset to Langston Hughes, June 15, 1925, box 61, LHP.
165. Feminist critics who deplore or struggle with this ending include McDowell, "Neglected Dimension of Jessie Redmon Fauset," 879–95; and Gilbert and Gubar, "Ain't I a New Woman," in *No Man's Land*, ed. Gilbert and Gubar.
166. Fauset, *There Is Confusion*, 291.
167. Ibid., 284.
168. Ibid., 191.
169. Ducille, *Coupling Convention*, 93.
170. Fauset, *There Is Confusion*, 83–84.
171. Ibid., 261.
172. Ibid., 81.
173. Ibid., 258–68.
174. Fauset, *Chinaberry Tree*, 121.
175. Ibid., 8.
176. Ibid., 124.
177. Ibid., 59.
178. Ibid., 62.
179. Ibid., 121.
180. Ibid., 132.
181. Ibid., 131.
182. Ibid., 207–11.
183. Ibid., 213.
184. Ibid., 226.
185. Ibid., 228.
186. Ibid., 251–52.
187. Welter, "Cult of True Womanhood," 151–74.
188. Fauset, *Chinaberry Tree*, 265.
189. Ibid., 256.
190. Ibid., 131.
191. Ibid., 132.
192. Jessie Fauset to W. E. B. Du Bois, February 16, 1905, reel 1, *Du Bois Papers*.
193. Vincent, *Keep Cool*, 147.
194. Jacques Garvey, ed., *Philosophy and Opinions*, 138.
195. Jacques Garvey, *Garvey and Garveyism*, 270–71.

Epilogue

1. Alice Woodby McKane to Herbert J. Seligmann, December 21, 1921, Subject File Marcus Garvey, part II, reel 35, *NAACP Papers*.
2. Lewis, *When Harlem Was in Vogue*, 44.
3. Sicherman et al., eds., *Notable American Women*, s.v. "Eunice Hunton Carter."
4. Height, *Open Wide the Freedom Gates*, 83.
5. Collins, *Black Feminist Thought*, 22–33.
6. Davis, *Lifting As They Climb*, 14–15.

7. More, *Leading the Race*, 5–6.

8. "An Account of Addresses by Washington and Mrs. Washington," September 12, 1898, *BTW Papers*, 4:464.

9. Gordon, "Black and White Visions of Welfare," 578.

10. Hull, ed., *Give Us Each Day*, 17–18; Georgia Douglas Johnson to Harold Jackman, September 19, 1938, Harold Jackman–Countee Cullen Memorial Collection, Atlanta University Center Archives.

11. Jessie Fauset to Joel Spingarn, June 6, 1927, Joel E. Spingarn Papers, Manuscript and Rare Books Division, NYPL.

12. Hedgeman, *Trumpet Sounds*, 55.

13. Gaines, *Uplifting the Race*, xi–xv; Higginbotham, *Righteous Discontent*, 185–229.

14. Wolcott, "Bible, Bath, and Broom"; Gordon, "Black and White Visions of Welfare," 578.

15. Jones, *Labor of Love, Labor of Sorrow*, 57.

16. Davis, *Lifting As We Climb*, 72, 78–81.

17. Rouse, "Out of the Shadow of Tuskegee," 39.

18. *Negro World*, February 12, 1927.

19. Collins, *Black Feminist Thought*, 19–33; bell hooks, *Feminist Theory*.

20. See Cecelia Cabaniss Saunders to Reverdy Ransom, March 12, 1947, cited in Weisenfeld, *African American Women and Christian Activism*, 201.

21. Robertson, "Deeper Even Than Race?" 384.

22. Chafe, *Civilities and Civil Rights*, 243.

23. Irvin-Smith, *Marcus Garvey's Footsoldiers*, 59.

24. Jacques Garvey, "Role of Women in Liberation Struggles," *Massachusetts Review*, 109–2.

25. Hedgeman, *Trumpet Sounds*, 44.

26. Excerpts from Speech by Addie Waites Hunton at the Twenty-Third Annual Conference of the NAACP, May 17–22, [1932], part 1, reel 9, *NAACP Papers*, cited in Lutz, "Dizzy Steps to Heaven," 261.

27. Burroughs, "With All Thy Getting."

28. For a discussion of Bakhtin's double-voiced discourse, see Higginbotham, "African-American Women's History and the Metalanguage of Race," 266–67.

29. Hurston to Margrit Sabloniere, December 3, 1955, cited in Boyd, *Wrapped in Rainbows*, 424.

30. Hurston, "Court Order Can't Make Races Mix," *Orlando Sentinel*, August 11, 1955, cited in Boyd, *Wrapped in Rainbows*, 424.

Bibliography

Manuscripts and Archival Sources

ATLANTA UNIVERSITY CENTER, ATLANTA

Harold Jackman–Countee Cullen Memorial Collection

BEINECKE RARE BOOK AND MANUSCRIPT LIBRARY, YALE COLLECTION OF AMERICAN LITERATURE, YALE UNIVERSITY, NEW HAVEN, CONN.

Claude McKay Collection
James Weldon Johnson Collection
Langston Hughes Papers

BRITISH NEWSPAPER LIBRARY, LONDON

Tuskegee Institute Newspaper Clippings File

BUTLER LIBRARY, RARE BOOKS AND MANUSCRIPTS, COLUMBIA UNIVERSITY, NEW YORK, N.Y.

L. S. Gumby Papers

FISK UNIVERSITY SPECIAL COLLECTIONS, FISK UNIVERSITY, NASHVILLE

Marcus Garvey Memorial Collection
Amy Jacques Garvey Papers

INDIANA HISTORICAL SOCIETY, INDIANAPOLIS

Madam Walker Collection

MANUSCRIPT DIVISION, LIBRARY OF CONGRESS, WASHINGTON, D.C.

Booker T. Washington Papers
Countee Cullen Papers
Harmon Foundation Files
Mary Church Terrell Papers
Mary McLeod Bethune Papers, Bethune Foundation Collection.
Nannie Helen Burroughs Papers
National Association for the Advancement of Colored Peoples Papers

Records of the National Negro Business League: Proceedings of the Annual Meeting of the National Negro Business League

MARY MCLEOD BETHUNE COUNCIL HOUSE, WASHINGTON, D.C.

National Council of Negro Women Papers

MOORLAND-SPINGARN RESEARCH CENTER, HOWARD UNIVERSITY, WASHINGTON, D.C.

Alain Locke Collection
Mary Church Terrell Papers

NATIONAL ARCHIVES, COLLEGE PARK, MD.

Records of the FBI. Acting Chief to R. W. Flourney, Esq., Chief Bureau of Citizenship, State Department, January 4, 1919, reel 761 OG336880, RG 65 FBI M1085761.
Records of the War Department General and Special Staffs, Correspondence of the Military Intelligence Division Relating to Negro Subversion. Reel 5, M1440S.
Report of R. W. Finch. "Japanese Intrigue with Negroes and Other Dark Skinned Radicals." March 5, 1919, file 10218-296, RG 165.
The World Forum. January 1919. From file 10218-296, RG 165.

NEW YORK CITY YWCA ARCHIVES, LEXINGTON AVENUE, NEW YORK

Cecelia Cabaniss Saunders, "A Half Century of the Young Women's Christian Association" (draft typescript, 1955)
Executive Committee Minutes of the 15th Street Association, YWCA of the City of New York
Minutes of the Board of Directors of the YWCA of the City of New York

NEW YORK PUBLIC LIBRARY, MANUSCRIPTS AND ARCHIVES DIVISION, FIFTH AVENUE BRANCH, NEW YORK

Carl Van Vechten Papers
Joel E. Spingarn Papers

SCHOMBURG CENTER FOR RESEARCH IN BLACK CULTURE, RARE BOOKS, NEW YORK

Arthur Schomburg Papers
Hatch-Billops Collection

YWCA OF THE USA, EMPIRE STATE BUILDING, NEW YORK

National Board Archives: Series 3 A: Reel 107.7—107.8: Inter-Racial practices, Negro Branches, 1924–1940
Eva Bowles, "Negro Women and the YWCA of the United States"
Annie Kate Gilbert, "Early Policies Regarding Branches: 1926–1940"
Council on Colored Work Minutes: 1907–1920
Colored Work Committee Summary of Minutes, compiled in 1931 from 1919 to 1931

Newspapers and Journals

Association Monthly, 1907–1922
Chicago Defender, 1913–1924
The Crisis, 1912–1935
Colored American Review, March 1916–August 1916
Messenger, 1918–1926
National Notes, 1897–1929
Negro World, 1921–1927
New York Age, 1906–1923
New York Amsterdam News, 1925–1938
Pittsburgh Courier, April–September 1918, 1926, 1930, 1943
Walker News, May 1928–September 1931

Published Primary Sources

Anthony, Susan B., and Ida Husted Harper, eds. *The History of Woman Suffrage: 1883– 1900,* vol. 4. Indianapolis: Hollenbeck Press, 1902.

Bell, Juliet O., and Wilkins, Helen J. *Interracial Practices in Community YWCAs: A Study under the Auspices of the Commission to Gather Interracial Experience as Requested by the 16th National Convention of the YWCAS of the USA.* New York: National Board of the YWCA, 1944.

Bethune, Mary McLeod. "My Last Will and Testament." *Ebony,* August 10, 1955.

Burroughs, Nannie Helen. "Report of the Work of Baptist Women: Twentieth Annual Report in Journal of the Twentieth Annual Session of the Woman's Convention Auxiliary to the National Baptist Convention, Held with the Second Baptist Church, Indianapolis, Indiana, September 8–13, 1920," 318–26, 332–47. Reprinted in *African American Religious History: A Documentary Witness,* edited by Milton C. Sernett. 2nd ed. Durham, N.C.: Duke University Press, 1999.

———. "Unload the Leeches and Parasitic 'Toms' and Take Promise Land." *Louisiana Weekly,* December 23, 1933, box 6, NHB-LOC.

———. "Up from the Depth," reprinted in *Rhetoric of Racial Revolt,* edited by Roy L. Hill. Denver: Golden Bell Press, 1964.

———. "With All Thy Getting." *Southern Workman* 56 (1927). In box 47, NHB-LOC.

Cullen, Countee, ed. *Caroling Dusk: An Anthology of Verse by Black Poets of the Twenties.* 1927; New York: Carol Publishing Group, 1993.

Davis, Elizabeth Lindsay. *Lifting As They Climb.* 1933; New York: G. K. Hall, 1996.

Du Bois, W. E. B. *The Correspondence of W. E. B. Du Bois,* vol. 1, *Selections, 1877–1934.* Edited by Herbert Aptheker. Amherst: University of Massachusetts Press, 1973.

———. *Dusk of Dawn.* New York: Harcourt, Brace, 1940.

———. *The Souls of Black Folk.* In *The Norton Anthology of African American Literature,* edited by Henry Louis Gates Jr. and Nellie McKay. New York: Norton, 1997.

Dunbar-Nelson Alice. "Negro Women and War Relief." In *Scott's Official History of the American Negro in the World War,* edited by Emmet J. Scott. Chicago: Homewood, 1919; reprint, New York: Arno, 1969. Also available online at <http://www.lib.byu.edu/~rdh/wwi/comment/Scott/SCh27.htm>, accessed on September 30, 2006.

Fauset, Jessie. *The Chinaberry Tree*. 1931; reprint, New York: G. K. Hall, 1995.
———. *Comedy: American Style*. 1933; reprint, College Park, Md.: McGrath, 1969.
———. *Plum Bun: A Novel without a Moral*. 1929; reprint, Boston: Beacon Press, 1990.
———. *There Is Confusion*. Foreword by Thaddious M. Davis. 1924; reprint, Boston: Northeastern University Press, 1989.
Harlan, Louis, ed. *The Booker T. Washington Papers*. 14 vols. Urbana: University of Illinois Press, 1972–1989.
Hedgeman, Anna Arnold. *The Trumpet Sounds: A Memoir of Negro Leadership*. New York: Holt, Rinehart, and Winston, 1964.
Hill, Robert A., et al., eds. *The Marcus Garvey and Universal Negro Improvement Association Papers*. Vols. 1, 3, and 4. Berkeley, Calif.: University of California Press, 1985.
Hughes, Langston. *The Big Sea: An Autobiography*. New York: Thunder's Mouth Press, 1986.
Hunton, Addie W. *Beginnings among Colored Women*. New York: Young Women's Christian Association, 1913.
Hunton, Addie W., and Kathryn M. Johnson. *Two Colored Women with the American Expeditionary Forces*. New York: G. K. Hall, 1997.
Irvin-Smith, Jeanette. *Marcus Garvey's Footsoldiers of the Universal Negro Improvement Association*. Trenton, N.J.: Africa World Press, 1989.
Jacques Garvey, Amy. *Garvey and Garveyism*. 1963. London: Macmillan, 1970.
———, ed. *Philosophy and Opinions of Marcus Garvey; or, Africa for the Africans*. 1923, 1925; reprint, Dover, Mass.: Majority Press, 1986.
———. "The Role of Women in Liberation Struggles." *Massachusetts Review* 13 (1972): 54–55.
Johnson, James Weldon. *Black Manhattan*. 1933. Reprint, New York: Da Capo Press, 1991.
———. *Negro Americans, What Now?* 1934. Reprint, New York: Da Capo Press, 1973.
Kornweibel, Theodore, ed. *Federal Surveillance of Afro-Americans 1917–1925: The First World War, the Red Scare, and the Garvey Movement*. Frederick, Md.: University Publications of America, 1986.
Lane, Linda Rochelle. *A Documentary History of Mrs. Booker T. Washington*. Lewiston, N.Y.: Edward Mellen Press, 2001.
Lerner, Gerda, ed. *Black Women in White America: A Documentary History*. New York: Vintage Books, 1972.
Locke, Alain. *The New Negro*. New York: Atheneum, 1925.
Madam C. J. Walker Beauty Manual: A Thorough Treatise Covering all Branches of Beauty Culture. Indianapolis: Madam Walker Manufacturing Company, 1928.
Mary McLeod Bethune Papers. Bethesda, Md.: University Publications of America, 1996.
McCluskey, Audrey Thomas, and Elaine M. Smith, eds. *Mary McLeod Bethune: Building a Better World: Essays and Selected Documents*. Bloomington: Indiana University Press, 1999.
McKay, Claude. *Home to Harlem*. New York: Harper and Bros., 1928.
———. *A Long Way from Home*. New York: Harcourt, Brace, and World, 1970.

National Association of Colored Women's Clubs Papers. Bethesda, Md.: University Publications of America, 1993–1994.

Olcott, Jane. *The Work of Colored Women.* New York: War Work Council of the National Board, YWCA, 1919.

Papers of the NAACP. Frederick, Md.: University Publications of America, 1982–1997.

Papers of W. E. B. Du Bois. Microfilm. Amherst: University of Massachusetts, 1980.

Ransom, Reverdy C. *The Pilgrimage of Reverdy Ransom's Son.* Nashville: AME Sunday School Union, n.d.

Reed, Beverly. "Amy Jacques Garvey-Black, Beautiful and Free." *Ebony,* June 1971.

Sims, Mary. *The First Twenty Five Years. Being a Summary of the Work of the YWCA of the USA, 1906–1931.* New York: YWCA, 1932.

———. *An Unfolding Purpose.* New York: National Board of YWCA, 1950.

Starkey, Marion L. "Jessie Fauset." *Southern Workman,* May 1932, 217–20.

Terrell, Mary Church. *A Colored Woman in a White World.* Washington, D.C.: 1940; reprint, New York: G. K. Hall, 1996.

Van Vechten, Carl. *Keep a-Inchin' Along: Selected Writings of Carl Van Vechten about Black Art and Letters.* Edited by Bruce Kellner. Westport, Conn., and London: Greenwood Press, 1979.

———. *Nigger Heaven.* New York: Knopf, 1926.

Walrond, Eric. "Review of Jessie Fauset's *There Is Confusion.*" *New Republic,* July 9, 1924.

Washington, Booker T. *Up from Slavery.* 1901; New York: Dover, 1995.

Wright, Richard. "Review of Their Eyes Were Watching God," *New Masses,* October 5, 1937. Reprinted in *Zora Neale Hurston: Critical Perspectives Past and Present,* edited by Henry Louis Gates Jr. and Anthony Appiah. New York: Amistad, 1993.

Woolf, Virginia. *Three Guineas.* New York: Harbinger, 1938.

Secondary Sources

Adeleke, Tunde. *UnAfrican Americans: Nineteenth-Century Black Nationalists and the Civilizing Mission.* Lexington: University Press of Kentucky, 1998.

———. *Without Regard to Race: The Other Martin Robison Delany.* Jackson: University Press of Mississippi, 2003.

Adi, Hakim., and Marika Sherwood. *The 1945 Manchester Pan-African Congress Revisited.* London: New Beacon Books, 1995.

Adler, Karen. "'Always Leading Our Men in Service and Sacrifice': Amy Jacques Garvey, Feminist Black Nationalist." *Gender and Society* 6 (1992): 346–75.

Anderson, Benedict. *Imagined Communities: Reflections on the Origin and Spread of Nationalism.* Rev. ed. London: Verso, 1991.

Anderson, Jervis. *A. Philip Randolph: A Biographical Portrait.* New York: Harcourt Brace Jovanovich, 1973.

———. *This Was Harlem: A Cultural Portrait, 1900–1950.* New York: Farrar, Straus, Giroux, 1982.

Asante, Molefi Kete. *Kernet, Afrocentricity, and Knowledge.* Trenton: Africa World Press, 1990.

Bair, Barbara. "Pan Africanism as Process: Adelaide Casely Hayford, Garveyism, and the Cultural Roots of Nationalism." In *Imagining Home: Class, Culture, and Nationalism in the African Diaspora*, edited by Sidney Lemelle and Robin D. G. Kelley, 121–44. New York: Verso, 1994.

———. "True Women, Real Men: Gender, Ideology, and Social Roles in the Garvey Movement." In *Gendered Domains: Rethinking Public and Private in Woman's History*, edited by Dorothy O. Helly and Susan M. Reverby, 154–66. Ithaca, N.Y.: Cornell University Press, 1992.

Baker, Houston A. *Blues, Ideology, and Afro-American Literature: A Vernacular Theory*. Chicago: University of Chicago Press, 1984.

Barbeau Arthur E., and Henri Florette. *Unknown Soldiers: Black American Troops in World War 1*. Philadelphia: Temple University Press, 1974.

Barnett, Evelyn Brooks. "Nannie Burroughs and the Education of Black Women." In *The Afro-American Woman: Struggles and Images*, edited by Sharon Harley and Rosalyn Terborg-Penn, 97–108. Baltimore: Black Classic Press, 1997.

———. "Religion, Politics, and Gender: The Leadership of Nannie Helen Burroughs." *Journal of Religious Thought* 44 (winter-spring 1988): 7–22.

Batker, Carol J. "'Love Me Like I Like to Be': The Sexual Politics of Hurston's *Their Eyes Were Watching God*, the Classic Blues, and the Black Women's Club Movement." *African American Review* 32, no. 2 (1998): 199–213.

———. *Reforming Fictions: Native, African, and Jewish American Women's Literature and Journalism in the Progressive Era*. New York: Columbia University Press, 2000.

Bennett, Lerone. *Pioneers in Protest*. Chicago: Johnson, 1968.

Biggart, Nicole. *Charismatic Capitalism: Direct Selling Organizations in America*. Chicago: University of Chicago Press, 1989.

Bone, Robert A. *The Negro Novel in America*. Rev. ed. New Haven: Yale University Press, 1965.

Boyd, Valerie. *Wrapped in Rainbows: The Life of Zora Neale Hurston*. London: Virago, 2003.

Bracey, John R., August Meier, and Elliot Rudwick, eds. *Black Nationalism in America*. Indianapolis: Bobbs-Merrill, 1970.

Bundles, A'Lelia. "Madam C. J. Walker." *American History*, August 1996.

———. *On Her Own Ground: The Life and Times of Madam C. J. Walker*. New York: Scribner, 2001.

———. "Sharing the Wealth." *Radcliffe Quarterly*, December 1991.

Carby, Hazel V. "It Jus Be's Dat Way Sometime: The Sexual Politics of Women's Blues." *Radical America* 20, no. 4: 238–49.

———. "Policing the Black Woman's Body in an Urban Context." *Critical Inquiry* 18 (1992): 738–55.

———. *Race Men*. Cambridge, Mass.: Harvard University Press, 1998.

———. *Reconstructing Womanhood: The Emergence of the Afro-American Woman Novelist*. Oxford: Oxford University Press, 1987.

Cash, Floris Barnett. *African American Women and Social Action: The Clubwoman and*

Volunteerism from Jim Crow to the New Deal, 1896–1926. Westport, Conn.: Greenwood, 2001.
Cell, John. *The Highest Stage of White Supremacy: The Origins of Segregation in South Africa and the American South*. Cambridge, England: Cambridge University Press, 1982.
Chafe, William. *Civilities and Civil Rights: Greensboro, North Carolina, and the Black Struggle for Freedom*. New York: Oxford University Press, 1980.
Chilton, John. *Billie's Blues: A Survey of Billie Holiday's Career, 1933–1959*. London: Quartet Books, 1977.
Christian, Barbara. *Black Feminist Criticism: Perspectives on Black Women Writers*. New York: Pergamon Press, 1985.
Collier-Thomas, Bettye. "National Council of Negro Women." In *Black Women in America: An Historical Encyclopedia*, volume 2, edited by Darlene Clark Hine, Elsa Barclay Brown, and Rosalyn Terborg-Penn, 853–864. Brooklyn, N.Y.: Carlson Publishing, 1992.
Collins, Patricia Hill. *Black Feminist Thought: Knowledge, Consciousness, and the Politics of Empowerment*. New York: Routledge, 1990.
———. "Producing the Mothers of the Nation: Race, Class, and Contemporary U.S. Population Politics." In *Women, Citizenship, and Difference*, edited by Nira Yuval-Davis and Pnina Werbner, 118–29. London: Zed, 1999.
Cott, Nancy F. *The Grounding of Modern Feminism*. New Haven: Yale University Press, 1987.
Cronon, E. David. *Black Moses: The Story of Marcus Garvey and the Universal Negro Improvement Association*. Madison: University of Wisconsin Press, 1955.
Cruse, Harold. *The Crisis of the Negro Intellectual*. 1967; New York: New York Review of Books, 2005.
Davies, Carol Boyce. *Black Women, Writing, and Identity: Migrations of the Subject*. New York: Routledge, 1994.
Davis, Angela. *Blues Legacies and Black Feminism*. New York: Vintage Books, 1999.
———. *Women, Race, and Class*. New York: Vintage Books, 1983.
Davis, Arthur Paul. *From the Dark Tower: Afro-American Writers, 1900 to 1960*. Washington, D.C.: Howard University Press, 1974.
Davis, Charles T., and Daniel Walden, eds. *On Being Black: Writings by Afro-Americans from Frederick Douglass to the Present*. Greenwich, Conn.: Fawcett, 1970.
Davis, Clarice Winn. "Eva del Vakia Bowles." In *Dictionary of Negro Biography*, edited by Rayford W. Logan and Michael R. Winson. New York: Norton, 1982.
Dodson, Dan W. *The Role of the YWCA in a Changing Era: The YWCA Study of YMCA-YWCA Cooperative Experiences*. New York: National Board of the YWCA, 1960.
Douglas, Ann. *Terrible Honesty: Mongrel Manhattan in the 1920s*. New York: Papermac, 1995.
Ducille, Ann. "Blues Notes on Black Sexuality: Sex and the Texts of Jessie Fauset and Nella Larsen." In *American Sexual Politics: Sex, Gender and Race since the Civil War*, edited by John C. Faut and Maura Shaw Tantillo, 193–219. Chicago: University of Chicago Press, 1993.

———. *The Coupling Convention: Sex, Text, and Tradition in Black Women's Fiction.* New York: Oxford University Press, 1993.

Duster, Alfreda M. *Crusade for Justice: The Autobiography of Ida B. Wells.* Chicago: University of Chicago Press, 1970.

Easter, O. V. *Nannie Helen Burroughs.* New York: Garland Publishing, 1995.

Enloe, Cynthia. *Bananas, Beaches, and Bases: Making Feminist Sense of International Politics.* London: Pandora, 1989.

Evans, Sara M. "Women's History and Political Theory." In *Visible Women: New Essays on American Activism,* edited by Nancy A. Hewitt and Suzanne Lesbock, 119–40. Urbana: University of Illinois Press, 1993.

Fairclough, Adam. *Better Day Coming: Blacks and Equality, 1890–2000.* New York: Penguin, 2001.

Ford-Smith, Honor. "Women and the Garvey Movement in Jamaica." In *Garvey: His Work and Impact,* edited by Rupert Lewis and Patrick Bryan, 73–86. Mona, Jamaica: Institute of Social and Economic Research, 1988.

Foreman, P. Gabrielle. "Looking Back from Zora, or Talking Out Both Sides My Mouth for Those Who Have Two Ears." *Black American Literature Forum* 24 (1990): 649–66.

Fout, John C., and Maura Shaw Tantillo. *American Sexual Politics: Sex, Gender, and Race since the Civil War.* Chicago: University of Chicago Press, 1993.

Fox, Stephen R. *The Guardian of Boston: William Monroe Trotter.* New York: Atheneum, 1970.

Franklin, John Hope. *From Slavery to Freedom: A History of Negro Americans.* 3rd ed. New York: Knopf, 1967.

Frazier, E. Franklin. *Black Bourgeoisie.* New York: Collier Books, 1962.

———. *The Negro Family in the United States.* Chicago: University of Chicago Press, 1939.

Freedman, Estelle B. "Separatism as Strategy: Female Institution Building and American Feminism, 1870–1930." *Feminist Studies* 1979, 5 (3): 512–29.

Gaines, Kevin. *Uplifting the Race: Black Leadership, Politics, and Culture in the Twentieth Century.* Chapel Hill: University of North Carolina Press, 1996.

Garland, Anne Witte. *Women Activists Challenging the Abuse of Power.* New York: Feminist Press, 1988.

Gatewood, William B. *Aristocrats of Color: The Black Elite, 1880–1920.* Bloomington: Indiana University Press, 1990.

Gayle, Addison. "The Black Aesthetic." In *The Norton Anthology of African American Literature,* edited by Henry Louis Gates Jr. and Nellie McKay. New York: Norton, 1997.

Giddings, Paula. *When and Where I Enter: The Impact of Black Women on Race and Sex in America.* New York: Bantam, 1984.

Gilbert, Sandra M., and Susan Gubar. *No Man's Land: The Place of the Woman Writer in the Twentieth Century.* New Haven: Yale University Press, 1989.

Gilmore, Glenda. *Gender and Jim Crow: Women and the Politics of White Supremacy in North Carolina, 1896–1920.* Chapel Hill: University of North Carolina Press, 1996.

Gilroy, Paul. *The Black Atlantic: Modernity and the Double Consciousness*. Cambridge, Mass.: Harvard University Press, 1993.

———. "One Nation under a Groove: The Cultural Politics of 'Race' and Racism in Britain." In *Anatomy of Racism*, edited by David Theo Goldberg, 263–82. Minneapolis: University of Minnesota Press, 1990.

Gordon, Ann D., and Bettye Collier-Thomas, eds. *African American Women and the Vote, 1837–1965*. Amherst: University of Massachusetts Press, 1997.

Gordon, Linda. "Black and White Visions of Welfare: Women's Welfare Activism, 1890–1945." *Journal of American History* 79 (1991): 559–90.

Greene, J. Lee. *Time's Unfading Garden: Anne Spencer's Life and Poetry*. Baton Rouge: Louisiana State University Press, 1977.

Guy-Sheftall, Beverly. *Daughters of Sorrow: Attitudes toward Black Women, 1880–1920*. Brooklyn, N.Y.: Carlson Publishing, 1990.

Hall, Jacqueline Dowd. *Revolt against Chivalry: Jessie Daniel Ames and Women's Campaign against Lynching*. New York: Columbia University Press, 1979.

Hanson, Joyce A. *Mary McLeod Bethune and Black Women's Political Activism*. Columbia: University of Missouri Press, 2003.

Harley, Sharon. "Nannie Helen Burroughs: 'The Black Goddess of Liberty.'" *Journal of Negro History* 81 (1996): 62–71.

———. "When Your Work Is Not Who You Are: The Development of a Working-Class Consciousness among Afro-American Women." In *Gender, Class, Race, and Reform in the Progressive Era*, edited by Noralee Frankel and Nancy S. Dye, 42–55. Lexington: University Press of Kentucky, 1991.

Harley, Sharon, and Rosalyn Terborg-Penn, eds. *The Afro-American Woman: Struggles and Images*. Baltimore: Black Classic Press, 1997.

Harrison, Daphne Duval. *Black Pearls: Blues Queens of the 1920s*. New Brunswick, N.J.: Rutgers University Press, 1988.

Haynes, Elizabeth Ross. "Negroes in Domestic Service in the United States." *Journal of Negro History* 8 (1923): 384–442.

Height, Dorothy. *Open Wide the Freedom Gates: A Memoir*. New York: Public Affairs, 2003.

Helly, Dorothy O., and Susan Reverby. *Gendered Domains: Rethinking Public and Private in Women's History*. Ithaca, N.Y.: Cornell University Press, 1992.

Hewitt, Nancy A. "Beyond the Search for Sisterhood: American Women's History in the 1980s." *Social History* 10 (1985): 299–321.

Hewitt, Nancy A., and Suzanne Lesbock, eds. *Visible Women: New Essays on American Activism*. Urbana: University of Illinois Press, 1993.

Higginbotham, Evelyn. "African-American Women's History and the Metalanguage of Race." *SIGNS* 17, no. 2 (winter 1991): 251–74.

———. "Clubwomen and Electoral Politics in the 1920s." In *African American Women and the Vote, 1837–1965*, edited by Ann D. Gordon with Bettye Collier Thomas. Amherst, Mass.: University of Massachusetts Press, 1997.

———. *Righteous Discontent: The Women's Movement in the Black Baptist Church, 1880–1920*. Cambridge, Mass.: Harvard University Press, 1993.

Hill, Robert. "Making Noise: Marcus Garvey's Dada, August 1922." In *Picturing Us: African American Identity in Photography*, edited by Deborah Willis, 180–205. New York: New Press, 1994.

Hine, Darlene Clark, ed. *Black Women in United States History*. 8 vols. Brooklyn: Carlson Publishing, 1990–1995.

———. *Black Women in White: Racial Conflict and Cooperation in the Nursing Profession, 1890–1950*. Bloomington: Indiana University Press, 1989.

Hine, Darlene Clark, Elsa Barclay Brown, and Rosalyn Terborg-Penn, eds. *Black Women in America: An Historical Encyclopedia*. Vols. 1 and 2. Brooklyn: Carlson Publishing, 1992.

Hine, Darlene Clark, and Kathleen Thompson. *A Shining Thread of Hope: The History of Black Women in America*. New York: Broadway, 1998.

Hobsbawm, Eric. "Ethnicity and Nationalism in Europe Today," *Anthropology Today*, February 8, 1992.

———. *Nations and Nationalism since 1870*. Cambridge: Cambridge University Press, 1991.

Holt, Rackham. *Mary McLeod Bethune: A Biography*. Garden City, N.Y.: Doubleday, 1964.

Honey, Maureen. *Shadowed Dreams: Women's Poetry of the Harlem Renaissance*. New Brunswick, N.J.: Rutgers University Press, 1989.

hooks, bell. *Feminist Theory: From Margin to Center.* 2nd ed. Cambridge, Mass.: South End Press, 2000.

Hull, Gloria T. *Color, Sex, and Poetry: Three Women Writers of the Harlem Renaissance*. Bloomington: Indiana University Press, 1987.

———, ed. *Give Us Each Day: The Diary of Alice Dunbar-Nelson*. New York and London: Norton, 1984.

Hunter, Tera. *To Joy My Freedom: Southern Black Women's Lives and Labors After the Civil War*. Cambridge, Mass.: Harvard University Press, 1997.

———. "The Correct Thing: Charlotte Hawkins Brown and the Palmer Institute." In *Black Women in United States History*, edited by Darlene Clark Hine, 3:696–98. Brooklyn, N.Y.: Carlson Publishing, 1990.

James, Winston. *Holding Aloft the Banner of Ethiopia: Caribbean Radicalism in Early Twentieth-Century America*. London: Verso, 1998.

Jayawardena, Kumari. *Feminism and Nationalism in the Third World*. London: Zed Books, 1986.

Johnson, Abbey Arthur. "Literary Midwife: Jessie Redmon Fauset and the Harlem Renaissance." *Phylon* 21 (1978): 143–53.

Johnson, Karen A. *Uplifting the Women and the Race: The Educational Philosophies and Social Activism of Anna Julia Cooper and Nannie Helen Burroughs*. New York: Garland Publishing, 2000.

Jones, Jacqueline. *American Work: Four Centuries of Black and White Labor*. New York: Norton, 1998.

———. *Labor of Love, Labor of Sorrow: Black Women, Work, and the Family, from Slavery to the Present*. New York: Vintage Books, 1995.

Jones, Leroi. "The Myth of a Negro Literature." In *On Being Black: Writings By Afro Americans from Frederick Douglass to the Present*, edited by Charles T. Davis and Daniel Walden, 293–301. Greenwich, Conn.: Fawcett Publications, 1970.

Kandivoti, Deniz, ed. Special issue "Gender and Nationalism," in *Nations and Nationalism*, 6 (4) 2000: 491–638.

Kelley, Robin D. G. "'We Are Not What We Seem': Rethinking Working Class Opposition in the Jim Crow South." *Journal of American History* 80, no. 1 (June 1993): 75–112.

Lasch-Quinn, Elisabeth. *Black Neighbors: Race and the Limits of Reform in the American Settlement House Movement, 1890–1945*. Chapel Hill: University of North Carolina Press, 1993.

Latham, Charles. "Historical Sketch." *Madam C. J. Walker Collection Guide* (1993). <www.indianahistory.org/library/manuscripts/collection_guides/m0399.html>, accessed April 5, 2001.

Lawrence, Paul. *Nationalism: History and Theory*. Harlow, England: Pearson, 2005.

Lemelle, Sidney, and Robin D. G. Kelley. "Introduction: Imagining Home: Pan-Africanism Revisited." In *Imagining Home: Class, Culture, and Nationalism in the African Diaspora*, edited by Sidney Lemelle and Robin D. G. Kelley, 1–16. London: Verso, 1994.

Lemke, Sieglinde. Introduction to *Lifting As They Climb*, by Elizabeth Lindsay Davis, xv–xxxiii. New York: G. K. Hall, 1996.

Levenstein, Harvey. *Seductive Journey: American Tourists in France from Jefferson to the Jazz Age*. Chicago: University of Chicago Press, 1998.

Lewis, David Levering. *W. E. B. Du Bois: The Fight for Equality and the American Century, 1919–1963*. New York: Henry Holt, 2000.

———. *When Harlem Was in Vogue*. New York: Oxford University Press, 1989.

Lewis, Rupert, and Patrick Bryan. *Garvey: His Work and Impact*. Trenton: Africa World Press, 1991.

Lowry, Beverly. *Her Dream of Dreams: The Rise and Triumph of Madam C. J. Walker*. New York: Knopf, 2003.

Lutz, Christine. "'The Dizzy Steps to Heaven': The Hunton Family, 1850–1970." Ph.D. diss., Georgia State University, 2001.

Marable, Manning. "Groundings with My Sisters: Patriarchy and the Exploitation of Black Women." *Journal of Ethnic Studies* 11 (1982): 1–39.

———. *Race, Reform, Rebellion: The Second Reconstruction in Black America, 1945–1982*. London: Macmillan, 1984.

Marks, Carole. *Farewell—We're Good and Gone: The Great Black Migration*. Bloomington: Indiana University Press, 1989.

Marks, Carole, and Diana Edkins. *The Power of Pride: Stylemakers and Rulebreakers in the Harlem Renaissance*. New York: Crown Publishers, 1999.

Martin, Tony, ed. *African Fundamentalism: A Literary and Cultural Anthology of Garvey's Harlem Renaissance*. Dover, Mass.: Majority Press, 1991.

———. *Literary Garveyism: Garvey, Black Arts, and the Harlem Renaissance*. Dover, Mass.: Majority Press, 1983.

———. *Marcus Garvey, Hero: A First Biography*. Dover, Mass.: Majority Press, 1983.

———. "Women in the Garvey Movement." In *Garvey: His Work and Impact*, edited by Rupert Lewis and Patrick Bryan, 67–72. Trenton: Africa World Press, 1991.

McClendon, Jacquelyn Y. *The Politics of Color in the Fiction of Jessie Fauset and Nella Larsen*. Charlottesville: University Press of Virginia, 1995.

McDonnaugh, Maxine. "Sister Samad: Living the Garvey Life." *Jamaica Journal* 20 (1987): 78–84.

McDowell, Deborah E. "Introduction: Regulating Midwives." In *Plum Bun: A Novel without a Moral*, by Jessie Fauset, ix–xxxiii. Boston: Beacon Press, 1990.

———. "The Neglected Dimension of Jessie Redmon Fauset." In *Black Women in United States History*, edited by Darlene Clark Hine, 3: 879–95. Brooklyn, N.Y.: Carlson Publishing, 1990.

McKissack, Patricia C., and Fredrick McKissack. *Madam C. J. Walker: Self-Made Millionaire*. Hillside, N.J., and Aldershot: Enslow, 1992.

Meier, August, and Elliot Rudwick. "The Boycott Movement against Jim Crow Streetcars in the South, 1900–1906." *Journal of American History* 55 (1969): 756–75.

Mexnaric, Silva. "Gender as an Ethno-Marker: Rape, War, and Identity Politics in the Former Yugoslavia." In *Identity, Politics, and Women*, edited by Valentine Moghadam, 76–97. Boulder, Colo.: Westview Press, 1994.

Mitchell, Michele. *Righteous Propaganda: African Americans and the Politics of Racial Destiny after Reconstruction*. Chapel Hill: University of North Carolina Press, 2004.

Mjagkij, Nina. *Light in the Darkness: African Americans and the YMCA, 1852–1946*. Lexington: University Press of Kentucky, 1994.

Mjagkij, Nina, and Margaret Spratt, eds. *Men and Women Adrift: The YMCA and the YWCA in the City*. New York: New York University Press, 1997.

Moore, Jacqueline M. *Booker T. Washington, W. E. B. Du Bois, and the Struggle for Racial Uplift*. Wilmington, Del.: Scholarly Resources, 2003.

———. *Leading the Race: The Transformation of the Black Elite in the Nation's Capital, 1880–1920*. Charlottesville: University Press of Virginia, 1999.

Moses, Wilson Jeremiah. *The Golden Age of Black Nationalism, 1850–1925*. 1978; paperback ed., Oxford: Oxford University Press, 1988.

Moton, Robert Russa. *Finding a Way Out: An Autobiography*. Garden City, N.Y.: Doubleday, 1920.

Neihart, Ben. *Rough Amusements: The True Story of A'Lelia Walker, Patroness of the Harlem Renaissance's Down-Low Culture*. New York: Bloomsbury, 2003.

Neverdon-Morton, Cynthia. "Advancement of the Race through African American Women's Organizations in the South, 1895–1925." In *African American Women and the Vote, 1837–1965*, edited by Ann D. Gordon and Bettye Collier-Thomas. Amherst: University of Massachusetts Press, 1997.

———. *Afro-American Women of the South and the Advancement of the Race, 1895–1920*. Knoxville: University of Tennessee Press, 1989.

———. "The Black Women's Struggle for Equality in the South, 1895–1925." In *The Afro-American Woman: Struggles and Images*, edited by Sharon Harley and Rosalyn Terborg-Penn, 43–57. Baltimore: Black Classic Press, 1997.

———. "Self-Help Programs as Educative Activities of Black Women in the South, 1895–1925: Focus on Four Key Areas." *Journal of Negro Education* 51 (1982): 207–21.
Pateman, Carol. *The Sexual Contract.* Cambridge, England: Polity, 1988.
Peiss, Kathy. "'Vital Industry' and Women's Ventures: Conceptualizing Gender in Twentieth Century Business History." *Business History Review* 72, no. 2 (1998): 218–41.
Perkins, Carol O. "The Pragmatic Idealism of Mary McLeod Bethune." *Sage* 1 (1988): 30–36.
Plastas, Melinda. "'A Band of Noble Women': The WILPF and the Politics and Consciousness of Race in the Women's Peace Movement, 1915–1945." Ph.D. diss., State University of New York, 2001.
Rhodes, Jane. *Mary Ann Shadd Cary: The Black Press and Protest in the Nineteenth Century.* Bloomington: Indiana University Press, 1998.
Robertson, Nancy. "'Deeper Even Than Race?': White Women and the Politics of Christian Sisterhood in the Young Women's Christian Association, 1906–1945." Ph.D. diss., New York University, 1997.
Robnett, Belinda. *How Long, How Long?: African-American Women in the Struggle for Civil Rights.* Oxford: Oxford University Press, 1997.
Roses, Lorraine Elena, and Ruth Elizabeth Randolph, eds. *Harlem Renaissance and Beyond: Literary Biographies of 100 Black Women Writers, 1900–1945.* Cambridge, Mass.: Harvard University Press, 1990.
Rouse, Jacqueline Anne. *Lugenia Burns Hope, Black Southern Reformer.* Athens: University of Georgia Press, 1989.
———. "Out of the Shadow of Tuskegee: Margaret Murray Washington, Social Activism, and Race Vindication." *Journal of Negro History* 81 (1996): 31–46.
Salem, Dorothy C. "Black Women and the NAACP, 1909–1922: An Encounter with Race, Class, and Gender." In *Black Women in America*, edited by Kim Marie Vaz, 54–70. Thousand Oaks, Calif.: Sage Publications, 1995.
———. *To Better Our World: Black Women in Organized Reform, 1890–1920.* Brooklyn, N.Y.: Carlson Publishing, 1990.
Sarkar, Kumari Tanika. *Hindu Wife, Hindu Nation: Community, Religion, and Cultural Nationalism.* Bloomington: Indiana University Press, 2002.
Scharf, Lois, and Joan M. Jensen, eds. *Decades of Discontent: The Women's Movement, 1920–1940.* Westport, Conn.: Greenwood Press, 1983.
Scruggs, Charles W. "Alain Locke and Walter White: Their Struggle for Control of the Harlem Renaissance." *Black American Literature Forum* 14 (1980): 91–99.
Seraille, William. "Henrietta Vinton Davis and the Garvey Movement." In *Black Women in United States History*, edited by Darlene Clark Hine, 4: 1073–91. Brooklyn: Carlson Publishing, 1990.
Sernett, Milton C. *African American Religious History: A Documentary Witness.* 2nd ed. Durham, N.C.: Duke University Press, 1999.
Shaw, Stephanie. "Black Club Women and the Creation of the National Association of Club Women." *Journal of Women's History* 3 (1991): 10–25.
———. *What a Woman Ought to Be and Do: Black Professional Women Workers during the Jim Crow Era.* Chicago: University of Chicago Press, 1996.

Sicherman, Barbara, et al., eds. *Notable American Women: The Modern Period: A Biographical Dictionary.* Cambridge, Mass.: Belknap Press of Harvard University Press, 1980.

Sinnette, Eleanor. "The Brownies' Book: A Pioneer Publication for Children." *Freedomways* 5 (1965): 133–42.

Sluga, Glenda. "Female and National Self-Determination: A Gender Re-reading of the 'Apogee of Nationalism.'" *Nations and Nationalism* 6 (4) (2000): 495–521.

Smith, Anthony. *The Ethnic Origins of Nations.* Oxford: Blackwell, 1986.

Smith, Elaine M. "Mary McLeod Bethune's 'Last Will and Testament': A Legacy for Race Vindication." *Journal of Negro History* 81 (1996): 105–22.

Smith, Karen Manners. "New Paths to Power: 1890–1920." In *No Small Courage: A History of Women in the United States,* edited by Nancy F. Cott, 353–412. Oxford: Oxford University Press, 2000.

Smith, Susan. *Sick and Tired of Being Sick and Tired: Black Women's Health Activism in America, 1890–1950.* Philadelphia: University of Pennsylvania Press, 1995.

Stein, Judith. *The World of Marcus Garvey: Race and Class in Modern Society.* Baton Rouge: Louisiana State University Press, 1986.

Stephens, Michelle Ann. *Black Empire: The Masculine Global Imaginary of Caribbean Intellectuals in the United States, 1914–1962.* Durham, N.C.: Duke University Press, 2005.

Stuckey, Sterling. *Slave Culture: Nationalist Theory and the Foundations of Black America.* Oxford: Oxford University Press, 1987.

Summers, Martin. *Manliness and Its Discontents: The Black Middle Class and the Transformation of Masculinity, 1900–1930.* Chapel Hill: University of North Carolina Press, 2004.

Sylvander, Carolyn Wedin. *Jessie Redmon Fauset: Black American Writer.* Troy, N.Y.: Whitson, 1981.

Tate, Gayle T. "Prophesy and Transformation: The Contours of Lewis Woodson's Nationalism." *Journal of Black Studies* 29, no. 2 (1998): 211–12.

Taylor, Traki L. "Womanhood Glorified: Nannie Helen Burroughs and the National Training School for Women and Girls Inc., 1900–1961." *Journal of African American History* 87 (autumn 2002): 390–402.

Taylor, Ula Y. "'As-Salaam Alaikum, My Sister, Peace Be Unto You': The Honorable Elijah Muhammad and the Women Who Followed Him." *Race and Society* 1 (1998): 177–96.

———. *The Veiled Garvey: The Life and Times of Amy Jacques Garvey.* Chapel Hill: University of North Carolina Press, 2002.

Terborg-Penn, Rosalyn. "African American Women and the Vote: An Overview." In *African American Women and the Vote,* edited by Ann D. Gordon with Bettye Collier-Thomas, 10–24. Amherst: University of Massachusetts Press, 1997.

———. *African American Women in the Struggle for the Vote, 1850–1920.* Bloomington: Indiana University Press, 1998.

———. "Discrimination against Afro-American Women in the Woman's Movement,

1830–1920." In *The Afro-American Woman: Struggles and Images*, edited by Sharon Harley and Rosalyn Terborg-Penn, 17–27. Baltimore: Black Classic Press, 1997.

Turner, W. Burghart. "Joel Augustus Rogers: Afro-American Historian." *Negro History Bulletin* 25 (1972): 35–38.

Tyson, Timothy B. "Robert F. Williams, 'Black Power,' and the Roots of the African American Freedom Struggle." *Journal of American History* 85 (1998): 540–70.

Vandenbuerg-Daves, Jodi. "The Manly Pursuit of a Partnership between the Sexes: The Debate over YMCA Programs for Women and Girls, 1914–1933." *Journal of American History* 78 (1992): 1324–46.

Vela, Ramón G. "The Washington–Du Bois Controversy: Ideological Conflict and Its Consequences." *Studies in American Political Development* 16, no. 1 (2002): 88–109.

Vincent, Theodore. *Black Power and the Garvey Movement*. Berkeley, Calif.: Ramparts Press, 1971.

———. *Keep Cool: The Black Activists Who Built the Jazz Age*. London: Pluto Press, 1995.

———, ed. *Voices of a Black Nation: Political Journalism in the Harlem Renaissance*. Trenton: Africa World Press, 1990.

Walby, Sylvia. "Is Citizenship Gendered?" *Sociology* 28: 2 (1994): 379–95.

Wall, Cheryl A. "Passing for What? Aspects of Identity in Nella Larsen's Novels." In *Analysis and Assessment, 1980–1994*, edited by Cary D. Wintz, 87–102. New York: Garland, 1996.

Washington, James Melvin. *Frustrated Fellowship: The Black Baptist Quest for Social Power*. Macon: Mercer Press, 1982.

Weisenfeld, Judith. *African American Women and Christian Activism, 1904–1945*. Cambridge, Mass.: Harvard University Press, 1997.

Welter, Barbara. "The Cult of True Womanhood: 1829–1860." *American Quarterly* 18 (1966): 151–74.

West, Cynthia S'thembile. "Nation Builders: Female Activism in the Nation of Islam, 1960–1970." Ph.D. diss., Temple University, 1994.

West, Lois A., ed. *Feminist Nationalism*. New York: Routledge, 1997.

———. "Introduction: Feminism Constructs Nationalism." In *Feminist Nationalism*, edited by Lois A. West, xi–xxxvi. New York: Routledge, 1997.

West, Robin. *Caring for Justice*. New York: New York University Press, 1997.

White, Deborah Gray. "The Cost of Club Work: The Price of Black Feminism." In *Visible Women: New Essays on American Activism*, edited by Nancy A. Hewitt and Suzanne Lesbock, 247–69. Urbana: University of Illinois Press, 1993.

———. *Too Heavy a Load: Black Women in Defense of Themselves, 1894–1994*. New York: Norton, 1999.

White, E. Frances. "Africa on My Mind: Gender, CounterDiscourse, and African American Nationalism." In *Dark Continent of Our Bodies: Black Feminism and the Politics of Respectability*, 117–50. Philadelphia: Temple University Press, 2001.

Wilson, Bobby M. "Race in Commodity Exchange and Consumption: Separate but Equal." *Annals of the Association of American Geographers* 95, no. 3 (2005): 587–606.

Wolcott, Victoria. "'Bible, Bath, and Broom': Nannie Helen Burroughs's National Training School and African-American Racial Uplift." *Journal of Women's History* 9 (spring 1997): 88–110.

———. *Remaking Respectability: African American Women in Interwar Detroit.* Chapel Hill: University of North Carolina Press, 2001.

Yard, Lionel M. *Biography of Amy Ashwood Garvey, 1897–1969: Co-founder of the Universal Negro Improvement Association.* Washington, D.C.: Associated Publishers, 1990.

Yuval-Davis, Nira. *Gender and Nation.* London: SAGE, 1997.

Zald, Mayer N. *Organizational Change: The Political Economy of the YMCA.* Chicago: University of Chicago Press, 1970.

Index

Accommodationism: integrationism, compatibility with, 3; NAACP, and hostility toward, 141; NTS and, 41; politics of respectability and, 36; segregation and, 191; sexual respectability and, 40; as strategy, 3; Trotter, opposition to, 120; Madam Walker, distanced from, 19; and Booker T. Washington, 4, 94, 141; and Margaret Murray Washington, 23, 24; to white norms, 36
Addams, Jane, 168
Adeleke, Tunde, 6, 8
Alexander, Lillian, 60, 214n75
American Colonization Society, 7
American Nurses Association, 86
Ames, Jessie Daniel, 57
Andrews, Regina, 32, 180, 214n75, 237n114
Anthony, Susan B., 21, 91
Anti-Lynching: mentioned, 2; Anti-Lynching Crusaders, 145, 238n137; legislation, 48, 57, 121; NAACP campaign for, 230n78; Ida B. Wells and, 54, 120; white women and, 57. *See also* Association of Southern Women for the Prevention of Lynching
Ashwood, Amy: help in launching UNIA, 151, 156; role as Garvey's wife, 156–57, 159, 165
Association for the Study of Negro Life and History, 205
Association Monthly (YWCA magazine), xii, 77, 79, 84
Association of Black Women Historians, 205
Association of Southern Women for the Prevention of Lynching (ASWPL), 57, 219n192
ASWPL. *See* Association of Southern Women for the Prevention of Lynching
Authentic blackness: in blues and folk, as markers of, 186–87; in *Chinaberry Tree*, 194–95, 196–97; Fauset lacking in, 179–80; gender and racial identity as markers of, 185, 198; middle class as lacking, 10; in *There Is Confusion*, 188

Baker, Houston A., 10, 238n143
Baptist Church, 34–35, 41, 49, 132. *See also* National Baptist Convention
Baraka, Amiri (Leroi Jones), 5, 186
Barnett, Evelyn Brooks. *See* Higginbotham, Evelyn
Bennett, Gwendolyn, 178, 180; "To Usward," 183
Bethune, Mary McLeod, xii, 1, 2, 13, 15, 17, 18, 65; A'Lelia, eulogy at funeral of, 2; appeal to whites, 50; ASWPL, attitude to, 57; black nationalism and, 50–51; Burroughs, relationship with, 43, 49; Colored Branch of YWCA and, 103, 105, 201; early life and career, 50; educator, 50–52; Fourth Pan-African Congress, helped to organize, 214n75; Dorothy Height, relationship with, 201; ICWDR, member of, 27, 30; married name of, 216n118; NACW and, 28, 29, 52–56, 201, 218n180; NAWE, member of, 47, 49; NCNW, role in, 2, 47, 59–61, 62; as New Deal administrator, 51, 52, 206; NWC and, 56–57; "pragmatic idealism" and, 51, 218n171; Eleanor Roosevelt, relationship with, 62; Madam Walker, relationship with, 2, 53, 108, 126, 129; Mary Waring, dispute with, 59–60. *See also* Daytona Normal and Industrial School; National Council of Negro Women
Biggart, Nicole, 108, 226n3
Big Sea, The (Hughes), 136, 183
Birth of a Nation (film), 28
Black Aesthetic, 5, 11

Black Arts Movement, 49
Black Atlantic, The (Gilroy), 8
Black Cross Nurses, 153, 155, 158, 233n12
Black Dispatch (Oklahoma City), 41
Black feminism: authentic racial identity and, 10, 188, 190, 193; black nationalism, compatible with, 2, 7, 8, 9, 12, 13, 14, 34–35, 42, 44, 64, 65, 67, 93, 103, 151, 169, 171, 174, 175, 191, 194, 206, 207; class status and, 10–11, 193; "community feminism" and, 164–65; definition of, 9–12; essentialist feminism and, 2, 9; NACW and, 16; pan-Africanism and, 126, 150, 154, 159, 170, 199; second wave feminism and, 64; shapers of, 1, 2, 7, 9, 15, 64, 109, 125, 126, 127, 148, 155, 162, 167, 170–72, 175, 176, 185, 186, 187, 192, 202–5; white feminism and, 8–9, 10, 95. *See also* Public-private divide; *individual black feminists*
Black nationalism: definitions of, 6, 9, 14; economic nationalism, strand of, 7, 38, 43, 51, 112, 126, 135, 171; gender and, 6–9, 14; as ideology or strategy, 207; imagined community model, 6, 7; integrationism and, 2, 3–6, 12, 13, 15, 33, 52, 59, 61, 151, 199, 209n1; masculine rhetoric of, 153–56, 157; nation-state model of, 6, 7, 210n32; patriarchy, apparently inherent in, 7–9; women as shapers and advocates of , 7, 9, 14, 154, 167, 171, 172, 174, 206, 207. *See also* black feminism; *individual black nationalists*
Black power movement, 64, 161
Black Star Line Shipping Company, 152
Blues: authentic blackness and, 10, 186–87; singers of, 11, 40, 186, 211n7, 234n43
Bone, Robert, 176, 186
Bontemps, Arna, on Jessie Fauset, 181. *See also* Fauset, Jessie Redmon
Bowles, Eva: mentioned, 1, 105; Bureau of Colored Work, 96, 98; Colored Work Committee (CWC) and, 68, 78–79, 96; Hostess Houses, 79–80, 222n57; ICWDR membership of, 28; on integration, 69, 104, 106; National Board and, 68, 99; National Secretary for Colored Work, 76; NCNW, founder member of, 60; and New York City Colored Branch, 71–73, 220n6; resignation from YWCA, 104, 206, 226n162; Madam Walker and, 126, 128, 230n77; white leadership, tactics for dealing with, 95, 105–6;

220n7; on World War I, 77, 85; YMCA, merger with, 95–96
Breedlove, Louvenia (sister of Madam Walker), 109
Breedlove, Minvera (mother of Madam Walker), 109
Breedlove, Owen (father of Madam Walker), 109
Brown, Charlotte Hawkins, 27, 38, 52, 59, 60, 99, 103, 126, 142, 214n75
Brown, Hallie Q., 46, 54, 56
Brownies' Book, The (children's magazine), 181–82, 237n121
Brown v. Board of Education, 208
Bundles, A'Lelia, 137, 143; Madam Walker, accounts of, 226n4; NNBL, on the founding of the 227n19; on Walker's desire for a missionary school in Africa, 229n55
Bureau of Investigations (later FBI), 124, 229n56, 229n72. *See also* Department of Justice
Burroughs, Nannie Helen, 1, 51, 65; as assimilationist, 35–36, 40; Bethune, work with, 49; black masculinity, engages with discourse on, 94, 158, 207; black men, critical of, 41, 44, 215n103; as black nationalist, 33–34, 37, 44, 48–49, 207; clubwomen, neglected in accounts of, 215n85; Department of Justice surveillance of, 30; Fourth Pan-African Congress, participant in, 214n75, 215n85; Harlem Renaissance, contributor to, 49; ICWDR, involvement in, 27, 30, 49; on integration, 37, 207; Jacques Garvey on, 49; NACW and, 43–44, 54; National Training School and, 2, 37–42; NAWE, 47, 49; NBC, 34–35; NLRCW, 44–47; NNBL, views on, 117; politics of respectability and, 35–36; on suffrage, 44–45; Madam Walker and, 41–42, 203, 216n120; Booker T. Washington, critical of, 33, 214n82; WC, 35–36, 215n93; white women, working with, 44–45, 48; women's work, dignity of 38–42, 203; YWCA and, 103. *See also* National Training School; National Association of Wage Earners; National League of Republican Colored Women

Carby, Hazel, 8, 177
Carter, Elizabeth, 27, 30, 54, 142

Carter, Eunice Hunton, 105, 201, 214n75
Cash, Floris, 16
Chenault, Lawrence, 146
Chinaberry Tree, The (Fauset), 151, 185, 187, 194–97, 198, 237n144, 238n147
Circle for Negro War Relief, 53, 100, 119, 228n37
Circle for Peace and Foreign Relations (CPFR), 31, 32, 62, 89, 95
Civil rights movement, 4, 34, 63, 150, 158, 200, 208
Clubwomen. *See* National Association of Colored Women. *See also individual clubwomen*
Collins, Patricia Hill, 12, 205
Colored American Review (periodical), 137, 148
Cooper, Anna Julia, 168, 169
Costigan-Wagner Bill, 57. *See also* Anti-Lynching
Cott, Nancy, 95, 219n206
CPFR. *See* Circle for Peace and Foreign Relations
Crisis, The, xii, 61; anti-lynching protest and, 48; Du Bois, editorship of, 61, 150, 176, 178, 232n1, 236n101; Fauset and, 1, 2, 26, 124, 127, 151, 175, 177–78, 180, 181–85, 191; Garvey, role in campaign against, 150, 201, 232n1; literary networks around, 201; readership below that of *Negro World*, 151; poems published by gender in, 236n103; Mae Walker Robinson wedding in, 144; J. A. Rogers, contributor to, 209n1; segregation, debate on, 61; State Department surveillance of, 122; Talbert, account of European trip for, 87; Madam Walker and, 107, 124, 230n78
Crummell, Alexander, 4
Crusader (newspaper), 162
Cruse, Harold, 5, 209n11
Cullen, Countee, xii, 146, 147, 177, 178, 179, 181
Cullen, Frederick, Rev., 122
Cullen, Ida, 147
Curtis, Helen, 28, 32, 78, 87, 88, 103, 145, 214n75, 222n52, 224n103

Dark Tower, 146–47, 232n144
Davis, Angela, 10, 92–93, 211n43, 234n43
Davis, Arthur, 186
Davis, Clarice Winn, 104
Davis, Elizabeth Lindsay, 53, 92
Davis, Henrietta Vinton, 155, 157, 172, 234n30

Daytona Normal and Industrial School (Daytona Educational and Industrial Training School for Girls), 50–53, 129, 217n164
Delany, Martin, 4, 7, 8
De Mena, Maymie L. T., Madame, 157–58, 234n32
Department of Justice: Garvey and, 123, 150, 151, 233n3; surveillance of black activists and, 30. *See also* Bureau of Investigations (later FBI)
Department of State: Paris Peace Convention, denies passports for travel to, 124, 125, 141; surveillance of black activists, 122
Depression (Great Depression), 58, 136, 201
Diaspora: clubwomen organizational networks across, 9, 25, 26, 27, 28, 31, 35, 171, 185; YWCA, as meeting place for women from across, 102
Dickerson, Addie, 27, 30, 32, 60, 142, 214n75
Dill, Augustus, 182
Dodge, Grace, 70, 74–75
Domestic servants: black women as, 36, 39–41, 77, 82, 203
Douglas, Aaron, 181
Douglas, Ann, 178
Douglass, Frederick, 3, 129; home of, 204
Du Bois, W. E. B. xii, 30; *The Brownies' Book* and, 182, 237n124; car ownership, views on, 114; as *The Crisis* editor, criticism of, 178, 236n101; *Dusk of Dawn*, 4; Fauset, relationship with, 176, 177–78, 181, 198, 236n98, 236n99, 237n117; Fourth Pan-African Congress and, 31–32, 175, 214n73; Garvey, opposition to, 123, 150, 152, 184, 232n1; Garveyites, criticism of, 13; gender politics of, 8, 177; Jacques Garvey and collaboration on Fifth Pan-African Congress, 175, 236n88; NNBL and, 227n19; Paris Peace Conference, attendance at, 124–25, 183; Augusta Savage's bust of, 199; Second Pan-African Congress, 175, 184; on segregation, 61; *Souls of Black Folk*, 4; Madam Walker, views on, 107, 135; Booker T. Washington, in oppositional framework with, 4, 17, 18, 38, 50, 51, 209n7, 212n12; and Margaret Murray Washington, 18, 19; World War I, support for black involvement in, 90, 118; YWCA and, 81
Ducille, Ann, 10, 193, 238n143

Dunbar High School, 177, 181, 236n93
Dunbar-Nelson, Alice, 2, 32, 86–87, 183, 203, 205, 209n2, 214n75
Dunbar, Paul, 183
Dusk of Dawn (Du Bois), 4

Ebony (magazine), 160, 161
Educators, 18, 24, 27, 34, 42, 52. *See also individual educators*
Emma Ransom House, 100, 105
Enloe, Cynthia, 9

Fairclough, Adam, 209n6
Fauset, Jessie Redmon, xii, 1, 14, 65, 150; articles by, 183–184,185; *The Brownies' Book*, role in, 182; *The Chinaberry Tree*, 151, 194–98, 237n114; compared to Jane Austen, 178; contemporary male criticism of, 178–80, 181; *The Crisis*, role at, 2, 124, 127, 177, 178, 180, 182–83; *Comedy: American Style*, 238n147; Du Bois and, 175–76, 177–78, 198, 236n98, 236n99, 237n117; early life, 176–77; female network, part of, 180, 182–83; Fourth Pan-African Congress and, 32, 175, 183, 214n75; Addie Hunton and, 171, 183; Jacques Garvey and, 150, 171, 175–76, 184–85, 198–99; on integration, 186, 198, 208; Alain Locke and, 180–81, 237n114; middle class, criticized as, 10, 17, 18, 176, 179, 186; NAACP and, 175, 177, 198; NACW and, 26, 185; as Pan-Africanist, 183–85, 187, 198, 205; *Plum Bun*, 183, 238n147; recent literary criticism on, 186–87; Second Pan-African Congress and, 26, 175, 184–85; *There Is Confusion*, 127, 151, 180, 188–94, 238n147; Villa Lewaro, desire to visit, 231n126; on white collectors of black art, 183; Women's Auxiliary, member of, 145, 238n137; working class characters in novels of, 193–94; YWCA and, 183, 237n119
Federal Bureau of Investigation (FBI). *See* Bureau of Investigations. *See also* Department of Justice
Female networks, xi–xii, 3, 6, 17, 27, 32, 46, 49, 52, 66, 99, 105, 108, 168, 201–2, 206; intergenerational networks, 65; international networks, 25
Fire!! (publication), 178
Fisher, Ruth, 81

Garvey, Amy Jacques. *See* Jacques Garvey, Amy
Garvey, Marcus, 1; appeal of, 151–52, 154; arrest and exile, 4, 123, 151; Ashwood, Amy, relationship with, 156–157, 165; bans joint membership of UNIA and NAACP, 169, 201; black masculinity, construction of, 153, 154, 197; black women challenge, 156; bust of, 199; campaign to get rid of, 123, 150, 232n1; Du Bois and, 150, 152, 184, 232n1; early historical assessments of, 233n7; founder of the UNIA, 150–51; ILPDR and, 122; Jacques Garvey, relationship with, 159, 161–165, 176, 167; parades and costumes, 152; A'Lelia Walker, relationship with, 145–146; Madam Walker, relationship with, 122–123, 125, 229n57; on World War I, 118
Garvey and Garveyism (Jacques Garvey), 159, 161, 206
Garvey Movement. *See* Universal Negro Improvement Association
Gayle, Addison, 5
Gibbs-Hunt, Ida, 25, 31, 214n75
Giddings, Paula, 57, 219n211
Gilroy, Paul, 8, 135
Granger, Lester B., 52
Griffith, D. W., 28
Grimke, Angelina Weld, 182

Hall, Jacqueline Dowd, 67
Harlem: mentioned, 14, 85, 103, 150, 152; black Americans move to, 100, 102, 221n33; Colored Branch of YWCA and, 2, 60, 74, 80, 100, 101, 102, 103, 104, 105, 128, 201, 206, 207; Dark Tower in, 146–47; economic boycott and, 171; Fauset's apartment in, 183; Amy Jacques Garvey speech in, 172; Marcus Garvey moves to, 151; Lelia College in, 111, 131; Liberty Hall in, 123, 146, 156, 172; novels about, 178, 179; Mae Walker Robinson wedding in, 144; UNIA headquarters in, 159; A'Lelia Walker as society hostess in, 136–37; Madam Walker moves to, 128, 130, 146; Walker agents in, 122, 131; white branch of YWCA in, 73, 74
Harlem Renaissance, xi, 1, 3, 5, 14, 32 34; African identity and, 25, 33; black literature of, 178; clubwomen's contribution to, 32–33, 49; Fauset and, 65, 150, 175–77, 236n102;

Jacques Garvey and, 65; Garveyism and, 3, 14, 150, 152, 199, 233n2; Locke's role in, 180–81; A'Lelia Walker and, 109, 146, 231n126, 226n4; Madam Walker and, 109, 126–27, 226n; whites and, 191; women artists and, 13, 181–83, 186–87 199; YWCA and, 128. *See also individual Harlem Renaissance writers*
Harley, Sharon, 33
Harper, Frances Ellen Watkins, 171
Hayford, Adelaide Casely, 26, 213n48
Haynes, Elizabeth Ross: *The Brownies' Book*, contributor to, 182; ICWDR and, 27, 28; NLRCW and, 217n142; *UnSung Heroes*, author of, 27; YWCA and, 75–76, 223n92
Hedgeman, Anna Arnold, 102, 103, 105, 206, 207–8
Height, Dorothy, 63, 104, 105, 201
Hewitt, Nancy, 10
Higginbotham, Evelyn (Evelyn Brooks Barnett): Burroughs and the politics of respectability, 34, 35–36; on the National Training School, 28; on NAWE, 47; race woman, definition of, 211n44
Hindu Indian National Congress, 174
History of Woman Suffrage, The (Anthony) 21
Hobsbawm, Eric J., 6, 8
Home to Harlem (McKay), 179
hooks, bell, 205
Hoover, Herbert, 46, 47
Hoover, J. Edgar, 30, 122
Hope, Lugenia Burns, 52, 69; on ASWPL, 57; Atlanta Neighborhood Union and, 220n1; Commission on Interracial Cooperation and, 225n138; Hostess House at Camp Upton, supervised by, 80; ICWDR and, 27, 28–29; NCNW and, 219n202; YWCA and, 96–99
Hopkins, Mary, 77, 84
Howard University, 96, 100, 105, 180
Hughes, Langston, 178, 181, 236n101; *The Big Sea*, 136, 183; "The Weary Blues," 146
Hughes, Revella, 145
Hunter, Jane, 28
Hunter, Tera, 10, 135, 238n145
Hunton, Addie Waites, 105, 119, 171, 205; *Beginnings Among Colored Women*, 69, 221n14; Bethune, mentor to, 201; black men, critical of, 94; Circle for Negro War Relief and, 119; CPFR and, 31; Fauset and, 183, 237n129;

ICWDR and, 27, 30; National Woman's Party and, 92; NCNW founding of, 60; suffrage and, 92; *Two Colored Women with the American Expeditionary Forces*, 87–89, 183; Pan-African Congress Movement and, 31–32, 183, 238n135; Women's Auxiliary, member of, 145; YMCA, canteen worker in France, 87, 88–89; YWCA and, 69, 72, 73, 75–76, 78, 81, 85, 104, 106, 206, 207
Hunton, William, A., 94
Hurston, Zora Neale, 1, 181, 199, 208, 237n107

ICWDR. *See* International Council of Women of the Darker Races
ILPDR. *See* International League of Peoples of the Darker Races
Integrationism: mentioned: 11, 12, 82, 206 ; Bethune and, 50, 51, 52, 55, 59–60; black nationalism, relationship to, 2, 3–6, 7, 14, 61, 186, 187, 209n1, 209n7; *Brown v. Board of Education*, 208; Burroughs on, 37, 48, 49, 207; clubwomen and, 13, 15, 33, 60, 65; *The Crisis* and, 184; Du Bois and, 61; Fauset and, 151, 186, 187, 190, 192, 194, 198, 199, 208; Garveyites on, 153; Hunton and, 207; Hurston and, 1, 208; as ideology, 207, 208; Jacques Garvey and, 151, 175, 100; NCNW, 60–61; racial uplift and, 37; as strategy of, 1, 13, 68–69, 207, 208; A'Lelia Walker and, 145; Madam Walker and, 14, 125; YWCA and, 66, 67, 68–69, 70, 71, 73, 74, 77, 96, 99, 104, 105, 106, 206, 220n5, 230n10
International Committee of Women for Permanent Peace, 87
International Council of Women, 56, 87, 105
International Council of Women of the Darker Races (ICWDR), 95, 123, 171, 204–5, 214n64; Bethune and, 55, 56; Burroughs and, 34, 35; CPRF, membership overlaps with, 30–31; founding of 2, 13, 24–31, 185; Fourth Pan-African Congress, building blocks for, 32; Hunton and, 89; NACW relationship to, 29, 58; NAWE, membership overlaps with, 47; NCNW, relationship to, 30, 60, 62; as separate black women's organization, 64, 65; Margaret Murray Washington and, 18, 25–26, 27, 29, 30, 31; white women, position on, 28–29

International League of Peoples of the Darker Races (ILPDR), 118, 122–24

Jackman, Harold, 147, 180, 232n144
Jackson, Mary E., 77, 82, 83, 84
Jackson, May Howard, 81
Jacques Garvey, Amy, 1, 14, 18, 65, 150; as able wife/rival to Marcus Garvey, 162–164, 165, 167; Ashwood, relationship with, 159, 165; black male Garveyites, criticism of, 162–63, 172–74, 160–62, 167; Burroughs and, 44, 49; Du Bois and, 236n88; Fauset and, 175–76, 183, 184, 189, 197, 198–99, 204; feminist black nationalism and, 151, 167, 170, 172, 174–75, 205, 206–7; Ula Y. Taylor and, 164–65; UNIA, role in, 158–59; Madam Walker, endorsement of, 126, 127; as wife and helpmate, 159, 160–62, 167; women's page and, 167–75
James, Winston, 173
Johnson, Georgia Douglas, 28, 32, 182, 183, 203, 205, 219n202
Johnson, James Weldon, 4, 5, 26, 61, 142, 221n33
Johnson, Karen, 38
Johnson, Kathryn, 87, 88, 89, 183
Johnson, Marie Peek, 78, 222n52
Johnson, Grace Nail, Mrs., 145
Jones, Leroi. *See* Baraka, Amiri

King, Martin Luther, 4
Kingston, Jamaica, 151, 152, 156, 157, 158
Knox, George, 113
Krasner, David, 152
Ku Klux Klan, 28

Larsen, Nella, 10, 182
Latham, Charles, 109
League of Nations, 26, 171, 183, 184
League of Women Voters, 61, 92
Lelia College, 110, 111, 131, 140
Lewis, David Levering, 146, 180, 233n2, 236n98
Liberty Hall, Harlem, 123, 146, 156, 172
Locke, Alain, 178, 179, 180–81, 237n114
Lowry, Beverly, 137
Lynching, 79, 89, 91, 222n45; in East St. Louis, 132–33; in Memphis, 133; Margaret Murray Washington critical of, 21; white women and, 20

Madam Walker Beauty Culturists Union Convention, 132, 230n96
Madam Walker Benevolent Association, 130–31, 230n81, 230n96
Madam Walker Manufacturing Company (Walker Company), xii, 113, 117, 121, 132, 137; agents and, 117, 127, 130–31; hair grower, product of, 53, 109, 110, 143; incorporation of, 110; marketing campaigns of, 108, 109, 110, 134–35, 138, 144–45, 226n6, 230n78. *See also* Lelia College; Ransom, Freeman B; Walker, A'Lelia; Walker, Madam C. J.
Malcolm X, 4
Malone, Annie Turbno (Madam Poro), 108, 110, 134
Martin, Tony, 150, 152, 159
Mason, Charlotte, 181
Matthews, Victoria Earle, 171
McCluskey, Audrey, 50–51
McDougald, Gertrude Elise Johnson, 83
McKane, Alice Woodby, 200
McKay, Claude: Du Bois, critical of, 236n101; Fauset, relationship with, 178, 179; UNIA conventions, views on, 152
Meier, August, 8, 209n7
Messenger (socialist magazine): readership of, 151; surveillance of, 122; on A'Lelia Walker, 143, 144, 147; Madam Walker, relationship with, 107, 122, 124, 135; World War I, position on, 118
Middle class: definitions of, 11, 18, 202–4; characters in Fauset's novels and, 176, 180, 186, 188, 192, 193, 194; compared to white middle class, 36, 40, 203; Fauset as representative of, 176, 186; integrationism, as synonymous with, 5, 187; problematic use of, 10–12, 18, 36, 203; relationship with working class, 17, 40, 203, 211n43, 211n7; terms used instead of, 11; YWCA, viewed as catering to, 82
Military Intelligence Division, 124, 141
Mitchell, Michele, 3, 8, 210n32,
Mjagkij, Nina, 94
Moorland, Jesse E., 94
Moses, Wilson J., 5, 8
Moton, Robert R., 145

NAACP. *See* National Association for the Advancement of Colored People
NACW. *See* National Association of Colored Women
NAWSA. *See* National American Women's Suffrage Association
Naidu, Sarojini, Mrs., 174
National American Women's Suffrage Association (NAWSA), 91–92; later League of Women Voters, 92
National Association for the Advancement of Colored People (NAACP): mentioned, 1, 58, 122, 127, 128, 141, 142; Du Bois and, 61, 125; Fauset and, 175, 177, 194, 198; Hunton and, 60, 72, 76, 89, 207; interracialism and, 48, 61, 69, 153; James Weldon Johnson and, 4, 26; UNIA, compared and relationship with, 150, 152, 153, 157, 169, 175, 200–201; Walkers and, 142, 144, 145, 153; Women's Auxiliary to, 2, 145
National Association of Colored Graduate Nurses, 86
National Association of Colored Women (NACW): Bethune and, 52–56, 57–58, 59; Burroughs and, 34, 43–44; commemorating black past, 204; conservative, viewed as, 16–17; Fauset and, 185; founding of, 2, 15, 92, 202; goals and aims, 15–16; headquarters, of 54; ICWDR, developed out of, 25–27, 29; limitations of, 58; lynching, protest against 48; "mistrissism," charges of, leveled against, 17; motto, 203–4; NCNW, relationship to, 62, 65, 219n200; NCW and, 56–57, 59; NLRCW, as offshoot of, 46; Richmond Convention and, 26, 185; suffrage, endorsement of, 23; pan-Africanism and, 25–27, 56; Madam Walker and, 128–29, 130, 131, 133; Mary Waring and, 59; Margaret Murray Washington and, 18, 19, 20–21, 24; women's networks and, 201; YWCA and, 76, 99. *See also National Notes*
National Association of Wage Earners (NAWE), 34, 44, 47, 48, 49
National Baptist Convention (NBC), 33, 34–35, 37, 38, 41, 42, 132, 154, 215n103
National Black Feminist Organization, 205
National Council of Negro Women (NCNW): assessment of, 62–64; Eunice Hunton Carter and, 105, 201; Colored Branch as first headquarters of, 2, 103, 105; founding of, 15, 29, 56–61, 219n202; NACW refuses to join, 219n200. *See also* Bethune, Mary McLeod; National Council of Women
National Council of Women (NCW), 20, 28; black clubwomen, relationship with, 56–57, 59, 60, 219n191
National Equal Rights League (NERL), 118, 120, 121, 122, 124, 200. *See also* Trotter, William Monroe
National Federation of Afro-American Women, 15, 20
National League of Colored Women, 15, 20
National League of Republican Colored Women (NLRCW), 34, 44, 46–47, 58, 62, 64, 65, 217n142
National Negro Business League (NNBL): Burroughs, critical of, 33, 228n30; founding of, 112, 227n19; Madam Walker's intervention at convention of, 113–14, 116–17, 118, 121, 227n16
National Notes (NACW publication), 16; Bethune and, 54; celebrates Madam Walker, 129; support for Republican Party, 46; Margaret Murray Washington and, 18, 21, 23, 27
National Organization for Women (NOW), 205
National Race Congress, 121, 124
National Training School (NTS): aims and curriculum, 38–40, 41; Burroughs and, 33; community involvement in, 37; defended from take over by NBC, 38, 41; graduates of, 42; historical debate on, 38; ICWDR founded at, 2, 27; motto, 37; racial pride and, 38–39, 41, 42, 47; *The Worker,* 41
National Urban League, 34, 48, 52
National Woman's Party, 92
National Women's Studies Association, 205
National Youth Administration, 50, 61
NAWSA. *See* National American Women's Suffrage Association
NAWE. *See* National Association of Wage Earners
NBC. *See* National Baptist Convention
NCNW. *See* National Council of Negro Women
NCW. *See* National Council of Women

Negro Americans, What Now? (Johnson), 4
Negro World (publication): Ashwood and, 156; Black Cross Nurses' health advice in, 233n12; black masculine language of, 94, 153; *The Crisis*, compared to, 184; Henrietta Vinton Davis, celebrated in, 234n30; Garvey articles in, 145, 153, 159; Hurston writes for, 199; Jacques Garvey articles in, 49, 126, 162–63, 164; Jacques Garvey role in, 151, 158–59, 162–63; readership of, 151, 233n3; reporter interviews Jacques Garvey, 161–62; surveillance of, 122; Madam and A'Lelia Walker's support for, 122, 145–146; Lucian B. Watkins, poet for, 237n121; women's page in, 167–74
Neihart, Ben, 113
NERL. *See* National Equal Rights League
New Deal, 4, 50, 51, 52, 58, 61, 206
New Negro, The (Locke), 181
New Negro movement: xi, 14, 127, 136, 150; masculine spirit of, 15, 65, 89, 93, 95, 178, 219–20n215; rhetoric of, 49, 119–20; women, participants in, 127, 136, 150, 170, 180, 188, 189. *See also individual New Negro writers*
New Republic (magazine), 179
Newsome, Effie Lee, 182, 183
New York Age, The, 19, 59; on Garvey, 152, 200, 233n1; on Madam Walker, 107, 117, 131, 142
New York City: center for black women's organizing, 17, 32, 66, 202; as segregated city, 74; working conditions of black women in, 83–84, 103. *See also* Young Women's Christian Association
Nigger Heaven (Van Vechten), 136, 179, 231n108
Nineteenth Amendment, 45, 47, 92, 93. *See also* Women's suffrage
NLRCW. *See* National League of Republican Colored Women
NNBL. *See* National Negro Business League
North-eastern Federation of Women's Clubs, 89, 92
NTS. *See* National Training School

Olcott, Jane, 71, 79, 82
Opportunity (publication), 236n103
"Our Women and What They Think" (women's page), 49, 126–27, 158–59, 160, 162, 167–74, 233n12. See also Jacques Garvey, Amy; *Negro World*

Ovington, Mary White, 142
Owen, Chandler, 118, 119, 122, 123, 223n78, 232n1

Pan-African Congress: first, 31; second, 26, 175, 184, 185, 238n135; third, 31; fourth, 26, 31–32, 33, 175, 183, 214n75; fifth, 175, 236n88
Pan-Africanism: black nationalism, relationship to, 6; clubwomen and, 24–33; feminism and, 154, 185, 186, 199; as movement, 25, 31, 33, 206; as strategy, 3, 4, 86
Paris Peace Conference, 120, 121, 122, 123, 183, 184
Paul, Alice, 92,
Peiss, Kathy, 108, 226n2
Peterson, Dorothy, 32, 214n75
Philosophies and Opinions (Garvey), 206
Pickens, William, Mrs., 145
Pinyon, Josephine, 85
Pittsburgh American (newspaper), 162
Plum Bun (Fauset), 180, 183, 238n147
Politics of respectability. *See* Higginbotham, Evelyn
Poston, Robert, 199
Powell, Adam Clayton, Sr., 122, 124
Procter and Gamble, 50
Progressive Era, 16, 58, 187, 220n1
Public-private divide, 10, 12, 173, 187, 234n43; feminist studies and, 160, 164–66; women's negotiation of, 12, 16, 45, 80, 135, 163–64, 165–66; 167, 169, 170

Race woman: Burroughs described as, 49; definition of, 11, 211n44; Madam Walker as, 107, 111, 112, 118, 125, 127, 128, 129, 133
Racial uplift, xi, 151; clubwomen and, 5, 62; Jacques Garvey and, 171; politics of respectability, as part of, 36–37, 203; racial solidarity and, 36–37; Madam Walker and, 13, 134; after World War I, 89
Randolph, A. Philip, 118, 122, 124, 141
Randolph, Florence, Rev., 32
Randolph, Lucille Green, 228n53
Ransom, Emma C., 73–75, 81, 99–100, 104, 106
Ransom, Freeman, B.: as business manager of Walker Company, 111, 135; career outside company, 122; A'Lelia Walker and, 141,

146–47; Madam Walker's advisor, 118, 121, 122, 124, 125; writer of advertising copy, 135
Ransom, Reverdy C., 73, 74
Reconstruction, 34, 64
Republican Party, 46–47, 122,
Ridley, Florida Ruffin, 78, 222n52
Rise and Triumph of Madam C. J. Walker, The (Lowry), 137
Robertson, Nancy, 68, 103, 104
Robinson, Lelia Walker. *See* Walker, A'Lelia
Robinson, Mae Walker, 144
Rogers, Joel A., 1, 209n1
Roosevelt, Eleanor, 62
Roosevelt, Franklin Delano, 50, 58, 61
Roosevelt, Theodore, 79
Rouse, Jacqueline Anne, 67
Ruffin, Adella, 97, 98

Saunders, Cecelia Cabaniss, 1, 60, 80–81, 104, 105, 106 126, 142, 206, 222n61; *A Half-Century*, xii, 100–102, 104
Savage, Augusta, 28, 199, 205
Schieffelin, William Jay, Col., 119
Schomburg, Arthur A., 122, 179
Schuyler, George: on *There Is Confusion*, 179; on A'Lelia Walker, 144; on Madam Walker, 107, 135
Scott, Emmet J.: as Booker T. Washington's secretary, 21; as War Department's advisor on Negro affairs, 122, 141–142
Segregation, xi, 91, 121, 202; Burroughs on, 48; Bethune on, 55, 206; Congress for World Democracy and, 121; Du Bois and NAACP fall out over, 61; Fauset's characters on, 190, 191; Hurston's views on, 1, 208; Shadd on, 7; UNIA, approach to, 199; Margaret Murray Washington on, 21; white women and, 91; in the workplace, 83; in the YWCA, 67, 69, 75, 93, 206
Seligmann, Herbert J., 200
Separate Spheres. *See* Public-private divide
Settlement-house movement, 17
Sexuality of black women: as represented in Fauset's novels, 195, 197; Garveyism and, 154; NTS and, 37
Shadd, Mary Ann, 7
Shaw, Stephanie, 17, 211n1, 211n9
Shillady, John H., 142

Sissle and Blake, 145
Slowe, Lucy, 96, 219n202
Smith, Honor Ford, 160
Social gospel, 66, 76
Sorbonne, 177
Souls of Black Folk, The (Du Bois), 4
Spence, Eulalie, 182
Spencer, Anne, 181
Spratt, Margaret, 67, 220n5
Stephens, Michelle Ann, 154, 233n2
Stewart, Maria, 7
Stewart, Sallie W., 58, 219n191, 219n195
Stuckey, Sterling, 5
Summers, Martin, 154
Surveillance of African Americans: 30, 122, 124, 142. *See also* Hoover, J. Edgar; Military Intelligence Division
Sylvander, Carolyn, 176

Talbert, Mary: Bethune, relationship with, 43; Fourth Pan-African Congress and, 214n75; as NACW president: 27, 35, 43; Second Pan-African Congress and, 238n135; Madam Walker and, 108, 126, 142; on YWCA racism, 87
Talented Tenth, 94, 178
Tandy, Vertnor, 141
Taylor, Thomas, 113
Taylor, Ula Y.: on "community feminism," 164–65; on gender and nationalism, 8, 210n32; on ICWDR, 214n64; on Jacques Garvey, 164–165, 173; on relationship between Jacques Garvey and Ashwood, 234n36
Teale, Georgia Myrtle, 105
Terrell, Mary Church, 205, 227n14; ICWDR, involvement in, 27, 30; NACW, first president of, 62; NCNW, skepticism concerning, 60; Niagara movement and, 233n10; NLRCW, member of, 217n142; on Red Cross racism, 87; Madam Walker, relationship with, 126; on white women, 87, 91; on World War I, 90–91
There Is Confusion (Fauset), 127, 151, 183, 188–94, 197, 198, 208, 238n147; Civic Club dinner, in honor of, 180; contemporaries' criticism of, 178–79; literary criticism on, 186–87
Three Guineas (Woolf), 8

Thurman, Wallace, 178
Trotter, William Monroe, 120, 121, 122, 124, 125, 228n41; in Trotter Bunch, 141
Truth, Sojourner, 113, 182
Turner, Victoria, 155
Tuskegee Institute: Bethune on, 51; Robert Moton and, 145; NTS, compared to, 38; Ransom and, 122; Madam Walker and, 117–18, 119, 120, 123, 143, 229n55; Booker T. Washington and, 110; Margaret Murray Washington and, 18, 19, 20, 21, 25, 26; women's roles at, 18; YWCA branch at, 70
Tuskegee Messenger (newspaper), 30
Tuskegee Negro Conference: Madam Walker and, 112–13
Tuskegee Wizard, 33. *See also* Washington, Booker T.
Tuskegee Women's Club, 24, 25, 113, 213n39
Two Colored Women with the American Expeditionary Forces, (Hunton and Johnson), 183

UN. *See* United Nations
UNIA. *See* Universal Negro Improvement Association
United Nations (UN), 62, 105, 201
Universal Negro Improvement Association (UNIA): 1922 Convention, 155–56; black masculinity, discourse on, 153–55, 158; founding and membership of, 151; Harlem Renaissance and, 152; Jacques Garvey's role in, 158–59, 161–63, 165, 171, 172, 174, 175; NAACP and, 17, 127, 150, 169, 201; Paris Peace Conference, chooses delegates to, 122; philosophy of, 199; A'Lelia Walker's support for, 145–46; represented in A'Lelia Walker's "Trip Around the World Campaign," 144; Madam Walker and, 123–25; women's roles in, 152–53, 155–56, 157–58, 199. *See also* Black Cross Nurses; Garvey, Jacques Garvey; Liberty Hall; *Negro World*; Universal African Motor Corps
Universal African Motor Corps, 153; 233n12
University of Pennsylvania, 176
Up from Slavery (Booker T. Washington), 21

Van Vechten, Carl: Fauset on, 192; *Nigger Heaven*, 136, 179, 231n108; A'Lelia Walker, relationship with, 232n148;
Villa Lewaro, 123, 138, 140–142. 146, 231n126
Vincent, Ted, 152

WA. *See* Women's Auxiliary
Walby, Sylvia, 166
Walker, A'Lelia (Lelia Walker Robinson), 1, 13, 108; 136th Street Beauty Parlor and, 138–40; Carl Van Vechten and, 136, 231n108, 231n109, 232n148; Dark Tower and, 146–47; funeral of, 2, 136; Harlem Renaissance and, 146; Lelia College and, 110, 111; marketing strategy of, 121, 134, 135–36, 137–38, 141, 143–44; Race Conference 1919 and, 141–142; race organizations and, 145–46; Randolph, Lucille Green and, 122; compared to Madam Walker, 137, 147; Women's Auxiliary and, 2
Walker, Charles J., 110
Walker Company. *See* Madam Walker Manufacturing Company
Walker, Madam C. J., 1, 5, 12, 13–14, 108, 124, 137, 148, 204, 205; and A'Lelia, 109, 137, 138, 140; agents of, 129–32, 134; anti-lynching crusaders and, 145, 230n78; automobile, ownership of; 114, 115; Bethune and, 53, 108; biographies of, 226n4; Burroughs and, 41–42, 43, 216n120, 203; death of, 134, 143; Fauset's fictional creation based on, 127, 185, 193, 203; Jacques Garvey on, 126, 185; legacy of, 148; ILPDR, involvement in, 118, 122, 123–24, 125; Garvey and, 122–23; "Madam," adopts title of, 110; Malone, Annie Turnbo and, 108, 110; marketing skills of, 107, 109, 111–12, 134, 135; NACW, involvement in, 128–29; NERL and, 118, 120; NNBL, speeches to, 113–14, 116, 117; Race Conference 1919 and, 141–42; Randolph, A. Philip and, 122; Ransom and, 111, 121–22, 124; "system" of, 107, 226n2; surveillance of, 142; Villa Lewaro and, 40–142; Booker T. Washington and, 110, 111, 112–18; Margaret Murray Washington and, 108, 117–18, 119, 126, 131; speaks to WC, 35; Wells-Barnett and, 120–21; Will of, 2; World War I and,

118–20, 142; YWCA and, 103, 127. *See also* Madam Walker Beauty Culturists Union Convention; Madam Walker Benevolent Association; Madam Walker Manufacturing Company
Walker, Maggie Lena, 35, 43, 47, 59, 103, 214n75, 217n142
Walker News, 127
Walrond, Eric, 179
Waring, Mary F. Dr., 43, 59–60, 87, 219n191
Washington, Booker T.: mentioned: xii, 22, 145, 204, 227n14; Bethune and, 51, 62, 121, 123; Burroughs and, 33, 38, 228n30; death of, 69, 131, 141; Du Bois and, 4, 17, 18, 38, 50–51, 94; NNBL, role as president of, 113, 116–18, 227n19; Trotter and, 120; Tuskegee and, 123, 145; Madam Walker and, 107, 108, 110, 111, 112–18, 227n16, 123, 131; Washington, Margaret Murray, as wife of, 18–19, 20, 21, 24; on women's suffrage, 23. *See also* Tuskegee Institute
Washington, D.C., 56, 113, 120, 121, 129, 171, 177, 180; female networks in, 2, 32, 177, 182; home of women's organizations, 2, 17, 27, 33, 49, 54, 202
Washington, Margaret Murray (Mrs. Booker T. Washington): mentioned: xii, 1, 13, 15, 17, 51, 65, 165, 203, 205; Bethune and, 52, 53, 54; children, views on, 22; conservative, accused of being, 18, 211–212n1; early life, 18–19; female networks, 2; ICWDR and, 24–30, 33, 185; NACW and, 20–21, 23, 24, 25–26; *National Notes,* 18, 21, 27; suffrage, views on, 22–24; Madam Walker and, 108, 117–18, 119, 126, 131; Washington, Booker T. and, 18, 19–21, 113; white women, criticism of, 20, 22; YWCA critical of, 69
WC. *See* Women's Convention
Weisenfeld, Judith, 68, 71, 220n5, 220n7
Wells-Barnett, Ida B., (Ida B. Wells), 54, 120–21, 122, 124, 141, 227n19, 233n10
West African Pilot, 159
West, Cornel, 8
Wheatley, Phyllis, 171
Wheeling, Laura, 182

White supremacy: white women and, 45, 57, 92–93; Madam Walker, challenge to, 111, 114, 124
White, Walter, 61
Who, 50
Wilberforce University, 70, 105
Williams, Bert, 191
Williams, George S., Mrs., 46
Williams, W. T. B., Mrs., 27
Wolcott, Victoria, 3, 11, 17, 36, 38, 40, 219–220n215
Women's Auxiliary (WA) to the NAACP, 2, 145, 238n137
Women's Christian Temperance Union, 20
Women's Convention, 33–37, 38, 40, 41, 48
Women's Era, xi, 13, 65
Women's suffrage, 22–24, 44–46, 47, 91–92
Women's Trade Union League, 83
Woodson, Carter G., 41, 205, 226n162
Woolf, Virginia, 8
Worker, The (NTS publication), 41
Working-class women: as authentic, 187; characters in Fauset's novels, 127, 188, 189, 193; Madam Walker Benevolent Association and, 131; middle class women, relationship with, 10, 11, 36, 40; NACW and, 129
World Forum, 3
World War I, 7, 17, 53; Fauset's views on, 183, 184, 185, 191, 194; Madam Walker and, 118; YWCA and, 66–68, 77, 78, 85, 90, 93, 95, 183, 213n58

Yard, Lionel, 156
YMCA. *See* Young Men's Christian Association
Young Men's Christian Association (YMCA), 113, 117, 122; World War I and, 87–89, 183, 194; YWCA and, 13, 66, 74, 93–96, 103–4
Young Women's Christian Association (YWCA), xii, 1, 13, 66, 69, 144, 146, 203, 207; Asheville Conference and, 70, 75, 98; Bureau of Colored Work, 96, 98; Colored Branch, Harlem, 2, 13, 66, 71–75, 99–103, 221n30; Colored Work Committee (CWC), 68, 76, 78, 82, 96, 100, 104; Fauset and, 183, 190; female networks and, 105–6, 201;

YWCA—*continued*
  founding of, 70; ICWDR and, 28; Lugenia Burns Hope and, 96–99; National Board of, 67, 68, 75–76, 99; Hostess Houses and, 79–80; hosts reception for Fourth Pan-African Congress, 32; Interracial Charter of, 67, 104, 206, 220n5, 225n141; NCNW and, 60; Patriotic League for Colored Girls and, 81, 82; Madam Walker and, 103, 111, 126, 128, 142, 144, 145; World War I, 77–89; YMCA, 93–96, 103–4

Yuval-Davis, Nira, 166

YWCA. *See* Young Women's Christian Association